ACTION SEMANTICS

Cambridge Tracts in Theoretical Computer Science

Managing Editor   Professor C.J. van Rijsbergen,
Department of Computing Science, University of Glasgow

Editorial Board

S. Abramsky, Department of Computing Science, Imperial College of Science
and Technology
P.H. Aczel, Department of Computer Science, University of Manchester
J.W. de Bakker, Centrum voor Wiskunde en Informatica, Amsterdam
J.A. Goguen, Programming Research Group, University of Oxford
J.V. Tucker, Department of Mathematics and Computer Science,
University College of Swansea

Titles in the series

ACTION SEMANTICS

PETER D. MOSSES
Department of Computer Science
Aarhus University, Denmark

CAMBRIDGE
UNIVERSITY PRESS

PUBLISHED BY THE PRESS SYNDICATE OF THE UNIVERSITY OF CAMBRIDGE
The Pitt Building, Trumpington Street, Cambridge, United Kingdom

CAMBRIDGE UNIVERSITY PRESS
The Edinburgh Building, Cambridge CB2 2RU, UK
40 West 20th Street, New York NY 10011–4211, USA
477 Williamstown Road, Port Melbourne, VIC 3207, Australia
Ruiz de Alarcón 13, 28014 Madrid, Spain
Dock House, The Waterfront, Cape Town 8001, South Africa

http://www.cambridge.org

First published 1992
First paperback edition 2005

A catalogue record for this book is available from the British Library

ISBN 0 521 40347 2 hardback
ISBN 0 521 61933 5 paperback

Contents

Appendices 230

List of Boxes

Preface

Formal semantics is a topic of major importance in the study of programming languages. Its applications include documenting language design, establishing standards for implementations, reasoning about programs, and generating compilers.

This book is about *action semantics*, a recently-developed framework for formal semantics. The primary aim of action semantics is to allow *useful* semantic descriptions of *realistic* programming languages.

Action semantics combines formality with many good pragmatic features. Regarding comprehensibility and accessibility, for instance, action semantic descriptions compete with informal language descriptions. Action semantic descriptions scale up smoothly from small example languages to full-blown practical languages. The addition of new constructs to a described language does not require reformulation of the already-given description. An action semantic description of one language can make widespread reuse of that of another, related language. All these pragmatic features are highly desirable. Action semantics is, however, the *only* semantic framework that enjoys them! (For syntax, context-free grammars have similar features, which perhaps accounts for their popularity in language reference manuals.)

Action semantics is *compositional*, like denotational semantics. The main difference between action semantics and denotational semantics concerns the universe of semantic entities: action semantics uses entities called *actions*, rather than the higher-order functions used with denotational semantics. Actions are inherently more operational than functions: when *performed*, actions process information *gradually*.

Primitive actions, and the various ways of combining actions, correspond to fundamental concepts of information processing. Action semantics provides a particular notation for expressing actions. The symbols of action notation are suggestive words, rather than cryptic signs, which makes it possible to get a broad impression of an action semantic description from a superficial reading, even without previous experience of action semantics. The action *combinators*, a notable feature of action notation, obey desirable algebraic laws that can be used for reasoning about semantic equivalence.

This book provides a comprehensive exposition of action semantics. It is aimed primarily at M.Sc. and Ph.D. students, and at researchers in semantics. It should also be accessible to senior undergraduates, and to professional programmers. No previous knowledge of formal semantics is assumed, although the reader should be prepared to meet a substantial amount of formal notation. Some familiarity with high-level programming languages is probably essential.

Organization

In general, this book explains concepts informally before introducing the associated formal notation. Relatively tedious formal details are deferred to the Appendices, which also provide a complete, self-contained reference manual for action semantics.

Part I introduces the concepts and formalism used in action semantics. First it motivates formal descriptions of programming languages, and discusses their main features. It then explains the particular kinds of formal specification used in action semantic descriptions of programming languages, giving a simple illustrative example. Finally it presents an unorthodox framework for algebraic specifications, and sketches the algebraic foundations of action semantics.

Part II introduces the details of action notation systematically, explaining the underlying concepts and the intended interpretation of the symbols. It is intended to be read *together with* Part III, which illustrates the use of action notation in semantic descriptions.

Some of the Appendices provide further details of the foundations of action notation, and summarize the explanations given throughout Part II. Appendix B specifies some algebraic properties of the entire action notation; this also reduces action notation to a reasonably small kernel. Appendix C defines the abstract syntax of the kernel, and gives the formal definition of its meaning, using structural operational semantics. Appendix D summarizes the informal explanations of the full action notation, for convenience of reference. Appendix E gives the complete algebraic specification of the data notation included in action notation.

Part III gives a progressive series of examples of action semantic descriptions. The programming constructs described all come from ADA. (No previous familiarity with ADA is required, as the necessary concepts are all explained here.) The examples not only describe a substantial sublanguage of ADA, they also serve as paradigms for description of other programming languages.

The description of constructs in the earlier examples remains *unchanged* in the later examples. This is in marked contrast to denotational semantics, where tedious reformulations of the earlier descriptions would be required for giving the later ones!

Appendix A collects the examples together, for convenience of reference—and to show how a medium-scale action semantic description looks in its entirety. It also provides the detailed specifications of semantic entities, which are omitted in Part III.

Part IV concludes by briefly relating action semantics to other frameworks, and by sketching its development. It cites the main sources for action semantics and the related frameworks, and mentions some current projects.

All the symbols used in the book are listed in an index, together with the numbers of the pages where they are explained and formally defined. The font used for the page numbers indicates whether a symbol is *standard* in action notation, or merely introduced *ad hoc* for use in examples. Moreover, when the index entry for a standard symbol is immediately followed by another entry for the corresponding abstract syntax, the symbol is in the *kernel* of action notation .

Each chapter starts with an overview, and concludes with a summary, navigational guidance about what to read next, and some exercises. You are strongly encouraged to do the exercises: they are intended to deepen and confirm the understanding of the material presented in each chapter, and some of them present interesting supplementary material.

The specification given on page x indicates (using action notation!) the suggested order of reading the various parts of this book.

> **N.B.** *At a first reading, you should read Parts II and III in parallel, so that you see an illustration of the use of each part of action notation immediately after its introduction. When revising, you should probably read Parts II and III separately.*

However, if you are already familiar with formal semantics, e.g., denotational semantics, you might prefer to ignore the suggested order and start from the Appendices, consulting the expository chapters for motivation or clarification only when necessary.

Tuition

This book originated from notes written for a course that I have given regularly at the Computer Science Department, Aarhus University, Denmark, since 1980. The course lasts about 15 weeks, with three 45-minute classes each week. I require the students to read the text and attempt the exercises prior to each class, which is devoted to discussion of any problems or issues arising from that reading, rather than to lectures as such. For a shorter course, one could omit the final chapters of Parts II and III, which treat concurrency, as well as much of the material in the Appendices.

I warn my students that they will be meeting a large amount of formal notation, as well as some unorthodox ideas. Some students are averse to the way that full details often get deferred to the Appendices. They are encouraged to make frequent excursions to the Appendices, to locate the details for themselves, using the modular structure of the Appendices and the symbol index for navigation.

Near the end of the course, I suspend classes for two weeks to let the students, working in groups of two or three, develop an action semantic description of a small programming language—as much as they can manage in 25 hours work. This not only documents the active participation of the students in the course, it also serves some important pedagogical purposes. For instance, it gives the students the opportunity to revise and assimilate further the material already covered; it gives them the opportunity to verify the inherent modularity of action semantics in their own descriptions; and it lets them check whether they have indeed acquired a *working* knowledge of action semantics. Appendix G provides an example of such an assignment. You are encouraged to attempt it after you finish reading Parts II and III.

Status

The penultimate version of this book (Version 9, November 1991) was not only class-tested in Aarhus, but also sent to more than 50 of my international colleagues. I have done my best to correct mistakes and improve the presentation, based on the feedback I have received. However, the book includes some largish formal specifications, and it is possible that there are still some bugs in them. Some tools that should help to discover lurking bugs are currently being developed.

I hope you will be able to correct any bugs that you find without too much trouble. Please send me a precise description of each bug as soon as you have identified it—preferably by e-mail, as described in Section 19.4.

Acknowledgments

Christopher Strachey taught me about his fundamental conceptual analysis of programming languages, and I later adopted it as the basis for the design of action notation. With Dana Scott he also originated denotational semantics, the starting point for the development of action semantics.

David Watt actively collaborated with me on the design of action notation, and on the action semantic description of realistic programming languages. His influence was crucial for the development of action semantics into a practical approach.

Silvio Meira, Ken Slonneger, and Bernhard Steffen bravely class-tested earlier versions of this book, and gave useful advice on how to improve the presentation.

A complete draft of this book circulated at the Marktoberdorf Summer School, 1991. The reactions of some of the participants, both to the book and to my lectures, had a significant influence on the subsequent versions.

The Computer Science Department at Aarhus University provided a very favourable environment for the development of action semantics. Brian Mayoh, Michael Schwartzbach, Paddy Krishnan, and Jens Palsberg read earlier versions of this book and gave valuable feedback. Numerous students explored the feasibility of using action semantics in their projects, giving valuable feedback about the applicability of the framework to the description of realistic programming languages.

The following persons kindly provided me with many pertinent and timely comments on the penultimate draft of this book: Valentin Antimirov, Deryck Brown, Jolanta Cybulka, Kyung-Goo Doh, Roope Kaivola, Paddy Krishnan, Peter Lauer, Vincenzo Manca, Jacek Martinek, Eugenio Moggi, Camille le Moniès de Sagazan, Hermano Moura, Martín Musicante, Jørgen Nørgaard, Arnd Pötzsch-Heffter, Horst Reichel, Teo Rus, Dave Schmidt, Ken Slonneger, Bernhard Steffen, Carolyn Talcott, and (with remarkable energy, considering the number of previous versions upon which he had previously commented) David Watt. Their general enthusiasm for the contents of the book was very encouraging. Prompted by some of their criticisms of the draft, I have made a significant reorganization of the material in Part I, so as to bring in a simple example of action semantics at an earlier point and to explain the unorthodox algebraic specification framework in more detail. Any remaining defects in the presentation are, of course, entirely my own responsibility.

Jaco de Bakker originally encouraged me to get my lecture notes on action semantics into publishable form. David Tranah made me aware of some problems with my writing style, gave useful typographical advice, and was remarkably patient when I failed to meet my own deadlines. The publisher's reviewers pointed out how to remedy several weaknesses in the organization of the material, and made many perceptive comments that helped me improve the final version.

Special thanks go to my family, who were very supportive while I was preparing this book for publication.

The development of action semantics has been partially funded by the Danish Science Research Council project DART (5.21.08.03).

Navigation

To whet your appetite for action notation, an *entirely formal* specification of the suggested order of reading this book is given on the next page, using action notation itself! It starts by specifying the sorts and functionalities of some *ad hoc* constants and operations. A few details are left unspecified—including the effect of reading the individual chapters...

needs: Action Notation.

- The Book   : text.
- number $= I \mid II \mid III \mid IV \mid A \mid B \mid C \mid D \mid E \mid F \mid G \mid$ natural[max 19].
- _ [_]   :: number, string $\rightarrow$ number (*partial*, *injective*).
- Part _ , Chapter _ , Appendix _ :: number $\rightarrow$ text (*partial*).
- read _   :: text $\rightarrow$ action (*total*).
- read _ together with _   :: text, text $\rightarrow$ action (*total*).

read The Book =
    read Part I and then
    read Part II together with Part III and then
    (read Part IV and read the Appendices) and then
    ((indivisibly read Part II and indivisibly read Part III) or escape).

read Part I ["Introduction"] =
    read Chapter 1 ["Language Descriptions"] and then
    read Chapter 2 ["Action Semantic Descriptions"] and then
    read Chapter 3 ["Algebraic Specifications"].

read Part II ["Action Notation"] together with Part III ["Semantic Descriptions"] =
    (read Chapter 4 ["Basic"] and read Chapter 11 ["Statements"]) and then
    (read Chapter 5 ["Data"] and read Chapter 12 ["Literals"]) and then
    (read Chapter 6 ["Functional"] and read Chapter 13 ["Expressions"]) and then
    (read Chapter 7 ["Declarative"] and read Chapter 14 ["Declarations"]) and then
    (read Chapter 8 ["Imperative"] and read Chapter 15 ["Variables"]) and then
    (read Chapter 9 ["Reflective"] and read Chapter 16 ["Subprograms"]) and then
    (read Chapter 10 ["Communicative"] and read Chapter 17 ["Tasks"]).

read Part IV ["Conclusion"] =
    read Chapter 18 ["Other Frameworks"] and then
    read Chapter 19 ["Development"].

read Part II =
    (read Chapter 4 and read Chapter 5) and then
    (read Chapter 6 and read Chapter 7 and read Chapter 8) and then
    read Chapter 9 and then read Chapter 10.

read Part III =
    (read Chapter 11 and read Chapter 12) and then read Chapter 13 and then
    read Chapter 14 and then read Chapter 15 and then read Chapter 16 and then
    read Chapter 17.

read the Appendices =
    read Appendix A ["AD Action Semantics"] and
    read Appendix B ["Action Notation"] and
    read Appendix C ["Operational Semantics"] and
    read Appendix D ["Informal Summary"] and
    read Appendix E ["Data Notation"] and
    read Appendix F ["Meta-Notation"].

Part I

Introduction

Part I introduces the concepts and formalism used in action semantics. First it motivates formal descriptions of programming languages, and discusses their main features. It then explains the particular kinds of formal specification used in action semantic descriptions of programming languages, giving a simple illustrative example. Finally it presents an unorthodox framework for algebraic specifications, and sketches the algebraic foundations of action semantics.

Navigation

- *Have you read the Preface? If not, please do so now—it explains how this book is organized.*

Chapter 1
Language Descriptions

- *Descriptions of programming languages have several important applications.*

- *Different applications require different features of descriptions.*

- *Informal descriptions are inadequate: formality is essential.*

- *Good pragmatic features are needed to make formal descriptions useful.*

- *Comprehensive language descriptions involve both syntax and semantics.*

- *Standards relate syntax and semantics to implementations.*

This chapter provides some background for the main topic of this book, namely the action semantic description of programming languages. We start by identifying some important uses for descriptions of programming languages. Although various uses require different features of descriptions, these requirements are not necessarily conflicting. Formality is a particularly important feature. We go on to consider the factorization of language descriptions into syntax and semantics, and discuss how they relate to the pragmatic issue of setting standards for programming languages.

1.1 Motivation

Programming languages are artificial languages. Programs written in them are used to control the execution of computers. There are many programming languages in existence. Some are simple, intended for special purposes; others are complex and general-purpose, for use in a wide variety of applications.

Even though programming languages lack many of the features of natural languages, such as vagueness, it is not at all easy to give accurate, comprehensive descriptions

3

of them. Which applications require descriptions of programming languages—and hence motivate the study of appropriate frameworks for such descriptions?

First, there is the programming language *design* process. Designers need to record decisions about particular language constructs, especially when the design is a team effort. This amounts to giving a partial description of the language. At a later stage, the formulation of a complete language description may be useful for drawing attention to neglected details, and for revealing irregularities in the overall design.

Once a language has been designed, it usually gets *implemented*, although in practice, design and implementation are often interleaved and iterated. A comprehensive description of the language is needed to convey the intentions of the language designers to the implementors—unless the designer and the implementor are the same person, of course. It is also needed for setting a definitive *standard* for implementations, so that programs can be transported between different implementations that conform to the standard, without modification.

A programmer needs a description of any new language in order to relate it to previously-known ones, and to understand it in terms of familiar concepts. The programmer also needs a description as a basis for *reasoning* about the correctness of particular programs in relation to their specifications, and for justifying program transformations.

Finally, theoreticians can obtain new *insight* into the general nature of programming languages by developing descriptions of them. This insight can then be exploited in the design of new, and perhaps more elegant, programming languages.

So we see that there are plenty of applications for descriptions of programming languages. But not all kinds of description are suitable for all purposes. The various applications mentioned above require different properties of descriptions, as we consider next.

1.2   Requirements

Which properties might language designers require of language descriptions? Well, design is an iterative process, so to start with, designers need *partial* descriptions that can easily be extended and modified. They also need descriptions that provide clear and concise documentation of individual language design decisions. For economy of effort, they might want to be able to reuse parts of descriptions of existing languages in the description of a new language. Finally, their completed language description should provide an appropriate basis for conveying the design to the implementors, and for setting standards.

The implementors of a language require a *complete* and unambiguous description of it—except that certain features, such as the order of subexpression evaluation, may have been deliberately left unspecified. Explicit indication of implementation techniques in the description may be helpful, but it might discourage alternative, perhaps more efficient, implementations. Ideally, the conformance of a purported implementation to a standard imposed by a language description should be verifiable.

A long-term aim is to generate complete, correct, and efficient implementations automatically from language descriptions, in the same way that parsers can be generated from grammars. There have already been some encouraging experiments in this direction. This application requires that the language descriptions can be directly related to machine operation.

What do programmers require? A language description should be easy to understand, and to relate to familiar programming concepts, without a major investment of effort in learning about the description technique itself. It should support program verification. And it shouldn't take up too much space on the shelf . . .

Theoreticians may require clear and elegant foundations for the exploited description technique, to support tractable reasoning about equivalence and other program features. They may take a *prescriptive* view of language description, considering only a restricted class of programming languages—those amenable to their favourite description technique—in the hope that this will prevent the design of 'big, bad, and ugly' languages. Or they may take a more liberal, *descriptive* view, requiring a universal description technique that can cope with any conceivable programming language, and hoping that poor language design will be evident from its description.

It seems highly unlikely that all the above requirements can be fully satisfied simultaneously. Certainly none of the previously available frameworks, reviewed in Chapter 18, appears to be suitable for use in all the above applications. This has led to the proposal of so-called *complementary* language descriptions, where several different techniques are used to give independent, but hopefully relatable, descriptions of 'the same' language.

The topic of this book, action semantics, avoids the need for complementary descriptions by making a *compromise* between the above requirements. An action semantic description is extremely modular, providing the high degree of extensibility, modifiability, and reusability required by language designers. It is also strongly suggestive of an operational understanding of the described language, and it has been found to be very well suited for generating compilers and interpreters, so implementors should be content. Programmers should find action semantic descriptions almost as easy to read as the usual reference manuals, without much preparation. On the other hand, although the foundations of action semantics are firm enough, the *theory* for reasoning about actions (and hence about programs) is still rather weak, and needs further development. This situation is in marked contrast to that of denotational semantics, where the theory[1] is strong, but severe pragmatic difficulties hinder its application to realistic programming languages.

Some of these claims for the virtues of action semantic descriptions can be supported by looking at examples. Let us postpone consideration of the extent to which action semantics meets the stated requirements until Part IV, after we have seen action semantics *in action!*

1.3   Features

One especially significant feature of language descriptions is whether or not they are *formal*. Let us distinguish between formal and informal descriptions as follows. Purely formal descriptions are expressed in well-defined, established notation, often borrowed from mathematics. Note that this notation itself may have been established either formally, using some previously-established *meta-notation*, or informally (but rigorously) as in most mathematical texts. Purely informal descriptions are expressed in natural languages, such as English.

Currently, the only comprehensive description of a programming language is usually its 'reference manual', which is mainly informal. Unfortunately, experience has shown that, even when carefully worded, such reference manuals are usually incomplete or inconsistent, or both, and open to misinterpretation. This is obviously undesirable, especially when such descriptions are used to guide implementors and to set standards. The existence of procedures for requesting clarification of international standards, which are generally based on reference manuals, confirms that misinterpretation is a problem. Moreover, informal descriptions can never provide a sound basis for reasoning about program correctness or equivalence.

To compensate for the vaguenesses of an informal language description, a formal *validation suite* of programs is sometimes used as the final arbiter of implementation correctness. By itself, however, such a validation suite is not much use as a language description. In any case, the correct processing of a validation suite by an implementation cannot guarantee analogous performance on other programs.

It might be imagined that informal descriptions should be easy to read, because they are written in a natural language; but in fact the (vain) attempt to be precise in a natural language leads to a rather stilted literary style that is tedious to read on a large scale. When well-written, however, informal descriptions can provide an easily-accessible guide to the fundamental concepts underlying a programming language;

---

[1]at least for dealing with deterministic, sequential programs

this seems to be their only real strength.

Formal descriptions have almost the opposite qualities to informal ones. They can be complete and consistent, and can be given a precise interpretation, appropriate for setting *definitive* standards. Questions about their consequences are answered by the theoretical foundations of the formal notation used. Formal descriptions can be used as the basis for systematic development and automatic generation of implementations. And it is one of their main strengths that they can provide a basis for sound reasoning about program correctness and equivalence.

On the other hand, it is often difficult to relate a formal description of a programming language to fundamental concepts, and to grasp the implications of the description for the implementation of programs. Poor notation, or excessively large and complex formulae can also lead to obscurity. Inferior formal descriptions can be unintentionally ambiguous or incomplete—even inconsistent! The mere use of formality does *not* ensure success.

One could consider the text of a *compiler*, or of an interpreter, as a formal definition of the language that it implements. The language used for writing it should already have a well-defined interpretation, of course: a so-called *meta-circular* interpreter, written using the language itself being interpreted, doesn't formally define anything at all! Unfortunately, practical compilers for realistic programming languages are somewhat unwieldy objects, and demand familiarity with particular target codes. Interpreters are generally more accessible, but still tend to have many details that are incidental to the implemented language.

In programming linguistics, as in the study of natural languages, it is useful to distinguish between *syntax* and *semantics*. The syntax of a programming language is concerned only with the *form* of programs: which programs are 'legal'? what are the connections and relations between the symbols and phrases that occur in them? Semantics deals with the *meaning* of legal programs.

Ideally, a comprehensive description of a programming language involves the specification of *syntactic entities*, of *semantic entities*, and of a *semantic function* that maps the former to the latter. The syntactic entities include the legal programs of the language, and the semantic entities include representations of the intended behaviours of these programs. To facilitate reasoning about parts of programs, the semantic function should give semantics not only to entire programs but also to their component phrases; and it should preferably be *compositional*, so that the semantics of a compound phrase is determined purely by the semantics of its components, independently of their other features.

Most frameworks for language description unfortunately do not provide a clear separation between syntactic and semantic entities, nor do they exploit compositional semantic functions. A notable exception is *denotational semantics*, from which action semantics was developed.

The distinction between the syntax and the semantics of a language is dependent on the division into structure and behaviour. At one extreme, structure could be trivial—arbitrary strings over an alphabet of symbols—and then the usual notion of program legality would have to be considered as a component of behaviour. At the other extreme, behaviour could be incorporated into a dynamic notion of structure. For comprehensive language descriptions, it is best to find a compromise such that separate descriptions of syntax and semantics provide a useful factorization of the entire description into parts with a simple interface.

1.4   Syntax

The syntax of a programming language determines the set of its legal programs, and the relationship between the symbols and phrases occurring in them.

We may divide syntax into *concrete* and *abstract* syntax. Concrete syntax involves *analysis*: the recognition of legal programs from texts (i.e., sequences of characters) and their unambiguous *parsing* into phrases. Abstract syntax deals only with the compositional *structure* of phrases of programs, ignoring how that structure might have been determined. In general, it is easier to define the semantics of programs on the basis of their abstract syntax, as explained later, rather than on their concrete syntax.

For comprehensive language descriptions, both kinds of syntax are needed—together with an indication of how they are related. Here, we are mainly concerned with semantic descriptions, so we emphasize abstract syntax, giving only a cursory explanation of concrete syntax and its relation to abstract syntax.

1.4.1   Concrete Syntax

Conventionally, concrete syntax is separated into *lexical* analysis and *phrase-structure* analysis. The task of lexical analysis is to group the characters of a program text into a *sequence* of legal *symbols*, or *lexemes*. That of phrase-structure analysis is to group these symbols into phrases, thereby constructing a *parse tree*, or *derivation tree*, with the symbols as leaves.

The main kinds of lexical symbol are, in the terminology used in [ANS83]:

- Delimiters: punctuation marks, mathematical signs (possibly multi-character);

- Words: alpha-numeric sequences, starting with a letter—these are usually divided into a set of *reserved words*, such as **begin** and **end**, and a set of *identifiers* used for naming program entities;

- Numeric literals: sequences of digits, decimal points, and signs indicating exponents and/or bases;

- Character and string literals: quoted characters and sequences of characters, usually with conventions for representing non-graphic characters;

- Comments: almost arbitrary sequences of characters, delimited by special sequences—these can sometimes be nested;

- Separators: space characters, format effectors, line terminators.

Comments and separators are generally allowed to occur freely between all other lexical symbols. But it would be tedious to describe that freedom as part of phrase-structure, so comments and separators—once recognized—are usually omitted from the sequence of symbols resulting from lexical analysis. (This, however, is inappropriate for languages such as OCCAM2, where indentation is significant for phrase-structure analysis.)

The various sorts of phrases in high-level programming languages can be classified primarily as follows:

- Declarations: these introduce identifiers to name program entities, and usually contain expressions or statements;

- Expressions: these resemble mathematical terms;

- Statements: simple and compound—they may contain declarations or expressions;

- Programs: proper combinations of declarations, expressions, and statements.

This classification is semantically significant, and can usually be made on the basis of so-called *context-free* structure analysis. Subsidiary classification deals with types, formal parameters, etc.

The parse tree produced by phrase-structure analysis of a program represents the recognized component relation between its phrases. It may also represent how the phrases have been classified.

Both lexical and phrase-structure analysis are required to be *unambiguous*: a sequence of characters making up a legal program must determine a unique sequence of symbols, which in turn must determine a unique parse tree. In the case of ambiguity, the programmer is left in doubt about the recognized structure of the program.

1.4.2   Abstract Syntax

Abstract syntax provides an appropriate interface between concrete syntax and semantics. It is usually obtained simply by ignoring those details of parse tree structure which have no semantic significance—leaving *abstract syntax trees* that represent just the essential compositional structure of programs.

For instance, in concrete syntax one usually sub-classifies compound arithmetic expressions into terms and factors, in order to avoid ambiguous parsing of sequences such as a+b*c. Factors are more restricted than terms, in that any additions that occur in factors have to be enclosed in grouping parentheses, whereas the parentheses are optional when additions occur in terms. The term a+b is not classified as a factor, so the only possible parsing for a+b*c is the one where b*c is grouped together. But the only semantically relevant features of an arithmetic expression are its subexpressions and its operator, so for abstract syntax we can ignore whether the expression is classified as a term or as a factor.

The symbols used for labeling the nodes in an abstract syntax tree may be the same as the lexical symbols of the corresponding concrete syntax. This is not essential, though, as the symbols are needed only to distinguish nodes for different constructs. For instance, while-statements and if-then-statements both have two components: a condition and a statement; extra symbols are required to label them distinctly, but these can be chosen arbitrarily. Similarly, when every statement is terminated by a semicolon in concrete syntax, the semicolons may be omitted in the corresponding abstract syntax, as they have no distinguishing effect. On the other hand, the lexical symbols from the concrete syntax do have considerable suggestive and mnemonic value. By retaining them as labels in abstract syntax trees—in the same order that they occur in the corresponding parse trees—much of the relation between concrete and abstract syntax can be made self-evident.

Another way of abstracting details of parse tree structure is to ignore the *order* of components, when this is semantically insignificant. For instance, the order in which the cases of a case-statement are written in the program text may be irrelevant; then one could take a *set* of cases, rather than an ordered list. Similarly, one might let declarations be (finite) maps on identifiers, instead of lists of pairs—thereby reflecting also that an identifier is not to be declared twice in the same sequence of declarations. This seems appealing, but on closer investigation turns out to have gone *too far* in abstraction, at least from a pragmatic point of view, as it complicates the definition of semantic functions on abstract syntax. In general, however, ignoring semantically irrelevant details of parse tree structure tends to simplify the definition of semantic functions.

It can happen that the compositional structure of programs derived from a given concrete syntax has a nesting that is inconvenient for a compositional semantics. We may then use an abstract syntax that corresponds to a rearrangement of the original structure, provided that we are prepared to specify the map from parse trees to abstract syntax trees. But when this map is complicated, the comprehensibility of the language description suffers considerably.

Some *programming environments* provide templates for constructing and editing abstract syntax trees, and for viewing them graphically, thereby allowing the use of concrete syntax to be avoided. Although this does not justify ignoring concrete syntax altogether when giving a comprehensive description of a programming language, it does underline the importance of abstract syntax, and further motivates that semantics should be defined on the basis of abstract, rather than concrete, syntax.

Section 2.1 provides a simple illustration of abstract syntax, and explains how to specify the structure of abstract syntax trees using *grammars*.

1.4.3 Context-Sensitive Syntax

Context-*free* syntax deals with those aspects of structure that can be described by context-free grammars, such as those written in the popular BNF formalism. Aspects which fall outside context-free syntax are called context-*sensitive* and include 'declaration of identifiers before use' and 'well-typedness of expressions'. Characteristic for them is that they involve a kind of matching between distant parts of programs that is inherently more complex than mere 'parenthesis-matching'.

The description of context-sensitive syntax can, in principle, be accomplished by use of so-called *attribute grammars*. Unfortunately, these are not always as perspicuous as context-free grammars. Moreover, context-sensitive abstract syntax makes a more complicated interface between concrete syntax and semantics than context-free abstract syntax does. Of course, this is to be expected, because the former generally captures more information than the latter. Attribute grammars cannot cope straightforwardly with so-called *dynamic scope rules* for declarations in programs.

An alternative way of defining context-sensitive syntax is by giving *inference rules* for well-formed phrases. Well-formedness is usually defined as a binary relation between context-dependent information and phrases, and the well-formedness of a compound phrase may depend on the well-formedness of its subphrases with modified context-dependent information. As with attribute grammars, this technique is not applicable when scope rules are dynamic.

Here, let us keep abstract syntax *context-free*, and describe context-sensitive aspects separately. This amounts to treating context-sensitive syntax as a kind of *seman-*

tics, called *static* semantics, because it depends only on the program structure, and does not involve program input. The input-dependent behaviour of a program is referred to as its *dynamic* semantics—or simply as its semantics, when this doesn't lead to confusion. Note that static semantics is just as essential an ingredient in a comprehensive language description as dynamic semantics, and that there are significant problems with program portability due to inconsistent implementation of static semantics by compiler front-ends. In this book, however, we are primarily concerned with dynamic semantics, although we may digress for a moment here to consider what static semantics might involve.

The simplest kind of static semantics is merely a *constraint* on programs: if a program violates the constraint, it is deemed to be illegal. Such a semantics may be given by a function mapping programs to truth-values, specified using auxiliary functions that map program parts and contextual information to truth-values. In practice, a thorough treatment of constraints would be more complicated, involving error messages about the cause of constraint violations. The dynamic semantics of programs may be defined independently of their static semantics: the dynamic semantics of an illegal program is of no interest, but it does no harm to define it anyway.

There are a few context-sensitive features that affect *grouping*, rather than legality. An obvious example is the declaration of *operator precedence* in programs themselves. Similarly, parsing may be guided by context-dependent type information. It would be awkward to deal with abstract syntax for (and the semantics of) ungrouped expressions! Fortunately, that is not necessary, as abstract syntax for grouped expressions merely reflects that grouping *has* been determined, somehow or other, by the program; it isn't affected by the means used to accomplish this, such as precedence, types, or ordinary grouping parentheses.

Static semantics may provide not only an indication of program legality, but also a tree according to a new (context-free) abstract syntax that incorporates context-dependent distinctions into the original abstract syntax. For instance, a static semantics for ADA might map the node corresponding to the expression A(X), to one with an auxiliary symbol that indicates whether the expression is actually an array component selection or a function call—this depends on the declaration for A. Then the dynamic semantics may be defined on the second abstract syntax. The (full) semantics of programs according to the original abstract syntax is simply obtained by composition of the specified static and dynamic semantics. Such factorization of semantics can substantially simplify the specification of dynamic semantics, but it has the disadvantage that the relation of the second abstract syntax to the original concrete syntax may be quite obscure.

Watt [WM87] has shown that action semantics can be useful for specifying static semantics, as well as dynamic semantics. The idea is to specify actions that *perform* type-checking, etc. Another interesting possibility is to *derive* a static semantics for a programming language from its dynamic semantics [DS92]. Here, however, to avoid distraction from our main purpose in this book, we henceforth ignore static semantics altogether, and concentrate on dynamic semantics.

1.5 Semantics

Consider an entire program in some programming language. What is the nature of its semantics?

First of all let us dismiss any effects that the program might have on human readers, e.g., evoking feelings of admiration or, perhaps more often, disgust. In contrast to philology, programming linguistics is not concerned with subjective qualities at all. The semantics of a program is dependent only on the objective *behaviour* that the program directly causes when executed by computers.[2]

Now computers are complex mechanisms, and all kinds of things can be observed to happen when they execute programs: lights flash, disc heads move, electric currents flow in circuits, characters appear on screens or on paper, etc. In order to consider programs that are specifically intended to control such physical behaviour, it is necessary to deal with these phenomena in their semantics.

But here, let us restrict our attention to programs in high-level programming languages, which generally deny the program direct control over the details of physical behaviour. The appropriate semantics of these programs is *implementation-independent*, consisting of just those features of program execution that are common to all implementations. This usually includes termination properties, but ignores efficiency considerations.

Thus the semantics of a program is an (abstract) entity that models the program's implementation-independent behaviour. The semantics of a programming language consists of the semantics of all its programs.

1.5.1 Semantic Functions

The semantics of a programming language can be captured by a *semantic function* that maps the abstract syntax of each program to the semantic entity representing its behaviour. How about the semantics of *parts* of programs, i.e., of phrases such as

---

[2]Usually, but not necessarily, electronic.

statements, declarations, expressions, etc.?

Well, one could say that the semantics of a phrase is already *implicit* in the semantics of all the programs in which it occurs. Thus two phrases have the same semantics if they are *interchangeable* in any program context, i.e., when replacing the one phrase by the other never affects the behaviour of the whole program. For example, two procedures that implement different algorithms for sorting have the same semantics, provided that program behaviour does not take account of efficiency. Any compositional semantics for phrases that has this property is called *fully abstract*.

For reasoning about phrases—their semantic equivalence, for instance—it is undesirable to have to consider all possible programs containing them, so we insist on *explicit* definition of semantics for all phrases. When the semantics of a compound phrase depends only on the semantics of its subphrases, not on other features (such as their structure) the semantics is called *compositional*. This guarantees that whenever two phrases have the same semantics, they are indeed interchangeable. But when they have different semantics, they may or may not be interchangeable: a compositional semantics is not necessarily fully abstract.

Action semantics, following denotational semantics, insists on compositionality, with the semantic function mapping not only entire programs but also all their component phrases to semantic entities. The semantics of a phrase thus entirely represents the *contribution* of the phrase to program semantics.

The semantic entities providing the semantics of parts of programs are usually more complex than those representing the behaviour of entire programs. For example, the semantics of a statement not only has to represent its direct contribution to observable program semantics (such as the relation between input and output) but also its *indirect* contribution by means of assignments to variables, etc.

Unfortunately, full abstractness is often difficult to obtain, at least when semantics is defined explicitly. In fact it has been shown *impossible* to give fully abstract *denotational* semantics for some rather simple programming languages [Plo77, Sto88]. In any case, a less-than-fully abstract semantics can be much simpler to specify, and the semantic equivalence that it provides between phrases may be adequate for most purposes. For instance, a semantics that is not fully abstract sets exactly the same standard for implementations as one that is fully abstract, provided the semantics of entire programs is the same, since requirements on implementations do not directly involve the semantics of phrases such as statements and expressions. So let us not demand full abstractness at all.

1.5.2 Semantic Entities

Semantic entities are used to represent the implementation-independent behaviour of programs, as well as the contributions that parts of programs make to overall behaviour. There are three kinds of semantic entity used in action semantics: *actions*, *data*, and *yielders*. The main kind is, of course, actions; data and yielders are subsidiary. The notation used in action semantics for specifying actions and the subsidiary semantic entities is called, unsurprisingly, *action notation*.

Actions are essentially dynamic, *computational* entities. The *performance* of an action directly represents information processing behaviour and reflects the gradual, step-wise nature of computation. Items of data are, in contrast, essentially static, *mathematical* entities, representing pieces of information, e.g., particular numbers. Of course actions are 'mathematical' too, in the sense that they are abstract, formally-defined entities, analogous to abstract machines as defined in automata theory. A yielder represents an *unevaluated* item of data, whose value depends on the *current information*, i.e., the previously-computed and input values that are available to the performance of the action in which the yielder occurs. For example, a yielder might always evaluate to the datum currently stored in a particular cell, which could change during the performance of an action.

Actions

A performance of an action, which may be part of an enclosing action, either:

- *completes*, corresponding to normal termination (the performance of the enclosing action proceeds normally); or

- *escapes*, corresponding to exceptional termination (parts of the enclosing action are skipped until the escape is trapped); or

- *fails*, corresponding to abandoning the performance of an action (the enclosing action performs an alternative action, if there is one, otherwise it fails too); or

- *diverges*, corresponding to nontermination (the enclosing action also diverges).

Actions can be used to represent the semantics of programs: action performances correspond to possible program behaviours. Furthermore, actions can represent the (perhaps indirect) contribution that *parts* of programs, such as statements and expressions, make to the semantics of entire programs.

An action may be nondeterministic, having different possible performances for the same initial information. Nondeterminism represents implementation-dependence, where the behaviour of a program (or the contribution of a part of it) may vary between different implementations—or even between different instants of time on the same implementation. Note that nondeterminism does not imply actual randomness: each implementation of a nondeterministic behaviour may be absolutely deterministic.

The information processed by action performance may be classified according to how far it tends to be propagated, as follows:

- *transient*: tuples of data, corresponding to intermediate results;

- *scoped*: bindings of tokens to data, corresponding to symbol tables;

- *stable*: data stored in cells, corresponding to the values assigned to variables;

- *permanent*: data communicated between distributed actions.

Transient information is made available to an action for immediate use. Scoped information, in contrast, may generally be referred to throughout an entire action, although it may also be hidden temporarily. Stable information can be changed, but not hidden, in the action, and it persists until explicitly destroyed. Permanent information cannot even be changed, merely augmented.

When an action is performed, transient information is given only on completion or escape, and scoped information is produced only on completion. In contrast, changes to stable information and extensions to permanent information are made *during* action performance, and are unaffected by subsequent divergence, failure, or escape.

The different kinds of information give rise to so-called *facets* of actions, focusing on the processing of at most one kind of information at a time:

- the *basic* facet, processing independently of information (control flows);

- the *functional* facet, processing transient information (actions are *given* and *give* data);

- the *declarative* facet, processing scoped information (actions *receive* and *produce* bindings);

- the *imperative* facet, processing stable information (actions *reserve* and *unreserve* cells of storage, and *change* the data stored in cells); and

- the *communicative* facet, processing permanent information (actions *send* messages, *receive* messages in buffers, and offer *contracts* to *agents*).

These facets of actions are independent. For instance, changing the data stored in a cell—or even unreserving the cell—does not affect any bindings. There are, however, some *directive* actions, which process a mixture of scoped and stable information, so as to provide finite representations of self-referential bindings. There are also some *hybrid* primitive actions and combinators, which involve more than one kind of information at once, such as an action that both reserves a cell of storage and gives it as transient data.

The standard notation for specifying actions consists of action *primitives*, which may involve yielders, and action *combinators*, which operate on one or two *subactions*.

Data

The information processed by actions consists of items of *data*, organized in structures that give access to the individual items. Data can include various familiar mathematical entities, such as truth-values, numbers, characters, strings, lists, sets, and maps. It can also include entities such as tokens, cells, and agents, used for accessing other items, and some compound entities with data components, such as messages and contracts. Actions themselves are not data, but they can be incorporated in so-called *abstractions*, which are data, and subsequently *enacted* back into actions. (Abstraction and enaction are a special case of so-called *reification* and *reflection*.) New kinds of data can be introduced *ad hoc*, for representing special pieces of information.

Yielders

Yielders are entities that can be *evaluated* to yield data during action performance. The data yielded may depend on the current information, i.e., the given transients, the received bindings, and the current state of the storage and buffer. In fact action notation provides primitive yielders that evaluate to compound data (tuples, maps, lists) representing entire slices of the current information, such as the current state of storage. Evaluation cannot affect the current information.

Compound yielders can be formed by the application of data operations to yielders. The data yielded by evaluating a compound yielder are the result of applying the operation to the data yielded by evaluating the operands. For instance, one can form the sum of two number yielders. Items of data are a special case of data yielders, and always yields themselves when evaluated.

1.6   Pragmatics

Let us conclude this chapter by considering the use of comprehensive language descriptions for setting *standards* for implementations.

The syntax of a programming language defines the set of legal programs, and the semantics of each program gives a representation of its implementation-independent behaviour. A standard for a programming language relates its syntax and semantics to properties of physical implementations, defining the class of *conforming* implementations. Thus it is concerned with the *pragmatics* of the language.

With syntax a standard may, for instance, require implementations to reject (with an informative error message) illegal programs, and perhaps allow them also to reject legal programs whose processing exceeds the available resources. It may allow national or typographical variations in the characters used to write programs.

It is important to realize in connection with semantics that the actual behaviour of a particular program may be allowed to vary between implementations—even between different runs on the same implementation! This variation may be represented in the semantics by loosely-specified entities, i.e., parameters, or by a nondeterministic relation between input and output. A standard may require certain parameters to be *implementation-defined*; the remaining ones are left *undefined*, and an implementation is free to choose. In ADA, for instance, the value of MAX_INT is implementation-defined, whereas the order of expression evaluation is generally left undefined.

Finally, note that although it may be feasible for a standard to *define* a class of implementations on the basis of syntactic and semantic descriptions, one may still not be able to *verify* that a particular implementation belongs to that class. In practice, it is feasible to verify only those implementations that have been developed systematically from language descriptions. A *validation suite* for a language is a particular set of programs that an implementation must process 'correctly' so as to be regarded as valid. The use of validation suites to test conformance to standards is a rather weak approximation to verification.

Summary

- *Various practitioners (designers, implementors, programmers) need descriptions of programming languages, but have differing requirements.*

- *Informal descriptions are inadequate, except for providing an accessible introduction to underlying concepts. Formal descriptions are adequate in theory, but often have pragmatic defects which discourage their use.*

- *Comprehensive language descriptions involve both syntax and semantics. Syntax concerns structure; semantics concerns behaviour.*

- *Concrete syntax concerns parsing of program texts into trees. Abstract syntax concerns only compositional, context-free structure of program trees. Context-sensitive syntax may be regarded as static semantics.*

- *Semantic functions map programs to representations of their behaviour, and parts of programs to representations of their contributions to program behaviour.*

- *When semantics is compositional, semantic equivalence implies interchangeability. When it is also fully abstract, semantic equivalence is the same as interchangeability. We demand compositionality, but not full abstractness.*

- *The semantic entities used in action semantics consist of actions, data, and data yielders. Actions represent information processing behaviour; they can be performed. Items of data represent pieces of information. Yielders in actions evaluate to data, determined by current information.*

- *Standards for implementations have to relate syntax and semantics to actual requirements, which is part of pragmatics.*

Navigation

- *Please try the exercises below. Then proceed to Chapter 2, which explains and illustrates how we formally specify abstract syntax, semantic functions, and semantic entities in this book.*

- *You could also make an excursion to Chapter 18 for a discussion of alternative frameworks for language description.*

Exercises

N.B. Some of the exercises in this book are based on the ADA Programming Language. ADA was chosen here primarily because its Reference Manual [ANS83, Geh83], although large, is quite accessible to the casual reader—thanks to its Glossary and copious cross-referencing. Moreover, our examples of action semantic descriptions involve constructs taken from ADA, and some of the exercises are concerned with extending or varying the examples.

1. Read through some of the ADA Reference Manual. Discuss how useful the style of language description used there might be for:

   (a) documentation of individual language design decisions during development;

   (b) setting definitive standards for implementations;

   (c) systematic development of implementations;

   (d) reasoning about programs.

2. Try to find some examples of incompleteness and/or inconsistency in the ADA Reference Manual. If you fail to find any, see [SIG89], which lists the official response to several hundred queries about details!

3. Make a list of the main implementation-dependent features of ADA, noting which are required to be implementation-defined, and which are intentionally left undefined. For example, find an undefined feature of expression evaluation in Section 4.5 of the ADA Reference Manual.

4. Consider the description of floating-point type-declarations in the ADA Reference Manual, Section 3.5.7, items 10 and 11. Discuss the advantages and disadvantages of using such equivalences in language descriptions.

5. Study the formal grammar specified in the ADA Reference Manual.

   (a) Draw the parse tree for the statement sequence null; P(A); .

   (b) Find an expression that has two different parse trees, thus showing that the grammar is ambiguous.

   (c) Which features of lexical symbols are not captured formally by the grammar?

6. List some of the context-sensitive constraints that ADA programs have to satisfy. For example, consider the visibility rules.

7. Various other frameworks for semantics, including structural operational semantics and axiomatic semantics, do not provide compositional semantic functions. Discuss whether compositionality in semantics is important.

8. Discuss the use of a validation suite for defining the syntax and semantics of a programming language. Which of the requirements mentioned in Section 1.2 does it meet?

Chapter 2

Action Semantic Descriptions

- *Action semantic descriptions are divided into modules.*

- *Grammars are used to specify abstract syntax.*

- *Semantic equations are used to specify semantic functions.*

- *Action semantics provides a standard notation for specifying semantic entities (actions, data, yielders).*

- *The standard notation can be extended and specialized by means of algebraic specifications.*

A semantic description consists of three main parts, concerned with specifying abstract syntax, semantic functions, and semantic entities. We specify these parts as separate *modules*, which, in larger specifications, may themselves be divided into *submodules*, just as we normally divide technical reports and textbooks into sections and subsections.

Let us adopt the following discipline in our modular specifications: each module has to have a *title*, and it has to be *self-contained*, in the sense that all the notation used in a module must be specified there too. Of course, when some module M uses notation that is already specified in another module M', there is no point in repeating all of M' literally in M: it is sufficient to *refer* to M' from M, using its title. Similarly, when the submodules M_i of a module M use some common notation, we may as well specify that notation just once, at the level of M, letting it be *inherited* by each M_i. A reference to a module M thus provides not only the notation specified directly in M and its submodules, but also that which is specified in modules referenced by M and in supermodules enclosing M.

The modular structure of an action semantic description is formally specified as follows.

Abstract Syntax .

Semantic Functions
     needs: **Abstract Syntax**, **Semantic Entities**.

Semantic Entities

We write titles of modules using initially capitalized words in **This Bold Font**. The specification above has three modules, with the obvious titles. We could give a title to the whole specification, if we wished; here let us simply inherit the title of the present chapter. Titles may be chosen freely, but it is a good idea to make them suggest the purpose of the module. The abstract syntax module and the semantic entities module are self-contained, and could be used independently. On the other hand, the semantic functions module *needs* the notation introduced by both the other modules, so its use implies their use too. Our notation for indicating modular structure is intended to be unobtrusive, and most of the time we shall disregard the modularization and focus on what is specified in the bodies of the modules. The bodies of the above modules are given later in this chapter. First, we note some practical points that are relevant mainly for larger semantic descriptions.

It is often helpful to divide the modules of semantic descriptions into *submodules*. For instance, suppose that we are describing the semantics of PASCAL. We might divide the abstract syntax module into submodules concerned with expressions, statements, and declarations. Similarly for the corresponding semantic functions module. We could also divide the semantic entities module into submodules dealing separately with numbers, arrays, procedures, etc. Such submodules might be reusable, with minor modifications, in other semantic descriptions.

Subdivision of modules does not require changes to already-specified module references, since a reference to a module implicitly provides all that its submodules specify. However, any dependencies between the new submodules have to be specified, which makes it counter-productive to carry subdivision to extremes. We refer to a submodule M_i of a module M by M/M_i, or just by M_i from within M itself.

We allow modules to be *mutually* dependent, and the order in which we present modules is immaterial. In abstract syntax, for instance, the specification of procedure declarations involves statements, and that of block statements involves declarations, so the corresponding modules have to be mutually dependent; similarly for the corresponding parts of the semantic equations. Most previous frameworks for modules insist on a strict hierarchy, thus forbidding mutual dependence.

A related point is that we are free to present modules in whatever order is most convenient for the reader. In semantic descriptions, it is preferable to present the specification of abstract syntax first, followed by the semantic functions, leaving the semantic entities to the end. This is assuming that the notation for semantic entities is well chosen, and its intended interpretation strongly suggested by the symbols used. When semantic entities are presented before the semantic functions, it can be difficult to appreciate them, independently of their usage. However, there is no need for us to be dogmatic about such matters, because the order in which modules are written has no effect at all on what they specify.

We may choose to specify a module *gradually*, by giving several incomplete specifications which, when combined, form the complete module. For clarity, the later specifications should explicitly indicate that a previous module with the same title is being *continued*. For instance, we may give an incomplete module that introduces some notation—and perhaps specifies its most essential properties—deferring the detailed definitions to an appendix where the module is completed. A similar effect could be achieved using extra submodules, but the accompanying specification of dependencies becomes a bit tedious on a large scale. An interactive module browser could let the user determine dynamically which partial views of each module are to be shown, which would be even better.

An extreme case of incomplete specification is giving only the modular structure, leaving out all the notation specified in the modules. For instance, the outline of modular structure of an action semantic description given above is itself a well-formed but incomplete specification. A completely empty module body is written as one or more periods '.'. Such an outline is especially useful when a specification involves a lot of modules, as do the Appendices of this book.

Finally, we use various devices to indicate that modules are submodules of other modules. For small specifications, indentation (formally equivalent to putting grouping parentheses around the indented part) is adequate for showing nesting structure. For larger specifications we either use absolute module titles of the form $/M_1/\cdots/M_n$, where M_1 is a top-level module, or we use numbered titles $m_1\cdots.m_n\ M$, where M is only the nth level title, as in ordinary technical documents. We allow informal text to be interjected freely between parts of our formal specifications. The reader should rely on typographical differences to distinguish between formal notation and informal text—something which otherwise is not quite so easy to do here as it is in most other formal frameworks ...

2.1   Abstract Syntax

Now let us consider how to specify abstract syntax. Reference manuals for programming languages generally use formal context-free *grammars*, augmented by some form of regular expressions, to specify *concrete* syntax. A formal grammar consists of a set of *productions*, involving *terminal* symbols, which may be characters or strings, as well as auxiliary *nonterminal* symbols. Formal grammars have excellent pragmatic properties, such as readability and modifiability; let us adapt them for specifying abstract syntax.

As an illustration, we specify an abstract syntax for a simple, impractical language, called SIMPLE, involving some basic statements and expressions. The main virtue of this example is that it nicely demonstrates the use of the formal notation that we use in action semantic descriptions, without the distracting (and sometimes tedious) details that arise when describing the semantics of realistic programming languages. Moreover, the SIMPLE language is a familiar example to readers who have studied previous frameworks for semantic description, such as denotational semantics, and most programmers will be able to recognize it as a much-restricted version of some high-level programming language that they have used. Hence we need not bother here to give an informal explanation of the intended semantics of SIMPLE, but focus our attention entirely on the *form* of its action semantic description.

grammar:

(1)   Statement = [[Identifier ":=" Expression]] |
                   [["if" Expression "then" Statement ⟨ "else" Statement ⟩$^?$]] |
                   [["while" Expression "do" Statement]] |
                   [["begin" Statements "end"]] .

(2)   Statements = ⟨ Statement ⟨ ";" Statement ⟩* ⟩ .

(3)   Expression = Numeral | Identifier | [["(" Expression ")"]] |
                   [[Expression Operator Expression]] .

(4)   Operator   = "+" | "−" | "*" | "≠" | "and" | "or" .

(5)   Numeral   = [[digit$^+$]] .

(6)   Identifier = [[letter (letter | digit)*]] .

closed.

Consider the grammar-like specification given above. It is the body of a module whose title, **Abstract Syntax**, is inherited from the present section. The module body consists mainly of a set of (numbered) equations. Ignoring the double brackets [[...]] for now, equations (3) and (4) have the same form as *productions* in a particular variant of BNF grammar—one that is commonly used for specifying concrete syntax in reference manuals, such as the ISO standard for PASCAL, differing a little from the variant used in the ADA reference manual. Terminal symbols are written as quoted strings of characters, such as "(" and "or". Nonterminal symbols are written as unquoted words, such as Expression, and we adopt the convention that they generally start with a capital letter, to avoid confusing them with symbols for semantic functions and entities, which we write using lower case letters. (Such conventions have no formal significance, and may be varied as desired.) The alternatives for each nonterminal symbol are started by =, separated by |, and terminated by a period.

The other equations above involve so-called *regular expressions*. In our notation, a regular expression is either a single symbol, or it consists of a *sequence* $\langle R_1 \dots R_n \rangle$, a grouped set of *alternatives* $(R_1 | \dots | R_n)$, an *optional* part $R^?$, an *optional repeatable* part R^*, or an *obligatory repeatable* part R^+. We do not use the rather inelegant notation for optional and repetitive parts provided by so-called EXTENDED BNF, despite its familiarity from reference manuals, because we have a better use for the brackets it uses for optional parts $[R]$, and its $\{R\}$ is hardly suggestive of ordered repetition! Moreover, EXTENDED BNF requires $R \{R\}$ to express that R is an *obligatory* repeatable part, whereas our R^+ avoids writing R twice.

The standard nonterminals digit and letter are always implicitly specified in our grammars, for convenience when specifying the lexical syntax of numerals and identifiers. The terminal symbols that they generate are single characters, rather than strings of characters. We make a distinction between a character, such as '0', and the string consisting of just that character, "0", following most programming languages.

In equation (1) the second alternative with the optional part $\langle$ "else" Statement $\rangle^?$ is equivalent to the following two alternatives:

$$[\![\text{ "if" Expression "then" Statement }]\!] \; | $$
$$[\![\text{ "if" Expression "then" Statement "else" Statement }]\!].$$

The use of such optional parts can often make grammars much more concise.

We could specify the abstract syntax of Statements in various ways. That shown in equation (2) earlier corresponds closely to the way that the *concrete* syntax of statements is usually specified in reference manuals. The usual style in texts on semantics corresponds to what we could write as:

$$\text{Statements} = \text{Statement} \; | \; [\![\text{ Statements ";" Statements }]\!] \; .$$

This is similar to the way we have specified the abstract syntax of expressions above. We then say that the nonterminal symbol Statements is *recursive*, both to the left and right. The choice of style doesn't matter much in the case of statements, because grouping is semantically irrelevant. It would matter if we were using grammars to specify *concrete* syntax: grammars with left and right recursive nonterminals are

always *ambiguous*, which makes them inappropriate as a basis for parsing—unless
disambiguation rules are specified as well. It also matters with *abstract* syntax for
expressions, which should be specified as shown in equation (3), since it is best to let
concrete syntax determine the grouping of subexpressions, and forget about how this
has been achieved when specifying abstract syntax, as mentioned in Section 1.4.2.

Note that occasionally, the use of recursive nonterminal symbols in abstract syntax
may needlessly complicate the semantic description. For instance, the abstract syntax
for **Digits** in Exercise 3 does *not* have a straightforward compositional semantics!

Recall that given a concrete syntax, we are free to choose *any* grammar for abstract
syntax—provided that we are prepared to specify how to map parse-trees to abstract
syntax trees. In this book, we do not bother with specifying concrete syntax formally
at all, but when we specify an abstract syntax we use ordinary lexical symbols as

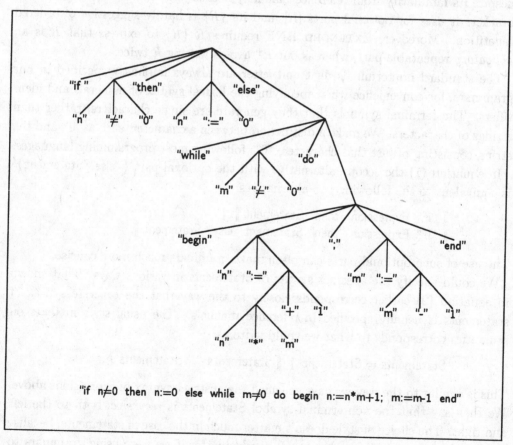

"if n≠0 then n:=0 else while m≠0 do begin n:=n*m+1; m:=m-1 end"

Box 2.1   An abstract syntax tree of a SIMPLE statement

terminal symbols in grammars, which makes it rather easy to imagine a corresponding concrete syntax (up to disambiguation of grouping, at least).

We have considered the form of the grammars that we use to specify abstract syntax. We defer the precise formal interpretation of a grammar as an *algebraic specification of sorts of trees* to Section 3.2. For now, it is enough to know that occurrences of ⟦ ... ⟧ indicate the construction of nodes of trees, and that strings are simply nodes whose branches are all single characters. We always write **grammar:** to ensure this interpretation of the subsequent equations. We also write **closed** at the end of a grammar, when all the productions have been given. The abstract syntax tree corresponding to a particular statement is shown in Box 2.1, for illustration. Notice that numerals and identifiers are *special cases* of expressions, rather than merely occurring as components of expressions. We do not indicate formally which nonterminal corresponds to entire *programs*, because we give the semantics of all phrases anyway. In the SIMPLE language, we may assume that a program consists of a single statement.

That concludes the explanation of how to specify abstract syntax for use in action semantic descriptions. See Section A.1 for a larger example.

2.2 Semantic Functions

In action semantics, we specify semantic functions by *semantic equations*. Each equation defines the semantics of a particular sort of phrase in terms of the semantics of its components, if any, using constants and operations for constructing semantic entities. The required compositionality of semantic functions is generally apparent from the semantic equations.

Mathematically, a set of semantic equations is simply an inductive definition of maps from syntax to semantics. Those familiar with algebraic semantics may understand the equations as a presentation of a target algebra; then the unique homomorphism to the target algebra from the initial algebra of abstract syntax corresponds to the semantic functions. Programmers may prefer to regard semantic equations as a definition of mutually-recursive functions by cases, as allowed, for instance, in the functional programming language HASKELL.

It is also possible to view a set of semantic equations as merely specifying a *translation* from programming language syntax to *notation* for semantic entities. But it is the semantic entities themselves that count, not the notation in which they are expressed: two phrases may get translated differently yet still have the same semantics.

As an illustration, let us specify the action semantics of SIMPLE on the basis of the abstract syntax given earlier. The semantic equations that define the required semantic functions are shown below in their entirety. The various symbols used in the right hand sides of the equations are explained in Part II. Most of them are rather suggestive of their intended operational interpretation, except perhaps for the combination unfolding ... unfold ..., which represents iteration. For now, we are concerned only with the *form* of semantic equations, not with the semantics that they specify.

introduces: execute _ , evaluate _ , the operation-result of _ , the value of _ .

- execute _ :: Statements → action [completing | diverging | storing] .

(1)   execute ⟦ I:Identifier ":=" E:Expression ⟧ =
        (give the cell bound to I and evaluate E)
        then store the given number#2 in the given cell#1 .

(2)   execute ⟦ "if" E:Expression "then" S_1:Statement ⟧ =
        evaluate E then
          | check the given truth-value and then execute S_1
          or
          | check not the given truth-value and then complete .

(3)   execute ⟦ "if" E:Expression "then" S_1:Statement "else" S_2:Statement ⟧ =
        evaluate E then
          | check the given truth-value and then execute S_1
          or
          | check not the given truth-value and then execute S_2 .

(4)   execute ⟦ "while" E:Expression "do" S:Statement ⟧ =
        unfolding
          | evaluate E then
            | check the given truth-value and then execute S
            | and then unfold
          or
            | check not the given truth-value and then complete .

(5)   execute ⟦ "begin" S:Statements "end" ⟧ = execute S .

(6)   execute ⟨ S_1:Statement ";" S_2:Statements ⟩ = execute S_1 and then execute S_2 .

- evaluate _ :: Expression → action [giving a value] .

(7)   evaluate N:Numeral = give the value of N .

(8)   evaluate I:Identifier =
        give the value bound to I or
        give the number stored in the cell bound to I .

(9)   evaluate ⟦ "(" E:Expression ")" ⟧ = evaluate E .

(10)   evaluate ⟦ E_1:Expression O:Operator E_2:Expression ⟧ =
        (evaluate E_1 and evaluate E_2) then give the operation-result of O .

- the operation-result of _ :: Operator → yielder [of a value] [using the given value[2]] .

(11) the operation-result of "+" = the number yielded by
the sum of (the given number#1, the given number#2) .

(12) the operation-result of "−" = the number yielded by
the difference of (the given number#1, the given number#2) .

(13) the operation-result of "*" = the number yielded by
the product of (the given number#1, the given number#2) .

(14) the operation-result of "≠" =
not (the given value#1 is the given value#2) .

(15) the operation-result of "and" =
both of (the given truth-value#1, the given truth-value#2) .

(16) the operation-result of "or" =
either of (the given truth-value#1, the given truth-value#2) .

- the value of _ :: Numeral → number .

(17) the value of N:Numeral = number & decimal N .

A semantic function always takes a single, syntactic argument and gives a semantic entity as result. The symbols used to denote semantic functions may be chosen freely; in this book we try to maximize their suggestiveness, at the expense of conciseness, but this is not obligatory. Each symbol generally consists of several words, e.g., the operation-result of _ , and the place-holder _ indicates where the argument goes.

It is usual to specify the *functionality* of each semantic function. For instance, evaluate _ :: Expression → action [giving a value] asserts that for every abstract syntax tree E for an expression, the semantic entity evaluate E is an action which, when performed, gives a value. The actual definition of evaluate E by the semantic equations is then required to be consistent with this.

The right hand sides of the semantic equations involve the standard notation for actions and data provided by action semantics. It must be emphasized that the notation is *absolutely formal*! The fact that it is possible to read it informally—and reasonably fluently—does not preclude reading it formally as well. The grouping of the symbols might not be completely obvious to those who have not seen action notation before, but it is in fact unambiguous. Some hints about the general form of action notation are given in the next section. All the formal symbols used are explained in Part II. For a summary one may refer to Appendix D. But for now, it is not necessary to understand the intended interpretation of action notation.

Each semantic equation defines the result of applying a particular semantic function to any abstract syntax tree whose root node has the indicated form, in terms of applying (perhaps different) semantic functions to the branches of the node. For instance, equation (2) above defines the application of the semantic function **execute** _ to nodes with four branches, where the first branch is the string "if", the second an expression E, the third "then", and the last branch is a statement S, in terms of **evaluate** E and **execute** S. Even though the presence of "if" as the first branch of a valid abstract syntax tree implies that the second branch is an expression and the fourth a statement, we specify this relation explicitly, as shown in equation (2), for technical reasons (explained in Section 3.3). Readers familiar with denotational semantics should observe that we do *not* write $[\![\, E \,]\!]$ and $[\![\, S \,]\!]$ on the right of the equation, since E and S by themselves already stand for trees. Nevertheless, we can still regard $[\![\, \ldots \,]\!]$ informally as separating syntactic symbols from semantic symbols in the left hand side of a semantic equation.

Since we allow regular expressions in our grammars, we have to be able to define semantic functions on nodes with an unbounded number of branches. Our technique for this is illustrated in equations (5) and (6) above. The use of the angle brackets $\langle \ldots \rangle$ instead of $[\![\, \ldots \,]\!]$ in equation (6) indicates that we are defining a function on a *tuple* of nodes, rather than on a single node. Tupling here is associative, i.e., $\langle\, x\, \langle\, y\ z\,\rangle\,\rangle$ is the same as $\langle\, \langle\, x\ y\,\rangle\ z\,\rangle$, so when tuple notation is used in the left hand side of a semantic equation, we have to ensure it cannot be matched in more than one way to a tuple argument. In equation (6) we insist that S_1 should match a *single* statement, whereas S_2 may match any sequence of statements; we could just as well interchange the restrictions. Incidentally, $\langle\, x\,\rangle$ is the same as x, regardless of whether x is itself a tuple or a node, and the empty tuple may be written as $\langle\ \rangle$. The formal interpretation of our tupling notation is explained in Section 3.2.

Sometimes, the semantics of a particular sort of node is uniform, i.e., independent of the deeper structure of the tree. Then the argument of the semantic function may be a single variable, restricted to the corresponding sort of node, and the right hand side of the semantic equation may involve the application of a different semantic function to the variable. See equations (7) and (8) for examples. When the semantics of a syntactic construct is that construct itself, considered as a semantic entity, as is the case for identifiers in the example above, we do not need to write a semantic function. In fact that is the case for numerals too: **decimal** _ is a *standard* operation mapping strings[1] to natural numbers, and N is its own semantics! Of course, we could define a semantic function corresponding to **decimal** _ rather easily, but here we keep the example as short as possible, and leave the specification of the semantics of numerals as an exercise, see Exercise 3.

---

[1] Strings are regarded as both syntactic *and* semantic entities.

When we define two different semantic functions f, g for the same syntactic construct x, we really intend *the* semantics of x to be (essentially) the *pair* $(f\ x,\ g\ x)$. It is usually notationally more convenient to define the components of such a pair separately than to define them together. In our example, we have both **evaluate** _ and **the value of** _ as semantic functions for numerals. Here, one of the two semantic functions is defined in terms of the other, but this need not be the case in general. Similarly for more than two semantic functions on the same syntactic constructs.

Each semantic function must be defined *consistently* and *completely* on the sort of abstract syntax tree for which it is required. Thus any tree of that sort must match the pattern in the left hand side of precisely one semantic equation for that function. When the right hand sides of equations involve applications of semantic functions only to branches of the tree matching the left hand side, well-definedness is ensured; otherwise, one has to check that no direct circularities are involved.

To see *how* our semantic equations define the semantics of statements, the reader might like to use them to work out the action corresponding to the SIMPLE statement if x $\neq$ 0 then x := x + 1. Starting from the application of **execute** _ to the abstract syntax tree of the statement, each application of a semantic function to a tree is replaced by the right hand side of the matching equation, with the variables E, S, etc., replaced by the corresponding subtrees, until no semantic functions remain. Clearly, the final result is independent of the order in which replacements are made.

2.3   Semantic Entities

To complete our semantic description of SIMPLE programs, we have to specify the notation that is used in the semantic equations for expressing semantic entities. In fact the standard notation provided by action semantics already includes notation for all the actions we need, so we refer to the module that specifies the standard notation as shown below.

includes: **Action Notation.**

We use **includes** here so as to make the notation specified in the module **Action Notation** available not only in the current module, **Semantic Entities**, but also in the module that refers to it, **Semantic Functions**. Had we used **needs** instead of **includes**, we would have to refer to **Action Notation** explicitly from **Semantic Functions**.

Action notation consists mainly of action *primitives* and *combinators*. Each primitive is concerned with one particular kind of information processing, and makes no contribution to the other kinds. Each combinator, on the other hand, expresses a particular mixture of control flow and how the various kinds of information flow. Action notation was designed with sufficient primitives and combinators for expressing most common patterns of information processing straightforwardly, i.e., not *simulating* one kind of information processing by another.

Action notation also incorporates a basic notation for *data*, including truth-values, rational numbers, lists, and finite maps.

The standard symbols used in action notation are ordinary English *words*. In fact action notation mimics natural language: terms standing for actions form imperative verb phrases involving conjunctions and adverbs, e.g., check it and then escape, whereas terms standing for data and yielders form noun phrases, e.g., the items of the given list. Definite and indefinite articles can be exploited appropriately, e.g., choose a cell then reserve the given cell. (This feature of action notation is reminiscent of Apple's HYPERCARD scripting language HYPERTALK [Goo87], and of COBOL.)

These simple principles for choice of symbols provide a surprisingly grammatical fragment of English, allowing specifications of actions to be made fluently readable—without sacrificing formality at all! To specify grouping unambiguously, we may use parentheses, but for large-scale grouping it is less obtrusive to use indentation, which we emphasize by vertical rules, as illustrated in the semantic equations for statements given earlier.

Compared to other formalisms, such as the so-called λ-*notation*, action notation may appear to lack conciseness: each symbol generally consists of several letters, rather than a single sign. But the comparison should also take into account that each action combinator usually corresponds to a complex pattern of applications and abstractions in λ-notation. For instance, (under the simplifying assumption of determinism!) the action term A_1 then A_2 might correspond to something like $\lambda\epsilon_1.\lambda\rho.\lambda\kappa.A_1\epsilon_1\rho(\lambda\epsilon_2.A_2\epsilon_2\rho\kappa)$. In any case, the increased length of each symbol seems to be far outweighed by its increased perspicuity. It would also be rather misleading to use familiar mathematical signs to express actions, whose essence is unashamedly computational. For some applications, however, such as formal reasoning about program equivalence on the basis of their action semantics, optimal conciseness may be highly desirable, and it would be appropriate to use abbreviations for our verbose symbols. The choice of abbreviations is left to the discretion of the user. Such changes of symbols do not affect the *essence* of action notation, which lies in the standard primitives and combinators, rather than in the standard verbose symbols.

The informal appearance and suggestive words of action notation should encourage programmers to read it, at first, rather casually, in the same way that they might read reference manuals. Having thus gained a broad impression of the intended actions, they may go on to read the specification more carefully, paying attention to the details. A more cryptic notation might discourage programmers from reading it altogether.

The intended interpretation of the standard notation for actions is specified operationally, once and for all, in Appendix C. All that one has to do before using action notation is to specify the information that is to be processed by actions, which may vary significantly according to the programming language being described. This may involve *extending* data notation with further sorts of data, and *specializing* standard sorts, using sort equations. Furthermore, it may be convenient to introduce formal *abbreviations* for commonly-occurring, conceptually-significant patterns of notation. Extensions, specializations, and abbreviations are all specified *algebraically*, as explained in detail in the next chapter. The specification below illustrates the use of sort equations to specialize some standard sorts of data, and to specify two nonstandard sorts of data for use in the semantic equations, namely value and number.

introduces: value , number .

(1)   datum   = cell | number | truth-value | □ .
(2)   token   = string of (letter, (letter | digit)*) .
(3)   bindable = cell | number .
(4)   storable = number .
(5)   value   = number | truth-value .
(6)   number ≤ integer .

We use the same symbol | for *sort union* as we used for combining alternatives in grammars. Thinking of sorts of data as *sets* (which isn't quite right, but close enough for now) we may regard | as ordinary set union; it is associative, commutative, and idempotent.[2] Although sort equations look a bit like the so-called domain equations used in denotational semantics, their formal interpretation is quite different. The next chapter explains sort equations in some detail. As well as equations we may specify sort inclusions, as in (6) above; in fact the use of □ in equation (1) also expresses an inclusion, as it leaves open what other sorts might be included in datum.

Let us not dwell on the intended interpretation of the semantic entities specified above, since the purpose of this chapter is merely to illustrate the form of action semantic descriptions, and the details of our simple example are not particularly interesting in themselves.

---

[2]Idempotency of _|_ means $X \mid X = X$.

Summary

- *Action semantic descriptions are divided into modules.*

- *In general, modules can be nested, and specified gradually. The titles of modules are used for reference. Mutual dependence is allowed.*

- *Our grammars for specifying abstract syntax are context-free. They allow regular expressions. Double brackets ⟦ ... ⟧ indicate node construction. Terminal symbols may be characters or strings. Abstract syntax is not concerned with parsing, so the possible ambiguity of grammars is irrelevant.*

- *Semantic equations are inductive definitions of semantic functions that map abstract syntax trees compositionally to semantic entities. The semantic equations for a particular semantic function must be exhaustive, and must not overlap.*

- *The standard notation provided by action semantics for semantic entities is called action notation. It includes notation for data and data yielders.*

- *Action notation can be extended* ad hoc *with new notation for data, and the information processed by actions can be specialized to include particular data. Abbreviations can be introduced. All this is specified algebraically, using an expressive meta-notation that also encompasses grammars and semantic equations, as explained in the next chapter.*

Navigation

- *If you would now like to see how a medium-scale action semantic description looks, make an excursion to Appendix A.*

- *Otherwise, proceed to Chapter 3 for an explanation of the simple, expressive, and somewhat unorthodox framework for algebraic specifications that we use in action semantics.*

Exercises

1. Study the grammar specified in the ADA Reference Manual.

   (a) Compare the form of BNF used for ADA with that used in our grammars. Discuss their relative merits.

(b) Give an appropriate abstract syntax for ADA's if-statement.

2. Consider the following alternative abstract syntax for SIMPLE Statements:

Statements = Statement | ⟦ Statements ";" Statements ⟧ .

(a) Draw a new abstract syntax tree for the statement shown in Box 2.1. Notice that there are several possibilities, corresponding to different groupings of statement sequences.

(b) Change the semantic equation for **Statements** to match the new abstract syntax.

(c) Discuss how the change to the abstract syntax might affect the relation between the abstract syntax and some given concrete syntax for SIMPLE.

3. Consider the following abstract syntax for decimal numerals:

Digits = digit | ⟦ Digits Digits ⟧ .

(a) Draw several abstract syntax trees for the numeral 102.

(b) Extend the semantic function **the value of _** for SIMPLE numerals to Digits, using the standard data notation for natural numbers: the constants 0, 1, ..., 10 and the operations sum (_ , _) and product (_ , _). Do not confuse the quoted character symbol '0' with the unquoted numerical constant 0! Hint: you may need to introduce a secondary semantic function for Digits.

(c) Repeat (a) and (b) after changing the rightmost occurrence of Digits above to digit. Now there is no need for a secondary semantic function! In fact to retain it prevents the semantics from being fully abstract. Can you see why?

(d) Finally, revert to the original abstract syntax for **Numeral** in SIMPLE and extend the semantic function **the value of _** to digit⁺, analogously to (c). Investigate how one might define the semantics of decimal *fractions* on the basis of the *same* abstract syntax.

4. Choose an abstract syntax for Roman numerals and specify the intended semantics. For example, the tree corresponding to "MCMXLVIII" should have semantics 1948; "DIV" should give 504.

Chapter 3

Algebraic Specifications

- *Algebraic specifications are used here for specifying standard notation for data, and for extending and specializing our standard notation for actions.*

- *Our unorthodox framework for algebraic specification copes well with partial operations, generic data, polymorphism, and nondeterminism.*

- *Algebraic specifications introduce symbols, assert axioms, and constrain models, as illustrated here by a natural example.*

- *The grammars and semantic equations used in action semantic descriptions can easily be regarded as algebraic specifications.*

- *The structural operational semantics of action notation is written as an algebraic specification of a transition function.*

This chapter is mainly concerned with the details of how we specify notation for data. It also introduces the foundations of action semantics. Some readers may prefer to defer the detailed study of the example given here, because when reading action semantic descriptions one may take it for granted that data can indeed be specified algebraically, and that foundations do exist. Moreover, action notation does not depend much on the unorthodox features of our algebraic specification framework. On the other hand, readers who are used to conventional algebraic specifications are advised to look closely at this chapter before proceeding, as they may otherwise find it difficult to reconcile our examples with their experience.

First, some standard terminology. An *algebra* consists essentially of a *universe*, or *carrier*, of *values*, together with some distinguished *operations* on values. Operations of no arguments are called *constants*. The *signature* of an algebra provides *symbols* for distinguishing the operations; we say also that an algebra provides an *interpretation* for the symbols in its signature. *Terms* are constructed from symbols and *variables*. In any particular algebra, an *assignment* of values to variables determines the values of terms.

An *algebraic specification* determines a signature, and restricts the class of all algebras with that signature using *axioms*: each algebra in the specified class has to *satisfy* all the axioms. We call an algebra in the specified class a *model* for the specification. An axiom is often just an equation between terms, universally quantified over all the variables that occur in it, but more general forms of axiom are allowed. A specification may also impose *constraints*, for instance to narrow its class of models to so-called *initial* algebras. Initial algebras are unique up to isomorphism, and can be regarded as *standard* models, as explained below. A class of specified algebras is generally called an *abstract data type*.

Most frameworks for algebraic specification support the notion of a *sort*. The essence of a sort is that it *classifies* the *individual* values of a universe, according to some common attributes. Thus a sort has an *extension*: the set of individuals that it classifies. But two sorts with the same extension may have different *intension*, and thus remain distinct. For instance, the sort of all integers greater than zero has the same extension as the sort of all natural numbers with a well-defined reciprocal, but these sorts may have different intension.

Now that we have some idea of *what* a sort is, let us consider *why* we should bother at all to specify sorts in algebraic specifications. Why is it useful to classify the individuals of a universe?

First of all, classification according to common properties is a fundamental *abstraction* principle, allowing us to perceive (or at least, to express our perception of) order amongst chaos. Simply by classifying a particular set of individuals together, we draw attention to the existence of *some* relationship between them.

Another important use of sorts is to allow us to specify the *functionalities* of operations, i.e., which sort of result each operation returns when applied to arguments of appropriate sorts. Some frameworks allow only one functionality to be specified for each operation, thus preventing so-called *overloading*, but this seems unfortunate: when exploited judiciously, overloading can be very useful. We might want to specify a print operation for all sorts of values, for example. Or we might want an if-then-else operation, where the sort of the second and third arguments could be arbitrary. Functionality specifications are commonly treated as part of signatures, but here we regard them as a particular kind of axiom.

When the extensions of sorts can overlap, we expect so-called *subsort polymorphism*. For example, the numerical product operation not only maps integers to integers, it also maps natural numbers to natural numbers; similarly for sorts classifying positive integers, the even or odd numbers, and for the singleton sorts classifying just zero or one! However, many restrictions of the sorts of arguments lead to uninteresting sorts of returned values, and it is pointless to specify these as functionalities.

In axioms, sorts are generally used for *restricting* assignments to *variables* to particular subsets of the universe. For instance, the product operation may be commutative on numbers but not on matrices; the commutativity axiom for product must then be restricted to numbers.

Most frameworks for algebraic specification treat sorts very differently from individuals. Typically, sorts are restricted to constants: no sort construction or restriction operations are allowed, not even union and intersection, nor can sorts be assigned to variables. Here, we go to the opposite extreme by regarding *sorts as values*! We can then have operations that map entire sorts to sorts. For example, an operation might map any sort S to the sort of lists whose components are all of sort S. A vacuous sort that includes no individuals at all turns out to be surprisingly useful, as it can represent undefined results of partial operations.

However, by focusing on sorts so much, we have been neglecting the *individuals*. It is important to bear in mind that we do not specify sorts for their own sake: it is the individual values, and the operations upon these, that are the real aim of an algebraic specification, and the sorts are only there to *facilitate* the specification. Where do individuals fit in, when sorts are regarded as values?

Think, for the moment, of sorts as sets. A singleton set is (in general) distinct from its only element. This is important in set theory, where one often considers sets of sets, and it would be inconvenient to treat singletons specially. But here, all we need to do is to classify *individuals* into sorts: we do not require sorts of sorts. Thus we can avoid introducing any distinction between a sort that classifies a single individual, and that individual itself. *An individual is merely a special case of a sort!* Let us refer to a sort as *proper* when it includes at least two individuals.

Another way of understanding our unorthodox treatment of sorts and individuals is to regard sorts as *nondeterministic choices* between individuals. A so-called Hobson's choice[1] of a single individual may be treated as a special case, where the nondeterminism has collapsed into determinism. Essentially, a sort is a collection of individuals; a collection consisting of a single individual is no different from that individual alone.

Once we have individuals as a special case of sorts, we immediately get the possibility of having operations that map individuals to sorts, for instance mapping a

---

[1]For readers unfamiliar with this idiom: 'option of taking the one offered or nothing [from T. Hobson, Cambridge carrier (d. 1631) who let out horses on this basis]'.

number n to the sort of lists of length at most n. We may also extend ordinary operations on individuals in a natural way to nontrivial sorts, under the assumption of *monotonicity*: as an argument sort increases, the result sort can only increase, or remain constant. The successor operation can be extended to map any sort of natural numbers to the sort of their individual successors, for example.

This is not the place for a comparison between our unorthodox algebraic specification framework and conventional frameworks, such as *many-sorted algebras* [GTW78, Wir90, Wir91] or *order-sorted algebras* [GM89]. Let our examples speak for themselves! Readers who wish to study the technical details of our framework should consult the paper 'Unified Algebras and Institutions' [Mos89b]; the use of sorts in various frameworks for algebraic specification is surveyed in [Mos92].

3.1   A Natural Example

Let us now consider an example of an algebraic specification. This is intended to illustrate not only concepts and techniques, but also the notation we use to write specifications. This notation is called a *meta-notation*, because it is for introducing and defining other notation.

The example is rather simple and familiar: it involves only truth-values, natural numbers, and a few of the usual operations on numbers. Nevertheless, it is sufficiently rich to exhibit most of the features of our meta-notation. Later chapters give examples with more intrinsic interest.

The modular structure of the example is as follows:

> **Truth-Values** .
>
> **Natural Numbers**
>
>> **Basics** .
>>
>> **Specifics**
>>> **needs:**   **Basics**, **Truth Values**.

Thus it has two main modules, the second being divided into two submodules entitled **Basics** and **Specifics**. It is possible to use **Truth-Values** and **Natural Numbers/Basics** independently, but a reference to the entire **Natural Numbers** module implicitly involves **Truth-Values** as well.[2] The module bodies are specified as follows.

---

[2]Similar, but not identical, modules are specified in Chapter 5 and Appendix E.

Truth Values

   introduces: truth-value , true , false .

   (1)   true : truth-value ;   false : truth-value .

   (2)   truth-value = true | false .

   (3)   nothing = true & false .

   closed .

Natural Numbers

Basics

   introduces: natural , 0 , successor _ .

   (1)   0 : natural .

   (2)   successor _ :: natural $\rightarrow$ natural (*total, injective*) .

   (3)   natural = 0 | successor natural   (*disjoint*) .

   closed .

Specifics

   introduces: 1 , sum (_ , _) , product (_ , _) .

   (1)   1 = successor 0 .

   (2)   sum (_ , _)   :: natural, natural $\rightarrow$ natural
                            (*total, associative, commutative, unit is* 0) .

   (3)   product (_ , _) :: natural, natural $\rightarrow$ natural
                            (*total, associative, commutative, unit is* 1) .

   (4)   sum (n:natural, 1) = successor n .

   (5)   product (n:natural, 0) = 0 .

   (6)   product (m:natural, successor n:natural) = sum (m, product (m, n)) .

   introduces: _ is _ .

   (7)   _ is _ :: natural, natural $\rightarrow$ truth-value (*total, commutative*) .

   (8) n : natural $\Rightarrow$ (n is n) = true .

   (9)   0 is successor (n:natural) = false .

   (10)   successor (m:natural) is successor (n:natural) = m is n .

3.1.1 Symbols

Let us first consider the *symbols* introduced by the various modules specified above.
We write each symbol using place-holders _ to indicate where any arguments should
go. Thus a symbol without place-holders, such as natural or 0, is always a constant.

When we apply operations to arguments in terms, we use *mixfix* notation,[3] writing the arguments instead of the place-holders and enclosing arguments in grouping
parentheses (...) only when necessary for disambiguation. Let us refer to an operation symbol as *infix*, *prefix*, *postfix*, or *outfix*, according to whether it starts and
finishes with place-holders, only finishes with a place-holder, only starts with a place-
holder, or only has internal place-holders, respectively. The operation symbol _ ,
invisible when used, is not allowed, to avoid ambiguity. Note that sum (_ , _) and
product (_ , _) are regarded as outfix operation symbols, because the parentheses
are part of the symbols.

It is convenient to adopt the following *precedence rule* in terms: outfixes have the
weakest precedence, followed first by infixes, then by prefixes, and postfixes have the
strongest precedence. Moreover, infixes are grouped to the left. Taking account of
precedence, a well-formed term usually has a unique grouping.

Parentheses may be inserted freely around terms, and other parts of specifications,
in order to enforce alternative grouping, provide disambiguation, or merely confirm an
already unambiguous grouping. Indentation—perhaps emphasized by a vertical line
or by enumeration—is equivalent to enclosing the indented part of the specification
in parentheses. Use of indentation helps to avoid the plethora of parentheses that
often plagues formal specifications.

Note that applications of prefix operations to arguments always require grouping
when the argument is an infix application, but not when it is a prefix or postfix
application. For instance, successor successor 0 is unambiguously grouped.[4] We could
insist on parentheses around arguments to the successor operation by introducing the
symbol successor (_) instead of successor _ .

All the symbols used in a module have to be introduced explicitly, except for the
built-in infixes _|_ and _&_, and the constant nothing, whose intended interpretation
is explained later. The introduction of a symbol merely allows that symbol to be used
(applied to the evident number of arguments) in the axioms of the enclosing module,
and in other modules that refer to that module. It does *not* restrict the interpretation
of the symbol. In particular, the introduction of a constant such as natural or 0 does

---

[3]So-called because of the way it generalizes infix, prefix, and postfix notation.
[4]We do not allow higher-order operations, so the grouping (successor successor) 0 need not be
considered.

not specify whether the constant is intended to stand for an individual, or for a proper sort comprising several individuals.

Those familiar with conventional algebraic specifications should note particularly that the mere introduction of an operation symbol here does *not* indicate any restriction on the sort of arguments of the operation. Formally, signatures are simply ranked alphabets. Specifications of functionalities are axioms. Thus terms are well-formed provided only that each operation symbols has the right *number* of argument terms, so sum (true is natural, truth-value) is just as well-formed as the term sum (1, 0) is 1.

Each symbol in a specification usually stands for the *same* entity throughout, regardless of the modularization. The ordinary introduction of a particular symbol serves only to make the symbol available, it does *not* create a distinct version of it! Thus a constant such as 0 must always stand for the same value, and if we needed to distinguish between, say, natural zero and 'real' zero, we would have to use different symbols for them. Sometimes, however, we may need an auxiliary symbol for local use in some module. We can restrict its use to the module by prefixing its introduction by **privately**. Formally, this corresponds to *translating* the symbol to a peculiar symbol formed from it using the sequence of titles that identifies the enclosing module. Thus when modules are combined, their privately-introduced symbols never clash with each other, nor with ordinarily-introduced ones.

3.1.2   Axioms

Apart from introducing some symbols, a module generally asserts some *axioms*, and perhaps a *constraint*. Let us consider the various forms of axiom first, starting with those illustrated in the module **Truth-Values** above.

Axiom (1) is the conjunction of two *individual inclusions* of the form $x : y$. Such an inclusion asserts both that x is an individual, and that the individual is included in the sort y. Because an individual is regarded as a special case of a sort, we can write $x : x$ to assert only that x is an individual, without specifying any (other) sort for it. Let us write $x!$ as an abbreviation for $x : x$, because the latter looks a bit paradoxical to those used to maintaining a separation between individuals and sorts. More generally, we can write $x \leq y$ to assert the *sort inclusion* of x as a subsort of y; it follows that all individuals included in x are also included in y. Sort inclusion is a partial order, so $x \leq y \leq x$ implies $x = y$. Note that $\leq$ is reserved for the sort inclusion relation, and should not be used as an operation symbol.

Axiom (2) is a *sort equation* identifying **truth-value** with the *sort union* true | false. This implies that both **true** and **false** are included in **truth-value**, which we already know from (1), but it also tells us that *nothing else* is included in **truth-value**.

Axiom (3) essentially prevents **true** and **false** from being the same individual by insisting that their *sort intersection* **true & false** is the vacuous sort **nothing**, which never includes any individuals.[5] Axioms (1) and (3) together can be conveniently abbreviated by inserting the word *individual* at the end of axiom (2). See Section F.2 for the precise schematic expansion of this and all the other formal abbreviations that we use to improve the conciseness *and* comprehensibility of our algebraic specifications. The operations _ | _ and _ & _ have the same properties as set union and intersection, i.e., they are the join and meet of a distributive lattice; see Section F.4 for the details. The final line of **Truth-Values** specifies the *constraint* **closed**, explained in Section 3.1.3.

Moving on to the **Basics** submodule of **Natural Numbers** above, axiom (1) is another individual inclusion. Axiom (2) specifies the *functionality* of the operation **successor** _ , with *total* and *injective* as *attributes*. By itself, the functionality specification **successor** _ :: **natural** → **natural** implies that whenever the argument is included in the sort **natural**, the result is included in **natural** too, but it leaves open whether the operation maps individuals to individuals, or to more general sorts. The attribute *total* implies that the result is an individual whenever the argument is an individual of the specified sort, i.e., **natural** here. Since 0:**natural**, it follows that any iterated application of **successor** to 0 returns an individual. The attribute *partial*, not illustrated here, is weaker than *total*, in that it allows the result to be either an individual or vacuous when the argument is an individual. The attribute *injective* specifies that the operation is a one-one function on individuals.

One may specify as many functionality axioms as desired for each operation symbol, even none at all! An operation symbol that has specified functionalities with disjoint argument sorts might be called *overloaded*, although we can also view this as *subsort polymorphism* by considering each functionality as a restriction of a single, unspecified functionality involving unions of the specified argument and result sorts.

The standard data notation used in action semantics makes good use of operations on sorts; it also uses nontrivial sorts to represent nondeterministic entities, with a sort corresponding to the choice between the individuals included in it. The built-in vacuous sort, written **nothing**, turns out to be a particularly convenient representation of lacking results of *partial operations*. One may also specify special *error values* if one wants to distinguish between different reasons for the lack of a normal result.

Ordinary operations like **successor** are mainly intended for application to individuals. However, that does not prevent us contemplating their application to more general sorts. For instance, we may apply the **successor** operation to the vacuous

---

[5] If **nothing** were specified to include individuals, our specifications would have only trivial models.

sort nothing, or to a proper sort such as 0 | 1 or natural. All operations are required to be *monotonic* with respect to sort inclusion. Thus from $s_1 \leq s_2$ we can infer successor $s_1 \leq$ successor s_2. This ensures that successor natural includes all the individuals successor^{i}0 for $i = 1, 2, \ldots$, i.e., all the positive integers. It is natural to let successor nothing = nothing, and successor $(0 \mid 1) = 1 \mid 2$ (where 1 and 2 abbreviate applications of successor _ to 0). Both *total* and *partial* imply the attributes *strict* (the operation maps nothing to nothing) and *linear* (the operation distributes over sort union) so we do not need to specify any further attributes than *total* to get the desired extension of successor _ to general sorts. Note that the attribute *injective* for an operation implies that the operation distributes over sort intersection; this property corresponds closely to one-oneness, at least for *total* operations.

Finally, axiom (3) of **Basics** asserts not only that any natural number is either 0 or in the range of successor _ , but also that 0 and the range of successor _ are *disjoint*, using an abbreviation in the same style as *individual*, explained earlier. Note that we cannot introduce an operation corresponding to disjoint sort union, since that would not be monotonic.

Now for **Specifics**. Axiom (1) is an individual equation, specifying that the new constant 1 is merely an *abbreviation* for what can already be written with the notation introduced by **Basics**. Note that we do *not* need to specify that 1 is an individual, included in natural, because that follows from the specified properties of 0 and successor _ .

Axiom (2) specifies the functionality of sum (_ , _). The attributes *associative*, *commutative*, and *unit is* 0 all abbreviate equations. We could specify further functionalities, to provide supplementary information about how the sort of result varies with the sorts of arguments. For example, we could specify sum (_ , _) :: positive-integer, positive-integer $\rightarrow$ positive-integer, where positive-integer = successor natural. Similarly for product (_ , _) in axiom (3).

Attributes are restricted by the specified functionality. For instance, those specified for sum (_ , _) and product (_ , _) apply when both arguments are included in natural, but not necessarily for other sorts of arguments. Thus an operation may have fewer attributes when extended to larger sorts of arguments, for example product (_ , _) is no longer total and commutative when extended from numbers to matrices, although it is still associative. When an operation is extended to sorts of arguments that are *disjoint* from the original ones, it may have entirely different properties on the new and old arguments—although in practice it is then advisable to use a different operation symbol, instead of overloading one that has already been specified. The attribute *restricted*, not illustrated here, has the effect of *preventing* extension of the operation to further sorts altogether.

In axiom (4), n is a *variable*. Variables are written in *this italic font*, with optional subscripts and primes. Variables are not explicitly introduced. They range over all proper and vacuous sorts, as well as individuals. Our specification framework is essentially *first-order*, so variables do not range over operations.

To restrict a variable x in an axiom to *individuals* of a particular sort S, we write $x{:}S$ instead of some occurrence of x in the axiom. For instance, $n{:}$natural restricts n to individual natural numbers. We can also restrict x merely to arbitrary *subsorts* of S by writing $x{\leq}S$, or to arbitrary *individuals* by writing $x!$. Formally, an axiom C containing a restricted variable $x{:}S$ in a term abbreviates a *conditional* axiom $x{:}S \Rightarrow C_0$, where C_0 is like C but has just x instead of $x{:}S$, and similarly for $x{\leq}S$ and $x!$. It is best, in general, to restrict all the variables that occur in axioms to particular sorts, to avoid defining operations unintentionally on other sorts of argument, which may have undesirable consequences.

Axiom (4) is sufficient to complete the specification of sum $(m,\ n)$, ensuring the intended interpretation whenever m and n are individuals of sort natural. This fact is not entirely obvious; see Exercise 4(c). Likewise, axioms (5) and (6) complete the specification of product $(m\ ,\ n)$. The restriction to *individuals* $n{:}$natural in axiom (5) is essential: by allowing n to be nothing we would get product (nothing, 0) = 0, but the strictness of product implies product (nothing, 0) = nothing. Similarly, the restriction $m{:}$natural in axiom (6) avoids the unfortunate consequences of allowing m to be a proper sort, such as 1 | 2, see Exercise 4(d).

An alternative style of specification is to define sum (_ , _) inductively, using primitive recursion, leaving it to the reader to discover attributes such as associativity and commutativity. When carried to the extreme, algebraic specifications written in such a style are simply functional programs, and have a straightforward operational semantics. Here, we are not concerned with executing our algebraic specifications, so we may write them as seems most informative.

The remaining axioms specify the operation _ is _ on the sort natural. As usual in algebraic specification frameworks, we represent relations on individuals, such as equality, by operations mapping individuals to the truth-values true and false. Here m is n is to be true when m is the same individual natural number as n, and false when m and n are different natural numbers; it is to be a vacuous sort when, for instance, m or n is a truth-value. Axioms (8–10) are sufficient to define _ is _ on natural numbers. Notice that when m and n are overlapping sorts of natural numbers, m is n must be true | false, i.e., the proper sort truth-value!

For reasons to be explained shortly, our axioms are restricted to being essentially so-called *positive Horn clauses* of the form of the form $F_1; \ldots; F_n \Rightarrow F$, where each of $F, F_1, \ldots, F_n$ is a basic formula: an equation $T_1 = T_2$, an individual inclusion $T_1 : T_2$, or a sort inclusion $T_1 \leq T_2$. Such a clause asserts that when all the antecedents F_i hold, so does consequent F. In fact we allow F to be also a conditional clause, or a conjunction, but such generalized clauses can be regarded as abbreviations for standard ones; see Exercise 6. We cannot directly express that some property is a consequence of a basic formula *not* holding, for instance that $m \neq n$ implies that m is n should be false. In fact we could specify that *indirectly*:

$$m = n \; ; \; (m \text{ is } n) = \text{false} \;\; \Rightarrow \;\; \text{true} = \text{false}$$

provided that we can be sure that true = false is an *absurdity* which can never hold. This can indeed be ensured by the use of *constraints*, as explained below; but this style of specification has the drawback of making reasoning more difficult than with the axioms given in **Specifics**, so we generally try to avoid specifications involving absurdity...

Our standard notation for data provides _ is _ on various sorts, i.e., this operation symbol is *overloaded*.[6] To make the task of defining it a bit easier, we may specify the general properties of _ is _ , once and for all, in a *generic* module, as follows:

Distinction

> **includes:**   **Truth-Values**.
>
> **introduces:**   s , _ is _ .
>
> (1)   _ is _ :: s, s $\rightarrow$ truth-value (*partial, commutative*) .
>
> (2) $x : s \Rightarrow (x \text{ is } x) = \text{true}$.
>
> (3) $x{:}s \text{ is } y{:}s = \text{true} \; ; \; y{:}s \text{ is } z{:}s = \text{true} \Rightarrow x \text{ is } z = \text{true}$.
>
> **open.**

The sort s is left open. We could emphasize this by specifying s = □, where □ is a formal abbreviation for the left hand side of the enclosing equation; this is more suggestive than writing s = s. In any case, s is not specified to include any individuals at all: we leave it to *instantiations* to provide the individuals. Notice that we let _ is _ be a *partial* equivalence relation, so that x is y may be neither true nor false for some x and y.

We may *instantiate* **Distinction** in two different ways. One way is to *translate* s to the intended sort symbol, e.g., in **Naturals/Specifics** we could put

> **includes:**   **Distinction** (natural *for* s).

---

[6]Because individuals are sorts, *all* operation symbols are overloaded! But some are more overloaded than others.

We could also translate _ is _ to another symbol, for instance eq (_ , _). Translating a symbol S to itself insists that the symbol is introduced in the referenced module, and the translation S *for* S may be abbreviated simply to S. We write a multi-symbol translation as $(S'_1$ *for* $S_1, \ldots, S'_n$ *for* $S_n)$. Untranslated symbols need not be mentioned.

The alternative way of instantiating a generic module is to *specialize* it by adding a sort inclusion axiom, e.g.,

> **includes: Distinction.** natural $\leq$ s .

Note that when we include also some other sorts in s, for instance truth-value, we might not intend to use the operation x is y with x and y from different sorts, in which case _ is _ can be left only partially specified on s.

3.1.3 Models

Finally, let us consider what *models* of our specifications look like, and the effect of *constraints* on models. A model of a specification consists of a *universe*, together with an *interpretation* for the constant and operation symbols introduced by the specification. The universe contains not only specified individuals, but also the specified sorts!

More precisely, the universe of a model is a *distributive lattice* of sorts with a bottom, closed under finite union and intersection and with union and intersection obeying the usual laws. The partial order of the lattice corresponds to sort inclusion. The individuals are merely a distinguished subset of the sorts; they usually occur somewhere near the bottom, but this is not required.

The interpretation of a constant symbol may be any value of the universe. That of an operation symbol must be a *monotonic* function on the lattice—but it is not required that the function be strict, linear, or in any sense continuous. The built-in constant nothing is interpreted as the bottom of the lattice, _ | _ as union, and _ & _ as intersection. The interpretation is required to satisfy all the axioms of the specification. Variables in axioms range over the entire universe, not just the individuals, although the effect of restricting variables to individuals can be achieved by use of individual inclusions as antecedents of clauses.

For instance, the diamond-shaped lattice structure indicated in Box 3.1 is a model of **Truth-Values**, assuming the filled-in circles indicate individuals. Similarly, the infinite lattice structure sketched there is a model of **Natural Numbers/Basics**. These models are in fact the models that the given specifications were *intended* to have. That is, they have no superfluous *junk*: values that cannot be expressed using the specified symbols, such as a third truth-value individual, or an unnatural number corresponding to infinity. Furthermore, they have no unintended *confusion*: identification of values, such as **true** and **false**, when their equality is not a logical consequence of the specified axioms; similarly for inclusion, and the property of being an individual.

Models with no junk and no confusion are called *standard models*. We use the *constraint* **closed** to restrict the models of a specification to standard models; see the bottom lines of **Truth-Values** and **Natural Numbers/Basics**. Once we have closed a module, we cannot add new individuals to its specified sorts, although we may add individuals to new sorts. For instance, we can refer to **Natural Numbers** when specifying a module providing negative numbers as well, and include the sort **natural** in a sort **integer** together with the negative integers, but the latter must *not* be included in the sort **natural**. We must also ensure that we do not specify axioms that equate different individuals, such as **true** and **false**, or the natural numbers 0 and **successor**^{i} for some $i \geq 1$. Once **Truth-Values** has been closed, **true** = **false** is an absurdity, never holding in any model of the closed specification.

It is pointless to specify a constraint to close **Natural Numbers/Specifics**,

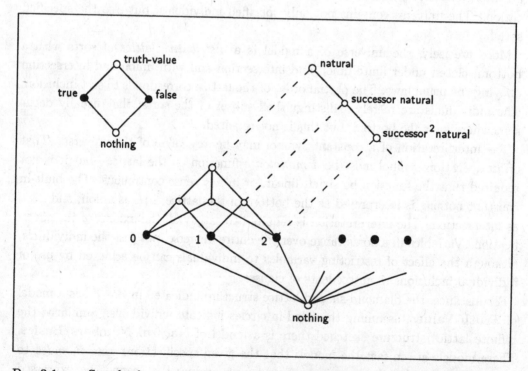

Box 3.1   Standard models of **Truth-Values** and **Natural Numbers/Basics**

because although it extends **Basics** and **Truth-Values** with new operations, it doesn't introduce any new individuals. We should definitely *not* close **Distinction**, because that would prevent s from including any individuals at all! We may write **open** to emphasize that a module still needs specializing.

A more general form of constraint, written **closed except** $M_1, \ldots, M_n$, closes the current module but leaves the submodules M_i open for later specialization. This is mainly used for specifying generic data, such as lists of unspecified items, as illustrated in Chapter 5.

Why do we need to use constraints at all? Wouldn't it be better to allow axioms to be more general than Horn clauses? For example, we might generalize to full first-order logic. But that wouldn't be sufficient: even such a simple structure as the linearly ordered natural numbers with addition and multiplication cannot be specified completely using any algorithmically-given[7] set of first-order formulae. This is just Gödel's well-known Incompleteness Theorem, which says any such set of formulae will always have a nonstandard model as well the standard one.

To be able to restrict specified classes of models to standard models, one has to go beyond first-order specifications. One could use second-order logic with the so-called ω-rule, or with a second-order induction rule (see Exercise 5) but this would entail a much more complicated mathematical foundation, not to mention the considerable pragmatic difficulties of finding proofs in such logics!

So we prefer to use constraints instead. And just at this point our restriction of axioms to positive Horn clauses plays its rôle: such a specification *always* has a standard (initial) model. Moreover, this model can be constructed in a very natural way using ground terms (i.e., terms without variables) as values. If we were to allow other forms of axiom, such as disjunctions of equations, the property of the axioms always having a standard model would be lost. The models of the axioms can now be accepted or rejected, according to whether all the constraints are satisfied or not.

Thus, the combination of (first-order) positive Horn clauses and constraints, together with our unorthodox treatment of sorts as values, provides a framework that is quite adequate for specifying the data that we need for use in action semantics. Further explanation of the foundations of the framework, which is called *unified algebras*, is out of the scope of this book, and readers who are interested in the topic should consult [Mos89b]. Appendix F summarizes the entire meta-notation. Chapter 5 introduces the algebraic specification of our standard notation for data, which is given in full in Appendix E.

---

[7]recursively-enumerable

3.2   Grammars

Recall the grammar used to specify the abstract of a simple programming language in Section 2.1. It consists of a number of equations. Let us see how it can be regarded as an algebraic specification.

With conventional frameworks for algebraic specification, one can only treat the alternatives of a context-free grammar as specifying *functionalities*. One introduces each nonterminal symbol as a sort symbol, and creates an operation symbol for each alternative, with an argument position for each nonterminal occurring in it [GTWW77]. For instance, one gets an operation symbol ⟦ "if" _ "then" _ ⟧ with the functionality of mapping Expression and Statement arguments into a Statement result. The initial model of the resulting specification—without any axioms at all—provides an algebra of abstract syntax trees, up to isomorphism.

However, thanks to the various unorthodox features of our algebraic specification framework here, we have an alternative, somewhat more direct way of regarding grammars algebraically: we take the productions of a grammar literally, as *sort equations*! We introduce the nonterminal symbols of the grammar as constants. Terminal symbols are strings or characters; we include a standard notation for them, with a constant symbol for each individual character c, written with single quotes 'c', and with strings of characters written with double quotes "$c_1 \ldots c_n$". For any number of arguments, ⟦ _ ... _ ⟧ is a standard, total operation that constructs nodes of trees from branches. A string is simply a node whose branches are all characters, for instance "if" is the same as ⟦ 'i' 'f' ⟧.

With these constant and operation symbols available, the term ⟦ "if" Expression "then" Statement ⟧ is well-formed! It is interpreted as a sort that includes any tree whose root node has four branches, the first being the string "if", the second being a tree included in the sort Expression, and similarly for the remaining branches. The production for Statement equates Statement to the union of several sorts of tree. The | separating the alternatives is, of course, our sort union operation, written infix. Notice that when specifying Operator we make a sort union from *individual* strings.

One especially nice feature of this algebraic interpretation of grammars is that replacing a nonterminal by the union of its alternatives does not affect the specified abstract syntax trees at all. We may *always* replace a term by another one that can be shown to be equal to it! For instance, in the example grammar given in Section 2.1, we may replace Operator in ⟦ Expression Operator Expression⟧ by the specified sort of string. The node construction operation distributes over sort union, so we get:

$$⟦ \text{Expression "+" Expression}⟧ \mid ⟦ \text{Expression "–" Expression}⟧ \mid \ldots$$

This *flexibility* is quite useful in practice, because it ensures that the abstract syntax trees specified by a grammar are not dependent on the internal organization, or style, of the grammar.

How about the *regular expressions* that we allow in our grammars? Let $\langle \_ \ldots \_ \rangle$ be an operation symbol for any number of arguments. In contrast to $[\![\_ \ldots \_]\!]$, the operation $\langle \_ \ldots \_ \rangle$ constructs non-nested sequences, called *tuples*, rather than nodes, which can be nested. Thus $\langle$ ";" Statement $\rangle$ is a sort of tuples with two components, the first being always the string ";", the second being a tree of sort Statement. When the t_i are tuples, the branches of $[\![t_1 \ldots t_n]\!]$ are all the components of the t_i, in other words the components of the *concatenation* of the t_i.

It is straightforward to specify the operations $\_^?$, $\_^*$, and $\_^+$ as *tuple sort constructors*. This is done in Section E.2 in connection with the tuple concatenation operation $(\_ , \_)$. Section E.8 specifies the node and tuple notation used for trees.

We write **grammar:** at the start of the specification in Section 2.1 as a formal abbreviation for the introduction of each symbol that occurs on the left hand side of the subsequent equations, i.e., each nonterminal of the grammar, and the inclusion of our standard notation for characters, strings, trees, and tuples. In general, we write the constraint **closed** at the end, so that in any model the specified sorts only include trees that can be *finitely* constructed, with different terms denoting different trees unless their equality can be deduced from our specifications.

3.3 Semantic Equations

Semantic equations involve semantic functions, abstract syntax, and semantic entities, as illustrated in Section 2.2. The algebraic interpretation of the notation for nodes and tuples, and of symbols used in grammars, was explained in the previous section. Without further ado, we can regard semantic equations as ordinary algebraic axioms.

However, recall that we insist that each variable occurring in a semantic equation gets explicitly *restricted* to individuals of some particular sort of tree. Such variable restrictions abbreviate antecedents of clauses, so our semantic 'equations' are essentially conditional. It would be dangerous to omit these restrictions, because without them, the vacuous sort nothing could be assigned to variables in semantic equations. The strictness of $[\![\_ \ldots \_]\!]$ on nothing might then cause some unwelcome identifications of semantic entities!

The only other point worth mentioning here is that when semantic equations are divided into modules, one can avoid having to specify inter-module dependencies by leaving the actual introduction of the symbols for semantic functions at the original level, so that it gets inherited by all the submodules.

3.4   Structural Operational Semantics

To conclude this chapter, let us see how our algebraic specification framework can be used to present a *structural operational semantics* (*SOS*) for a programming language. The technique described here is exploited in Appendix C to define the operational semantics of our standard action notation. You may defer reading this section until you need to look at Appendix C if you wish.

The key idea is to use a transition *function* mapping individual configurations to arbitrary *sorts* of configurations, rather than a transition *relation* between configurations. It is notationally just as easy to specify a function as a relation, and by allowing proper sorts as results we can still cope with nondeterminism. Moreover, we can specify the result to be a single individual when the transition from a particular configuration is deterministic, rather than leaving determinism implicit; we can even specify directly that a configuration is blocked, using a vacuous sort such as nothing!

A less significant point is that we use positive Horn clauses instead of inference rules. The only drawback of this seems to be that meta-proofs using induction on the length of inference become less immediate, because one has to consider the inference rules for Horn clause logic. Perhaps our ⇒ doesn't look as nice as the horizontal line used in inference rules, but this could easily be fixed, by allowing ⇒ to be written very long and thin, with the antecedents of the clause written on top and the consequent below...

The following example serves to illustrate the basic technique of SOS, as well as our style of specification. It should also prepare the reader for looking at the SOS of standard action notation given in Appendix C, although it requires a major effort to become properly familiar with that description.

The example deals with a fragment of the simple programming language that we used to illustrate action semantic descriptions in Chapter 2. A state, or configuration, is a pair (S, i), where S is a syntactic entity—a statement or an expression—and i is some semantic entity representing the current information, for example the values stored in cells. For brevity, we do not bother here to specify the notation for semantic entities, nor transitions for constructs that directly affect or refer to these entities.

introduces: stepped _ , evaluated _ .

- stepped _ :: (Statements, info) → (Statements$^?$, info).

(1)   stepped $(S_1, i) \geq (S_1':\text{Statements}, i':\text{info}) \Rightarrow$
      stepped $(\langle S_1:\text{Statement } ";" \ S_2:\text{Statements} \rangle, i:\text{info}) \geq (\langle S_1' \ ";" \ S_2 \rangle, i')$.

(2)   stepped $(S_1, i) \geq i' : \text{info} \Rightarrow$
      stepped $(\langle S_1:\text{Statement } ";" \ S_2:\text{Statements} \rangle, i:\text{info}) \geq (S_2, i')$.

(3)   evaluated (E, i) = true $\Rightarrow$
       stepped ($[\![$ "while" E:Expression "do" S:Statement $]\!]$, i:info) =
              $(\langle S$ ";" $[\![$ "while" E "do" S $]\!] \rangle, i)$.

(4)   evaluated (E, i) = false $\Rightarrow$
       stepped ($[\![$ "while" E:Expression "do" S:Statement $]\!]$, i:info) = i.

   • evaluated _ :: _ (Expression, info) $\rightarrow$ value.

(5)   evaluated $(N$:Numeral, i:info) = number & decimal N.

(6)   evaluated (E_1, i) = n_1 : number ;   evaluated (E_2, i) = n_2 : number $\Rightarrow$
       evaluated ($[\![$ E_1:Expression "+" E_2:Expression $]\!]$, i:info) = number & sum (n_1, n_2).

...

In fact for this simple programming language, the transitions are deterministic, so stepped _ is an ordinary partial operation, i.e., stepped (S, i) is at most a single individual when S and i are individuals. Nevertheless, stepped _ is specified in such a way that it would be easy to add nondeterminism.

Summary

- *Algebraic specifications involve individuals, operations, and sorts. The main unorthodox feature of our framework is that both individuals and sorts are treated as values, with individuals being a special case of sorts.*

- *As axioms we allow not only equations but also individual and sort inclusions. Moreover, these can be combined in positive Horn clauses.*

- *We allow constraints to standard (initial) models, perhaps leaving part of the specification open for later specialization.*

- *Models of our specifications are lattices of sorts, but the sorts are mainly there only to facilitate specification of the individuals.*

- *Algebraic specifications are used here for specifying standard notation for data, and for extending and specializing our standard notation for actions.*

- *The grammars and semantic equations used in action semantic descriptions have a simple algebraic interpretation.*

- *We can write a structural operational semantics as an algebraic specification of a transition function from individual configurations to sorts.*

Navigation

- *If you would now like to see a summary of our entire meta-notation, make an excursion to Appendix F.*

- *To see how a medium-sized algebraic specification looks, make an excursion to Appendix E.*

- *To see how the structural operational semantic description of action notation looks, make an excursion to Appendix C.*

- *Otherwise, proceed to Part II and Part III for a presentation of action notation and its use in action semantic descriptions.*

Exercises

1. What properties do you expect of _|_ , _&_ , and **nothing**? Specify them formally, without using attributes. (You can check your answer with Section F.4, where all the intended properties are specified.)

2. Consider the module **Truth-Values** in Section 3.1.

   (a) What difference would it make to the standard model of the specification to omit axioms (2) and (3)? Draw a diagram. Similarly for omitting just axiom (3).

   (b) Suppose that we specify the following:

   > **includes:**   **Truth-Values**.
   > **introduces:**   maybe .   maybe : truth-value .

   What is the relationship between **true**, **false**, and **maybe** in models of this specification? What difference would it make if we added the specification of **maybe** directly to **Truth-Values** before constraining it?

3. Consider the submodule **Natural Numbers/Basics** in Section 3.1.

   (a) Characterize those sets of natural numbers which are the extensions of expressible sorts.

   (b) Specify an operation **predecessor** _ to give the predecessor of each positive integer. Discuss pros and cons of alternative treatments of **predecessor** 0 (e.g., leaving it unspecified, equating it to **nothing**, equating it to 0).

4. Consider the submodule **Natural Numbers/Specifics** in Section 3.1.

   (a) Give an example of a set of natural numbers that is the extension of a sort expressible in **Specifics** but not in **Basics**.

   (b) Specify Horn clauses that correspond to the functionality and attributes of the operation sum (_ , _). (The formal meaning of functionalities and attributes is explained in Section F.2.2.2.)

   (c) Show that any term sum (successor^{i}0, successor^{j}0), where $i, j \geq 0$, is provably-equal to successor^{i+j}0, using the specified axioms. Does it follow that sum is completely defined on individual natural numbers?

   (d) The operation product (_ , _) was specified to be *total*, which implies *linear*, i.e., product $(x \mid y, z)$ = product $(x, z) \mid$ product (y, z); similarly for sum (_ , _). Investigate the consequences of this and the following (inadvisable) generalization of axiom (7):

   $$\text{product } (m \leq \text{natural, successor } n \leq \text{natural}) =$$
   $$\text{sum } (m, \text{ product } (m, n)) \ .$$

5. Here are Peano's axioms for the natural numbers, formulated in *second-order logic with equality*:

   $$\forall n \ (\ 0 \neq s(n) \ );$$
   $$\forall m \forall n \ (\ s(m) = s(n) \ \Rightarrow \ m = n \ );$$
   $$\forall P \ (\ (\ P(0) \wedge \forall n \ (\ P(n) \ \Rightarrow \ P(s(n)) \ ) \ ) \ \Rightarrow \ \forall n \ (P(n)) \ ).$$

   Compare these axioms with our specification of the constraint **closed** in **Natural Numbers/Basics** given in Section 3.1. Which of the axioms here prevent *junk*? Which of them prevent *confusion*?

6. Our algebraic specification framework allows axioms to be *positive Horn clauses* of the form $(F_1; \ldots ; F_n) \Rightarrow F$, where $F, F_1, \ldots, F_n$ are basic formulae $T_1 = T_2$, $T_1 : T_2, T_1 \leq T_2$. Argue that it does not make any real difference to allow the conclusion of a Horn clause, F, to be itself a Horn clause, or a conjunction of Horn clauses. Would it make a real difference to allow Horn clauses in the hypotheses F_i of axioms?

Part II

Action Notation

Part II introduces the details of action notation systematically, explaining the underlying concepts and the intended interpretation of the symbols. It is intended to be read together with Part III, which illustrates the use of action notation in semantic descriptions.

Some of the Appendices provide further details of the foundations of action notation, and summarize the explanations given throughout Part II. Appendix B specifies some algebraic properties of the entire action notation; this also reduces action notation to a reasonably small kernel. Appendix C defines the abstract syntax of the kernel, and gives the formal definition of its meaning, using structural operational semantics. Appendix D summarizes the informal explanations of the full action notation, for convenience of reference. Appendix E gives the complete algebraic specification of the data notation included in action notation.

Navigation

- *If this is your first reading, proceed* in parallel *through Parts II and III: Chapter 4, Chapter 11, Chapter 5, Chapter 12, and so on. This way, you see an illustration of the use of each part of action notation immediately after its introduction.*

- *Alternatively, you could look at each chapter of Part III before the corresponding chapter of Part II. This way, the illustrations in Part III motivate the action notation introduced in Part II.*

- *If you are revising, and would like an uninterrupted presentation of action notation, proceed straight through Part II.*

- *When you have finished Part II, take a look at Appendix D, which fills in some details omitted in Part II.*

Chapter 4

Basic

- *Actions are semantic entities, used to represent behaviour.*

- *Action notation includes a basic action notation for specifying control flow.*

- *Basic actions are not explicitly concerned with any particular kind of information.*

- *Chapter 11 illustrates the use of basic action notation in the semantic description of statements.*

Actions are semantic entities that represent potential information-processing behaviour, i.e., the semantics of programs and of their component phrases, such as statements. Each *performance* of an action corresponds to a possible behaviour.

In this chapter, we restrict our attention to the actions provided by *basic* action notation. These basic actions are closely related to fundamental concepts of *control flow*. In subsequent chapters, we enhance basic actions to process various kinds of information, and introduce further actions.

Before we look at our formal notation for actions, let us consider the concepts of control flow that underlie the intended interpretation of the notation. An action performance consists of some atomic *steps*, made by one or more *agents*. For now we only consider single-agent performances, and we assume that in any particular performance, steps occur in a definite order, rather than concurrently. This ensures that the *current* information available when performing a step is well-defined, and that conflicting changes to the current information cannot arise. Chapter 10 explains multi-agent performances, where a dynamically-changing distributed system of agents proceeds to perform separate actions with 'true' concurrency, with asynchronous sending of messages between agents.

Thus an action performance is just a sequence of steps, and a set of possible performances is a set of step sequences. It is perhaps tempting to regard a set of step sequences as an arbitrary *partially-ordered* set of steps, with the order representing some kind of causality. For our purposes here, however, it is simpler to deal directly with the fundamental ways of relating steps when *combining* sequences, which are as follows:

- The step sequences may be *sequenced*, with all of one of them always preceding all of the other;

- They may be *interleaved*, with no inherent order between the steps of the two sequences; or

- They may be provided as mutually-exclusive *alternatives*, not both occurring.

Moreover, a finite sequence of steps may be made into a single *indivisible* step, to ensure that the steps follow each other directly, without interruption. If you are familiar with formal language theory, you may prefer to regard a set of sequences as a language. Then sequencing corresponds to language concatenation, interleaving to language 'shuffle', and mutual exclusion to language union. Indivisibility does not have a direct counterpart as a language operation, but corresponds to regarding the strings of one language as the alphabet of another.

Other ways of relating step sequences could be imagined, for instance synchronized interleaving, but they do not seem to be nearly so fundamental for control flow as those discussed above. In any case, they can usually be *analyzed* in terms of control flow together with the various kinds of information processing introduced in the subsequent chapters.

An action performance may be finite and *terminate*, or it may be infinitely long and *diverge*. When it terminates, it may be that performance of the enclosing action is to continue normally. Sometimes, however, the termination of a performance is supposed to *escape* from the normal performance, and skip further actions until a *trap* is reached. Let us refer to this as *abnormal* termination. We shall also say that a normally-terminating action performance *completes*, whereas an abnormally-terminating one *escapes*.

A final kind of termination, called *failure*, is one that indicates the *abortion* of the current *alternative*. The performance should then *back-track* to try any remaining alternatives. As with escape above, the effect is to skip some actions. The main difference is that the order in which alternatives are tried is unspecified. Moreover, some kinds of information processing, such as destructive changes to stored information or irrevocable message transmission, make back-tracking unrealistic. They involve a *commitment* to the current alternative, similar to the effect of cut in PROLOG. We may regard commitment as a fundamental concept of control flow, irrespective of what information is being processed.

Consideration of the above concepts led to the design of the basic part of action notation, which is introduced in detail below. The primitive actions correspond to the various kinds of termination and commitment, and the action combinators correspond to sequencing, interleaving, and providing alternatives. Diverging performances can arise from *unfolding*, which allows finite expression of infinite actions.

The basic action notation enjoys some pleasant algebraic laws, for instance all the combinators are associative and have units. Two actions that are algebraically equivalent may be used interchangeably, and the differences between their performances are immaterial. More generally, we may regard two actions as *equivalent* whenever there is no conclusive *test*, formulated using other actions, that can reveal any difference between them.

An equivalence class of actions is somewhat analogous to a mathematical function, and action notation specifies actions in the same way that the λ-notation specifies functions. When we use actions as semantic entities, we take them 'up to equivalence'.

The module below specifies the functionality of each symbol of basic action notation. That, together with the following informal explanation, should be adequate preparation for reading Chapter 11, which illustrates the use of basic action notation. Of course the informal explanation is not definitive: it leaves out many details, and may be open to misinterpretation.

We defer the full *definition* of action notation to the Appendices. Appendix B gives an algebraic specification of the entire action notation, divided into modules in the same way as Part II. The algebraic laws also reduce action notation to a reasonably small kernel. Appendix C specifies the abstract syntax of the kernel, gives its structural operational semantics (in the style explained in Section 3.4) and defines an action equivalence that includes the specified laws. Unfortunately, the formal details in Appendix C are quite demanding, and their study at this stage would delay the illustrations in Part III too much. In any case, you should find it easier to read the Appendices after becoming acquainted with the full action notation and its use through reading Parts II and III.

Although one could imagine performing a proper *sort* of actions by choosing between the individual actions included in it, as proposed in [Mos89a], let us here restrict performance to individuals, and keep our notation for proper sorts of actions separate from that for expressing individual actions. The symbol action denotes the sort of *all* actions—not just the purely basic actions that can be expressed using only the symbols explained in this chapter.

4.1   Actions

- complete   : action .
- escape   : action .
- fail   : action .
- commit   : action .
- diverge   : action .
- unfold   : action .
- unfolding _ :: action → action (*total*) .
- indivisibly _ :: action → action (*partial*) .
- _ or _   :: action, action → action (*total, associative, commutative,*
                                         idempotent, unit is fail) .
- _ and _   :: action, action → action (*total, associative, unit is* complete) .
- _ and then _ :: action, action → action (*total, associative, unit is* complete) .
- _ trap _   :: action, action → action (*total, associative, unit is* escape) .

Performance of the primitive action complete takes a single step and terminates normally, so that normal sequencing and interleaving continue. The basic combination A_1 and then A_2 combines the actions A_1, A_2 into a compound action that represents their normal, left-to-right sequencing, performing A_2 only when A_1 completes. complete is the unit for _ and then _.

Similarly, performance of escape terminates abnormally, causing normal sequencing and interleaving to be suspended until a trap is reached. The action A_1 trap A_2 sets A_2 as the trap action to be performed when A_1 escapes. Once an escape has been trapped, normal sequencing and interleaving are resumed. escape is, perhaps a bit surprisingly, the unit for _ trap _.

The performance of fail aborts, causing the alternative currently being performed to be abandoned and, if possible, some other alternative to be performed instead, i.e., *back-tracking*. The action A_1 or A_2 represents implementation-dependent choice between alternative actions, although if A_1, A_2 are such that one or the other of them is always bound to fail, the choice is deterministic. The action fail is the unit for _ or _. The primitive action commit discards all alternatives other than the one currently chosen, so that a subsequent failure does not lead to trying them instead.

The action A_1 and A_2 represents implementation-dependent order of performance of the indivisible subactions of A_1, A_2. When these subactions cannot 'interfere' with each other, it indicates that their order of performance is simply irrelevant. The combinator _ and _ is commutative on the basic actions considered here, but not on the functional actions introduced in the next chapter.

A performance of A_1 **and** A_2 arbitrarily interleaves the steps of performances of A_1, A_2 until both have completed, or until one of them escapes or fails. When the performance diverges, it may be 'unfair', for instance letting A_1 make infinitely-many steps but only finitely-many of A_2. A performance of the unary 'combination' **indivisibly** A consists of a terminating performance of A, made into a single step. In fact A should not be able to diverge at all, but it is algorithmically undecidable whether actions (in the full action notation) can diverge or not.

Performance of **diverge** never terminates. In fact **diverge** is an abbreviation for **unfold**-ing **unfold**, where **unfolding** A performs A but whenever it reaches the dummy action **unfold**, it performs A instead. You may prefer to regard **unfolding** A as an abbreviation for an action, generally infinite, formed by continually substituting A for **unfold** in A. (To avoid syntactic 'singularities' in action terms, substitute **complete and then** A instead of just A.) The action **unfolding** A is mostly used in the semantics of iterative constructs, with **unfold** occurring exactly once in A, but it can also be used with several occurrences of **unfold**.

That is all the notation for *individual* basic actions. The remaining notation is for general use in expressing proper *sorts* of actions. These sorts enable the specification of the precise functionalities of action combinators, as shown in Section B.9, and of the results of semantic functions, as illustrated in Part III and Appendix A.

4.2 /Action Notation/Facets

4.2.1 Outcomes

- outcome = completing | escaping | committing | diverging | failing | □ .
- failing = nothing .

The sort **outcome** includes auxiliary entities that are used for specifying sorts of actions according to *performance possibilities*. The outcomes **completing**, **escaping**, **diverging**, and **failing** allow normal termination, abnormal termination, nontermina-tion, and failure, respectively. Most actions that use information fail when that infor-mation is not currently available to their performance, so we let **failing** be included in *every* outcome as an implicit possibility, which is achieved by simply equating it to **nothing**. The outcome **committing** allows commitment *during* performance, irrespec-tive of termination possibilities.

Sort union $O_1 | O_2$ is used for combining outcomes. For instance, we may specify the outcome possibilities **completing | escaping**, excluding the possibility of divergence and commitment—but still allowing failure, implicitly. The basic outcomes considered in this chapter are mutually disjoint. Further sorts of outcomes are considered in later chapters. See Section B.9 for the full specification of outcomes.

4.2.2 Actions

- _ [_] :: action, outcome → action .

When A is a sort of action and O is a sort of outcome, $A\,[O]$ is the subsort of A with just those actions which, whenever performed, have an outcome included O. For instance, we may write action [completing | escaping]. Note that this is a proper supersort of action [completing] | action [escaping]. For example, the action complete or escape is included in the former sort but not in the latter. Thus $A\,[O]$ is not *linear* in O. Of course, like all our operations, it is monotone, so including more possibilities in O cannot exclude actions already in $A\,[O]$.

When O does not include diverging, the sort action $[O]$ only contains actions that are guaranteed to terminate. It does not include actions that contain any occurrence of unfolding, unless they are equivalent to other actions that do not have it.

So much for *basic* action notation. Basic actions are, of course, not of much use by themselves, since any basic action is essentially equivalent to a choice between completing, escaping, failing, or diverging—with or without committing. But when we add some information-processing actions to basic actions, as in Chapter 6, we quickly get a *Turing-complete* notation, where any computable function can be expressed.

The symbols that we use in basic action notation are quite verbose, and you might be thinking how much more concise we could be by using mathematical signs and punctuation marks, for instance writing A_1 and then A_2 as $A_1; A_2$, following most programming languages. But the full action notation is quite rich in combinators, and it seems impossible to find sufficiently suggestive mathematical signs or punctuation marks for them all. In the interests of uniformity, we stick to verbose symbols for action notation, and use signs such as ';' only in our meta-notation; see Section F.1.1 for the full list. You are welcome to introduce your own abbreviations, using whatever symbols you like—so long as this does not cause ambiguity, of course.

The following action term shows how we may write basic action notation, using vertical lines to specify the grouping. Chapter 11 provides further illustrations.

$$A = \text{unfolding}$$
$$\left|\ \left|\ \begin{array}{l}\text{complete or escape}\\\text{and then unfold}\end{array}\right.\right.$$
$$\left|\ \text{or complete}\ .\right.$$

A = unfolding
    | | complete or escape
    | and then unfold
    | or complete .

Summary

- *Basic action notation is for specifying flow of control.*

- *A performance of an action either completes, escapes, fails, or diverges.*

- *Actions may be nondeterministic. Failure requires back-tracking to try alternative actions. Committing cuts away all the alternatives.*

- *Arbitrary interleaving represents unspecified, implementation-dependent order of performance.*

- *Completing and escaping play analogous rôles in relation to normal, respectively abnormal sequencing, but different ones in relation to interleaving.*

- *Sorts of actions are expressed using sorts of outcomes.*

Navigation

- *Now look at Chapter 11, which gives an illustrative example of the use of basic action notation, before proceeding with Part II.*

- *If you would like a more detailed informal explanation of basic actions, see Section D.1.1.*

- *You could also make an excursion to Section B.1.1, which gives an algebraic specification of basic action notation.*

Exercises

1. Determine for which outcome sorts O the following actions are included in the sort action $[O]$:

    $A_1 =$ escape and diverge .

    $A_2 =$ unfolding
          | | | complete or escape
          | | and then unfold
          | or complete .

2. For each combinator of basic action notation:

(a) Does it preserve determinism, i.e., is the compound action deterministic when its subactions are?

(b) Is it strict in fail, i.e., is the compound action equivalent to fail when one of its subactions is?

3. Suppose that A_1, A_2 are arbitrary actions, possibly processing and changing information. Would you expect the following basic combinations of A_1, A_2 to be equivalent? If not, give an example that demonstrates their inequivalence.

$$A = \text{indivisibly } A_1 \text{ and indivisibly } A_2 \text{ .}$$
$$A' = |\ A_1 \text{ and then } A_2$$
$$\text{or}$$
$$|\ A_2 \text{ and then } A_1 \text{ .}$$

(Hint: consider performing A, A' interleaved with some other action.) How about the following pair?

$$A'' = \text{indivisibly } A_1 \text{ and indivisibly } A_2 \text{ .}$$
$$A''' = |\ \text{indivisibly } A_1 \text{ and then indivisibly } A_2$$
$$\text{or}$$
$$|\ \text{indivisibly } A_2 \text{ and then indivisibly } A_1 \text{ .}$$

4. A nondeterministic choice between two actions is called *angelic* when diverging alternative performances are disregarded whenever possible; it is called *demonic* when a diverging alternative is always chosen whenever possible. Compare the obligations made on implementations by the combinator _ or _ , angelic choice, and demonic choice.

5. Consider a cash dispensing machine that can serve two customers at once. Represent the control flow using basic actions, introducing constants for primitive actions that correspond to the various duties of the machine: reading a bank card, checking the PIN, reading the desired amount, checking the account is in credit, dispensing the cash, giving a receipt, etc. Try not to overspecify the order of performance of the various actions, but take care of the possibility that two customers might have cards for the same account!

Chapter 5

Data

- *Action notation includes a data notation for general use.*

- *Standard data consists of tuples, truth-values, numbers, characters, strings, lists, trees, sets, and maps.*

- *Some of the operations of data notation are intended for use mainly on proper sorts, rather than on mere individuals.*

- *Appendix E gives the full algebraic specification of data notation.*

Consider an implementation of a high-level programming language. When a program is run, the information processed by it is represented entirely by sequences of bits: 0's and 1's. The programmer, however, does not usually have to deal with this representation directly. The program can be regarded as processing *abstract* entities, such as numbers, arrays, and sets. Indeed, standards for high-level programming languages generally leave the binary representation of information unspecified.

Recall from Chapter 1 that the semantics of a program is an entity which represents the implementation-independent aspects of its information processing behaviour, and that the semantics of a phrase is an entity which represents its contribution to overall behaviour. In action semantics, these entities are generally actions. The information processed by programs is represented by items of *data*, which correspond directly to abstract entities such as numbers rather than to bit sequences.

Various sorts of data are needed for the semantics of general-purpose high-level programming languages, not only 'mathematical' values such as numbers and lists, but also abstract entities of computational origins such as variables, procedures, packages, and so on.

67

It would be futile to try to provide standard notation for all possible sorts of data. Apart from the excessive amount of notation that would be needed, future programming languages may involve sorts of data previously unconceived . Let us restrict the standard data notation included in action notation to a small collection of generally useful abstract data types. Action semantics allows further abstract data types to be specified *ad hoc* when required, so the data to be processed by actions is not constrained. Our standard data notation involves the following sorts of data:

Tuples: ordered, single-level collections of components. Single components are 1-tuples. Unary operations on tuples represent operations with varying numbers of arguments.

Truth Values: the usual 'Booleans'. Truth-valued operations represent predicates.

Numbers: unbounded exact rational numbers. Restriction to bounded numbers can easily be expressed using sort intersection. A loosely-specified sort of approximate rational numbers can be specialized to represent the usual types of implemented 'real' numbers (fixed-point, floating-point).

Characters: a loosely-specified character set. ASCII characters are provided too.

Lists: ordered collections of items. A tree is simply a leaf or a possibly-nested list.

Strings: unbounded, non-nested lists of characters, representing lexical symbols.

Syntax: trees with only characters as leaves, used to represent abstract syntax. Strings are a special case of syntax trees.

Sets: unordered, possibly-nested collections.

Maps: unordered, indexed collections.

Lists, sets, maps and tuples are always *finite*, and their components are individuals, not vacuous or proper sorts. Action notation provides some further sorts of data, such as storage cells and abstractions. These are described in the subsequent chapters of Part II, together with the actions that involve them. In fact abstractions can be used to represent infinite and *lazy* data, as explained in Chapter 9.

Readers who are familiar with denotational semantics might like to compare our standard sorts of data with the basic domains and domain constructors provided by the λ-notation. Tuple sorts here correspond only roughly to Cartesian products of domains: our tupling is associative, and components have to be totally-defined. Our map sorts correspond to finitely-indexed products of domains. Set sorts correspond to simple kinds of power domains. A major difference is that we use sort union, rather than a separated sum of domains. The fact that sort union is associate, commutative, and idempotent—in contrast to separated sum—means we can really think of it as set union. We can still discriminate between *disjoint* subsorts of individuals. Of course, what we don't have in our data notation is something corresponding to domains of higher-order functions, although the sort of abstractions does correspond to a particular 'lifted' domain of functions.

When an action semantic description of a particular programming language requires other sorts of data, they have to be specified algebraically, *ad hoc*. Suppose, for instance, that we are describing a programming language that involves the concept of an 'array variable'. Then we introduce a corresponding sort symbol, say **array-variable**, and specify notation for expressing individual array variables.

But we should avoid the temptation to equate **array-variable** with some given sort of data, such as a sort of lists, even when the given operations are close to those that we require, because that would reduce the modifiability of the semantic description. When specifying **array-variable** abstractly, we may also insist on its disjointness from other sorts of data, so that we may discriminate between the various sorts of data without having to manipulate special 'tags'.

On the other hand, some of the sorts of data provided by action notation, in connection with particular actions, correspond directly to basic concepts. For instance, the sort **cell** corresponds to the notion of a simple variable. Then we may use the given sort directly, or introduce a synonym for it, without unduly jeopardizing modifiability.

In the rest of this chapter, we consider only the *standard* data notation. Part III illustrates the *ad hoc* specification of other sorts of data that are needed for the semantic description of a particular programming language.

Most of the symbols of our standard data notation are quite suggestive of their intended interpretation. Note that sometimes the same word is used both as a sort symbol, and in the symbol for an operation that constructs individuals of that sort. For instance, the operation **list of** _ constructs individuals of sort **list**.

Unary operation symbols are generally prefix, the only exceptions being the tuple sort operations $\_^*$, $\_^+$, and $\_^?$ (also the operations such as $\_1$ that provide decimal notation for natural numbers). Since operations cannot be applied to other operations, composite applications of unary operations $f \_$, $g \_$ can be written unambiguously as $f\ g\ x$ without parentheses. Associative binary operations are generally specified as unary operations on tuples, for instance **sum** _ is an operation mapping tuples of numbers to numbers; but since a pair of numbers can be written (m, n), we can still use the same notation as in Chapter 3 for binary sums, namely **sum** (m, n).

Below, operations that are specified as having the attribute *total* or *partial* are usually intended for use on individuals, rather than on proper sorts. A constant stands for an individual only when this is specified explicitly, using $x : y$ or by writing *individual* at the end of a sort equation $y = \ldots \mid x \mid \ldots$; other constants denote proper sorts.

Let us now take a quick look at some of the main features of data notation, which is specified in full, algebraically, in Appendix E. Here we consider only the main constants and operations and their most fundamental properties. We use the same modular structure as Appendix E, so that it should be easy to locate the detailed definition of a particular symbol, if desired, without having to consult the symbol index. Here is an outline of the main modules. The intermodule dependency, and a list of all the submodules, is specified at the beginning of Appendix E.

/Data Notation

> **General** .
>
> **Instant** .
>
> **Tuples** .
>
> **Truth-Values** .
>
> **Numbers** .
>
> **Characters** .
>
> **Lists** .
>
> **Strings** .
>
> **Syntax** .
>
> **Sets** .
>
> **Maps** .

/Action Notation/Basic/Data

Since the symbols of data notation are mostly quite suggestive of their intended interpretation, it is *not* necessary to commit them all to memory! However, you should at least look briefly at the functionalities specified in this chapter, so that you are likely to recognize the standard symbols of data notation as such when you see them in use. You may also find it helpful to study the diagram in Box 5.1 on page 86, which summarizes the main inclusions between some of the standard sorts of data. The diagram is a so-called *Hasse* diagram, where a sloping line between two sort symbols indicates that the sort at the lower end is included in the sort at the upper end. Note that many other sorts, not indicated in the diagram, can be expressed by terms.

5.1   /Data Notation

A reference to **Data Notation** includes the specialization of characters to the ASCII character set in **Characters/ASCII**, whereas a reference to the submodule **Data Notation/General** includes everything except for that.

5.1.1   General

includes: **Tuples, Truth-Values, Numbers, Characters/Alphanumerics, Lists, Strings, Syntax, Sets, Maps.**

The **Instant** modules below specify properties of operations on the individuals of an *unspecified* sort s. We *instantiate* them by translating s to some other constant, as explained and illustrated in Section 3.1.2.

5.1.2   Instant

Distinction

- s   = □ .
- _ is _ :: s, s → truth-value (*partial, commutative*) .

Partial Order

includes: **Distinction.**

- _ is _   :: s, s → truth-value (*total, commutative*) .
- _ is less than _   :: s, s → truth-value (*total*) .
- _ is greater than _ :: s, s → truth-value (*total*) .

Total Order

includes: **Partial Order.**

- _ [min _] :: s, s → s (*partial*) .
- _ [max _] :: s, s → s (*partial*) .

In the submodule **Distinction** the intention is for the operation _ is _ to represent a *partial* equivalence relation, with ordinary equivalence relations and equality as special cases. The full specification of **Distinction**, including the usual axioms that characterize partial equivalence relations, is given in Appendix E. Actually, it needs the module that specifies our standard data notation truth-values, which is explained later, in Section 5.1.4, but you have already seen some of that notation in Section 3.1. Note that x is y may be specified to be true even when the algebraic equality relation $x = y$ doesn't hold, for individuals x, y of sort s.

The mark □ is allowed generally in terms in our meta-notation. It is read as 'to be filled in later'. Formally, it stands for the left hand side of the enclosing equation. Thus s = □ specifies merely the obvious fact s = s, while suggesting that s has been left open, and could be identified with any other sort.

Partial Order extends **Distinction** with the operations m is less than n and m is greater than n. When we use this module, we only need to define m is less than n, as the other operation is already defined in terms of that. **Partial Order** also insists that the operations are *total*, giving true or false when applied to any two individuals of sort s. What may be partial about the order is that we may have *all* of x is less than y, x is y, and x is greater than y, equal to false for particular x, y. For instance, set inclusion is a partial order: any two disjoint sets are incomparable. See Appendix E for the detailed axioms.

Total Order specializes **Partial Order** by insisting that whenever two of x is less than y, x is y, and x is greater than y are false, the third one must be true. All the standard sorts of numbers in our data notation instantiate **Total Order**. It also provides the *restriction* operations y [min x] and y [max x] which give y when it is at least, respectively at most, x, otherwise they give nothing. Although these restriction operations are ordinary partial operations, we generally exploit their natural extensions to proper sorts, to express subsorts of ordered data. For instance natural [min 1] [max 10] expresses the subsort 1 | 2 | ... | 10 of the natural numbers—once **Total Order** has been instantiated by translating s to natural, as in **Numbers/Naturals**. The compositional order of the two restrictions on natural is immaterial, of course. It is one of the strengths of our unorthodox algebraic specification framework that sort restriction operations can be specified straightforwardly.

The next module of our data notation provides *tuples*. Compared to **Truth-Values** and **Numbers**, which follow, it is a rather 'advanced' module, providing several sort-constructing operations. We should not defer it, however, because almost all the other modules provide unary operations on tuples, representing operations on arbitrary numbers of arguments. Let us at least leave out some of the less important operations in the overview here. As usual, the full details are given in Appendix E.

5.1.3 Tuples

Generics

- component = □ .

Basics

- tuple ≥ component .
- ( ) : tuple .
- (_ , _) :: tuple, tuple → tuple (*total, associative, unit is* ( )) .
- _? :: tuple → tuple .
- _* :: tuple → tuple .
- _+ :: tuple → tuple .
- _- :: tuple, natural → tuple .

Specifics

- count _ :: tuple → natural (*total*) .
- first _ :: tuple → component (*partial*) .
- rest _ :: tuple → tuple (*partial*) .
- equal _ :: (component+, component+) → truth-value (*partial*) .
- distinct _ :: (component+, component+) → truth-value (*partial*) .
- strictly-increasing _ :: (component+, component+) → truth-value (*partial*) .
- strictly-decreasing _ :: (component+, component+) → truth-value (*partial*) .
- _ is _ :: tuple, tuple → truth-value (*partial*) .
- component# _ _ :: positive-integer, tuple → component (*partial*) .

The module **Tuples** specifies a *generic* abstract data type. It is intended to be instantiated by *including* particular sorts of data in the sort **component**, whose specification in the submodule **Generics** below is left **open** in Appendix E.

As we shall see, binary operations such as **sum** on numbers can be generalized to unary operations on tuples of arbitrary length. Tuples also provide a convenient representation of transient information, which is considered in Chapter 6. Finally, notation for sorts of tuples allows us to get the effect of regular expressions in grammars, as explained in Section 3.2.

The sort **component** is a subsort of **tuple**, corresponding to 1-tuples. ( ) is, of course, the empty tuple. Tuples *cannot* be nested, so (t_1, t_2) is the associative *concatenation* of the tuples t_1 and t_2, giving a pair when both t_1 and t_2 are single components, and ignoring one of the t_i when it is the empty tuple. Let us write a triple with components t_1, t_2, and t_3 as (t_1, t_2, t_3), omitting a pair of parentheses—it doesn't matter where!—and similarly for n-tuples in general, essentially treating the parentheses in (_ , _) as ordinary grouping parentheses around an infix comma operation symbol.

The remaining operations in **Basics** above are for expressing *sorts* of tuples. Actually, we already have some useful notation for proper sorts of tuples: when s_1 and s_2 are proper sorts, (s_1, s_2) is precisely the sort of individual tuples (t_1, t_2) where $t_1{:}s_1$ and $t_2{:}s_2$. Now $s^?$ is the union of s with the individual sort $(\ )$, which gives the effect of an *optional* subtuple of sort s when used in a concatenation; s^+ is the union of s and the sort (s^+, s^+), corresponding to the sort of nonempty tuples with components of sort s; and s^* is the same as $(s^+)^?$, allowing also the empty tuple. The sort s here may be just a subsort of **component**, or it may be a more general sort of tuples. For instance, if a and b are subsorts of **component**, $(a, (b, a)^*)$ is the sort of tuples with components alternately of sorts a and b, starting and finishing with a.

Sort expressions formed from component sorts using the empty tuple, concatenation, union, and $\_^*$ correspond exactly to regular expressions, as studied in formal language theory and exploited for pattern-matching, etc., in the operating system UNIX. We also have the operation $\_^{\_}$ for expressing sorts: c^n is the sort of n-tuples with components of sort c, when n is (usually) an individual natural number. This involves our standard notation for natural numbers, which is explained later, in Section 5.1.5.1, but you have already seen some of that notation in Section 3.1.

The tuple operations provided by **Specifics** are intended for use on individual arguments. For instance, **count** t is simply the number of components in the tuple t; we shall use it later to measure the lengths of lists and the cardinalities of sets. The remaining operations on tuples are quite straightforward. For instance, **equal** $\_$ is defined in terms of $\_$ **is** $\_$. Let us move on to look at our notation for truth-values.

5.1.4   Truth-Values

Basics

- truth-value = true **|** false (*individual*) .

Specifics

- if $\_$ then $\_$ else $\_$ :: truth-value, x, $y \rightarrow x$ **|** y (*linear*) .
- when $\_$ then $\_$ :: truth-value, $x \rightarrow x$ (*partial*) .
- there is $\_$ :: $x \rightarrow$ true (*total*) .
- not $\_$ :: truth-value $\rightarrow$ truth-value (*total*) .
- both $\_$ :: (truth-value, truth-value) $\rightarrow$ truth-value
            (*total, associative, commutative, idempotent, unit is* true) .
- either $\_$ :: (truth-value, truth-value) $\rightarrow$ truth-value
            (*total, associative, commutative, idempotent, unit is* false) .

- all _   :: truth-value* → truth-value
                 (*total, associative, commutative, idempotent, unit is* true) .

- any _   :: truth-value* → truth-value
                 (*total, associative, commutative, idempotent, unit is* false) .

- _ is _   :: truth-value, truth-value → truth-value (*total*) .

A module similar to **Basics** was given in full, and explained in detail, in Section 3.1.

Specifics provides a useful collection of operations on truth-values. The value of if t then x else y is either x or y whenever t is an individual truth-value, regardless of the sorts of x and y. It is non-*strict*, although in other respects it is just like an ordinary *total* operation. For instance if t then x else nothing is equal to x when t is equal to true; this can also be expressed, more concisely, by when t then x. We shall use there is x to check that x is not vacuous: it is true whenever x includes some individual (of any sort).

The other operations correspond to the usual Boolean operations. The unary operations all $(t_1, \ldots, t_n)$ and any $(t_1, \ldots, t_n)$ apply to arbitrary n-tuples of truth-values, generalizing the usual binary conjunction both (t_1, t_2) and disjunction either (t_1, t_2).

5.1.5 Numbers

5.1.5.1 Naturals

Basics

- natural   = 0 | positive-integer (*disjoint*) .
- 0   : natural .
- successor _ :: natural → positive-integer (*total, injective*) .

Specifics

- 1 , 2 , 3 , 4 , 5 , 6 , 7 , 8 , 9 : natural .
- _0 , _1 , _2 , _3 , _4 , _5 , _6 , _7 , _8 , _9 :: natural → natural (*total*) .
- sum _   :: natural* → natural
              (*total, associative, commutative, unit is* 0) .
- product _   :: natural* → natural
              (*total, associative, commutative, unit is* 1).
- exponent _ :: (natural, natural) → natural (*total*).
- integer-quotient _ :: (natural, natural) → natural (*partial*) .
- integer-remainder _ :: (natural, natural) → natural (*partial*) .

A simplified version of the notation specified in **Naturals/Basics** was explained in detail in Chapter 3. Here we have **positive-integer** as a (slight!) abbreviation for the term **successor natural**.

As might be expected, juxtaposed digits such as **10** are interpreted decimally. Let us avoid 'invisible' operations such as _ _ , since their introduction might cause irremovable ambiguity in our terms.

integer-quotient (m, n) and **integer-remainder** (m, n) are both *partial*, giving nothing when n is 0. No predecessor operation is specified for naturals. However, **predecessor** _ is specified as a *total* operation on *integers*. We can therefore express the *partial* predecessor of a natural number n using the sort intersection **natural & predecessor** n. The value of **predecessor 0** is an individual, but included in a sort **negative-integer** that is disjoint from **natural**, hence **natural & predecessor 0** is **nothing**, which we may use to represent an error.

5.1.5.2   Integers

Basics

- integer   = 0 | nonzero-integer (*disjoint*) .

- nonzero-integer = positive-integer | negative-integer (*disjoint*) .

- successor _   :: integer → integer (*total, injective*) .

- predecessor _   :: integer → integer (*total, injective*) .

Specifics

- negation _ :: integer → integer (*total*) .

- absolute _ :: integer → natural (*total*) .

- difference _ :: (integer, integer) → integer (*total*) .

The sort **natural** is a subsort of **integer**. For brevity, let us not bother to specify here how the arithmetic operations on natural numbers, such as **sum** _ , extend to integer arguments. Similarly we take it for granted that **Total Order** gets appropriately instantiated in all our numeric data types. As usual, see Appendix E for all the formal details.

The integers are unbounded, but it is easy to express partial bounded arithmetic using sort intersection, as for **predecessor** _ on natural numbers. Chapter 12 illustrates an alternative approach that allows several disjoint 'types' of numbers.

5.1.5.3 Rationals

Basics

- rational   = 0 | nonzero-rational (*disjoint*) .
- nonzero-rational = positive-rational | negative-rational (*disjoint*).
- positive-integer ≤ positive-rational ;   negative-integer ≤ negative-rational .
- quotient _   :: integer, nonzero-integer → rational (*total*) .

Specifics

- quotient _ :: rational, nonzero-rational → rational (*total*) .
- truncation _ :: rational → integer (*total*) .
- fraction _   :: rational → rational (*total*) .

The sort **integer** is a subsort of **rational**. The arithmetic operations on rational numbers are *exact*. Most programming languages allow *approximate* implementations of rational arithmetic, which we can specify using the following notation.

5.1.5.4 Approximations

Generics

- approximation ≤ rational .
- min-approximation, max-approximation : approximation .

Basics

- interval _   :: rational → rational (*strict*) .
- approximately _ :: rational → rational (*strict, linear*) .

The sort **approximation** is an arbitrary finite subsort of **rational**, corresponding to the numbers actually implemented on a computer. It can be specialized to correspond to *fixed-point* or *floating-point* implementations. The constants **min-approximation** and **max-approximation** are simply the numerically-smallest and largest individuals of sort **approximation**.

For any sort r ≤ **rational**, **interval** r is the smallest rational interval that includes r, regarded as a subsort of **rational**, whereas **approximately** r insists that the bounds of the interval are of sort **approximation**, and is **nothing** when r is entirely outside the interval from **min-approximation** to **max-approximation**. Chapter 12 illustrates how these operations can be used to specify minimal accuracy for approximate arithmetic. Here we really exploit the extension of ordinary operations from individuals to sorts provided by our unorthodox algebraic specification framework.

5.1.6   Characters

Basics

- character $= \square$.
- character of _ :: natural $\rightarrow$ character (*partial, injective*) .
- code _   :: character $\rightarrow$ natural (*total, injective*) .

Alphanumerics

- character $\geq$ digit | letter (*disjoint*) .
- digit   = '0' | '1' | '2' | '3' | '4' | '5' | '6' | '7' | '8' | '9' (*individual*) .
- letter   = lowercase letter | uppercase letter (*disjoint*) .
- lowercase letter = 'a' | ... | 'z' (*individual*) .
- uppercase letter = 'A' | ... | 'Z' (*individual*) .
- lowercase _   :: character $\rightarrow$ character (*total*) .
- uppercase _   :: character $\rightarrow$ character (*total*) .

ASCII

- code _   :: character $\rightarrow$ natural [max octal "177"] (*total*) .
- character = graphic-character | control-character .

The sort character is loosely-specified in **Basics**, and can be specialized as desired. In particular, the codes of characters can be defined arbitrarily, except that code _ is required to be one-one. **Alphanumerics** provides singly-quoted symbols for letters and digits. The operations lowercase _ and uppercase _ are identity on non-letter characters. **ASCII** extends **Alphanumerics** with graphic and control characters, and defines the 7-bit character codes. (The 8-bit ISO Latin character sets should be provided as well, if they become adopted in programming languages.)

Note that a reference to the entire module **Characters** implicitly refers to the submodule **ASCII**. To avoid this, one may refer just to **Characters/Basics** or to **Characters/Alphanumerics**.

5.1.7 Lists/Flat

Generics

- item = □ .

Basics

- flat-list = list of item* .
- list of _ :: item* → flat-list (*total, injective*) .

Specifics

- _ [_]   :: flat-list, item → flat-list .
- items _   :: flat-list → item* (*total, injective*) .
- head _   :: flat-list → item (*partial*) .
- tail _   :: flat-list → flat-list (*partial*) .
- empty-list   : flat-list .
- concatenation _ :: flat-list* → flat-list (*total, associative, unit is* empty-list) .

Let's look at the notation for flat lists before their generalization to nested lists. We shall instantiate the generic abstract data type of lists by including particular sorts of data in item, rather than by translating item to some other sort symbol. Of course, if we include, say, both truth-value and integer in item, it follows that their union truth-value | integer is also included, so we must admit 'heterogeneous' lists. However, we shall provide some notation to express subsorts of lists that have restricted sorts of items, so one will hardly notice the presence of the heterogeneous lists. In any case, the only *really* homogeneous lists are those whose items are all one particular individual!

In **Basics** a flat list consists of an ordered collection of individual items. Using the notation for tuples explained in Section 5.1.3, we may write list of $(i_1, \ldots, i_n)$ to specify the list whose items are $i_1, \ldots, i_n$. Note that one cannot specify lists whose items are themselves tuples! For instance, list of $((1, 2), (3, 4))$ is the *same* list as list of $(1, 2, 3, 4)$.

In **Specifics**, $l[i]$ is the restriction of the list sort l to those individual lists whose items are *all* of sort i. This is a good example of an operation that is neither *strict* nor *linear*, for instance flat-list[nothing] includes the individual empty-list and list[0 | 1] includes the individual list of (0, 1) which is not included in flat-list[0] | flat-list[1]. Of course like all operations $l[i]$ has to be monotonic with respect to subsort inclusion.

The operation items *l* gives the tuple of items of a flat list *l*, so that for instance count items *l* can be used to give the length of *l*, where count is defined on arbitrary tuples.

5.1.8   Lists/Nested

Generics

- leaf = item | □ .

Basics

- list   = list of tree* .
- tree   = leaf | list (*disjoint*) .
- list of _ :: tree* → list (*total, injective*) .

Specifics

- _ [_]   :: list, tree → list .
- branches _   :: list → tree* (*total, injective*) .
- leaves _   :: tree → leaf* (*total, injective*) .
- head _   :: list → tree (*partial*) .
- tail _   :: list → list (*partial*) .
- empty-list   : list .
- concatenation _ :: list* → list (*total, associative, unit is* empty-list) .

Now for nested lists. A nested list is essentially a *tree*! Whereas lists are constructed from items, trees are constructed from leaves. By letting the sort leaf include item, we obtain that nested lists include flat lists, as one might expect. That explains **Generics**. In **Basics**, we let tree abbreviate the sort union of leaf and list. The operation list of _ is now extended from tuples of items to tuples of trees: its restriction to items still constructs flat lists, of course. Notice that leaf and list are disjoint. Thus we *cannot* include, say, flat lists of items as *leaves* of nested trees. But we can write list of tree*, which (assuming leaves are simply items) gives the required sort of trees.

The notation provided by **Specifics** for nested lists corresponds closely to that explained previously in connection with flat lists. Instead of the single operation items _ , we now have the operations branches _ and leaves _ , which are the two natural generalizations of items _ to nested lists: branches *l* is the tuple of immediate components of the list *l*, whereas leaves *t* collects all the leaves in the tree, however much they are nested inside lists—perhaps not at all. In Appendix E it is generalized to tuples of trees.

5.1.9   Strings

Basics

- character $\leq$ item .
- string   = flat-list [character] .
- string of _   :: character* $\rightarrow$ string (*total, injective*) .
- characters _ :: string $\rightarrow$ character* (*total, injective*) .
- ""   : string .
- _ ^ _   :: string, string $\rightarrow$ string (*total, associative, unit is* "") .

Alphanumerics

- lowercase _ :: string $\rightarrow$ string (*total*) .
- uppercase _ :: string $\rightarrow$ string (*total*) .
- decimal _   :: string of digit$^+$ $\rightarrow$ natural (*total*) .
- octal _   :: string of octal-digit$^+$ $\rightarrow$ natural (*total*) .
- octal-digit = '0' | '1' | '2' | '3' | '4' | '5' | '6' | '7' .

We represent strings simply as flat lists of characters, so we can express a string with characters 'c_1', ..., 'c_n' as list of ('c_1', ..., 'c_n'). For conciseness let us also allow the notation "$c_1 \ldots c_n$" for such a string, although unfortunately we cannot specify the symbol "_ ... _" algebraically in our framework. "" is the empty string, and $s_1 \,\hat{}\, s_2$ expresses the concatenation of the strings s_1 and s_2.

Alphanumerics provides some notation that is often useful in practice: the extensions from characters to strings of the operations lowercase _ and uppercase _ , and operations for evaluating strings of digits to natural numbers.

5.1.10   Syntax

Basics

- syntax-tree = character | list [syntax-tree] (*disjoint*) .

Specifics

- [ ]   : syntax-tree .
- [_]   :: syntax-tree* $\rightarrow$ syntax-tree (*total*) .
- [_ _] :: syntax-tree*, syntax-tree* $\rightarrow$ syntax-tree (*total*) .

   ...

- ⟨ ⟩   : syntax-tree* .
- ⟨ _ ⟩   :: syntax-tree* → syntax-tree* (*total*) .
- ⟨ _ _ ⟩ :: syntax-tree*, syntax-tree* → syntax-tree* (*total*) .

  ...

Syntax trees are trees whose leaves are only characters. They are used primarily for representing *syntactic* entities, in particular the abstract syntax of programs. Note that strings are simply syntax trees whose *branches* are all characters.

The operations ⟦ _ ... _ ⟧ in **Specifics** above allow us to write specifications of particular sorts of tree perspicuously as productions of *grammars*, and to write semantic equations similar to those used in denotational semantics. As mentioned in Section 3.2, ⟦ t_1 ... t_n ⟧ is the syntax tree whose branches are the concatenation of the *tuples* t_1, ..., t_n. The operations ⟨ _ ... _ ⟩ are for use in connection with regular expressions, which we express using the general notation for tuples, explained in Section 5.1.3.

5.1.11   Sets

Generics

- nonset-element = □ .
- _ is _   :: nonset-element, nonset-element → truth-value (*total*) .

Basics

- set   = set of element* .
- element = nonset-element | set (*disjoint*) .
- set of _ :: element* → set (*total*) .

Specifics

- _ [_]   :: set, element → set .
- elements _   :: set → element* (*strict, linear*) .
- empty-set   : set .
- _ [in _]   :: element, set → element (*partial*) .
- _ [not in _]   :: element, set → element (*partial*) .

Sets are specified in much the same way as nested lists, but of course different operations are provided for combination and inspection. As the symbols are quite self-explanatory, only a few operations are mentioned here; see Appendix E for the remaining details. Note, however, that the elements of sets cannot themselves be tuples.

Sets are not much use unless we can ask whether a particular element is *in* a particular set. Clearly, this requires *distinguishing* between particular *elements*, hence we demand a total equality operation _ is _ on the sort element.

e [in *s*] is the restriction of the sort of element *e* to those individuals *e'* for which *e'* is in *s* is true. The complementary restriction is *e* [not in *s*]. The analogous operation on *sorts s* cannot be provided, as it is not monotonic with respect to subsort inclusion.

5.1.12 Maps

Generics

- nonmap-range = □ .

Basics

- map   = disjoint-union (map of element to range)* .
- range   = nonmap-range | map (*disjoint*) .
- map of _ to _ :: element, range → map (*total, injective*) .
- empty-map   : map .
- disjoint-union _ :: map* → map
  (*partial, associative, commutative, unit is* empty-map) .
- mapped-set _   :: map → set (*total*) .

Specifics

- _ [_ to _]   :: map, element, range → map .
- _ at _   :: map, element → range (*partial*) .
- overlay _   :: map* → map
  (*total, associative, idempotent, unit is* empty-map) .
- _ restricted to _ :: map, set → map (*total*) .
- _ omitting _   :: map, set → map (*total*) .

Maps play an important rôle in connection with action notation, as they are used to represent various kinds of information, such as bindings and storage. We may imagine a map as the graph of a finite function, i.e., a set of pairs such that no value occurs more than once as the first component of a pair.

In contrast to lists and sets, maps involve two unspecified sorts, **element** and **nonmap-range**. So as to be able to determine the **mapped-set** of a map, we take **element** to be the same as for sets, whereas **nonmap-range** is arbitrary.

The notation for constructing maps is not quite as neat as that for lists and sets: **map of** e **to** r gives a single-point map, and **disjoint-union** $(m_1, \ldots, m_n)$ combines the maps $m_1, \ldots, m_n$, provided that their mapped-sets are mutually disjoint. **overlay** $(m_1, \ldots, m_n)$ also combines the maps, giving the same result as the basic operation **disjoint-union** $(m_1, \ldots, m_n)$ when their mapped-sets are disjoint, but taking the first value provided by $m_1, \ldots, m_n$ when they overlap. Thus for example **overlay (map of 'x' to 1, map of 'y' to 2, map of 'x' to 3)** is the same map as **disjoint-union (map of 'x' to 1, map of 'y' to 2)**. m [e **to** r] is the restriction of the map sort m to those individual maps that only map elements in e to values in r, for instance **map [character to natural]**.

5.2   /Action Notation/Basic/Data

includes: **Data Notation/General** .

- **datum**   ≤ **component** .
- **datum**   ≥ **truth-value** | **rational** | **character** | **list** |
                    set | **map** | **abstraction** (*disjoint*) .
- **distinct-datum** ≤ **datum** .
- **distinct-datum** ≥ **truth-value** | **rational** | **character** | **list [distinct-datum]** |
                    set [distinct-datum] | **map [distinct-datum to distinct-datum]** .

includes: **Data Notation/Instant/Distinction** (**distinct-datum** *for* s) .

- **data**   = **datum***.
- **a** _ , **an** _ , **the** _ , **of** _ , **some** _ :: **data** → **data** (*total*) .

Action notation provides the sort **datum**, which is intended to include all the individual items of data used in an action semantic description. It already includes the standard data provided by data notation, and any extra data used should be specified to be included as well. The subsort **abstraction** of **data** involves actions and is defined in Chapter 9. The sort **data** includes all tuples whose components are of sort **datum**.

The sort **distinct-datum** is the restriction of **datum** to individuals for which the operation _ **is** _ is at least partially specified; it does *not* include **abstraction**. Only distinct data can be elements of sets and maps. To specify concisely that all the individuals of the sorts $s_1, \ldots, s_n$ are always distinct from each other, we may write the single axiom distinct $(x_1{:}s_1, \ldots, x_n{:}s_n) = $ true.

Finally, action notation provides the operations a d, an d, the d, of d, and some d purely for fluency of expression when specifying data d. For instance, we may write an integer or the integer instead of just integer, and similarly for the negation of 42 and the product of (6, 7). We may also write sort restrictions such as list [of natural]. Formally, operations such as of _ are specified as *identity* on data.

Caveat: When one introduces new symbols, e.g., to specify *ad hoc* semantic entities, one must be careful: if the notation contains both oops _ and oops of _ , the term oops of x is ambiguous, due to the presence of of _ . Although one can force the grouping oops (of x), one cannot force the alternative grouping at all! Similarly for operation symbols involving the other 'noise' words. Despite this drawback, it still seems worthwhile to provide of _ , etc., as action notation reads very tersely without them.

Summary

- *Data notation provides tuples, truth-values, numbers, characters, lists, strings, syntax trees, sets, and maps.*

- *Tuple notation includes a form of regular expressions.*

- *Tuples are used to provide operations of arbitrarily-many arguments..*

- *Various sorts, such as* component, *are left open for later specialization.*

- *The arithmetic operations are exact, but can be used to specify the accuracy of implementable operations on approximate numbers.*

- *Basic characters can be specialized to any desired character set, such as ASCII.*

- *Lists, sets, and maps can be nested, whereas tuples can only be concatenated.*

- *Trees includes leaves and nested lists. Flat lists of items are a special case of trees.*

- *Syntax trees have only characters as leaves. Strings are flat lists of characters, hence also syntax trees.*

- *Data notation can be extended ad hoc with algebraically-specified special data.*

- *Action notation includes general data notation.*

Navigation

- *Now look at Chapter 12, which gives an illustrative example of the use of data notation, before proceeding with Part II.*

- *You could also make an excursion to Appendix E, which gives the complete algebraic specification of data notation.*

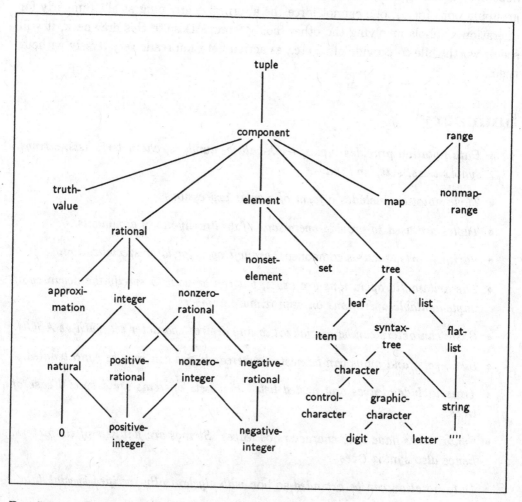

Box 5.1   Some inclusions between standard sorts of data

Exercises

1. Introduce and define operations for bounded integer arithmetic, leaving the bounds (say minimum-integer and maximum-integer) loosely specified. For instance, let bounded-sum $(i_1, i_2) =$ nothing when sum (i_1, i_2) is out of bounds.

2. Introduce explicit error individuals of sort error, to be disjoint from rational. Indicate how the specification of numbers in Appendix E should be changed so all numeric operations become *total* functions on rational | error.

3. Specify an operation frontier _ that maps any tree to the *string* formed from all the characters that form the leaves of the tree. Hint: express it directly in terms of the standard operations on trees.

4. Give a module that specifies an operation component-sort _ , intended to map any tuple to the least sort that includes all its components.

5. Specialize the specification of approximate numbers to correspond to a particular type of fixed-point 'real' numbers (e.g., as in ADA). What changes would be needed to represent a floating-point type of real numbers instead?

Chapter 6

Functional

- *Action notation includes a functional action notation for specifying data flow.*

- *Functional actions are concerned with transient information.*

- *Chapter 13 illustrates the use of functional action notation in the semantic description of expressions and statements.*

So far, we have considered actions and data separately: basic action notation does not involve data at all, nor does data notation involve actions. This chapter introduces *functional* actions that do involve data, as well as *yielders* that can occur in actions.

The information that actions can process is classified as transient, scoped, stable, or permanent, according to how far it tends to be propagated. Functional actions are concerned with processing *transient* information, which generally isn't propagated very far during action performance. The transient information current at the start of an action may still be current at the start of the action's direct subactions. However, almost all primitive actions, and a few combinators, prevent the propagation of transient information, so it usually disappears rather quickly.

Transient information represents intermediate values computed during program execution. For example, it may represent the values of some subexpressions, prior to the application of an arithmetic operation to them. Transient information typically corresponds to data which implementations put in registers, or on a stack.

Each item of transient information consists of a single individual of sort **datum**. We represent a collection of transients as a *tuple*, so as to be able to keep track of each item. Thus the entire tuple is an individual of sort **data**, which Chapter 5 introduced as an abbreviation for **datum***.

Recall that an action performance may complete, escape, fail, or diverge. When it completes or escapes, it always *gives* transient information, i.e., a data tuple.

The empty tuple represents the lack of transient information, and a tuple with just one component is, of course, already a single datum. When a performance fails or diverges, it never gives any transients at all.

An action performance is always *given* the *current* transient information. This may be either the entire transient information given *to* the performance of an *enclosing* action, or that given *by* the already-terminated performance of an *immediately preceding* action.

Primitive actions may involve *yielders*, which are *evaluated* to yield data with reference to all the current information, transient or otherwise. Ordinary data are a special case of yielders, always evaluating to themselves without reference to the current information. In general, evaluation of a compound yielder involves evaluation of all its components, with reference to the same information. Evaluation cannot affect the current information directly, and it always yields some (perhaps vacuous) *sort* of data, so the order of evaluation of several yielders in the same primitive action is insignificant. Most primitive actions require their yielders to evaluate to individuals, and fail when any of them yields the vacuous sort, nothing; a few of them allow evaluation of yielders to yield proper sorts as well as individuals.

Functional actions are closely related to fundamental concepts of *data flow*, rather than control flow. Data has to be computed before it can flow, though, so specifying data flow does at least partially specify control.

The transient information given to an action (henceforth, let us drop the tedious emphasis on 'performance') represent the influx of data. When the action is a combination of two subactions, the transients may be given to both the subactions, or just to one.

The transients given by an action represents the resulting data, which may have been computed, or merely copied, from the transients given to the action. Now when an action is a combination of two subactions, the transients given by the combination are either the *concatenation* of all the transients given by both subactions, or else just the transients given by the subaction that made the last step of the performance.

Functional actions that merely complete or fail, depending on the current information, can be used to *guard* alternatives. Choices between guarded alternatives are generally more deterministic than those between unguarded alternatives. When the guard of one alternative checks some condition, and that of another checks the negation of that condition, the nondeterministic choice reduces to an ordinary deterministic conditional choice. Similarly, guards that check for mutually-exclusive cases make choices deterministic. When the cases are not exhaustive, however, the lack of a guard on an alternative does *not* represent a 'default' or 'otherwise' case, since it can *always* be chosen! Instead, we have to use a guard that is complementary to all the other cases—or use traps and escapes, as illustrated in Chapter 17.

The functional action notation introduced below extends the basic action notation and data notation with a few primitive actions, one new combinator, and some notation for yielders. It corresponds to a simple yet quite expressive functional programming language—hence the name—with the transients given to an action corresponding to the arguments of a function. Actually, functional programming languages fall into two distinct groups: those based on *application* of functions to arguments, such as STANDARD ML [MTH90], and those based on *composition* of functions, without explicit mention of arguments, such as FP [Bac78]. Functional action notation belongs to the latter group. The presence of nondeterministic choice, however, is unconventional in a functional programming language.

Functional action notation was designed for convenient use in action semantic descriptions of programming languages, rather than for writing large-scale programs. Compared to most functional programming languages, its syntax is rather meagre. Evaluation in action notation is *eager*, whereas many functional programming languages use *lazy* evaluation. However, Chapter 9 introduces so-called abstractions, whereby actions can be incorporated in data, and this allows action notation to achieve the same effect as lazy evaluation, as well as to represent passing functions as arguments to other functions.

6.1 Actions

- give _   :: yielder → action .

- escape with _ :: yielder → action .

- regive   : action .

- choose _   :: yielder → action .

- check _   :: yielder → action .

- _ then _   :: action, action → action (*total, associative, unit is* regive) .

The primitive action give Y completes, giving the data yielded by evaluating the yielder Y, provided that this is an individual; it fails when Y yields nothing. Giving the empty tuple corresponds to completing without giving any transients at all, and give ( ) is equivalent to complete. The primitive action regive gives all the transients that are given to it, thereby propagating them. regive is actually an abbreviation for give the given data, but it is important enough to merit a constant symbol. The action escape with Y escapes, giving the data yielded by Y.

The action **choose** Y generalizes **give** Y to make a choice between the individuals of a *sort* yielded by Y. For instance, **choose a natural** gives an arbitrary individual of the sort **natural**. The use of a sort, rather than an individual set, as an argument is essential here, since our sets are always finite. In any case, we may easily express the choice of an element of a set s of natural numbers as **choose a natural [in s]**, using a sort restriction operation provided by **Data Notation/Sets**. As with **give** Y, **choose** Y fails if Y yields **nothing**. Failure after a completed choice does *not* cause back-tracking to try other choices! **choose** Y represents an implementation-dependent choice of data, rather than a choice between alternative actions to perform.

If you are familiar with the use of so-called power domains to model nondeterminism in denotational semantics, you may know that unbounded nondeterministic choices such as **choose a natural** present the dilemma between abandoning *continuity*, or including nontermination as a possible choice. Yet the operational semantics of unbounded nondeterminism is straightforward.

The action **check** Y requires Y to yield a truth-value; it completes when the value is true, otherwise it fails, without committing. It is used for guarding alternatives. For instance, (**check** Y **and then** A_1) **or** (**check not** Y **and then** A_2) expresses a deterministic choice between A_1 and A_2, depending on the condition Y.

The functional action combination A_1 **then** A_2 represents ordinary functional composition of A_1 and A_2: the transients given to the whole action are propagated only to A_1, the transients given by A_1 on completion are given only to A_2, and only the transients given by A_2 are given by the whole action. See Box 6.1. Regarding control flow, A_1 **then** A_2 specifies normal sequencing, as in A_1 **and then** A_2. When A_1 doesn't give any transients and A_2 doesn't refer to any given transients, A_1 **then** A_2 may be used interchangeably with A_1 **and then** A_2. The action **regive** is the unit for _ **then** _ .

Primitive basic actions generally do not give any transients at all, except for **escape**, which is like **regive** in giving all the transients given to it. Actually, **escape with** Y is an abbreviation for **give** Y **then escape**.

The basic action combination A_1 **and** A_2 passes given transients to both the subactions, and concatenates the transients given by the subactions when they both complete; similarly for A_1 **and then** A_2. See Box 6.1. But with abnormal sequencing A_1 **trap** A_2, the transients given to the combination are passed only to A_1, and A_2 is given only the transients given by the escape from A_1, so it resembles A_1 **then** A_2 regarding data flow. Finally, each alternative of A_1 **or** A_2, when performed, is given the same transients as the combination, and of course the combination gives only the transients given by the non-failing alternative performed, if any.

Whereas the data flow in A_1 **then** A_2 is analogous to that in ordinary function composition $g \circ f$ (at least when the functions are strict) the data flow in A_1 **and** A_2

is analogous to so-called *target-tupling* of functions, sometimes written $[f, g]$ and defined by $[f, g](x) = (f(x), g(x))$.

6.2   Yielders

- given _   :: data $\rightarrow$ yielder (*strict*) .
- given _#_ :: datum, positive-integer $\rightarrow$ yielder (*strict*) .
- it   : yielder .
- them   : yielder .

The yielder **given** Y yields all the data given to its evaluation, provided that this is of the data sort Y. For instance **the given truth-value** (where 'the' is optional) yields **true** or **false** when the given data consists of that single individual of sort **truth-value**. Otherwise it yields nothing. Similarly, **given** $Y\#n$ yields the n'th individual component of a given tuple, for $n > 0$, provided that this component is of sort Y.

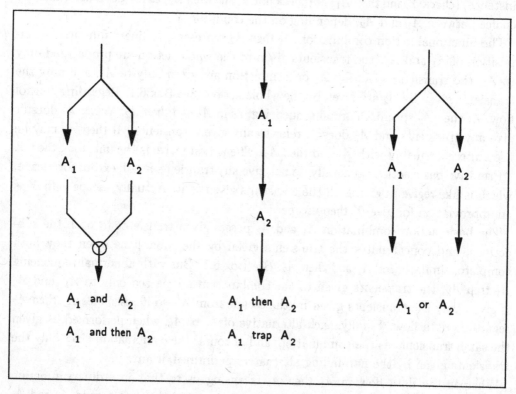

Box 6.1   Fundamental patterns of data flow

The yielders **it** and **them** both yield all the given data, but **it** insists that there should be only a single component datum. In fact **it** always yields the same as the given datum, and **them** yields the same as the given data.

It is primarily the presence of A_1 **then** A_2 in functional action notation that causes the *transience* of transient data. This combinator does *not* automatically make the given transients available to A_2, so unless A_1 propagates them, they simply disappear. A common beginner's mistake in writing functional actions is to refer to a transient after it has disappeared, as in **check there is given a positive-integer then give the predecessor of the given positive integer**, where the **check** action does *not* pass on the given transient. To correct this mistake, either change 'then' to 'and then', or add 'and give it' to the checking action.

6.3   /Action Notation/Basic/Yielders

- yielder $\geq$ data .
- the _ yielded by _ :: data, yielder $\rightarrow$ yielder .
- *data-operation*   :: yielder, ... $\rightarrow$ yielder .

The above notation for yielders is for general use in action notation. The sort yielder includes all yielders, including **data** as a subsort. The yielder **the** d **yielded by** Y evaluates to the same individual as Y, when that is of sort d, otherwise it yields nothing. This is only useful when d is a proper subsort of the sort of data that can be yielded by Y, or to make a formal comment about the sort of data yielded by Y, when that is a subsort of d. For instance, we may write **the natural yielded by the predecessor of the given natural**, where predecessor of 0 is not a natural number; or we may write **the natural yielded by the absolute of the given integer**, just for emphasis.

Each *data-operation*, i.e., operation specified only with functionalities involving subsorts of **data**, extends to arguments of sort **yielder** as well. An application of the data-operation yields whatever results from applying it to the data yielded by evaluating the arguments. For instance **the successor of the given natural** involves an application of the operation **successor** _ to the yielder **given natural**, and evaluates to $n+1$ when the current transient information consists of the single natural number n.

Finally, we continue with the notation provided in Chapter 4 for expressing subsorts of actions, and extend it with analogous operations for subsorts of yielders.

6.4 /Action Notation/Facets (*continued*)

6.4.1 Outcomes (*continued*)

- outcome   = □ | giving data | escaping with data | □ .
- giving _   :: data → outcome (*strict, linear*) .
- escaping with _ :: data → outcome (*strict, linear*) .
- completing   = giving ( ) .
- escaping   = escaping with given data .

For any data sort d, the outcome giving d allows normal termination giving transients included in d. Note that the number of components in the given transients has to match the number of components in d exactly, because for instance natural is *not* a subsort of natural², i.e., (natural, natural). However, an outcome sort such as giving natural* covers any number of natural transients—as does giving data, of course. The basic outcome completing abbreviates giving ( ), where ( ) is the empty tuple of data, thus it corresponds to the outcomes of actions that give no transients at all when they complete.

Similarly, escaping with d allows abnormal termination giving transients included in the data sort d. But observe that escaping abbreviates escaping with data, in accordance with the difference between complete and escape regarding dataflow.

The notation for outcomes is used together with the notation $A\ [O]$, as explained in Chapter 4.

6.4.2 Incomes

- income   = given data | □ .
- given _   :: data → income (*strict, linear*) .
- given _#_   :: data, positive-integer → income (*strict, linear*) .

The sort income is, like outcome, a sort of auxiliary entities that are used for specifying sorts of actions and yielders.

For any data sort d, the income sort given d allows use of given transients of the data sort d. This is the same notation that we use for yielders themselves, which makes the intended interpretation of the notation for incomes particularly self-evident. Note that for example given natural has to be included in given integer, by monotonicity from natural $\leq$ integer. The income given $d\#p$ allows use of the p'th component of the given transients, this being of datum sort d.

Further notation for incomes is provided in later chapters. The notation for incomes is used together with the following notation for subsorts of actions and yielders.

6.4.3 Actions (*continued*)

- _ [using _] :: action, income → action .

When A is a sort of action and I is a sort of income, A [using I] restricts A to those actions which, whenever performed, perhaps evaluate yielders that refer at most to the current information indicated by I. Compare Y [using I], where Y is a sort of yielder, below.

Restrictions regarding incomes and outcomes can be composed. For example, we may write action [giving a truth-value] [using a given integer]. The order in which the restrictions are written is immaterial.

6.4.4 Yielders

- _ [_]   :: yielder, data → yielder .
- _ [using _] :: yielder, income → yielder .

Recall that yielder is the sort of all yielders. When Y is a sort of yielder and d is a sort of data, Y [d] restricts Y to those yielders which, whenever evaluated, yield data included in d. The sort term Y [of d] is equivalent to Y [d], since 'of' here is merely an application of the operation of _ , which is the identity function on data, but a yielder [of an integer] reads a bit more naturally than yielder [integer].

When I is a sort of income, Y [using I] restricts Y to those yielders which, whenever evaluated, refer at most to the current information indicated by I.

As with incomes and outcomes above, restrictions regarding incomes and yielded data can be composed. For example, we may write yielder [of a truth-value] [using a given integer]. Again, the order in which the restrictions are written is immaterial.

That is all the standard notation for sort restrictions, although we shall introduce a few more constants for incomes and outcomes in subsequent chapters. The full notation is specified in Section B.9. *Caveat*: The notation for subsorts of actions and yielders has been much less stable than that for individual actions and yielders during the development of action semantics, and the version used in this book was introduced only recently. It is much simpler than the previous version (used in [Wat91]), and not quite so expressive. We have not yet had much experience of exploiting the algebraic properties of sort restrictions, given in Section B.9, for verifying that particular actions are included in the expected sorts, nor has the notation for incomes and outcomes been related formally to the operational semantics of action notation. It may be that some adjustments to Section B.9 will be required.

Summary

- *Functional action notation is for specifying transient information processing, i.e., data flow.*

- *A performance of an action is given a tuple of transient data, and gives a tuple of transient data if it completes or escapes.*

- *The combinators _ then _ and _ trap _ pass transients from their first subaction to the second one. All the other combinators introduced so far pass given transients to both their subactions, and concatenate any transients given by the subactions.*

- *Yielders include primitives that refer to particular components of the current transients, and can be combined using ordinary data operations.*

- *Sorts of actions are expressed using incomes and outcomes, whereas sorts of yielders are expressed using incomes and sorts of yielded data.*

Navigation

- *Now look at Chapter 13, which gives an illustrative example of the use of functional action notation, before proceeding with Part II.*

- *If you would like a more detailed informal explanation of functional actions, see Section D.2 and Section D.1.2.*

- *You could also make an excursion to Section B.2 and Section B.1.2, which give an algebraic specification of functional action notation.*

Exercises

1. Determine what the following action gives when it is given an integer i.

    unfolding
    | check (the given integer is less than 1) and then give 1
    or
    | check (the given integer is greater than 0) and then
    | | give it and
    | | give the predecessor of it then unfold
    | then give the product of (the given integer#1, the given integer#2) .

2. Practice programming with functional actions by modifying the action specified in the preceding exercise:

   (a) to use so-called tail recursion, i.e., **unfold** gives the final result;

   (b) to give a tuple of all the products computed during the performance.

3. On which subsort of functional actions is _ **and** _ commutative? Express it formally, using the notation for outcome restrictions. Discuss the usefulness of the properties of combinators, such as commutativity and associativity.

4. Find an action that specifies the flow of data indicated by the following diagram:

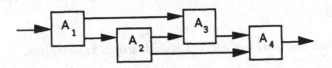

   Consider whether one could introduce further (binary) combinators to facilitate the specification of such patterns of data flow.

5. Let A be an action of sort **action [completing | escaping] [using a given integer]**. Specify an action, say **iterate** A **up to** n, that performs A some number n times (or until A escapes), giving $1, 2, \ldots, n$ to the various performances of A, which are to be interleaved, not sequenced. Use an unfolding, rather than specifying the action recursively. Consider whether your action would have the intended effect when n is replaced by a yielder, such as **the given integer**; if not, investigate how to change it to achieve that.

6. Compare the functional part of Action Notation with the functional programming language FP [Bac78]. In particular, discuss whether the nested tupling used in FP has any advantages or disadvantages compared to the tupling used here.

Chapter 7

Declarative

- *Action notation includes a declarative action notation for specifying scopes of bindings.*

- *Declarative actions are concerned with scoped information.*

- *Chapter 14 illustrates the use of declarative action notation in the semantic description of declarations, expressions, and statements.*

Declarative actions are concerned with processing *scoped* information, which generally gets propagated further than transient information. The scoped information current at the start of an action is often current throughout the action—although it may get temporarily hidden by other scoped information within the action. It disappears at the end of its scope.

Scoped information represents the associations, called *bindings*, which declarations in programs establish between identifiers and entities such as constants, variables, procedures, etc.[1] Implementations usually represent bindings by some form of *symbol-table*.

Programming languages are often characterized as having *static* or *dynamic* scopes for bindings. The difference concerns whether or not it is possible to determine from the program text, before running the program with its input, which declarations establish the bindings of which identifiers. For efficiency, compilers extract the required information from the symbol table during compilation, so that it isn't needed when the compiled code is run.

---

[1]Declarative actions have nothing to do with 'declarative programming' in logic programming languages.

The possibility of dynamic bindings only arises when the programming language contains procedures, or similar constructs, where the body of the procedure can be called from various parts of the program: the bindings current at each call might be different. (This is a second sense of the word 'dynamic': the declaration binding a particular identifier may *change* during a run of the program.) We defer further consideration of static versus dynamic bindings to Chapter 9, where the abstractions that are used to represent procedures are explained.

Another distinction concerning scopes of bindings is that between *block* and *modular* structure. With block structure, the *local* bindings established by declarations at outer levels are also available at inner levels of structure, unless hidden by redeclarations. With modular structure, however, each module must explicitly *import* any bindings required from other modules.

We represent bindings as maps from *tokens* to individual items of *bindable* data. Tokens correspond directly to the identifiers used in programs, which are ofter just strings of letters and digits.

When an action performance completes, it always *produces* a binding map. The empty map represents the lack of bindings. When the performance escapes, fails, or diverges, however, it never produces any binding map at all.

An action performance always *receives* the *current* scoped information. As with transient information, this may be the entire bindings received by the performance of an *enclosing* action, or the bindings produced by the already-terminated performance of a *preceding* action. But there are further possibilities with scoped information, allowing bindings to be *overridden* by new bindings for the same tokens. For instance, the bindings received by A_2 in a combination of A_1 with A_2 may be the map obtained by overlaying the bindings received by the entire combination with those produced by A_1, so that the latter bindings may hide the former. Here, overlaying does not change a map, it merely returns a different map.

The bindings produced by an action represent just the effect of that action itself. They do not, in general, include any of the bindings received by the action. When an action is a combination of two subactions, the bindings produced by the combination may be the *disjoint union* of the bindings produced by both subactions, with failure occurring if the subactions produce bindings for the same token; they may be the *overlay* of the bindings produced by the first subaction with those produced by the second subaction; or they may be just the bindings produced by the second subaction. Other combinations can easily be imagined, see Exercise 3, but they seem to be less fundamental than those described.

Block structure limits the scope of local bindings to the block body. This corresponds to overlaying received, nonlocal bindings with the local bindings, and passing the resulting bindings to the block body, which does not itself produce any bindings at all. Nested blocks thus correspond to a disciplined *stacking* of bindings, with those most recently pushed onto the stack overriding any earlier ones for the same tokens. This lets the local bindings at each block level accumulate. Sometimes, nonlocal bindings that are about to be overridden by local bindings are hidden at the start of the block, so that two uses of the same token at the same block level cannot refer to different bindings. Such hiding can be represented by producing a binding to a special datum that is not ordinarily bindable.

With modular structure, on the other hand, the module *body* does produce bindings. These are not necessarily produced by the module declaration itself, though: the corresponding binding map may be merely bound to the module identifier. The scope of the bindings is thus restricted to the module body that produced them, and to where they are imported by reproducing the binding map.

Box 7.1 depicts various common ways that bindings flow between actions. Notice the difference between the way that disjoint union and overlaying of bindings is indicated.

How about self-referential bindings? Often, self-reference is regarded as a fundamental binding concept, corresponding directly to *recursive* declarations of procedures, etc., and similarly for mutual reference. However, self-referential bindings are inherently *infinite* entities. To produce such entities by a finite amount of processing requires them to be represented finitely by *cyclic* data structures. This leads us to consider *indirect* bindings, which can be subsequently *redirected* to entities that contain the indirect bindings. Such indirect bindings involve a *hybrid* of scoped information (the bindings themselves) and stable information (the redirections), the latter being similar to the storage considered in the next chapter.

Indirect bindings are not only useful for finite representation of self-referential bindings, but also correspond closely to features such as *forward* procedure declarations, where an *interface* is declared separately from a body. In fact it is quite difficult to describe the semantics of forward procedure declarations in terms of self-referential bindings, because one has to deal simultaneously with two different bindings for a forward procedure identifier, and to arrange for the one to get incorporated in the other. Most attempts at semantic descriptions of languages that allow forward declarations, PASCAL for instance, duck this problem by starting from a really abstract syntax, where procedure bodies have already been joined with the corresponding heads—but then it is quite difficult to see the precise scope of the forward procedure identifiers, and to relate the specified abstract syntax to the familiar concrete syntax for the language.

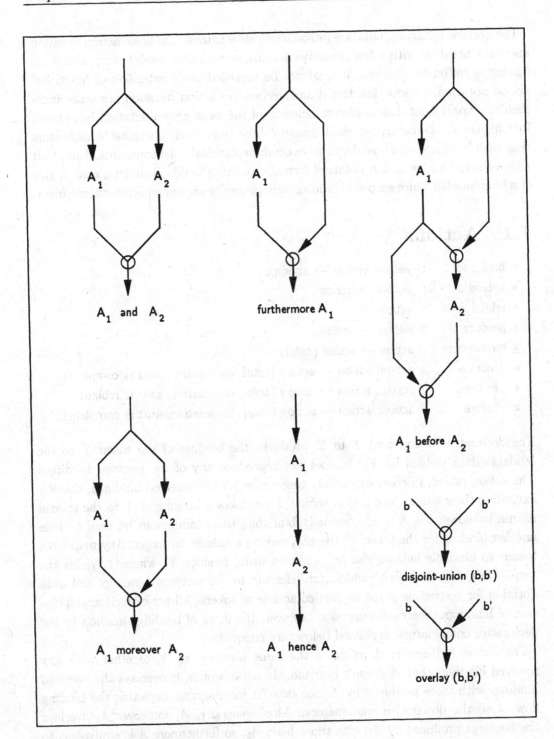

Box 7.1   Various binding flows

The declarative action notation introduced below extends the basic action notation and data notation with a few primitive actions, several new combinators, and some further notation for yielders. It need not be regarded as an extension of functional action notation, because functional and declarative action notation are quite independent, apart from their common inclusion of the basic action notation introduced in Chapter 4. However, we shall consider how basic and functional combinators deal with bindings, and how declarative combinators deal with transients. Note that although declarative action notation formally includes nondeterministic choice, this is seldom needed, since scopes of bindings are generally implementation-independent.

7.1   Actions

- bind _ to _   :: yielder, yielder → action .
- unbind _   :: yielder → action .
- rebind   : action .
- produce _   :: yielder → action .
- furthermore _ :: action → action (*total*) .
- _ moreover _ :: action, action → action (*total, associative, unit is* complete) .
- _ hence _   :: action, action → action (*total, associative, unit is* rebind) .
- _ before _   :: action, action → action (*total, associative, unit is* complete) .

The declarative action bind T to Y produces the binding of the token T to the bindable data yielded by Y. It does *not* reproduce any of the received bindings! The action rebind, in contrast, merely reproduces all the received bindings, thereby extending their scope. The action unbind T produces a binding of T to the special datum unknown, which is not normally bindable; this binding can be used to hide another binding for the token T, thereby making a hole in its scope. Any map from tokens to bindable entities can be produced using produce Y, where Y yields the map. This, together with yielders for referring to the received bindings and data notation for restricting maps to particular sets of tokens, allows explicit manipulation of bindings. For most purposes, however, the flows of bindings implicit in the declarative combinators, explained below, are adequate.

The action furthermore A produces the same bindings as A, together with any received bindings that A doesn't override. In other words, it overlays the received bindings with those produced by A. See Box 7.1 for diagrams depicting the binding flow of all the declarative combinators. More generally, A_1 moreover A_2 overlays the bindings produced by A_1 with those from A_2, so furthermore A is equivalent to rebind moreover A. This pattern of binding flow occurs so frequently in the semantics of block structured languages that it is worth having **furthermore** A as a standard abbreviation in action notation.

The combination A_1 **hence** A_2 lets the bindings produced by A_1 be received by A_2, which limits their scope—unless they get reproduced by A_2. It is analogous to functional composition. The unit for _ **hence** _ is **rebind**. The compound combination **furthermore** A_1 **hence** A_2 (recall that prefixes have higher precedence than infixes!) corresponds to ordinary block structure, with A_1 being the block head and A_2 the block body: nonlocal bindings, received by the combination, are also received by A_2 unless they are overridden by the local bindings produced by A_1.

The action A_1 **before** A_2 represents sequencing of declarations. Like **furthermore** A_1 **hence** A_2, it lets A_2 receive bindings from A_1, together with any bindings received by the whole action that are not thereby overridden. The combination produces all the bindings produced by A_2, as well as any produced by A_1 that are not overridden by A_2. Thus A_2 may rebind a token that was bound, or hidden, by A_1. Note that the bindings received by the combination are not reproduced at all, unless one of A_1, A_2 explicitly reproduces them.

The basic and functional combinators, such as A_1 **and** A_2, all pass the *received* bindings to their subactions without further ado—analogously to the way A_1 **and** A_2 passes all the given data to both A_1 and A_2. They are similarly unbiased when it comes to combining the bindings produced by their subactions: they produce the *disjoint union* of the bindings, providing this is defined, otherwise they simply fail.

Box 7.1 shows the various ways in which bindings can flow. Notice the pattern that results from replacing A_1 in A_1 **hence** A_2 by **furthermore** A; this occurs rather often in practice. See also the exercises at the end of the chapter.

There are further combinators, deferred to the Appendices, which correspond to hybrids of the above declarative combinators with various basic and functional combinators. For instance, _ **thence** _ is a hybrid of _ **then** _ and _ **hence** _ , with the combination A_1 **thence** A_2 passing transients *as well as* bindings from A_1 to A_2. See Section D.8 for the details, which are quite straightforward.

Nevertheless, even with the hybrid combinators, some mixtures of control, data, and binding flow are still difficult to express directly, and one may have to to resort to manipulating bindings as transient data and using **produce** Y. The combinators provided in declarative action notation are a compromise between generality and simplicity.

Let us also defer the details of notation for indirect bindings to the Appendices, to avoid extending this chapter unduly. The use of indirect bindings is not illustrated in Part III at all, for simplicity, so we don't need to deal with it just now. Appendix A extends the language described in Part III with constructs whose action semantics does involve the use of indirect bindings, so one may look there for illustrations, but it is perhaps best to leave that until one has become reasonably familiar with the rest of action notation.

To give an impression of the notation used for indirect bindings, the main actions are indirectly bind T to Y and redirect T to Y, where T is a token and Y yields data of sort bindable, or unknown. The action recursively bind T to Y abbreviates

> | furthermore indirectly bind T to unknown
> hence
> | redirect T to Y and
> | bind T to the redirection bound to T .

The sorts bindable and redirection are disjoint, so one may refer both to the bindable bound to T and, as above, to the redirection bound to T. Usually, one doesn't need to deal explicitly with redirections at all.

7.2 Yielders

- current bindings : yielder .
- the _ bound to _ :: bindable, yielder → yielder .
- _ receiving _   :: yielder, yielder → yielder (*total*) .

The yielder current bindings evaluates to a map that represents the received bindings. Thus the mapped-set of the current bindings yields the set of currently-bound tokens. The yielder the d bound to T evaluates to the current binding for the particular token T, provided that it is of data sort d, otherwise it yields nothing. This is the case also when the binding is indirect.

Note that when unbind T has been used to *hide* a binding for T, the d bound to T yields unknown rather than nothing, and T is in mapped-set of the current bindings yields true.

The yielder Y_1 receiving Y_2 is the only compound yielder where the component yielders are evaluated with different information. The yielder Y_2 is evaluated with all the current information, to yield a binding map b. The yielder Y_1 is then evaluated with that binding map, together with the rest of the current information. For instance, the value bound to "x" receiving the given bindings refers to some *given*, i.e. transient, binding map for the bound value of "x", not to the current, *received* bindings. This is the same as the given bindings at "x", except when the given binding for "x" is indirect, when the latter yielder evaluates to the indirection itself, rather than to the bindable datum to which the binding has been redirected.

7.3   Data

- bindings $\geq$ map [token to bindable | unknown] .
- token $\leq$ distinct-datum .
- bindable $\leq$ data .
- unknown : datum .
- known _ :: bindings $\rightarrow$ bindings (*total*) .

The sorts token and bindable are left to be specified by the user of action notation. Tokens are usually strings of letters and digits, corresponding to identifiers used in programs. Bindable values are always a proper subsort of data, since the individual datum unknown, used to indicate a hidden binding, is not included in bindable. Standard action notation does not include any particular data in token and bindable *a priori*, so they may be defined arbitrarily. The bindings map known b is obtained by omitting any hidden bindings from b, but it is not often needed in practice.

7.4   /Action Notation/Facets (*continued*)

7.4.1   Outcomes (*continued*)

- outcome = □ | binding | □ .

The outcome binding allows normal termination producing bindings. It is convenient to let binding include also the possibility of normal termination producing *no* bindings! The notation for outcomes is used together with the notation $A\,[O]$ for sorts of actions, as explained in Chapter 4. Note that we may combine binding with the outcome giving d using sort union. When we specify binding alone, the outcome completing is implicit.

7.4.2   Incomes (*continued*)

- income = □ | current bindings | □ .

The income current bindings (which is also used as a yielder) allows use of received bindings. The notation for incomes is used together with the notation $A\,[\text{using } I]$ for sorts of actions and $Y\,[\text{using } I]$ for sorts of yielders, as explained in Chapter 6. We may combine current bindings with given d using sort union. Note that the sort action [using given data | current bindings] is strictly larger than the union of action [using given data] and action [using current bindings], and similarly for yielders.

Summary

- *Declarative action notation is for specifying scoped information processing, i.e., the flow of bindings.*

- *A performance of an action receives a binding map, and produces a generally-unrelated binding map when it completes.*

- *The combinators _ hence _ and _ before _ pass bindings from the first action to the second one, and imply sequencing. All the other combinators introduced so far pass all received bindings to both their actions; and they produce the disjoint union of the bindings produced by the actions, except for _ moreover _ which, like _ before _ , overlays the produced bindings.*

- *Declarative yielders refer to the current bindings, in toto or individually.*

- *The* outcome *binding allows production of bindings (perhaps none); the* income current bindings *allows reference to received bindings.*

Navigation

- *Now look at Chapter 14, which gives an illustrative example of the use of declarative action notation, before proceeding with Part II.*

- *If you would like a more detailed informal explanation of declarative actions, see Section D.3.*

- *You could also make an excursion to Section B.3, which gives an algebraic specification of declarative action notation.*

Exercises

1. Let A_1 = bind "x" to 0, A_2 = bind "y" to the successor of the integer bound to "x", and A_3 = bind "x" to the successor of the integer bound to "x". For each of the actions below, determine which bindings must be received for its performance to complete, and what bindings it then produces:

    A_1 and A_2 ;
    A_1 hence A_2 ;
    A_1 moreover A_3 ;
    A_1 before A_3 .

2. Let A_1, A_2, A_3 be arbitrary actions.

   (a) Draw diagrams indicating the binding flows in the following combinations:
       - furthermore A_1 hence furthermore A_2 hence A_3 ;
       - furthermore (A_1 before A_2) hence A_3 .

   By comparing the bindings received and produced by A_1, A_2, and A_3, argue that the two actions are equivalent.

   (b) Draw diagrams for the two different groupings of the combination A_1 before A_2 before A_3 (ignoring the rule about infixes always grouping to the left) and argue that they are equivalent.

3. Consider sequential combinations A of actions A_1, A_2. There are various possibilities for the relationship between the bindings received and produced by A, A_1, and A_2: the bindings may be disjoint unions or overlays of other bindings, or they may be a copy of some other bindings, or they may be empty.

   (a) Make a systematic list of the possibilities, accompanied by diagrams in the style of Box 7.1. Hint: the magnitude of the task can be reduced dramatically by observing that the cases where bindings are empty can be obtained as instances of the other cases, inserting 'complete hence' or 'hence complete' as appropriate.

   (b) Consider the possibility of treating received bindings as for A_1 before A_2, but producing the disjoint union of the bindings produced by A_1, A_2 (when this is defined). Try to express it using the standard combinators. If you fail, express it with the help of the primitive action produce Y.

4. Show how to simulate declarative actions using functional actions. Hint: let the first component of transient data always be a binding map.

Chapter 8

Imperative

- *Action notation includes an imperative action notation for specifying changes to storage.*

- *Imperative actions are concerned with stable information.*

- *Chapter 15 illustrates the use of imperative action notation in the semantic description of variable declarations, assignment statements, and expressions.*

Imperative actions are concerned with processing *stable* information, which generally gets propagated further than transient and scoped information, remaining current until some primitive action changes it. Stable information consists of a collection of independent items, and each change only affects one item. Changes are destructive, rather than temporary, so they can only be reversed if a copy of the destroyed item is available.

Stable information represents the values assigned to *variables* in programs. An assignment is regarded as an order to the computer, rather than as an assertion, hence the adjective 'imperative' for the processing of stable information.

Implementations represent stable information using random-access memory, or secondary storage devices such as magnetic tapes and discs, which in fact can only store single bits—but lots of them! Particular bit-patterns in memory correspond to values, although different occurrences of the same bit-pattern may represent many different abstract values, such as characters and numbers. However, the representation of values by bit-patterns is generally implementation-dependent, so we are justified in ignoring it in semantic descriptions.

In action notation we represent stable information by a map from storage *cells* to individual items of *storable* data. Cells correspond to the addresses, or locations, of areas in random-access memory that can accommodate (the binary representation of)

entire, abstract values. For instance, a cell for storing a character might correspond
to a single byte of memory, whereas a cell for storing a high-precision real number
might correspond to two whole words of memory, each consisting of several bytes. A
compound value, such as a list, is generally stored in a collection of cells, so that its
components may be changed individually; when a list is stored in a single cell, it can
only be changed monolithically, to a whole new list.

We make very few assumptions about the properties of cells. This avoids bias
towards any particular storage architecture, as well as keeping things simple. Cells are
always distinguishable, but they do not have to be ordered. There may be an infinite
number of *potential* cells, although only finitely many of them can be *reserved*, i.e.,
in use, at once. (Such idealized unbounded storage is convenient, and familiar from
the Turing machine model of computation. It could be implemented by a magnetic
tape unit together with a factory for making new tapes!)

In the absence of further assumptions about cells, the choice of which particular
cells to allocate for use is immaterial, and can be made nondeterministically, reflecting implementation dependence. When cells are ordered, however, implementations
might be required to use blocks of adjacent cells to represent variables for storing
compound values, so that 'relative addressing' between cells is well-defined. Then
the basic notion is that of choosing nondeterministically between the available contiguous blocks. The extreme case is when implementations are required to allocate
successive cells, as with stack-based storage, where the choice of the next cell is always
deterministic.

An action performance is always given *access* to the current storage. It may make
changes to the storage by reserving cells, unreserving cells, and storing data in
reserved cells. Because action performances by a single agent consist of sequences
of steps, changes to storage occur sequentially, and different references to storage by
yielders in a particular primitive action find the same datum stored in the same cell.
Later, in Chapter 10, we consider distributed systems of agents, each with a separate local storage, and then changes to different local storages need not be sequential;
nevertheless, the result of evaluating yielders in a primitive action remains insensitive
to order of evaluation, because the local storage of an agent can only be changed by
the agent itself.

The imperative action notation introduced below extends the basic action notation
with a few primitive actions. This extension is independent of the extensions to
functional and declarative action notation. No new combinators are necessary, since
stable information processing follows the flow of control, which is specified by the
basic action combinators.

8.1   Actions

- store _ in _ :: yielder, yielder → action .
- unstore _ :: yielder → action .
- reserve _ :: yielder → action .
- unreserve _ :: yielder → action .

The imperative action store Y_1 in Y_2 changes the data stored in the cell yielded by Y_2 to the storable data yielded by Y_1. The cell concerned must have been previously reserved, using reserve Y, otherwise the storing action fails. Here, Y has to yield a particular, individual cell. However, standard action notation doesn't provide any operations for identifying individual cells! So how can we make use of reserve Y?

In practice, we do not usually want to be specific about *which* cell to reserve: all we require is some cell that is not currently reserved. Thus the solution is to choose a cell *nondeterministically*. Action notation provides allocate Y for this purpose, where Y yields a subsort of cell. In particular, allocate a cell abbreviates the following hybrid action:

> indivisibly
> | choose a cell [not in the mapped-set of the current storage] then
> | reserve the given cell and give it .

Reserved cells can be made available for reuse by unreserve Y, where Y yields an individual cell. Whether or not cells are reused usually makes no difference to the outcome of action performances, but it can be useful to indicate explicitly that a particular use of a particular cell is finished. However, unreserving a cell may leave so-called *dangling references*, for example through the binding of some token to the cell—causing confusion if the cell gets reused. The action unstore Y merely removes the data stored in the cell, leaving it as if freshly reserved.

All the above actions commit the performance to the current alternative, since the storage information originally available to any other alternative actions is now out of date. This reflects that an implementation is *not* expected to back-track through destructive changes.

8.2   Yielders

- current storage   : yielder .
- the _ stored in _ :: storable, yielder → yielder .

The yielder **the** d **stored in** Y yields the data currently stored in the cell yielded by Y, provided that it is of the sort d. Otherwise it yields **nothing**. The yielder **current storage** is analogous to **current bindings**, and takes a snapshot of the current state of the storage. Action notation does not provide an action for restoring such a snapshot, but it is not too difficult to define such an action, as might be necessary in connection with database transactions, for instance.

8.3 Data

- storage   = map [cell to storable | uninitialized] .
- cell   ≤ distinct-datum .
- storable ≤ data .
- uninitialized : datum .
- initialized _ :: storage → storage (*total*) .

The sort **cell** is left unspecified, and may be regarded as an implementation-dependent parameter of action notation. It may be specialized as desired, for instance by introducing subsorts for cells capable of storing particular sorts of data, or by introducing an enumeration of all the cells. The sort **storable** is to be specified by the user of action notation; it may be equated with any subsort of **data** that does not include the datum **uninitialized**, which is stored in cells when they are reserved or unstored. The storage **initialized** s is the map obtained by omitting any cells that store **uninitialized** in the storage s, and is mainly used to ascertain the set of initialized cells.

8.4 /Action Notation/Facets (*continued*)

8.4.1 Outcomes (*continued*)

- outcome = □ | storing | □ .
- storing   ≥ committing .

The outcome **storing** implies the outcome **committing**. It allows making changes to storage, i.e., performing the primitive imperative actions explained earlier in this chapter. Specifying **storing** says nothing at all about termination possibilities. It is convenient to let **storing** include the possibility *not* making any changes at all!

The notation for outcomes is used together with the notation $A\ [O]$ for sorts of actions, as explained in Chapter 4. We combine **storing** with other outcomes using sort union.

8.4.2 Incomes (*continued*)

- income = □ | current storage | □ .

The income **current storage** (which may also be used as a yielder) allows reference to storage. The notation for incomes is used together with the notation A [using I] for sorts of actions and Y [using I] for sorts of yielders, as explained in Chapter 6. We may combine **current storage** with other incomes using sort union.

Summary

- *Imperative action notation is for specifying stable information processing, i.e., changes to storage.*

- *Cells of storage have to be reserved before data can be stored in them. They can be made available for reuse by unreserving them.*

- *A performance of an action has access to the storage, and may make changes during the performance, regardless of whether it completes, escapes, fails, or diverges.*

- *Changes to storage are always committing, causing alternative actions to be discarded.*

- *Imperative yielders refer to the data currently stored in cells.*

- *The outcome* storing *allows changes to storage (perhaps none); the income* current storage *allows reference to stored data.*

Navigation

- *Now look at Chapter 15, which gives an illustrative example of the use of imperative action notation, before proceeding with Part II.*

- *If you would like a more detailed informal explanation of imperative actions, see Section D.4.*

- *You could also make an excursion to Section B.4, which gives an algebraic specification of imperative action notation.*

Exercises

1. Would you expect the following actions to be equivalent?

   A_1 = store 0 in the given cell and then store 1 in the given cell ;

   A_2 = store 1 in the given cell .

   What numbers could be stored in the given cell after performing the following action?

   $A_3 = $ | store 0 in the given cell and then
   store the successor of (the integer stored in the given cell)
       in the given cell
   and store 2 in the given cell .

2. The action below is supposed to be given a pair of reserved cells, with an arbitrary integer n stored in the first cell, and 1 stored in the second cell.

   unfolding
     | check (the integer stored in the given cell#1 is less than 1)
   or
       check (the integer stored in the given cell#1 is greater than 0)
       and then
       store the product of (the integer stored in the given cell#1,
                       the integer stored in the given cell#2)
          in the given cell#2
       and then
       store the predecessor of (the integer stored in the given cell#1)
          in the given cell#1
       and then unfold .

   (a) Determine what value is stored in the second cell when the performance completes.

   (b) Change the action above so that the products are calculated *after* the unfolds. Can it be done without allocating further cells?

   (c) Compare the action above with that in Exercise 1 in Chapter 6. If action notation were to be used as a programming language, would it be more convenient to use functional or imperative actions—or a mixture—for such algorithms as that illustrated?

3. Specify a representation of variables for storing *lists* of numbers, together with actions for allocating lists of given length, changing components of lists to given numbers, and copying lists. Hint: represent a variable as a list of cells.

Chapter 9

Reflective

- *Reflective action notation is for specifying abstractions and their enaction.*

- *Abstractions are data that incorporate actions. The incorporated action can be supplied with transients and bindings.*

- *Chapter 16 illustrates the use of reflective action notation in the semantic description of procedure declarations.*

An *abstraction* is a datum that merely incorporates a particular action. It corresponds to the 'code' for the action, which could be implemented as a sequence of machine instructions, or as a pointer to such a sequence. We use abstractions to represent the semantics of programming constructs such as procedures.

We may form an abstraction directly from an action. The abstraction, just like any other datum, can then be given as a transient, bound to a token, etc. Ultimately, the abstraction should be *enacted*, so as to perform the incorporated action.

Forming an abstraction may be regarded as a kind of *reification*, and enacting it as *reflection*. Reification and reflection are general concepts concerned with passing from components of an implicit, underlying computational state to values that can be manipulated explicitly, and vice versa [FW84]. Thus the evaluation of yielders for referring to the given transients, current bindings, etc., can also be regarded as reification, with the performance of primitive actions such as **give** Y and **produce** Y corresponding to reflection.

The action incorporated in an abstraction is usually performed in a context different to that where the abstraction itself occurs. This raises a question about what information is current at the start of the performance of the incorporated action: is it that which was current at *abstraction-time*, when the abstraction was originally formed? or that which is current at *enaction-time*, i.e., just prior to the performance?

114

The answer depends partly on the kind of information considered. Suppose that an abstraction is representing a parameterized procedure of a program. Let A be the incorporated action.

There is generally no *transient* information current at abstraction-time at all. The transient information current at enaction-time usually consists of the procedure abstraction itself, and the values of its parameters, but it is only the latter information that is required by A. For parameterless procedures, A requires no transient information at all.

The *scoped* information, i.e., bindings, current at enaction-time is generally different from that current at abstraction-time, since the enaction may correspond to a call of the procedure from an inner block, or from a different module. Letting the abstraction-time bindings be received by the incorporated action corresponds to *static* bindings for the procedure. References to received bindings during the performance of A then always yield the same datum, regardless of the context of the performance. Letting the enaction-time bindings be received by A corresponds to *dynamic* bindings. Another possibility is that all the dependency of the procedure body is supposed to be indicated explicitly by its parameters. Then neither the abstraction-time bindings nor the enaction-time bindings should be received by A.

The *stable* information, i.e., storage, current at abstraction-time is irrelevant to performances of A. Access to the storage current at enaction-time is generally required.

We cater for this variety of information supply as follows. The performance of the incorporated action is given no transients and receives no bindings at all, so whatever is required must be already *incorporated* in the abstraction before it is enacted. On the other hand, the performance has access to the current storage, as usual.

To ensure that when the abstraction that incorporates an action A is enacted, A is given some particular transient data d, we may replace A by give d then A. Similarly, to ensure that some particular binding map b is received by A we may replace A by produce b hence A. Now produce b hence (give d then A) is equivalent to give d then (produce b hence A), so the supplies of transients and bindings are independent of each other, and can be made in either order. Moreover, give d' then give d then A is equivalent to give d then A, since d is data, not a yielder, so once transient data has been supplied, further supplies are ignored; similarly for bindings.

This simple form of supply of data and bindings is usually adequate in practice, and we introduce notation for abstraction yielders that supports it, allowing one to forget about the details of the replacement of incorporated actions. For generality, reflective action notation also allows *gradual* supply of both transients and bindings, but we shall not dwell here on how this is achieved.

The abstraction formed by incorporating the current bindings in an abstraction is a *closure*.[1] When we form a closure at abstraction-time, we ensure static bindings. On the other hand, when we defer closure formation until enaction-time, bindings are dynamic. The enaction of an abstraction without forming any closure from it prevents the incorporated action from referring to any received bindings when performed. Notice that static and dynamic bindings can coexist, except that once a particular abstraction has been supplied with static bindings, we cannot subsequently change the bindings to dynamic ones, of course.

If we bind a token to an abstraction *a* that incorporates an action *A* and then, in the scope of that binding, enact the closure of the abstraction—thus providing dynamic bindings—*A* may refer to *a*, via the token. But this is not possible with static bindings, since the token should be bound to a closure that already incorporates the binding that is about to be produced! Instead, it is necessary to produce an *indirect* binding for the token, and then *redirect* the binding to a closure, which thus incorporates itself, but only indirectly. Indirect bindings are hybrid information. They resemble bindings to cells, but the indirection is not apparent when referring to bound values. Recall the discussion in Chapter 7.

Abstractions are the quintessence of delayed, or *lazy*, evaluation: yielders in the incorporated action are *never* evaluated before the abstraction is enacted. We can represent an infinite list lazily by an abstraction which, when enacted, gives the head of the list and an *abstraction* that lazily represents the tail of the list. Even more lazily, we might want to avoid recomputation of the head of the list on subsequent reference to it. This is called *memoization* in the functional programming community; it can be represented using imperative actions. Roughly, the idea is to put abstractions in cells, then replace the abstractions by the values that they give when they get enacted for the first—and last—time.

The reflective action notation explained below extends the basic, functional, and declarative action notation.

9.1   Actions

- enact _ :: yielder → action .

The action **enact** Y performs the action incorporated in the abstraction yielded by Y. The performance of the incorporated action is not given any transient data, nor does it receive any bindings. However, transients and/or bindings may have already been supplied to the incorporated action, using the notation for yielders explained next.

---

[1]The name 'closure' comes from the notion of a closed term in logic. Closures are also referred to as 'funargs' in the LISP community.

9.2   Yielders

- application _ to _ :: yielder, yielder → yielder .
- closure _   :: yielder → yielder .

Suppose that Y_1 yields abstraction of A, and that Y_2 yields data d. Then the yielder application Y_1 to Y_2 evaluates to abstraction of (give d then A). Similarly, when current bindings evaluates to b, closure Y_1 yields abstraction of (produce b hence A). When both are used together, the order is immaterial.

The uniform use of the closure of abstraction of A instead of just abstraction of A (which is explained below) ensures so-called static bindings for abstractions. Then enact the given abstraction performs A, letting it receive the bindings that were current when the closure of abstraction of A was evaluated. The pattern enact the application of the given abstraction#1 to the rest of the given data is useful for supplying parametric data to the abstraction, whereas enact the closure of the given abstraction provides dynamic bindings—unless static bindings were already supplied, that is.

The action notation for producing and redirecting indirect bindings, mentioned briefly in Chapter 7, allows the specification of self-referential closures with static bindings. In particular, recursively bind T to the closure of abstraction of A allows A to refer statically to the closure that incorporates it.

9.3   Data

- abstraction   ≤ datum .
- abstraction of _ :: action → abstraction (*total*) .
- *action-operation* :: abstraction, ... → abstraction (*total*) .
- provision _   :: data → abstraction (*total*) .
- production _   :: bindings → abstraction (*total*) .

The sort abstraction is a subsort of datum. When A is an action, abstraction of A is the abstraction that incorporates just A. Yielders in A only get evaluated if and when A gets performed, not before.

Any *action-operation*, i.e., combinator, can be used to form compound abstractions. As might be expected, abstraction distributes over combinators, for instance

$$\text{(abstraction of } A_1) \text{ and then (abstraction of } A_2) =$$
$$\text{abstraction of } (A_1 \text{ and then } A_2) .$$

The operations provision _ and production _ are useful when applied to yielders. When *d* is data, the datum provision *d* is simply abstraction of give *d*, and similarly for production *b* where *b* is a binding map. Note that provision of it does *not* evaluate to the abstraction abstraction of give it, where the evaluation of it is delayed to enaction time!

Summary

- *Reflective action notation is for specifying abstractions and their enaction.*

- *Abstractions are reified actions. They can be supplied with transients and bindings, but not with storage. Further supply of the same kind of information is ignored.*

- *Supplying bindings forms a closure. Bindings are static when closures are always formed at abstraction-time, and dynamic when closures are formed at enaction-time. Abstractions with static and dynamic bindings can be mixed.*

- *Abstractions can be combined using action combinators.*

- *Abstractions are only useful when they are ultimately enacted.*

Navigation

- *Now look at Chapter 16, which gives an illustrative example of the use of reflective action notation, before proceeding with Part II.*

- *If you would like a more detailed informal explanation of reflective actions, see Section D.5.*

- *You could also make an excursion to Section B.5, which gives an algebraic specification of reflective action notation.*

- *You may leave a detailed study of action notation for indirect bindings until later, as it is not much used. The details can be found in Section B.7, an informal explanation in Section D.7, and its use is illustrated in the semantics of packages and subprograms in Appendix A.*

Exercises

1. Compare the action specified below with that in Exercise 1 in Chapter 6.

   > recursively bind "fact" to the closure of abstraction of
   > | | check (the given integer is less than 1) and then give 1
   > | or
   > | | check (the given integer is greater than 0) and then
   > | | | give it and
   > | | | enact the application of the abstraction bound to "fact"
   > | | | to the predecessor of it
   > | | then give product (the given integer#1, the given integer#2)
   > hence enact the application of the abstraction bound to "fact"
   > to the given integer .

   Assuming that **recursively bind** T **to** Y has the expected effect (or by considering indirect bindings, if you prefer) simulate the performance of the above action, given the integer 3.

2. Consider the action specified in the previous exercise. Change it so that the scopes of bindings are dynamic, rather than static, avoiding the use of 'recursively'. Simulate a performance of the new action.

3. Specify an action which gives an abstraction corresponding to the *lazy* infinite list of the natural numbers. When the abstraction is enacted, it should give a pair consisting of 0 and an abstraction which, when enacted, gives a pair consisting of 1 and so on. Define also an operation for accessing the nth item in an arbitrary lazy list represented in the same way.

4. Show how to use imperative action notation so that the recomputation of items in lazy lists in the preceding exercise is avoided. Hint: one is allowed to replace an abstraction stored in a cell by some other datum, for instance a number. Discuss whether or not the avoidance of recomputation can be relevant to semantics of programming languages.

5. (This one assumes that you are familiar with the λ-notation.) Consider the basic, functional and reflective parts of action notation. Compare the expressiveness of this notation with that of the λ-notation. For instance, 'Currying' takes a function of two arguments into a higher-order function which, when applied to the first argument, returns a function of the remaining argument; thus applying the Curried version of addition to 1 returns the successor function. Can an analogous operation on abstractions be expressed?

Chapter 10

Communicative

- *Action notation includes a communicative action notation for specifying information processing by distributed systems of agents.*

- *Communicative actions are concerned with permanent information.*

- *Chapter 17 illustrates the use of communicative action notation in the semantic description of tasks and entry calls.*

So far, we have dealt with sequential performance of actions by a single agent in isolation. Let us now consider concurrent performance by a *distributed system* of agents, where each agent can *communicate* with the other agents, sending and receiving *messages* and offering *contracts*. Even when only one agent is active, this generalizes action performance sufficiently to allow the representation of *interactive* input-output behaviour, where nonterminating information processing is especially significant.

An agent represents the identity of a single process, embedded in a universal communication *medium*, or 'ether'. Implementations of processes may run them on physically separate processors, linked by buses or networks, or on a single processor using time-sharing. Of course each processor itself may consist of a number of connected parts, such as CPU, memory modules, video cards, etc. Agents may correspond to the behaviours of such special-purpose subprocessors, as well as to processes specified directly in high-level programming languages.

Communication between agents is *asynchronous*: to send a message, an agent emits the message into the medium, with another agent specified as the receiver, and then carries on performing, not waiting until the message has been delivered to the other agent. For simplicity, we assume that message transmission is reliable, that is, messages never get lost, though the order in which they arrive need not correspond to

120

the order in which they were sent. Imagining some ideal universal time-scale, one could say that each message transmission takes arbitrary but finite time.

Each message transmission constitutes a piece of *permanent* information: there is no way to 'undo' a communication once it has been initiated, the most one can do is to send another message telling the recipient to ignore the first one—unless it is too late! Therefore communication commits action performance to the current alternative, just like changes to storage do.

Messages transmitted to an agent are put into an unbounded *buffer* as they arrive. The arrival of a message does *not* interrupt the action being performed, and it remains unnoticed until the action itself inspects the buffer. An agent that doesn't have anything better to do may *wait* patiently for the arrival of a particular sort of message, continually inspecting the buffer. Messages can be *removed* from the buffer, to indicate that they have been dealt with and to avoid confusion with new messages of the same sort.

Every message carries the identity of the agent that sent it, and of the agent that is to receive it. It also has a contents, which can be an arbitrary datum—even an abstraction (incorporating an action) or the identity of an agent. Each transmitted message has a serial-number, determined by the sending agent, which distinguishes it from all other transmitted messages.

Initially, only one distinguished agent, the *user* agent, has an action to perform, and all the other agents are inactive. An active agent may offer *contracts* to inactive agents, specifying actions to be performed. Let us call this *subcontracting* actions to agents. The number of active agents is always finite, but may be unbounded.

A performance of a system of agents consists of the performance of the user agent's action, together with the performances of those actions that get subcontracted to other agents—until the *user agent* terminates. Further processing by subcontracted agents is simply ignored.

The performances by different agents are not synchronized at all: they may proceed at arbitrary, and varying, rates. On an ideal universal time-scale, each performance step may take an arbitrary but finite time, just like message transmissions. Thus steps of different agents may overlap in time, representing so-called *true concurrency*—which is different from interleaving, at least conceptually. Moreover, a performance by one agent cannot hinder the performances of other agents, so the collective performance of the distributed actions proceeds *fairly*, in that the next step of an agent cannot be delayed forever.

It would be inappropriate to select an agent for a subcontract by nondeterministic choice from the sort of currently inactive agents, in the same way that cells of storage are allocated, since choices made simultaneously by different agents might conflict. In fact the notions of 'current' and 'simultaneous' aren't even well-defined when agents are physically distributed! The selection of an agent for a subcontract may require communication, for instance between agents competing for selection, or between agents and some administrative process. Let us merely assume the existence of an action that initiates the selection of an inactive agent, leaving it open just *how* selection is to be achieved. Agents are never reused, even when they complete the subcontracted action, to avoid possible confusion about messages intended for previously subcontracted performances. (Reusable agents would correspond more to *processors* than to *processes*.) Note that it is *not* possible to deactivate an agent: all one can do is to ignore any messages that it sends.

Each agent has its own buffer and storage. The cells allocated on an agent refer to its local storage, and are distinct from those allocated on other agents. Shared storage is not provided, but can be represented using auxiliary agents that respond to messages about allocating, changing, and inspecting their local cells. The action incorporated in a contract is always performed with no given transients, no received bindings, all its cells of storage unreserved, and an empty buffer.

The asynchronous primitives sketched above are quite implementable, and reasonably simple. They seem to be adequate for representing various higher-level communication notions, such as *broadcasting*, *distributed termination*, and *rendezvous*. For example, we may represent simple forms of rendezvous using an acknowledgment message; we can also represent more complex forms, involving arbitration between competing rendezvous, using auxiliary agents that correspond to *channels*. An agent may subcontract a number of actions that all start by reporting back the identity of their performing agents to the contracting agent, which may then send them the identities of the other agents, to permit direct communication between the subcontracted agents.

On the other hand, it is not so easy to express lower-level notions, such as *interruptive* behaviour, where one agent is supposed to be able to suspend the performance by another agent at any stage, perhaps allowing it to be resumed later. Neither is it easy to represent so-called *light-weight processes*, or *threads*, having common access to the same storage. Of course, we can interleave actions on a single agent, but there is no direct support in action notation for controlling such actions individually, for instance suspending or aborting them.

If one finds the standard communicative action notation introduced below insufficiently expressive, one may extend it with abbreviations which, when used together in a disciplined way, represent such concepts as interrupts in terms of asynchronous message *protocols*. A more costly alternative would be to *replace* this part of action notation with a different (or extended) set of primitive actions, redefining the operational semantics of the entire action notation—and verifying that the algebraic laws in Appendix B still hold! In this case, one should take care to preserve the main feature of action notation: the simplicity of its intended interpretation.

Incidentally, an asynchronous communication through a medium *could* be regarded as a succession of *synchronous* communications between the various parts of the medium. Then a cable connection, say, would consist of a multitude of adjacent bits of wire, each of which would receive a message (some electrons) at one side, then—a little later—pass it on at the other side. Of course, there is no problem with the idea of synchronous communication in such a context, because it occurs *at a point*, where the bits of wire touch. But when the aim is to represent communication between truly distributed agents, where message transmission between agents can take time, it seems that synchronous communication is best avoided.

Specification frameworks that involve synchronization generally ignore the time delays which result from message transmission. Such an abstraction from reality may lead to an elegant theory. But the behaviour of systems predicted by the theory may be difficult to achieve when distribution becomes large-scale, so that the time taken to synchronize becomes a major factor. In fact it seems to be impossible to implement general synchronization at all, in a truly distributed way, without introducing some arbitrary priorities between communications. See the work on *actor systems* [Agh86] for further motivation for asynchronous systems.

An action performance has access to the current buffer, as well as to the identity of the performing agent and the contracting agent. The communicative action notation explained below extends the basic and reflective action notation with a few primitive actions and one new combinator, as well as some yielders and ordinary data.

10.1 Actions

- send _   :: yielder → primitive-action .
- remove _   :: yielder → primitive-action .
- offer _   :: yielder → primitive-action .
- patiently _ :: action → action (*partial*) .

The primitive action send Y, where Y yields a *sort* of message, initiates the transmission of a message. The usual form of Y is a message [to Y_1] [containing Y_2], where Y_1 and Y_2 are individuals. The sort yielded by Y is implicitly restricted to messages from the performing agent, with the next local serial number, and this should determine an individual message.

In the action **remove** Y, the yielder Y should itself evaluate to an *individual* message. The message gets deleted from the buffer, provided that it is already there, otherwise the action fails.

The primitive action **offer** Y, where Y yields a sort of contract, initiates the arrangement of a contract with another, perhaps only partially specified, agent. The usual form of Y is **a contract [to an agent] [containing abstraction of** A**]**, where A is the action to be performed according to the contract.

The compound action **patiently** A represents *busy waiting* while A fails. Each performance of A is indivisible, so that further messages cannot arrive in the buffer in the middle of A's performance. A is given the same transients and receives the same bindings as the compound action. Usually, A performs primitive communicative actions, as illustrated in the definition of **receive** Y below; it may also make changes to storage, for instance a time-out can be represented by decrementing the contents of a cell until zero is reached.

The communicative actions above are used to define some standard hybrid actions. The action **receive** Y is an abbreviation for

> patiently
> | choose a Y [in set of items of the current buffer] then
> | remove the given message and give it

thus waiting indefinitely for a message of the sort specified by Y to arrive. The action **subordinate** Y abbreviates

> offer a contract [to Y] [containing abstraction of subordinate-action]
> and then
> | receive a message [from Y] [containing an agent] then
> | give the contents of the given message .

where **subordinate-action** abbreviates

> send a message [to the contracting-agent]
>   [containing the performing-agent] then
> receive a message [from the contracting-agent]
>   [containing an abstraction] then
> enact the contents of the given message .

By using **subordinate an agent** several times, an agent get several agents ready before sending them the abstractions that they are intended to enact. This allows the identities of all the agents to be supplied to the abstractions when sending them, so that the subordinated agents may communicate with each other directly.

10.2 Yielders

- current buffer : yielder .
- performing-agent , contracting-agent : yielder .

The yielder current buffer evaluates to the list of messages that have arrived in the buffer, but which have not yet been removed. The messages are listed in the order of their arrival.

The yielder performing-agent yields the identity of the agent that is performing the action in which it is evaluated, whereas contracting-agent yields that of the agent that offered the contract for the action.

10.3 Data

- agent $\leq$ distinct-datum .

- user-agent   : agent .

- buffer   = flat-list [of message] .

- communication $\leq$ distinct-datum .

- communication = message | contract .

- sendable $\leq$ data .

- sendable   = abstraction | agent | □ .

- contents _   :: message $\rightarrow$ sendable (*total*) ,
                       contract $\rightarrow$ abstraction (*total*) .

- sender _   :: communication $\rightarrow$ agent (*total*) .

- receiver _   :: message $\rightarrow$ agent (*total*) ,
                       contract $\rightarrow$ agent (*strict*, *linear*) .

- serial _   :: communication $\rightarrow$ natural (*total*) .

- _ [containing _] :: message, sendable $\rightarrow$ message (*partial*) ,
                       contract, abstraction $\rightarrow$ contract (*partial*) .

- _ [from _]   :: communication, agent $\rightarrow$ communication (*partial*) .

- _ [to _]   :: message, agent $\rightarrow$ message (*partial*) ,
                       contract, agent $\rightarrow$ contract (*strict*) .

- _ [at _]   :: communication, natural $\rightarrow$ communication (*partial*) .

The sort **agent** is unspecified, as the number and distribution of processors is usually implementation-dependent. It may be partitioned *ad hoc* into subsorts of agents intended for performing particular actions. The user-agent is the distinguished agent that initially is the only one with a contract.

The representation of **buffer** as a sort of list allows the use of standard data notation for inspecting the buffer. The sort **message** is determined by **sendable**, which is loosely-specified to include **abstraction** and **agent**, for use in subordinate *Y*, and should be extended with any other data that is to be sent in messages. An individual of sort **contract** contains an abstraction, incorporating the action to be subcontracted, and it is addressed to the *sort* of agents to which the contract is offered.

The remaining notation for communicative data is rather straightforward. The operations **contents** *d*, **sender** *d*, **receiver** *d*, and **serial** *d* select the indicated component of a message *d*, whereas d_1[containing d_2] , d_1[from d_2], d_1[to d_2], and d_1[at d_2] restrict the sort of message or contract d_1 to those individuals that have the corresponding component of sort d_2.

10.4   /Action Notation/Facets (*continued*)

10.4.1   Outcomes (*continued*)

- outcome   = □ | communicating .

- communicating ≥ committing .

The outcome **communicating** implies the outcome **committing**. It allows sending messages, offering contracts, and removing messages from the buffer, i.e., performing the primitive communicative actions explained earlier in this chapter. Specifying **communicating** says nothing at all about termination possibilities. It is convenient to let **communicating** include the possibility *not* communicating at all!

10.4.2   Incomes (*continued*)

- income = □ | current buffer | □ .

The income **current buffer** (which may also be used as a yielder) allows reference to the message buffer.

Summary

- *Communicative action notation is for specifying permanent information processing, i.e., sending and removal of messages, offers of contracts.*

- *Primitive communicative actions are always committing, causing alternative actions to be discarded.*

- *The combinator* patiently _ *iterates an action while it fails, and is useful for specifying busy waiting.*

- *Communicative yielders refer to the current buffer of messages, and to the identities of the performing and contracting agents.*

Navigation

- *Now look at Chapter 17, which gives an illustrative example of the use of communicative action notation, before proceeding to Part IV.*

- *If you would like a more detailed informal explanation of imperative actions, see Section D.6.*

- *You could also make an excursion to Section B.6, which gives an algebraic specification of imperative action notation.*

Exercises

1. Let us introduce the following abbreviation:

   write n:natural = send a message [to the user-agent] [containing n] .

   Using write 0 and write 1, give actions whose performances have precisely the following possibilities:

   (a) infinitely-many write 0s;

   (b) infinitely-many write 1s, or any finite number of write 1s followed by infinitely-many write 0s.

   Try also to find an action that avoids the possibility of infinitely-many write 1's in (b) above.

2. Specify an action that treats messages containing small natural numbers as urgent: if there are several pending messages containing numbers, it is to give the one with a minimal contents, otherwise it is to give the next message containing a number to arrive. Hint: contemplate the definition of **receive** Y, and count upwards.

3. There is no way for one agent to deactivate another agent. Discuss whether or not this is a weakness of the communicative action notation. Is such a facility necessary? Can it be simulated by a particular communication protocol?

4. Specify an action that represents a *server* for shared storage, responding to messages whose contents indicate whether to allocate, change, or inspect a shared cell.

5. (Harder!) Specify a distributed system of agents to compute the factorial function, with each agent only allowed to calculate one product. The user agent should subcontract the computation of factorial, then wait for the result.

Part III
Semantic Descriptions

Part III gives a progressive series of examples of action semantic descriptions. The programming constructs described all come from ADA. (No previous familiarity with ADA is required, as the necessary concepts are all explained here.) The examples not only describe a substantial sublanguage of ADA, they also serve as paradigms for description of other programming languages. The description of constructs in the earlier examples remains *unchanged* in the later examples. This is in marked contrast to denotational semantics, where tedious reformulations of the earlier descriptions would be required when giving the later ones! Appendix A collects the examples together, for convenience of reference—and to show how a medium-scale action semantic description looks in its entirety. It also specifies the detailed specifications of semantic entities that are omitted in Part III.

Navigation

- *If this is your first reading, proceed* in parallel *through Parts II and III: Chapter 4, Chapter 11, Chapter 5, Chapter 12, and so on. This way, you see an illustration of the use of each part of action notation immediately after its introduction.*

- *If you are already familiar with high-level programming languages, you could alternatively look at each chapter of Part III before the corresponding chapter of Part II. This way, the illustrations in Part III motivate the action notation introduced in Part II.*

- *If you are revising, and would like an uninterrupted presentation of examples of action semantic descriptions, proceed straight through Part III.*

- *When you have finished Part III, take a good look at Appendix A, which not only fills in all the details omitted in Part III but also illustrates some further techniques.*

Chapter 11

Statements

- *Basic statements include sequencing, choices, loops, and exits.*

- *The semantic description of statements illustrates the use of the basic action notation introduced in Chapter 4.*

- *No special semantic entities are required.*

Statements, sometimes called *commands*, are basic constructs of many programming languages. Together with other constructs, they mainly serve to specify the order in which parts of a program are *intended* to be performed. We call the performance of a statement its *execution*.

Implementations usually follow the intended order of performance, although any order providing the same observable behaviour is allowed. Moreover, when the intended order is only partially specified, implementations are free to choose any order consistent with the specified order. Of course, when different orders of performance can lead to different observable behaviours, an implementation only provides one of the possible behaviours in each execution.

The so-called *imperative* programming languages contain a wide variety of statements. This is in contrast to *functional* programming languages, where the primary concern is with data rather than with order of performance. Most statements, however, have other kinds of phrases as components, such as expressions and declarations. The few statements that do not involve other kinds of construct don't provide much of a programming language: they allow for sequences, nondeterministic choices, and loops, but not much else. Nevertheless, the semantic description of these simple statements does provide some illustration of the use of the basic action notation introduced in Chapter 4.

The description of statements below begins the action semantic description of a substantial illustrative language called AD, which is a sublanguage of ADA. Actually, the name 'A' would have better reflected the relative sizes of our language and ADA! Subsequent chapters of Part III gradually extend the description. Appendix A gives the full description of AD, which collects together all the illustrations given throughout Part III, as well as covering some details that they omit.

The form of the action semantic description of AD is in accordance with Chapter 2. Its modular structure is as follows:

/AD

> **Abstract Syntax**
> > **Statements**
> **Semantic Functions**
> > **needs:**   **Abstract Syntax, Semantic Entities.**
> > **Statements**
> **Semantic Entities**

Subsequent chapters introduce further submodules of **Abstract Syntax** and **Semantic Functions**, and some submodules of **Semantic Entities**. This subdivision facilitates navigation, as well as comparison with Appendix A, which uses the same submodules.

The grammar below specifies our first fragment of AD abstract syntax. The symbols, both terminal and nonterminal, used in the grammar are very close to those used for concrete syntax in the ADA Reference Manual.

11.1   /AD/Abstract Syntax

11.1.1   Statements

grammar:

- Statement = ⟦ "null" ";" ⟧ |
  ⟦ "select" Alternatives "end" "select" ";" ⟧ |
  ⟦ "loop" Statement⁺ "end" "loop" ";" ⟧ |
  ⟦ "exit" ";" ⟧ |
  ⟦ "begin" Statement⁺ "end" ";" ⟧ | □ .
- Alternative = Statement⁺ | □ .
- Alternatives = ⟨ Alternative ⟨ "or" Alternative ⟩* ⟩ .

Both **Statement**$^+$ and **Alternatives** are sorts of tuple, including **Statement** and **Alternative**, which are sorts of tree. We could easily eliminate **Alternatives** from the grammar, but it turns out to be a convenient abbreviation in our semantic equations below.

A □ formally stands for the left hand side of the enclosing equation. Its use above thus weakens the equalities to inclusions, and allows us to extend the specified sorts with further individuals in subsequent chapters. There is no need to use it at all when a complete description is given in one go, as in Appendix A.

The concrete syntax of many programming languages treats ";" as a separator between statements, rather than as a statement terminator. We could reflect this in the abstract syntax, if desired, by removing the ";"s from the productions for **Statement**, and specifying **Statements** analogously to **Alternatives**, as illustrated in Section 2.1. When ";"s are optional in concrete syntax, we could omit them altogether from abstract syntax without making the intended relation between concrete and abstract syntax less obvious.

A compound statement ⟦ "begin" S "end" ";" ⟧ is semantically equivalent to S, so we could omit it from our abstract syntax, but it is preferable to leave it in and *confirm* its expected semantics in the semantic equations below. A loop statement is intended to execute its component statements until an exit statement is reached; however, the exit statement only terminates a single level of looping. (This informal description should give you a rough idea of the intended semantics, but it is not intended to be complete.)

If you are familiar with ADA, you may have noticed that AD allows *unguarded* alternatives in select statements, whereas the syntax of ADA is more restrictive in this respect. Moreover, the semantics of the select statement is non-iterative here. These variations are purely for simplicity of illustration in this chapter, and Chapter 17 provides a form of select statement that is much closer to that of ADA.

11.2 /AD/Semantic Functions

11.2.1 Statements

introduces: execute _ , select _ .

11.2.1.1 Executing Statements

- execute _ :: Statement$^+$ → action
  [completing | escaping | diverging | committing] .

(1)   execute ⟨ S_1:Statement S_2:Statement$^+$ ⟩ = execute S_1 and then execute S_2 .

The following semantic equations cover the subsort **Statement** of **Statement**⁺.

(2)   execute ⟦ "null" ";" ⟧ = complete .

(3)   execute ⟦ "select" A:Alternatives "end" "select" ";" ⟧ = select A .

(4)   execute ⟦ "loop" S:Statement⁺ "end" "loop" ";" ⟧ =
    | unfolding
    | | execute S and then unfold
    trap complete .

Without the 'trap complete' above, an exit statement would terminate all enclosing statements.

(5)   execute ⟦ "exit" ";" ⟧ = escape .

(6)   execute ⟦ "begin" S:Statement⁺ "end" ";" ⟧ = execute S .

11.2.1.2   Selecting Alternatives

 • select _ :: Alternatives → [completing | escaping | diverging | committing] action .

(1)   select S:Statement⁺ = commit and then execute S .

The commitment above is actually redundant, since execution of the statements considered in this chapter cannot fail; but its presence emphasizes that an implementation is *not* obliged to try other alternatives if a failure occurs in the selected one.

The form of the above semantic equation is not entirely orthodox: one component of the semantics of a statement sequence is equated to an action that involves another component of the semantics of the *same* sequence. Used incautiously, such equations could introduce circularity, and thereby undermine the well-definedness of the semantic functions. For instance, had we defined **execute** S:Statement⁺ in terms of **select** S, neither **execute** _ nor **select** _ would now be well-defined on statement sequences.

Here it is easy to see that no circularity arises, and to replace the given equation with some orthodox ones without changing the specified semantics (Exercise 4).

(2)   select ⟨ A_1:Alternative "or" A_2:Alternatives ⟩ = select A_1 or select A_2 .

11.3   /AD/Semantic Entities

includes: Action Notation/Basic .

We do not have to extend or specialize basic action notation for this simple illustration.

Summary

- *We introduce corresponding submodules of* **Abstract Syntax** *and* **Semantic Functions** *to help navigation when we extend* AD *in subsequent chapters. Such submodules are not necessary in small-scale descriptions.*

- *Our abstract syntax for* AD *statements is strongly suggestive of* ADA *concrete syntax. We represent sequences using tuples of trees. The use of □ to leave sorts open for extension is not necessary in complete descriptions.*

- *The semantic equations define each semantic function on the entire syntactic sort for which it is used. The equations for basic statements remain largely unchanged when further statements and other constructs are allowed.*

- *The semantic entities representing statement execution are actions. Only basic actions are needed for the description of basic statements that do not involve other kinds of phrase.*

Navigation

- *Now look at Chapter 5, which introduces basic data, before proceeding with Part III.*

- *Don't forget to try the exercises below!*

Exercises

1. Let S be a sequence of AD statements. Is the statement with abstract syntax ⟦ "loop" S ⟦ "exit" ";" ⟧ "end" "loop" ";" ⟧ always semantically equivalent to S? If not, find an S that shows a difference regarding possible outcomes.

2. Argue that the AD statement ⟦ "loop" ⟦ "exit" ";" ⟧ S "end" ";" ⟧ is semantically equivalent to ⟦ "null" ";" ⟧.

3. Replace the exit statement of AD by ⟦ "repeat" ";" ⟧, which is supposed to repeat the execution of the enclosing loop statement. A loop statement without any repeat statement is now supposed to terminate after the first execution of the body, without iterating. Modify the semantic description accordingly.

4. Replace the unorthodox semantic equation for selecting statement sequences by some orthodox ones.

Chapter 12

Literals

- *Literals are lexical symbols including numerals, characters, and strings.*

- *The semantic description of literals is facilitated by standard operations on strings.*

- *The semantic entities required are specified* ad hoc, *exploiting the general data notation introduced in Chapter 5.*

Literals are the simplest constructs of programming languages, with regard to both syntax and semantics. Typical examples are *numeric literals*, i.e., numerals, and *string literals*.

The description of literals is not very challenging. But we have to take care to avoid overspecification that might place unintended and impractical burdens on implementations.

For instance, it might be imagined that we could adapt the description of binary numerals in Chapter 2 immediately to decimal integer numerals, such as those in ADA. However, in the absence of syntactic limits on the length of numerals, the corresponding semantic entities would be arbitrarily-large numbers. Practical programming languages generally put implementation-dependent bounds on the magnitude of numbers. In ADA, the constants MIN_INT and MAX_INT bound the *required* integers, although implementations are *allowed* to provide further integer 'types' with implementation-dependent bounds.

The semantics of an integer numeral is the expected mathematical value only when that lies within bounds. Otherwise it should be some entity that represents a numeric error. The situation with literals for so-called 'real' numbers is similar, although it is necessary to take account of implementation-dependent lower bounds on the *accuracy* of 'real' numbers, as well as bounds on their magnitude. In practice, implementations provide only a finite set of rational numbers as approximate real numbers. In ADA, for instance, implementations may provide various 'fixed' and 'floating' point types with specified minimum accuracy of arithmetic operations.

The main effort in describing the intended semantics of numerals lies in specifying the semantic entities, i.e., the sorts of data representing implemented numbers, and the appropriate arithmetic operations upon them.

The description of string literals poses similar problems. Syntax does not restrict their length, but practical implementations should be allowed to impose bounds, as in ADA, where the length of strings is bounded by the largest integer. Thus the semantics of a string isn't always just the corresponding list of characters.

The literals described below correspond to a simplified version of literals in ADA.

/AD

> **Abstract Syntax** (*continued*)
>> **Literals**   •
>
> **Semantic Functions** (*continued*)
>> **Literals**   •
>
> **Semantic Entities** (*continued*)
>> **Sorts**   •
>> **Values**   •
>> **Numbers**   •
>> **Characters**   •
>> **Arrays**   •

12.1   /AD/Abstract Syntax (*continued*)

12.1.1   Literals

grammar:
- Literal   = Numeric-Literal | Character-Literal | String-Literal .
- Numeric-Literal = [[digit$^+$]] | [[digit$^+$ '.' digit$^+$]] .
- Character-Literal = [[''' graphic-character ''']] .
- String-Literal   = [['"' graphic-character* '"']] .

Literals are regarded as lexical symbols in ADA. We make our abstract syntax for AD easy to relate to the concrete syntax of ADA by using characters instead of strings as terminal symbols in the grammar above.

12.2   /AD/Semantic Functions (*continued*)

12.2.1   Literals

introduces: the value of _ .

- the value of _ :: Literal → value .

12.2.1.1   Numerals

- the value of _ :: Numeric-Literal → number .

(1)   the value of $[\![\ d\text{:digit}^+\ ]\!]$ = integer-number of decimal $[\![\ d\ ]\!]$.

(2)   the value of $[\![\ d_1\text{:digit}^+\ \text{'.'}\ d_2\text{:digit}^+\ ]\!]$ =
        real-number of the sum of (decimal $[\![\ d_1\ ]\!]$,
            the product of (decimal $[\![\ d_2\ ]\!]$,
                the exponent of (decimal "10", the negation of the count of d_2))) .

The operation decimal _ is a standard operation on strings, see Section 5.1.9; similarly count _ is the standard operation that returns the number of components in any sort of tuple, see Section 5.1.3. We could define these operations as semantic functions, but it wouldn't be very exciting, so we take this short-cut. Formally, we are regarding a digit sequence as its own semantics, i.e., a string! No abstractness is lost, though, because leading zeros in digit sequences *are* significant in the fractional parts of real numbers.

The use of $[\![\ \ldots\ ]\!]$ in the right hand sides of the semantic equations above is atypical. It is needed because decimal _ expects its argument to be a string, not a tuple of characters.

12.2.1.2   Characters

- the value of _ :: Character-Literal → character .

(1)   the value of $[\![\ \text{''' } c\text{:graphic-character '''}\ ]\!]$ = c .

Here we assume that both the syntax and the semantics of AD employ the same character-set, namely ASCII. Otherwise, we would have to define the semantics of each individual character literal separately—a tedious task.

.2.2.1.3 Strings

- the value of _ :: String-Literal → string-array .

1)   the value of ⟦ '"' *s*:graphic-character* '"' ⟧ = array of *s* .

n ADA, strings are a special case of array values, and we let AD be the same. Oth-
:rwise, we could let the semantics of a string literal be the corresponding individual
>f the standard sort string, i.e., simply a list of characters.

12.3   /AD/Semantic Entities (*continued*)

Note that in general, we shall only sketch the main properties of our *ad hoc* notation
or semantic entities in the rest of Part III. The full specifications, including the
letails of inter-module dependencies, are given in Section A.3. However, mostly it
should be possible to get quite a good understanding of the semantics of AD from
?art III alone, without consulting Section A.3.

ncludes: **Action Notation/Basic/Data** .

12.3.1   Sorts

- datum = value | □ .

The sort **datum** in action notation is supposed to include all individual items of
lata used in a particular semantic description. We introduce the sort **value** *ad hoc*,
corresponding to the informal concept of a value in ADA. It is specified below, but
.eft open for extension in subsequent chapters.

12.3.2   Values

- value = number | character | string-array | □ .

12.3.3   Numbers

- number   = integer-number | real-number .
- integer-number of _ :: integer → integer-number (*partial*) .
- real-number of _   :: rational → real-number (*partial*) .

You might like to know that **integer-number** and **real-number** are specified to be (possibly disjoint) abstract *copies* of bounded subsorts of the standard **integer** and **rational**, respectively, and that the usual arithmetic operations on them are provided. An alternative, but less general, technique is to equate **integer-number** and **real-number** with subsorts of **integer** and **rational**, and provide nonstandard arithmetic operations on them. Note that then we would not be able to specify **integer-number** and **real-number** to be disjoint.

12.3.4   Characters

includes: Data Notation/Characters/ASCII .

12.3.5   Arrays

- array of _ :: character* → string-array (*partial*) .

Had we specified **array of _** to be a *total* operation, implementations would be obliged to support arrays of unbounded size. In fact Appendix A specifies that all arrays whose length doesn't exceed the maximum integer number should exist, following ADA.

Summary

- *We use characters as terminal symbols when specifying the grammar of lexical symbols such as literals, so that lexical symbols are represented as strings, rather than more general tree structures.*

- *To avoid tedious semantic equations, we use standard operations on strings and tuples to specify the semantics of numeric literals.*

- *The semantic entities representing values of numeric and string literals are closely related to, but disjoint from, standard numbers and strings. We defer the details of their specification to Appendix A.*

Navigation

- *If you are curious about the full specification of the semantic entities used here, see the modules* **Numbers** *and* **Arrays** *in Appendix A. However, most of the operations specified in there are not yet needed.*

- *Now look at Chapter 6, which introduces functional actions, before proceeding with Part III.*

Exercises

1. The full specification of numbers in Appendix A allows trivial implementations where *all* literals are regarded as errors! Consider what minimum requirements could be put on the implementation-dependent bounds on numbers, so that programmers would be sure of 'enough' numbers (and strings) yet implementors would not have difficulty in providing *exactly* the specified sort of numbers. (This corresponds to specifying what are called *model* numbers in the ADA Reference Manual.)

2. Extend the description of AD literals to include ADA's remaining literals.

3. Investigate whether your favourite programming language demands any properties of real arithmetic. If so, try to capture them in a formal algebraic specification, extending the module **Data Notation/Numbers/Approximations**.

4. The ISO Standard for PASCAL avoids commitment to ASCII. The characters allowed in strings are implementation-defined. The values of these (and perhaps other) characters belong to the type denoted char. The indices of the character values in char start from 0; the indices of those corresponding to digits are supposed to be numerically-ordered and contiguous, whereas those corresponding to English letters are only supposed to be alphabetically-ordered, and need not be contiguous.

   Give a formal specification of sorts and operations corresponding to the PASCAL type char. Discuss the possible effects of the looseness of this specification on the portability of PASCAL programs.

Chapter 13

Expressions

- *Expressions include arithmetic and Boolean operations. Statements involving expressions include conditionals, while-loops, and guarded alternatives.*

- *The semantic description of expressions and statements illustrates the use of the functional action notation introduced in Chapter 6.*

- *Semantic entities are the same as for literals, although further operations on them are needed now.*

Expressions in programming languages resemble mathematical terms. Syntactically, both expressions and terms are generally formed from literal *constants*, such as numerals, and *variables*, using mathematical *operators*, such as +. Semantically, both expressions and terms are *evaluated* to particular values.

There are, however, some distinctive differences between expressions and terms. *Function calls* in expressions may lead to divergence, whereas the application of a mathematical function in a term to arguments outside its domain of definition is merely *undefined*. Expression evaluation may even involve execution of statements. The notion of a program variable in an expression is quite different from that of a mathematical variable in a term, as explained in detail in Chapter 15. The order of evaluation of subexpressions in an expression may affect the value given—although in most programming languages, the order of evaluation is deliberately left implementation-dependent, which prevents program(mer)s from relying on any particular order. Whether or not a particular subexpression gets evaluated may also affect the outcome of the evaluation, and some expression constructs conditionally avoid the evaluation of particular subexpressions.

Thus the semantics of an expression is inherently more computational than that of a mathematical term, and it is appropriate to represent it by an action. The action, if and when its performance completes, gives the value of the expression as an item of transient information. We use the functional actions introduced in Chapter 6, together with the basic actions introduced in Chapter 4, to specify the intended order, or lack of order, of subexpression evaluation, as well as how the given values are processed.

The following specification is an extension of the semantic descriptions given in the preceding chapters, augmenting AD with some basic expressions, and with basic statements that involve expressions. The overview of its modular structure below omits the **Literals** submodules, which remain unchanged. Thus one sees just the titles of the modules whose bodies are specified in the present chapter, and the overview can be used as a table of contents. It uses (*continued*) to distinguish between new modules and modules that are extensions of previous specifications.

/AD

Abstract Syntax (*continued*)

> **Expressions**
> > **needs: Literals.**
> **Statements** (*continued*)
> > **needs: Expressions.**

Semantic Functions (*continued*)

> **Expressions**
> > **needs: Literals.**
> **Statements** (*continued*)
> > **needs: Expressions.**

Semantic Entities (*continued*)

> **Sorts** (*continued*)
> **Values** (*continued*)
> **Numbers** (*continued*)
> **Arrays** (*continued*)

13.1   /AD/Abstract Syntax (*continued*)

13.1.1   Expressions

grammar:

- Expression   = Literal | ⟦ "(" Expression ")" ⟧ |
                     ⟦ Unary-Operator Expression ⟧ |
                     ⟦ Expression Binary-Operator Expression ⟧ |
                     ⟦ Expression Control-Operator Expression ⟧ | □ .
- Unary-Operator = "+" | "−" | "abs" | "not" .
- Binary-Operator = "+" | "−" | "&" | "*" | "/" |
                     "mod" | "rem" | "=" | "/=" |
                     "<" | "<=" | ">" | ">=" |
                     "and" | "or" | "xor" .
- Control-Operator = ⟨ "and" "then" ⟩ | ⟨ "or" "else" ⟩ .

The distinction between control operators and binary operators is semantically relevant, since the intended order of evaluation of their operands is different.

We make no attempt to distinguish syntactically between expressions according
to the sort of entity to which they evaluate: truth-values, numbers, arrays. Such
distinctions between expressions would not simplify the semantic description at all,
and they would in any case have to be abandoned in the next chapter, where identifiers
with context-dependent types are included in expressions.

13.1.2   Statements (*continued*)

grammar:

- Statement = □ | ⟦ "if" Expression "then" Statement⁺
                        ⟨ "else" Statement⁺ ⟩? "end" "if" ";" ⟧ |
                ⟦ "while" Expression "loop" Statement⁺ "end" "loop" ";" ⟧ .
- Alternative = □ | ⟦ "when" Expression "=>" Statement⁺ ⟧ .

The use of the same module names as before lets us extend our previous specifications. Notice that the old statement constructs can now have the new statements
as components. Of course this is only possible because the syntax of *both* old and
new statements is specified using □ to indicate the possibility of further constructs.
It doesn't make any formal difference where the □ occurs in relation to the other
constructs; let us agree to put it at the end in the first equation that we ever specify
for a sort of phrase, and at the beginning in subsequent ones.

13.2 /AD/Semantic Functions (*continued*)

13.2.1 Expressions

introduces: evaluate _ ,
the unary-operation-result of _ ,
the binary-operation-result of _ .

13.2.1.1 Evaluating Expressions

- evaluate _ :: Expression → action [giving a value] [using nothing] .

The above functionality assertion is not formally necessary: it is merely a consequence of the semantic equations below, as could be verified using the algebraic specification of sort restrictions in Section B.9.[1] We could also be less precise about the sort of action that is used to represent the semantics of expression evaluation, omitting one or both of the sort restrictions concerning outcomes and incomes. However, in practice it seems quite helpful—both for the reader and the writer of a semantic description—to be as precise as possible when specifying the functionalities of semantic functions.

The penalty for being so precise is that we will have to *change* the specification of the functionality of evaluate _ later, when we include expressions whose evaluation can diverge in AD. This penalty is, however, hardly so severe as to discourage precise specification of functionalities during the gradual development of a larger action semantic description.

(1)   evaluate L:Literal = give the value of L .

(2)   evaluate 〚 "(" E:Expression ")" 〛 = evaluate E .

(3)   evaluate 〚 O:Unary-Operator E:Expression 〛 =
     evaluate E then give the unary-operation-result of O .

(4)   evaluate 〚 E_1:Expression O:Binary-Operator E_2:Expression 〛 =
     | evaluate E_1 and evaluate E_2
     then give the binary-operation-result of O .

The use of the combinator _ and _ above indicates that the order of expression evaluation is implementation-dependent. When expression evaluation can only complete, giving a value, all orders are equivalent, so here we can read _ and _ as indicating that the order of evaluation is *irrelevant*. When a language insists on left-to-right order of evaluation, this can be specified by using the combinator _ and then _ instead of _ and _ above.

---

[1]Not all such verifications have yet been carried out.

The evaluation of an expression may give any individual of sort **value**. We leave it to the semantics of operators, specified below, to insist on individuals of particular sorts—numbers, for instance. For simplicity, we do not bother with precise error messages in case the given operands are *not* of the right sort for a particular operator: we merely let the application of the corresponding operation yield **nothing**, so that the action which gives it must fail. In any case, errors arising due to wrong sorts of operands are statically detectable in most languages, and should therefore be the concern of a static semantic description, not of the dynamic semantics that we are developing here.

(5)   evaluate ⟦ E_1:Expression "or" "else" E_2:Expression ⟧ =
    evaluate E_1 then
      | | check the given truth-value then give true
      | or
      | | check not the given truth-value then evaluate E_2 .

(6)   evaluate ⟦ E_1:Expression "and" "then" E_2:Expression ⟧ =
    evaluate E_1 then
      | | check the given truth-value then evaluate E_2
      | or
      | | check not the given truth-value then give false .

Whether E_2 gets evaluated at all depends on the value given by evaluating E_1. Notice the difference between the way we specify the semantics of expressions that involve binary operators, and of those that involve the control operators ⟨ "and" "then" ⟩, ⟨ "or" "else" ⟩. Treating the two kinds of operators the same way leads to a less perspicuous semantic description, it seems.

13.2.1.2   Operating Unary Operators

- the unary-operation-result of _ :: Unary-Operator →
    yielder [of value] [using given value] .

Assuming that applications of operators to operands should never diverge or escape, we may represent the semantics of an operator as a yielder. Otherwise, we could use actions here too. But note that we cannot let the semantics of an operator be simply an algebraic operation, since our meta-notation is first-order, and does not treat operations as entities themselves.

(1)   the unary-operation-result of "+" = the given number .
(2)   the unary-operation-result of "−" = the negation of the given number .
(3)   the unary-operation-result of "abs" = the absolute of the given number .
(4)   the unary-operation-result of "not" = not the given truth-value .

13.2.1.3 Operating Binary Operators

- the binary-operation-result of _ :: Binary-Operator →
  yielder [of value] [using given (value,value)] .

We could also write **a given value#1 | a given value#2** instead of given (value,value) above. The following equations are a bit tedious:

(1) the binary-operation-result of "+" =
   the sum of (the given number#1, the given number#2) .

(2) the binary-operation-result of "−" =
   the difference of (the given number#1, the given number#2) .

(3) the binary-operation-result of " & " =
   the concatenation of (the given string-array#1, the given string-array#2) .

(4) the binary-operation-result of "*" =
   the product of (the given number#1, the given number#2) .

(5) the binary-operation-result of "/" =
   the quotient of (the given number#1, the given number#2) .

(6) the binary-operation-result of "mod" =
   the modulo of (the given number#1, the given number#2) .

(7) the binary-operation-result of "rem" =
   the remainder of (the given number#1, the given number#2) .

(8) the binary-operation-result of "=" =
   the given value#1 is the given value#2 .

(9) the binary-operation-result of "/=" =
   not (the given value#1 is the given value#2) .

(10) the binary-operation-result of "<" =
   the given number#1 is less than the given number#2 .

(11) the binary-operation-result of "<=" =
   not (the given number#1 is greater than the given number#2) .

(12) the binary-operation-result of ">" =
   the given number#1 is greater than the given number#2 .

(13) the binary-operation-result of ">=" =
   not (the given number#1 is less than the given number#2) .

(14) the binary-operation-result of "and" =
   both of (the given truth-value#1, the given truth-value#2) .

(15) the binary-operation-result of "or" =
   either of (the given truth-value#1, the given truth-value#2) .

(16) the binary-operation-result of "xor" =
   not (the given truth-value#1 is the given truth-value#2) .

13.2.2 Statements (*continued*)

13.2.2.1 Executing Statements (*continued*)

- execute _ :: Statement$^+$ → action
  [completing | escaping | diverging | committing] .

(1)   execute ⟦ "if" E:Expression "then" S:Statement$^+$ "end" "if" ";" ⟧ =
       evaluate E then
         | | check the given truth-value and then execute S
         | or check not the given truth-value .

Since **check** D doesn't give any data, and **execute** S doesn't refer to given data, it doesn't make any difference whether we use _ **and then** _ or _ **then** _ to combine them above. But we shouldn't use _ **and** _ ! Do you see why not? Hint: it concerns divergence.

It is important not to omit 'or check not the given truth-value' above, for then the execution of an if-then statement with a false condition would fail, rather than simply completing.

(2)   execute ⟦ "if" E:Expression "then" S_1:Statement$^+$
                    "else" S_2:Statement$^+$ "end" "if" ";" ⟧ =
       evaluate E then
         | | check the given truth-value and then execute S_1
         | or
         | | check not the given truth-value and then execute S_2 .

(3)   execute ⟦ "while" E "loop" S:Statement$^+$ "end" "loop" ";" ⟧ =
       unfolding
         | | evaluate E then
         | | | check the given truth-value and then execute S and then unfold
         | | or check not the given truth-value
       trap complete .

Compare the above semantic equation with that for loop statements in Chapter 11.

13.2.2.2 Selecting Alternatives (*continued*)

- select _ :: Alternatives → [completing | escaping | diverging | committing] action .

(1)   select ⟦ "when" E:Expression "=>" S:Statement$^+$ ⟧ =
       evaluate E then
         | check the given truth-value and then commit and then execute S .

Here, the intention is that the selection of the alternative should indeed fail when the condition evaluates to false. We could suggest this by specifying **failing** as a possible outcome of the sort of actions in the functionality of **select** _ , although formally it makes no difference, because failure is always regarded as a possible outcome.

13.3   /AD/Semantic Entities (*continued*)

includes: **Action Notation/Basic/Yielders** .

includes: **Action Notation/Functional** .

13.3.1   **Values** (*continued*)

- value = number | character | string-array | truth-value | □ .

As it is important to bear in mind precisely which items of data are classified as values, we reiterate our previous specification of **value** above, as well as adding **truth-value** to it.

13.3.2   **Numbers** (*continued*)

- number   = integer-number | real-number .

- min-integer , max-integer : integer .

- integer-number of _   :: integer → integer-number (*partial*) .

- real-number of _   :: rational → real-number (*partial*) .

- negation _ , absolute _   :: number → number (*partial*) .

- sum _ , difference _ , product _ , quotient _ ::
                    number^2 → number (*partial*) .

- modulo _ , remainder _   :: integer-number^2 → integer-number (*partial*) .

- _ is _ , _ is less than _ , _ is greater than _ ::
                    integer-number, integer-number → truth-value (*total*) ,
                    real-number, real-number → truth-value (*total*) .

As usual, the detailed specification of semantic entities is deferred to Appendix A.

13.3.3   Arrays (*continued*)

- empty-array   = array of ( ) .
- concatenation _   :: string-array^2 → string-array
                        (*partial, associative, unit is* empty-array) .
- _ is _   :: string-array, string-array → truth-value (*total*) .

Summary

- *The semantic entities representing expression evaluation are actions.*

- *We need only basic and functional actions for the description of statements and expressions that do not involve other kinds of phrases.*

- *We let the semantics of an operator be a yielder.*

Navigation

- *If you are curious about the full specification of the semantic entities used here, see the corresponding modules in Appendix A.*

- *Now look at Chapter 7, which introduces declarative actions, before proceeding with Part III.*

Exercises

1. Specify an alternative abstract syntax for expressions, distinguishing truth-valued and numeric expressions. Specify appropriate semantic functions, and compare them with those above.

2. Try to give semantic equations for the expressions ⟦ E_1 "and" "then" E_2 ⟧ and ⟦ E_1 "or" "else" E_2 ⟧ using a semantic function for Control-Operator.

3. (a) Consider what changes would be needed in our semantic equations for expressions and operators if we wanted to use actions, rather than yielders, to represent the semantics of operators.

   (b) Suppose that we want an erroneous expression evaluation, such as division by zero, to give rise to an *escape*, rather than a failure. Investigate how this could be achieved without changing the semantics of operators to actions. Hint: see Exercise 2 in Chapter 5.

4. Assuming that sum $_-$ is commutative, argue that the expressions $[\![\ E_1\ \text{"+"}\ E_2\ ]\!]$ and $[\![\ E_2\ \text{"+"}\ E_1\ ]\!]$ are always equivalent, for any E_1, E_2: Expression.

5. Look at the details of the module **Numbers** in Appendix A. Try to relate them to the informal description of approximate arithmetic operations in the Ada Reference Manual. Hint: for simplicity, we are ignoring the notion of 'safe' numbers here.

6. Give an action semantic description of some 'pocket calculator' operation language, using basic and functional actions. Ignore any 'memory' operations.

7. Consider the abstract syntax specified below. The intended semantics of a program is that the individual instructions manipulate a *stack* of numbers. Some instructions put values on the top of the stack, whereas others apply particular operations to the top value(s), replacing it (them) by the result. The details of the instructions are left to your imagination. A program is merely a sequence of instructions: the input is the given stack, the output is the stack given by following the instructions.

       grammar:
       Program $= [\![\ \text{Instruction}^+\ ]\!]$.
       Instruction $= [\![\ \text{"push" Numeral}\ ]\!]$ | "pop" |
                         "add" | "subtract" | "multiply" |
                         "duplicate" | "exchange" .
       Numeral $= \square$.

Tuples provide a convenient representation of stacks. Using the notation for basic and functional actions, specify an appropriate action semantics for this stack-machine language. Compare your specification with any available specification of a conventional machine code.

Chapter 14

Declarations

- *Declarations include definitions of constants and packages. Expressions include identifiers, as well as aggregates for arrays and records and selection of components. Statements include blocks with local declarations.*

- *The semantic description of declarations, etc., illustrates the use of the declarative action notation introduced in Chapter 7.*

- *Semantic entities now include general array and record values, and packages.*

Declarations in programs are constructs that are similar to mathematical definitions, in that they introduce symbols and determine their interpretation. The symbols introduced are called *identifiers*. Declarations are said to *bind* identifiers to their interpretation.

The *scope* of a declaration is the part of the program in which its binding is valid. This is usually the rest of the *block* statement in which it occurs, except for inner blocks where the same identifier is re-declared, thus making a hole in the scope of the outer-level declaration. Declarations can also occur in modules, which are called *packages* in ADA. A module may limit the scope of the declarations in it, and it declares a module identifier which may be used to *import* the bindings of the declarations into other modules.

The processing of a declaration is called its *elaboration*. Declarations may involve expressions that are to be evaluated, so their elaboration generally has a computational aspect—in contrast to mathematical definitions.

A *record* value is similar to a module or package entity, in that its *field* identifiers can be regarded as bound to component values. An *array* value generalizes strings by allowing arbitrary values as components, even nested array values themselves. The primary difference between record and array values is that reference to components of

records uses identifiers, which cannot be computed, whereas reference to components
of arrays uses values such as integers, which can be computed. Implementations use
different techniques to represent records and arrays, for efficiency.

Here is the overview of the modules specified in this chapter:

/AD

Abstract Syntax (*continued*)

    Declarations

        needs: **Identifiers, Expressions.**

    Statements (*continued*)

        needs: **Declarations.**

    Expressions (*continued*)

        needs: **Identifiers.**

    Identifiers

Semantic Functions (*continued*)

    Declarations

        needs: **Identifiers, Expressions.**

    Statements (*continued*)

        needs: **Declarations.**

    Expressions (*continued*)

        needs: **Identifiers.**

    Identifiers

Semantic Entities (*continued*)

    Sorts (*continued*)

    Values (*continued*)

    Arrays (*continued*)

    Records

    Packages

14.1   /AD/Abstract Syntax (*continued*)

14.1.1   Declarations

grammar:

- Declaration = 〚 Identifier ":" "constant" ":=" Expression ";" 〛 |
  〚 "package" Identifier "is" Declaration⁺ "end" ";" 〛 |
  〚 "use" Nominator ";" 〛 | □ .

We do not bother to allow types in the syntax of constant declarations, as they are irrelevant to our dynamic semantics for AD.

In ADA, packages are divided into *heads* and *bodies*, where only those entities declared *publicly* in the head of a package become available when the package is imported with a use declaration. The syntax shown above corresponds to package heads. We defer the semantic description of package bodies to Appendix A, as their semantics involves the redirection of indirect bindings, which is a topic left for advanced study.

14.1.2   Statements (*continued*)

grammar:

- Statement = □ | 〚 "declare" Declaration⁺ "begin" Statement⁺ "end" ";" 〛 .

A declare statement is a block. Some languages, PASCAL for instance, don't allow such anonymous blocks to occur in the middle of a statement sequence, only directly in other declarations, but the extra generality here doesn't complicate the semantic description noticeably.

14.1.3   Expressions (*continued*)

grammar:

- Nominator   = Identifier | 〚 Nominator "." Identifier 〛 .
- Name   = Identifier | 〚 Name "." Identifier 〛 |
                 〚 Name "(" Expression ")" 〛 | □ .
- Expression   = □ | Name |
                 〚 "(" Expressions ")" 〛 | 〚 "(" Associations ")" 〛 .
- Expressions = 〈 Expression 〈 "," Expression 〉* 〉 .
- Association   = 〚 Identifier "=>" Expression 〛 .
- Associations = 〈 Association 〈 "," Association 〉* 〉 .

The ADA syntax for names is essentially context-sensitive. Here we introduce **Nominator** as a subsort of **Name**, corresponding to names that may refer to entities of packages. It corresponds roughly to the ADA notion of an *expanded* name in the ADA Reference Manual, but includes identifiers.

The syntax of array component selection ⟦ **Name** "(" **Expression** ")" ⟧ cannot be separated from that of function calls, without access to context-dependent information about the types of values bound to identifiers. It could be argued that the appropriate technique is to let static semantics produce a different (context-free) abstract syntax where there is a clear separation between these constructs. Nevertheless, let us take an abstract syntax that is close to the original concrete syntax, so as to see when function declarations are introduced (in Chapter 16) how one can cope with such difficulties *without* introducing a separate static semantics.

The syntax of ordinary parenthesized expressions ⟦ "(" **Expression** ")" ⟧ is a special case of ⟦ "(" **Expressions** ")" ⟧, which ADA generally uses for expressing array values as *aggregates*. Because of this confusion, single-component array values in ADA have to be expressed using a syntax for aggregates like that of ⟦ "(" **Associations** ")" ⟧ above, but using array component indices instead of record field identifiers. We omit this more complicated syntax here, with the consequence that single-component array values cannot be expressed at all in AD.

14.1.4 Identifiers

grammar:

- **Identifier**   = □ .
- **Word**   = **Reserved-Word** | **Identifier** (*disjoint*) .
- **Word**   = ⟦ letter ⟨ letter | digit ⟩* ⟧ .
- **Reserved-Word** = "abs" | "and" | □ | "xor" .

The syntax of identifiers is not particularly exciting: alphanumeric sequences of characters, excluding some *reserved words*. The specification given here seems to be the most concise way to specify this, using *disjoint* to get the effect of sort difference—which is blatantly nonmonotonic as an operation on sorts, and therefore cannot be provided directly. Because of the awkwardness of specifying that identifiers do not include reserved words with context-free grammars, reference manuals usually leave the specification of identifiers informal. The □ in the production for **Reserved-Word** stands for the remaining reserved words of the full AD language; the full list can be found in Appendix A.

14.2   /AD/Semantic Functions (*continued*)

14.2.1   Declarations

introduces: elaborate _ .

14.2.1.1   Elaborating Declarations

- elaborate _ :: Declaration$^+$ → action [binding] [using current bindings] .

(1)   elaborate ⟨ D_1:Declaration D_2:Declaration$^+$ ⟩ =
         elaborate D_1 before elaborate D_2 .

The use of the combinator _ before _ in the semantics of declaration sequences allows later declarations to refer to the bindings produced by earlier declarations—but not the other way round. Mutually-recursive declarations are deferred to Appendix A, since they involve indirect bindings, which were not explained in detail in Chapter 7.

(2)   elaborate ⟦ I:Identifier ":" "constant" ":=" E:Expression ";" ⟧ =
         evaluate E then bind the token of I to the given value .

Somewhat contrary to the explanation of ADA constants in the Reference Manual, we let constants be bound directly to values, rather than to special 'variables' that cannot be assigned new values. Thus AD constants resemble *named numbers* in ADA. This allows us to defer consideration of variable declarations to the next chapter, and in any case has the advantage of simplicity.

(3)   elaborate ⟦ "package" I:Identifier "is" D:Declaration$^+$ "end" ";" ⟧ =
         elaborate D hence
         bind the token of I to package of the current bindings .

Note the use of _ hence _ in the semantics of packages, to ensure that *only* the bindings produced by the declarations D are incorporated into the package entity, without the bindings current for the elaboration of D. In ADA, the package identifier should be visible throughout D. To describe that would again involve the use of indirect bindings, so we don't bother to follow ADA on this point.

(4)   elaborate ⟦ "use" N:Nominator ";" ⟧ =
         produce the public-bindings of the package yielded by
             the entity nominated by N .

Above, we could omit 'the package yielded by', since public-bindings _ is *only* defined on package entities. But it serves to make explicit which sort of entity N is supposed to nominate (in a legal program).

Below, we are able to extend the previous description of the semantics of statements and expressions by merely adding new semantic equations *without making any changes to the semantic equations previously given!* This feature seems to be unique to action semantics, among frameworks for semantic description of programming languages. Algebraic specifications of abstract data types have similar extensibility.

14.2.2 Statements (*continued*)

14.2.2.1 Executing Statements (*continued*)

- execute _ :: Statement⁺ → action
  [completing | escaping | diverging] [using current bindings] .

In fact the previous functionality for execute _ is still valid, the one specified here is merely more precise.

(1)   execute ⟦ "declare" D:Declaration⁺ "begin" S:Statement⁺ "end" ";" ⟧ =
            furthermore elaborate D hence execute S .

Remember that prefixes take precedence over infixes!

14.2.3 Expressions (*continued*)

needs: **Identifiers** .
introduces: the entity nominated by _ , investigate _ .

14.2.3.1 Nominators

- the entity nominated by _ :: Nominator → yielder
  [of bindable] [using current bindings] .

(1)   the entity nominated by I:Identifier = the entity bound to the token of I .

(2)   the entity nominated by ⟦ N:Nominator "." I:Identifier ⟧ =
            the entity bound to the token of I receiving
            the public-bindings of the package yielded by the entity nominated by N .

An alternative technique here is to use the standard map operation _ at _ to retrieve the entity bound to the token of I in the package. But this only works so long as the binding is an ordinary, direct one, so the use of the yielder operation _ receiving _ is preferable.

14.2.3.2 Investigating Names

- investigate _ :: Name → action [giving an entity] [using current bindings] .

The sort Name is a subsort of Expression, so we might think of using evaluate _ to investigate the entities to which names refer. However, the sort entity is a proper supersort of value: at the moment, the difference is merely the sort package, but further differences are introduced in subsequent chapters. This makes it worthwhile to introduce investigate _ for names. Moreover, we get an additional benefit in Chapter 15, when the difference between investigation and evaluation becomes more pronounced.

(1)   investigate I:Identifier = give the entity bound to the token of I .

(2)   investigate ⟦ N:Name "." I:Identifier ⟧ =
          investigate N then
             produce the public-bindings of the given package or
             produce the component-bindings of the given record
          hence investigate I .

The use of _ or _ above makes apparent the syntactic overloading of "." for selecting from both records and packages. The alternatives cannot be given an entity that is both a record and a package at the same time, so at least one of them fails, due to the reference to a given datum yielding nothing. If the name N evaluates to give, say, a number or an array, both alternatives fail.

(3)   investigate ⟦ N:Name "(" E:Expression ")" ⟧ =
          | investigate N and evaluate E
          then give the component of (the given array-value#1,
                                              the given index-value#2) .

14.2.3.3 Evaluating Expressions (*continued*)

- evaluate _ :: Expression → action [giving a value] [using current bindings] .

(1)   evaluate I:Identifier = give the value bound to the token of I .

(2)   evaluate ⟦ N:Name "." I:Identifier ⟧ =
          investigate N then
             produce the public-bindings of the given package or
             produce the component-bindings of the given record
          hence evaluate I .

(3)   evaluate ⟦ N:Name "(" E:Expression ")" ⟧ =
          | investigate N and evaluate E
          then give the component of (the given array-value#1,
                                              the given index-value#2) .

ı)   evaluate ⟦ "(" *A*:Associations ")" ⟧ =
       evaluate *A* then
         give record of the bindings yielded by the given map .

- evaluate _ :: Expressions → action [giving value$^+$] [using current bindings] .

ı)   evaluate ⟨ E_1:Expression "," E_2:Expressions ⟩ = evaluate E_1 and evaluate E_2 .

Notice that a single expression is of sort Expressions, so we simply extend the semantic function evaluate _ , rather than introducing a new semantic function, which would require a semantic equation defining it on Expression.

4.2.3.4   Evaluating Associations

- evaluate _ :: Associations → action
       [giving a map [token to value]] [using current bindings] .

ı)   evaluate ⟦ *I*:Identifier "=>" *E*:Expression ⟧ =
       evaluate *E* then give map of the token of *I* to the given value .

2)   evaluate ⟨ A_1:Association "," A_2:Associations ⟩ =
       | evaluate A_1 and evaluate A_2
       then give disjoint-union of (the given map#1, the given map#2) .

If A_1 and A_2 contain associations for the same identifier, the attempt to give the combination of the maps to which they evaluate fails. But such associations would be banned by a static semantics, so their semantics is irrelevant.

14.2.4   Identifiers

introduces: the token of _ .

- the token of _ :: Identifier → token .

ı)   the token of *I*:Identifier = string & uppercase *I* .

Following ADA, let us canonicalize identifiers in AD by converting all letters to (for example) upper case. For languages where case differences are taken seriously, the semantic function the token of _ would simply be the identity function on identifiers, and then we could omit it altogether.

14.3   /AD/Semantic Entities (*continued*)

includes: Action Notation/Declarative .

14.3.1   Sorts (*continued*)

- entity   = value | package | □ .
- datum   = entity | bindings | □ .
- token   = string of (uppercase letter, (uppercase letter | digit)*) .
- bindable = entity | □ .

The sort entity corresponds to the ADA notion of entities, whereas the sorts datum, token, and bindable play a fixed rôle in action notation.

14.3.2   Values (*continued*)

- value   = simple-value | array-value | record-value (*disjoint*) .
- simple-value = truth-value | character | number | □ .

The details of the following modules are deferred to Appendix A.

14.3.3   Arrays (*continued*)

- array of _ :: value$^+$ → array-value (*partial*) .
- index-value = integer-number .
- component _ :: (array-value, index-value) → value (*partial*).

14.3.4   Records

- empty-record   = record of empty-map .
- record of _   :: empty-map → empty-record (*total*) ,
                          map [token to value] → record-value (*total*) .
- component-bindings _ :: record-value → map [token to value] (*total*) .
- _ is _   :: record-value, record-value → truth-value (*total*).

14.3.5   Packages

- package of _   :: bindings → package (*total*) .
- public-bindings _ :: package → bindings (*total*) .

Summary

- *The semantic entities representing declaration elaboration are actions.*

- *Basic, functional, and declarative actions are needed for the description of declarations.*

- *The semantics of an identifier is a token.*

- *A constant declaration binds a token directly to a value.*

- *A package declaration binds a token to a datum that incorporates the bindings produced by elaborating the packaged declarations.*

- *Adding declarations to* AD *does not require any changes to the semantic description of statements and expressions.*

Navigation

- *If you are curious about the full specification of the semantic entities used here, see the corresponding modules in Appendix A.*

- *Now look at Chapter 8, which introduces imperative actions, before proceeding with Part III.*

Exercises

1. Let S be an arbitrary sequence of statements. Consider the abstract syntax trees of the two blocks that might be written concretely as follows:

    S_1 = "declare x: constant := 1 ;

                        y: constant := 2 ;

          begin S end ;"

    S_2 = "declare x: constant := 1 ;

            begin declare y: constant := 2 ;

                   begin S end ;

          end ;"

Work out the action semantics of these statements according to the semantic equations, and argue for the equivalence of the two actions.

2. Read the description of scope rules for declarations in the ADA Reference Manual. Relate the description to the use of the various action combinators in our semantic description of AD.

3. Modify the semantics of constant declarations in AD so that (as in STANDARD PASCAL) any existing binding of an identifier is hidden on entry to a block if that same identifier is declared by the outermost declarations of the block. Hint: introduce an extra semantic function for declarations, returning the set of identifiers declared in them.

Chapter 15

Variables

- *Declarations of variables involve types, which indicate the values that may be assigned to the variables. Assignments are statements.*

- *The semantics of variable declarations and assignment statements illustrates the use of the imperative action notation introduced in Chapter 8.*

- *Semantic entities now include variables, types, and access values.*

In programs, *variables* are entities that refer to stored data. The *value* of a variable is the data to which it currently refers; a variable may be *assigned* a succession of different values.

This concept of a program variable is quite different from that of a mathematical variable. In mathematics, variables are used to stand for particular unknown values—often the arguments of functions being defined. Although these variables can be 'assigned' values, e.g., by function application, their values do not subsequently vary! In the scope of a variable, all occurrences of that variable refer to the same value. In fact mathematical variables correspond exactly to the *constant identifiers* of programming languages, described in Chapter 14.

A declaration of a variable in a program determines a *new* variable: one whose value is, in general, independent of that of the values of all other variables. This is called *allocating* the variable. The declaration then binds an identifier to the variable. Usually the declaration specifies the *type* of the variable, indicating what sort of value may be assigned to it. Not all programming languages insist on explicit declarations of variables: the first assignment to a variable may be treated as an implicit declaration, sometimes with the type indicated by the assigned value.

When the supply of variables might be finite, the semantics of programs *is* affected by whether or not variables allocated for locally-bound identifiers are *relinquished* on block exit. For instance, a block statement with local variables might be the body of a loop; if the local variables of the block are not relinquished, the supply might be exhausted after some number of iterations of the loop, leading to an error, which would not be a possibility otherwise.

An assignment to a variable does *not* affect the binding of the 'corresponding' variable identifier. The binding remains fixed throughout its scope. The assignment only affects the stored datum to which the variable refers. See the diagram in Box 15.1.

The distinction between variables and their identifiers allows a simple analysis of the notion of *sharing* or *aliasing* between variables: it is just when different identifiers are bound to the same variable. Whether one likes it or not, most practical programming languages do allow aliasing, e.g., when passing variables as parameters to procedures, as explained in Chapter 16. The same variable may be used for two different parameters, or the variable may be accessible both through a parameter and through a nonlocal binding.

Now, an occurrence of a variable identifier in the scope of its declaration could evaluate either to the variable bound to the identifier, or to the value of that variable. Whether the variable or its value is required generally depends on the *context* of the occurrence. For instance, the variable itself is required when the identifier occurs as the target of an assignment statement, conventionally written on the left of the assignment symbol ":=", whereas its value is required when the identifier occurs in an expression, such as on the right of ":=".

The value of the variable can be obtained from the variable, but obviously not *vice versa*. Going from a variable to its value is called *dereferencing*. Occasionally, programming languages insist that dereferencing be made explicit by use of a special

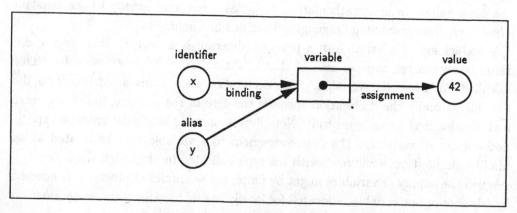

Box 15.1   Identifiers, variables, and values

operator; but usually dereferencing is left implicit in the context of the occurrence. Let us refer to dereferencing as a *coercion*. Another kind of coercion is the conversion between different types of value that is implicit in some operators, e.g., the conversion from integer to real in connection with numeric operators in ADA.

It is useful to distinguish between *simple* and *structured* variables. Simple variables, such as integer variables, are monolithic, and their values can only be changed by assigning them an entire new value. Structured variables, such as array variables, have subvariables as components, which allows assignments that change *part* of the value of the variable, leaving the other parts unaltered.

Typically, structured variables are formed in the same way as structured values. Wholesale assignment of one structured variable to another is, conceptually, the evaluation of the structured value already assigned to the former variable, followed by assignment of that value to the latter variable, component by component. Implementations are, of course, welcome to optimize this by eliminating the intermediate structured value—provided that the outcome is the same. Structured variables introduce further possibilities for aliasing: two different names, such as a(i) and a(j), may access the same component variable, depending on the values of i and j.

Many programming languages make a distinction between variables declared for local use, to be made available for reuse when the scope of the declaration is left, and variables that are allocated on a more permanent basis. Typically, local variables are implemented on a *stack*, whereas those whose allocation may extend beyond the scope of their declarations are implemented on a *heap*. The latter may be referred to via values known as *pointers*, *references*, or (in ADA) *accesses*. These values that give access to variables can be assigned to other variables—and to components of structured variables, which allows the creation of cyclic structures, such as graphs and two-way lists.

The problem of *dangling references* occurs when some means of referring to a variable, such as an access value or a binding, survives the extent of the variable's allocation. Once a variable has been relinquished, the storage for it might get reused immediately, perhaps for storing a different type of value. A reference to the value of the relinquished variable or an attempt to assign a new value to it may then have an unpredictable, implementation-dependent effect. An accurate semantic description has to reflect this possibility, independently of whether the supply of variables is finite or not.

Often, programming languages ensure that all variables declared locally in a block get automatically relinquished on block exit, without any possibility of dangling references to them. They restrict access values to reference heap-allocated variables. An implementation of a program may reuse a heap-allocated variable as soon as there is no longer any possibility of referring to it via an access value. Ascertaining which variables can be reused is known as *garbage collection*. It can be computationally expensive, so the program may be required to relinquish heap-allocated variables explicitly, whereby dangling references may get introduced, inadvertently.

Here is an overview of the modules that are specified in this chapter:

/AD

Abstract Syntax (*continued*)

Declarations (*continued*)
    needs: **Types**.

Types
    needs: **Identifiers, Expressions**.

Statements (*continued*)

Expressions (*continued*)

Semantic Functions (*continued*)

Declarations (*continued*)
    needs: **Types**.

Types
    needs: **Identifiers, Expressions**.

Statements (*continued*)

Expressions (*continued*)

Semantic Entities (*continued*)

Sorts (*continued*)

Values (*continued*)

Variables

Types

Accesses

Arrays (*continued*)

Records (*continued*)

15.1 /AD/Abstract Syntax (*continued*)

15.1.1 Declarations (*continued*)

grammar:

- Declaration = □ | ⟦ Identifier ":" Nominator ⟨ ":=" Expression ⟩? ";" ⟧ |
    ⟦ "type" Identifier "is" Type ";" ⟧ .

In the variable declaration ⟦ *I* ":" *N* ";" ⟧ the nominator *N* is supposed to nominate a type. In ⟦ *I* ":" *N* ":=" *E* ";" ⟧ the declared variable gets initialized to the value of the expression *E*.

15.1.2 Types

grammar:

- Type   = ⟦ "(" Enumerands ")" ⟧ |
    ⟦ "array" "(" Expression ".." Expression ")"
        "of" Nominator ⟧ |
    ⟦ "record" Component-Type⁺ "end" "record" ⟧ |
    ⟦ "access" Nominator ⟧ .

- Enumerands   = ⟨ Identifier ⟨ "," Identifier ⟩* ⟩ .
- Component-Type = ⟦ Identifier ":" Nominator ";" ⟧ .

As in ADA, simple types such as **integer** and **real** are treated as required identifiers, rather than as reserved words. Programs are run in the scope of bindings for all required identifiers, as specified in Chapter 17.

For simplicity, we omit so-called *variant* records from AD altogether.

15.1.3 Statements (*continued*)

grammar:

- Statement = □ | ⟦ Name ":=" Expression ";" ⟧ .

The name on the left of the assignment statement above may access an entire structured variable, in which case the expression on the right hand side should evaluate to a value with the same structure. Of course we cannot exclude mismatched assignments from our context-free abstract syntax, so we have to specify their semantics.

15.1.4   Expressions (*continued*)

grammar:

- Name   = □ | ⟦ Name "." "all" ⟧ .
- Expression   = □ | "null" | ⟦ "new" Nominator ⟧ .

The sort ⟦ Name "." "all" ⟧ is disjoint from the sort ⟦ Name "." Identifier ⟧ because "all" is included in Reserved-Word. This ADA syntax corresponds roughly to the syntax ⟦ Name "^" ⟧ for following pointers in PASCAL and other languages. For instance, if r and s are declared as variable identifiers of access type, the assignment of r.all to s.all copies the value of the variable accessed by r to the variable accessed by s, whereas the assignment of r to s merely sets the value of s to the access value of r.

The expression "null" evaluates to a dummy access value, whereas ⟦ "new" N ⟧ evaluates to a proper value that accesses a fresh variable of type N.

15.2   /AD/Semantic Functions (*continued*)

15.2.1   Declarations (*continued*)

15.2.1.1   Elaborating Declarations (*continued*)

- elaborate _ :: Declaration$^+$ → action
  [binding | storing] [using current bindings | current storage] .

We specified a more restrictive sort of action in the functionality of elaborate _ in Chapter 14, excluding the possibility of changing the store. The functionality now has to be changed, as above, to accommodate the actions specified in the semantic equations for variable declaration below.

(1)   elaborate ⟦ I:Identifier ":" N:Nominator ";" ⟧ =
         allocate a variable for the type yielded by the entity nominated by N
         then bind the token of I to the given variable .

The action allocate d for Y is *ad hoc*, see the module **Semantic Entities/Variables**.

(2)   elaborate ⟦ I:Identifier ":" N:Nominator ":=" E:Expression ";" ⟧ =
         | allocate a variable for the type yielded by the entity nominated by N
         | and evaluate E
         then
         | bind the token of I to the given variable#1 and
         | assign the given value#2 to the given variable#1 .

Non-declarative action combinators (such as _ and _ , _ then _) pass on received bindings to both their subactions, which is particularly useful for combining declaration elaborations with evaluations and assignments. The action assign Y_1 to Y_2 is *ad hoc*, see the module **Semantic Entities/Variables**. It generalizes store Y_1 in Y_2 from cells to arbitrary variables.

Whereas bindings produced by declarations automatically disappear at the end of their scope, locally-declared variables are not thereby automatically *relinquished*. Appendix A shows how to specify relinquishment by introducing an extra semantic function for declarations.

(3)   elaborate ⟦ "type" *I*:Identifier "is" *T*:Type ";" ⟧ =
        typify *T* then bind the token of *I* to the given type .

15.2.2   Types

introduces: typify _ , enumerate _ , the component-types of _ .

Type 'typification' resembles (and involves) expression evaluation, with the extra possibility of the declaration of enumeration types producing some bindings as well as giving a type.

We do not distinguish semantically between different occurrences of the same type structure—in marked contrast to the description of types in the ADA Reference Manual. That is because our only use for types in the dynamic semantics of AD is to determine the *structure* of variables to be allocated. We are assuming that type *checking* is the concern of a static semantics, which is 'somebody else's problem'...

15.2.2.1   Typifying Types

- typify _ :: Type → action
  [giving a type | binding] [using current bindings | current storage] .

(1)   typify ⟦ "(" *E*:Enumerands ")" ⟧ =
        give the enumeration-type and (give 0 then enumerate *E*) .

(2)   typify ⟦ "array" "(" E_1:Expression ".." E_2:Expression ")" "of" *N*:Nominator ⟧ =
        | evaluate E_1 and evaluate E_2 and give the entity nominated by *N*
        then give array-type of the given (index-value, index-value, type) .

(3)   typify ⟦ "record" *C*:Component-Type[+] "end" "record" ⟧ =
        give record-type of the component-types of *C* .

(4)   typify ⟦ "access" *N*:Nominator ⟧ = give the access-type .

The lack of dependence of access types on the type of variable accessed (the *designated* type) allows type declarations to refer to each other, and to themselves—provided that such references are protected by access types. In relation to implementation techniques, this possibility reflects the fact that values of access types are essentially addresses of variables, and can be represented in a fixed way, independently of the types of those variables. In AD, for instance, we allow such type declarations as type List is record Head:Integer; Tail:access List end . (The *incomplete* type declarations required in ADA are only relevant for static semantics, so we omit them in AD.)

15.2.2.2   Enumerating Constants

- enumerate _ :: Enumerands → action [binding] [using given natural] .

(1)   enumerate I:Identifier =
          bind the token of I to integer-number of the given natural .

(2)   enumerate ⟨ I:Identifier "," E:Enumerands ⟩ =
          enumerate I and
          | give the successor of the given natural then enumerate E .

15.2.2.3   Component Types

- the component-types of _ :: Component-Type⁺ → yielder
    [of map [token to type]] [using current bindings] .

(1)   the component-types of ⟦ I:Identifier ":" N:Nominator ";" ⟧ =
          map of the token of I to the type yielded by the entity nominated by N .

(2)   the component-types of ⟨ C_1:Component-Type C_2:Component-Type⁺ ⟩ =
          disjoint-union of (the component-types of C_1, the component-types of C_2) .

Below, as in the foregoing chapters, we are able to simply extend our previous semantic equations for AD statements, despite the inclusion of new features such as assignment statements. This may seem unsurprising, but an analogous development of a *denotational* semantics for AD would involve major reformulation of previous semantic equations in each chapter! Moreover, this important feature is intrinsic to action semantics, and not dependent on the precise order of our extensions.

15.2.3   Statements *(continued)*

15.2.3.1   Executing Statements *(continued)*

- execute _ :: Statement$^+$ → action
    [completing | escaping | diverging | storing]
    [using current bindings | current storage] .

(1)   execute ⟦ *N*:Name ":=" *E*:Expression ";" ⟧ =
    | access *N* and evaluate *E*
    then assign the given value#2 to the given variable#1 .

Of course, you already saw a somewhat simplified version of the above semantic equation in Section 2.2, in the action semantics of the language SIMPLE. There, the left hand side of the assignment was simply an identifier, and variables were represented directly by cells.

The definition of assign Y_1 to Y_2 in Appendix A caters for wholesale assignment of arrays and records, so it is quite complicated.

15.2.4   Expressions *(continued)*

introduces: access _ .

15.2.4.1   Accessing Names

- access _ :: Name → action
    [giving a variable] [using current bindings | current storage] .

(1)   access *N*:Name = investigate *N* then give the given variable .

Essentially, access _ is a semantically-restricted version of investigate _ .

Some of the semantic equations below *replace* equations previously specified in Chapter 13 and Chapter 14. Without these changes, however, the previous semantic equations would still specify *a* semantics for expressions, but it would not be the *intended* one. For instance, when x and y are variable identifiers, evaluate ⟦ x "+" y ⟧ would lead to failure, as the sum operation is not applicable to variables, only to numbers. On the other hand, had AD insisted on explicit dereferencing of variable identifiers (as in a few high-level languages, and commonly in assembler languages) no changes at all would have been required!

Notice that all the following changes to expression evaluation essentially consist of adding further *meaningful alternatives* to the previously-specified actions. This is very different from the tedious changes required to a conventional denotational description when adding imperative features to the described language.

15.2.4.2   Evaluating Expressions (*continued*)

- evaluate _ :: Expression → action
  [giving a value] [using current bindings | current storage] .

(1)   evaluate *I*:Identifier =
    give the entity bound to the token of *I* then
    | give (the given value | the value assigned to the given variable) .

Notice that when *I* is bound to a variable, evaluate *I* gives the value of the variable, whereas investigate *I* (and hence access *I*) gives the variable itself.

(2)   evaluate ⟦ *N*:Name "." *I*:Identifier ⟧ =
    investigate *N* then
      produce the public-bindings of the given package or
      produce the component-bindings of
        the record accessible from the given (value | variable)
    hence evaluate *I* .

(3)   evaluate ⟦ *N*:Name "." "all" ⟧ =
    evaluate *N* then
    give the value assigned to the variable accessible from the given access .

(4)   evaluate ⟦ *N*:Name "(" *E*:Expression ")" ⟧ =
    | investigate *N* and evaluate *E*
    then
      give the component of
        (the given array-value#1,
         the index-value yielded by the rest of the given data) or
      give the value assigned to the component of
        (the array-variable accessible from the given (access | variable)#1,
         the index-value yielded by the rest of the given data) .

(5)   evaluate "null" = give the null-access .

(6)   evaluate ⟦ "new" *N*:Nominator ⟧ =
    allocate a variable for the type yielded by the entity nominated by *N* then
    give access to the given variable .

The precise relationship between evaluate _ and access _ is that when performing access *N*:Name gives a variable, we have

    evaluate *N* = access *N* then give the value assigned to the given variable.

15.3   /AD/Semantic Entities (*continued*)

includes: Action Notation/Imperative .

15.3.1   Sorts (*continued*)

- entity   = value | package | variable | type | □ .
- datum = entity | bindings | natural | □ .
- storable = simple-value .

We introduce the sort variable *ad hoc*, corresponding to the intuitive concept of a variable in ADA. It is specified below, in the same way as value was specified in Chapter 12 and subsequent chapters. The sort storable consists of those values that can be stored in single cells, which represent simple variables.

15.3.2   Values (*continued*)

- value   = simple-value | array-value | record-value (*disjoint*) .
- simple-value = truth-value | character | number | access (*disjoint*) .

That concludes the specification of the module **Values**.

15.3.3   Variables

- variable   = simple-variable | array-variable | record-variable (*disjoint*) .
- assign _ to _   :: yielder [of value], yielder [of variable] → action [storing] .
- the _ assigned to _ :: value, yielder [of variable] → yielder [of value] .
- allocate _ for _   :: variable, yielder [of type] →
                         action [giving a variable | storing] .

See Appendix A for the definitions of the above actions, and of the remaining notation that is partially specified below. Notice that allocate _ for _ takes a sort of *variable* and an individual type, whereas the standard action allocate _ merely operates on a sort of *cell*.

15.3.4   Types

- type   = simple-type | array-type | record-type (*disjoint*) .
- simple-type = boolean-type | character-type | enumeration-type |
                integer-type | real-type | access-type (*individual*) .

Type entities are rather syntactic: essentially just a copy of the abstract syntax of types, with nominators replaced by the nominated types, and any expressions by their values. It would be more abstract to represent each type by an abstraction which, when enacted, allocated a variable of the appropriate structure; but the description given above turns out to be the most perspicuous.

15.3.5   Accesses

- null-access   : access .
- access to _   :: variable → access (*total*) .
- accessed-variable _   :: access → variable (*partial*) .
- the _ accessible from _ :: (value | variable), yielder [of value | variable] →
                                   yielder [of value | variable] .

Essentially, the sort access is a copy of variable, together with the extra value null-access. Note that the *v* accessible from *Y* includes the *v* yielded by *Y*, as well as other possibilities arising from dereferencing.

15.3.6   Arrays (*continued*)

- array   = array-value | array-variable .
- array of _   :: variable+ → array-variable (*partial*) .
- component _   :: (array-variable, index-value) → variable (*partial*) .
- array-type of _   :: (index-value², type) → array-type (*total*) .
- lower index-value _ , upper index-value _ ::
                                   array-type → index-value (*total*) .
- component-type _ :: array-type → type (*total*) .

15.3.7   Records (*continued*)

- record   = record-value | record-variable .
- empty-record   = record of empty-map .
- record of _   :: map [token to variable] → record-variable (*total*) .
- component-bindings _   :: record-variable → map [token to variable] (*total*) .
- record-type of _   :: map [token to type] → record-type (*total*) .
- component-type-bindings _ :: record-type → map [token to type] (*total*) .

Summary

- *Variable declarations allocate storage for variables, and bind identifiers to variables.*

- *Assignment statements change the values stored in variables.*

- *Accessing a variable identifier gives the variable itself; evaluating it gives the value last assigned to the variable.*

- *To allow implicit coercions from variables to their values (minor) modifications to previously-specified semantic equations are required, inserting extra alternatives.*

- *Structured variables generally have a similar representation to structured values.*

- *Type expressions are evaluated to closely-related semantic entities.*

Navigation

- *If you are curious about the full specification of the semantic entities used here, see the corresponding modules in Appendix A.*

- *Now look at Chapter 9, which introduces reflective actions, before proceeding with Part III.*

Exercises

1. Extend the syntax of Expression with a (non-ADA) construct of the form ⟦ Statement "result" Expression ⟧. The intended semantics is for the evaluation to consist of the execution of the statement followed by the evaluation of the component expression. Specify this formally.

2. Independently of the preceding exercise, extend the syntax of Statement with a construct ⟦ "result" Expression ";" ⟧, and let statements be included *as* expressions. The intended semantics is for the *evaluation* of an statement-expression to consist of its *execution* until a return statement is met; this gives the result of the statement-expression. Specify the intended semantics formally. For simplicity, you may like to prohibit the loop exit statement from occurring in statement-expressions.

3. Both the previous exercises involve expressions that can have so-called *side-effects*. Give an example, based on either of the extensions considered, where expression evaluation can give two different values.

4. Solutions to these exercises are given in Appendix A:

   (a) Specify an operation **dispose of** _ :: variable → action, intended to generalize **unreserve** _ to structured variables.

   (b) Change the semantic equation for block statements ⟦ "declare" D "begin" S "end" ";" ⟧ to relinquish locally-allocated variables at the end of executing the block—also when the execution terminates abnormally, due to an exit statement.

5. (Harder!) Change the representation of variables so that each variable is tagged with the type entity for which it is allocated. Change the actions **allocate** v **for** t and **assign** x **to** v accordingly (at least for simple variables) so that assignments *fail* when the value x is not of the sort indicated by the type of the variable v.

6. Change the semantic entities representing types so that each elaboration of a type declaration creates a *different* type. (This is significant when type-checking is incorporated in assignment, as in the previous exercise.) Hint: allocate cells for use as unique distinguishing labels—without storing anything in them!

7. (a) Extend the syntax of AD by allowing so-called *variant-parts* in the components of record types, as in ADA.

   (b) Specify the intended semantics.

Chapter 16

Subprograms

- *Subprograms are classified as procedures or functions.*

- *Procedures are parameterized statements. They may be declared, and then called with various actual parameters. Formal parameter declarations resemble incomplete constant and variable declarations.*

- *Functions are essentially parameterized expressions.*

- *The semantics of subprogram declarations and calls illustrates the use of the reflective action notation introduced in Chapter 9, as well as the declarative action notation introduced in Chapter 7.*

- *Semantic entities now include subprogram entities, which are formed from abstractions, and data that are used to distinguish subprogram returns from other reasons for abnormal termination of statement execution.*

A *procedure* is a construct that incorporates a statement, which is known as the *body* of the procedure. A procedure *declaration* binds an identifier to a procedure. A procedure *call* statement causes the body of the identified procedure to be executed. In a few languages, procedures are provided as *expressions*; then a procedure declaration may be written just like an ordinary constant declaration.

A *function* is like a procedure, but a function body is essentially an expression, rather than a statement: it has to return a result. A function call is a kind of expression. In practice, most conventional programming languages allow *impure* functions, where the body is a mixture of statements and an expression. They use various syntactic devices in function bodies to indicate the result: in PASCAL, the function identifier is regarded as a variable to which a result should be assigned before completing the body, although it may also be used for recursive calls; in ADA, execution of a special *return* statement gives the result, skipping any remaining statements; and in C, statements and expressions are merged, so that every statement execution gives a result, possibly null.

In the presence of impure functions, the evaluation of a function call in an expression can involve the execution of statements, giving the possibility of so-called *side-effects*: changes to storage that are not purely local to the function call. Moreover, expression evaluation can diverge. Then when the order of expression evaluation is left implementation-dependent, different orders of evaluation may have different outcomes, so that the semantics of an expression (and hence of a program) essentially becomes nondeterministic. Some languages ban programs whose overall behaviour is sensitive to implementation-dependent order of evaluation—but it is still necessary to describe the semantics of these programs: precisely to define whether they are to be banned or not!

Procedures and functions are collectively referred to as *subprograms*. A subprogram may be called from many different places in a program, some of which may be in the scope of declarations that are different from those where the subprogram itself is specified. Most programming languages let bindings be *static*, so that the declarations referred to by identifiers in the body of the subprogram do not depend on the particular call of the program. This corresponds to letting the subprogram incorporate the current bindings when it is specified, making a closure out of it. For dynamic bindings, the formation of the closure is delayed until the point of call of the subprogram. A few languages restrict closure to particular kinds of bindings, for instance to prevent direct reference to local variables of enclosing subprograms— either for the sake of efficiency, or to enforce a discipline of programming. Some languages mix static and dynamic bindings, for instance LISP provides alternative forms of function declaration.

Subprograms can have *parameters*. A subprogram declaration indicates the *formal* parameters, which often resemble ordinary variable declarations. A subprogram call specifies the *actual* parameters, which provides the values of the formal parameters. There are several so-called *modes* of passing each parameter:

- *Constant mode*: the formal parameter essentially identifies a constant; the actual parameter gives its value. This is also known as *call by value*.

- *Copy mode*: the formal parameter identifies a local variable; the actual parameter gives its *initial* value. This is sometimes referred to as 'value-mode'.

  There is a variant of copy mode where the final value of the variable identified by the formal parameter is copied back; then, of course, the actual parameter has to be variable, which is not required otherwise.

- *Reference mode*: the formal parameter identifies a nonlocal variable, given by the actual parameter.

- *Name mode*: the formal parameter essentially identifies a parameterless function; the actual parameter gives an expression, corresponding to the body of the function, to be evaluated each time the value of the formal parameter is required. This is also known as *call by name*.

Name mode parameters correspond closely to *lazy* entities in functional programming languages such as HASKELL, as they are not evaluated at all until required. There is a variant of name mode known as *call by need*, corresponding to *full laziness* or *memoization* in the terminology of functional programming: the value given by the first evaluation of the parameter is stored, so that subsequent evaluations may give it immediately. Although this is often regarded as a mere implementation technique, the semantics of name mode and call by need are generally different, for example in the presence of side effects.

ADA has three modes of parameter passing, called *in* mode, *in-out* mode, and *out* mode. These correspond *roughly* to constant mode, copy mode, and reference mode, although implementations are allowed to choose (for some types of parameters) between copying and referencing.

The modes of parameters are generally not evident from the syntax of calls: it is necessary to consult the declaration of the formal parameters of a subprogram to see whether the actual parameters are supposed to be variable or values.

Usually, the formal parameters indicate the *types* of actual parameters that are allowed in calls. These types are useful for modular type-checking of programs: the body of a subprogram can be checked independently of the calls. The types are also needed for allocating variables in copy mode. For functions, the type of result is generally indicated as well.

Various restrictions may be placed on the types of data that can be passed as parameters, and given as the results of function calls. Both simple and structured values and variables are usually allowed as parameters; only values are allowed as results, moreover these are often restricted to be simple values—although the use of access values can simulate returning variables and compound values. Packages and types are not usually allowed as parameters, nor as results.

As might be expected, functional programming languages allow functions to be passed as parameters and, in general, returned as results. But in fact also many conventional programming languages, PASCAL for instance, allow subprograms as parameters. ADA was a step backwards in that respect: it doesn't allow subprograms as parameters at all—except in connection with so-called *generic* declarations.

Name mode parameter passing is essentially a special case of passing a function as a parameter: the actual parameter in a call determines a function expression, thus avoiding the need for declaring the function separately.

Finally, there is the matter of the correspondence between formal and actual parameters. This may be indicated by *position*: the formal and actual parameters are paired off in the order that they are written. Or it may be indicated by *identifier*: each actual parameter specifies the corresponding formal parameter identifier. These constructs can even be mixed, although then it is usual to insist that the positional parameters come first. Formal parameters may provide *defaults* for missing actual parameters; then different calls of the same subprogram may have different numbers of actual parameters. This is more convenient with identified parameters than with positional ones.

/AD

Abstract Syntax (*continued*)

    Declarations (*continued*)

        needs: **Statements**.

    Statements (*continued*)

    Expressions (*continued*)

Semantic Functions (*continued*)

    Declarations (*continued*)

        needs: **Statements**.

    Statements (*continued*)

    Expressions (*continued*)

Semantic Entities (*continued*)

    Sorts (*continued*)

    Subprograms

        Modes

        Arguments

        Functions

        Procedures

        Escapes

        Errors

16.1   /AD/Abstract Syntax *(continued)*

16.1.1   Declarations *(continued)*

needs: Statements .

grammar:

- Declaration = □ | ⟦ "function" Identifier ⟨ "(" Formals ")" ⟩$^?$ "return" Nominator "is" Block ";" ⟧ | ⟦ "procedure" Identifier ⟨ "(" Formals ")" ⟩$^?$ "is" Block ";" ⟧ .

- Formal = ⟦ Identifier ":" Mode$^?$ Nominator ⟧ .

- Formals = ⟨ Formal ⟨ ";" Formal ⟩* ⟩ .

- Mode = "in" | ⟨ "in" "out" ⟩ | "out" .

Following ADA, parameterless functions and procedures omit the parentheses as well as the formals; and a missing formal parameter mode is equivalent to the mode "in". Functions are supposed to have only "in" mode formals.

16.1.2   Statements *(continued)*

grammar:

- Statement = □ | ⟦ Identifier ";" ⟧ |
  ⟦ Nominator "." Identifier ";" ⟧ |
  ⟦ Nominator "(" Actuals ")" ";" ⟧ |
  ⟦ "return" Expression$^?$ ";" ⟧ .

- Block = ⟨ Declaration* "begin" Statement$^+$ "end" ⟩ .

The first three new statement constructs above are procedure calls. The syntax of a procedure call could be specified to be simply a nominator, but it is a bit more convenient for the semantic equations in Chapter 17 when we separate the various forms of nominator, as here, because ⟦ N "." I ⟧ can also be a task entry call.

The return statement with no expression is intended for use in procedure bodies, whereas that with an expression is for use in function bodies. This restriction is actually context-free, but to specify it syntactically would require almost duplicating the entire grammar for statements!

A block is essentially a statement with some local declarations. In AD, following ADA, blocks can occur directly in ordinary statement sequences, whereas in PASCAL, for example, they can only occur in subprogram declarations.

16.1.3   Expressions (*continued*)

grammar:

- Name   = □ | ⟦ Name "(" Actuals ")" ⟧ .
- Actuals   = Expressions | Associations |
                  ⟨ Expressions "," Associations⟩ .

We have to include the syntax of function calls in the sort Name, since a parameterless function call is just a nominator, and a parameterized one can be confused with an array component selection—in the absence of context-sensitive information about the declarations of identifiers. The semantic equations below reveal how this syntactic confusion is resolved.

Note that we are allowing mixtures of positional and identified actual parameters, but insisting that any positional parameters come first, as in ADA.

16.2   /AD/Semantic Functions (*continued*)

16.2.1   Declarations (*continued*)

introduces: the mode of _ , the modes of _ , actualize _ .

16.2.1.1   Elaborating Declarations (*continued*)

- elaborate _ :: Declaration* → action
    [binding | diverging | storing] [using current bindings | current storage] .

Declaration elaboration may involve expression evaluation, which may now diverge (due to function calls) so we have to *change* the previous functionality to the one shown above. Similarly for other semantic functions that we extend below.

(1)   elaborate ⟨ ⟩ = complete .

(2)   elaborate ⟦ "function" I:Identifier "return" N:Nominator "is" B:Block ";" ⟧ =
          bind the token of I to
                    parameterless function of the closure of abstraction of
                    | execute B and then err "No returned value"
                    trap give the returned-value of the given function-return .

The use of closure _ above ensures static bindings: the execution of the block B when the function is called receives the same bindings as the declaration. These bindings, however, do not include that for I itself, so *self-referential*, or *recursive*, calls of the function are not possible. In fact it is easy to allow self-reference: just change 'bind' to 'recursively bind' in the semantics equations for **elaborate** D. But it is not quite so straightforward to allow *mutual* reference. Appendix A shows how this can be done, using indirect bindings (directly!).

Performance of the action **err** D may here be understood as a special kind of committed failure. Appendix A uses communicative action notation, illustrated in Chapter 17, to specify that an error message is to be sent before failing.

Notice that an enaction of an abstraction bound to a function identifier can only complete when the execution of the block escapes, giving a function-return. If the execution of the block escapes for any other reason, or completes, the enaction fails.

(3)   **elaborate** ⟦ "function" I:Identifier "(" F:Formals ")"
                        "return" N:Nominator "is" B:Block ";" ⟧ =
        bind the token of I **to**
            parameterized function of the closure of abstraction of
            | **furthermore actualize** F **thence**
            | | **execute** B **and then err** "No returned value"
            | **trap give the returned-value of the given function-return** .

The action **actualize** F gives a map that is used in the semantics of parameterized procedures below, in connection with in-out parameters. Here, we have no use for the map, since the formal parameters of functions are supposed to be always "in" parameters. We use **thence**, rather than **hence**, so as to forget about the given map.

(4)   **elaborate** ⟦ "procedure" I:Identifier "is" B:Block ";" ⟧ =
        bind the token of I **to**
            parameterless procedure of the closure of abstraction of
            | **execute** B
            | **trap check there is given a procedure-return** .

Above we see that enaction of the abstraction can complete when the block execution completes, i.e., without executing a return statement, in contrast to the semantics of function declarations.

(5)   **elaborate** ⟦ "procedure" I:Identifier "(" F:Formals ")" "is" B:Block ";" ⟧ =
        bind the token of I **to**
            parameterized modalized (the modes of F,
                procedure of the closure of abstraction of
                | **furthermore actualize** F **thence**
                | | **execute** B
                | | **trap check there is given a procedure-return**
                | **and then copy-back the given map [token to variable]**) .

The action copy-back Y is *ad hoc*, see Section 16.3.2. The performance of actualize F above not only *produces* bindings for the formal parameters, it also *gives* a map corresponding to the bindings for copy-mode parameters. This map is exploited to copy back the final values of the local formal parameter variables to the actual parameter variables.

The operation modalized (m, p) attaches the modes m to a procedure p, so that formal-modes of p can obtain them when procedure call statements are executed. See Section 16.3.2. If you look at the corresponding module of Appendix A, Section A.3.11, ignore everything concerning procedure *heads*, which are only relevant for the semantics of full AD.

16.2.1.2 Modes

- the mode of _ :: Mode$^?$ → mode .

(1)   the mode of ⟨ ⟩ = the constant-mode .

(2)   the mode of "in" = the constant-mode .

(3)   the mode of ⟨ "in" "out" ⟩ = the copy-mode .

(4)   the mode of "out" = the reference-mode .

16.2.1.3 Modes of Formal Parameters

- the modes of _ :: Formals → modes .

(1)   the modes of ⟦ I:Identifier ":" M:Mode$^?$ N:Nominator ⟧ =
         (the mode of M, map of the token of I to the mode of M).

(2)   the modes of ⟨ F_1:Formal ";" F_2:Formals ⟩ =
         the combined-modes of (the modes of F_1, the modes of F_2) .

We need not only a tuple of modes, but also a *map* from tokens to modes, for dealing with identified parameter associations. The sort modes is defined in refpr-se-sub.

16.2.1.4 Actualizing Formal Parameters

- actualize _ :: Formals → action
     [binding | giving a map [token to variable] | storing]
     [using given arguments | current bindings | current storage] .

The given arguments may be either a tuple of individual arguments, a map from tokens to arguments, or a tuple concatenated with a map, according to whether the actual parameters are passed by position or identifier. The map of tokens to variables given by actualization is used for copying-back the values of copy-mode parameters on procedure return.

(1)   actualize ⟦ I:identifier ":" M :"in" ? N:Nominator ⟧ =
       bind the token of I to the value yielded by
             (the first of the given arguments | (the given map at the token of I))
       and give the empty-map .

(2)   actualize ⟦ I:identifier ":" "out" N:Nominator ⟧ =
       bind the token of I to the variable yielded by
             (the first of the given arguments | (the given map at the token of I))
       and give the empty-map .

(3)   actualize ⟦ I:identifier ":" "in" "out" N:Nominator ⟧ =
       │ give the variable yielded by
       │   (the first of the given arguments | (the given map at the token of I))
       │ and allocate a variable for the type yielded by the entity nominated by N
       then
       │ bind the token of I to the given variable#2 and
       │ give map of the token of I to the given variable#1 and
       │ assign (the value assigned to the given variable#1)
       │   to the given variable#2 .

(4)   actualize ⟨ F_1:Formal ";" F_2:Formals ⟩ =
       │ actualize F_1 and
       │   │ give (the rest of the given (argument,arguments) | the given map)
       │   then actualize F_2
       then give the disjoint-union of (the given map#1, the given map#2) .

When the given **arguments** entity is just a map, the effect is for it to be passed on unchanged to actualize F_2 above. We don't bother to check that all named actual parameters correspond to formal parameters.

16.2.2   Statements (*continued*)

16.2.2.1   Executing Statements (*continued*)

  • execute _ :: Statement⁺ → action
       [completing | escaping with an escape-reason | diverging | storing]
       [using current bindings | current storage] .

Previously, we only used an escape to represent an exit from a loop. Now we need escapes also to represent returns from function and procedure block executions. Of course a return must not be prevented by an enclosing loop statement—although an untrapped exit in a function or procedure block is illegal, so we may let that fail. Thus we have to modify our previous semantics for loop statements to ensure the propagation of non-exit escapes.

The **trap** combinator is the only part of action notation that has rather poor modifiability: when one introduces a new sort of escape, one has to re-examine each occurrence of **trap**, and usually extend the action that follows it to specify explicitly how the new escapes are to be treated. But this doesn't involve large-scale changes at all, and in practice the burden of making the necessary changes is negligible.

(1)   execute ⟦ "loop" S:Statement$^+$ "end" "loop" ";" ⟧ =
      | unfolding
      | | execute S and then unfold
      trap
      | | check there is given an exit
      or
      | | check there is given a return and then escape .

Recall from Chapter 5 that there is x is either **true** or **nothing**—never **false**. Thus one shouldn't ever write something like check not there is given an exit, as it *always* fails.

(2)   execute ⟦ "exit" ";" ⟧ = escape with an exit .

(3)   execute ⟦ I:Identifier ";" ⟧ =
      enact the procedure-abstraction of
         the parameterless procedure bound to the token of I .

(4)   execute ⟦ N:Nominator "." I:Identifier ";" ⟧ =
      give the entity nominated by N then
      | produce the public-bindings of the given package hence
      | enact the procedure-abstraction of
      | the parameterless procedure bound to the token of I .

(5)   execute ⟦ N:Nominator "(" A:Actuals ")" ";" ⟧ =
      give the entity nominated by N then
      | give the procedure-abstraction of the given procedure and
      | give the formal-modes of the given parameterized procedure then
      | moderate A
      then enact the application of the given abstraction#1
            to the arguments yielded by the rest of the given data .

(6)   execute ⟦ "return" ";" ⟧ = escape with a procedure-return .

(7)   execute ⟦ "return" E:Expression ";" ⟧ =
      evaluate E then escape with function-return of the given value .

16.2.2.2   Executing Blocks

- execute _ :: Block → action
      [escaping with an escape-reason | diverging | storing]
      [using current bindings | current storage] .

(1)   execute ⟨ "begin" S:Statement⁺ "end" ⟩ = execute S .

(2)   execute ⟨ D:Declaration⁺ "begin" S:Statement⁺ "end" ⟩ =
      furthermore elaborate D hence execute S .

16.2.3   Expressions (continued)

introduces: moderate _ .

16.2.3.1   Investigating Names

- investigate _ :: Name → action
      [giving a (package | value | variable | parameterized function) | diverging | storing]
      [using current bindings | current storage] .

The syntactic confusion between function calls and other constructs requires us to
change a couple of earlier semantic equations for name investigation, as follows. These
changes would *not* be needed if parameterless function calls were indicated by empty
parentheses, and if parameterized function calls distinguished from array component
selections by using different kinds of brackets, as in most languages. But the changes
below merely add further alternatives to subactions, so from a pragmatic point of
view they are almost as simple as genuine extensions.

(1)   investigate I:Identifier =
      give the entity bound to the token of I then
      | give the given (package | value | variable | parameterized function) or
      | enact the function-abstraction of the given parameterless function .

Going from a parameterless function to its value is a kind of *coercion*.

(2)   investigate ⟦ N:Name "(" A:Actuals ")" ⟧ =
      | investigate N and evaluate A
      then
      | give the component of
      | (the array accessible from the given (value | variable)#1,
      | the index-value yielded by the rest of the given data) or
      | enact the application of
      | the function-abstraction of the given parameterized function#1
      | to the arguments yielded by the rest of the given data .

16.2.3.2   Accessing Expressions

- access _ :: Expression → action
  [giving a variable | diverging | storing] [using current bindings | current storage] .

We need to use access _ on expressions in the semantic equations for moderating actual parameters, below. In fact *legal* programs must have *names* as actual parameters of procedure calls whenever these correspond to out or in-out formal parameters; but we cannot restrict our context-free abstract syntax to legal programs.

(1) E & Name = nothing ⇒ access E:Expression = err "Illegal program" .

16.2.3.3   Evaluating Expressions (*continued*)

- evaluate _ :: Expression → action
  [giving a value | diverging | storing]
  [using current bindings | current storage] .

We have to change the semantic equations for evaluating expressions in the same ways as those for investigating names, for the same reasons as explained above.

(1)   evaluate I:Identifier =
           give the entity bound to the token of I then
           | give (the given value | the value assigned to the given variable) or
           | enact the function-abstraction of the given parameterless function .

(2)   evaluate ⟦ N:Name "(" A:Actuals ")" ⟧ =
           | investigate N and evaluate A
           then
           | give the component of
           | (the given array-value#1,
           | the index-value yielded by the rest of the given data) or
           | give the value assigned to the component of
           | (the array-variable accessible from the given (access | variable)#1,
           | the index-value yielded by the rest of the given data) or
           | enact the application of
           | the function-abstraction of the given parameterized function#1
           | to the arguments yielded by the rest of the given data .

The above semantic equation exploits the fact that actual parameters of functions are always of in-mode, so they can be evaluated in the same way as indices in array component selections. If this were not the case, we would have to discover whether N is bound to an array or to a function before evaluating the actuals.

16.2.3.4 Evaluating Actual Parameters

- evaluate _ :: Actuals → action
    [giving arguments | diverging | storing]
    [using current bindings | current storage] .

(1) evaluate ⟨ *E*:Expressions "," *A*:Associations ⟩ = evaluate *E* and evaluate *A* .

Here, *E* is the list of parameters passed by position, and *A* is the list of those passed by name. See Section 13.2.1.1 and Section 14.2.3.4 for the definition of evaluate _ on Expressions and Associations, respectively.

16.2.3.5 Moderating Actual Parameters

- moderate _ :: Expressions → action
    [giving argument[+] | diverging | storing]
    [using given modes | current bindings | current storage] .

Whereas ordinary evaluation of actual parameters is sufficient when these occur in function calls, it is dependent on modes when the parameters occur in procedure calls.

(1) moderate *E*:Expression =
        give the first of the given modes then
        | | check either (it is the reference-mode, it is the copy-mode)
        | | then access *E*
        | or
        | | check (it is the constant-mode)
        | | then evaluate *E* .

(2) moderate ⟨ *E*₁:Expression "," *E*₂:Expressions ⟩ =
        moderate *E*₁ and
        | give the rest of the given modes then moderate *E*₂ .

In fact an entity of sort modes consists of an arbitrary number of individual modes, followed by a map from formal parameter tokens to modes. In legal programs, there are never more positional actual parameters than formal parameters for each function and procedure, so rest _ never gets applied to a modes entity that consists only of a map. (It would return the empty tuple if it were to be so applied; that would provoke a failure when dealing with the next actual parameter.)

16.2.3.6   Moderating Associations

- moderate _ :: Associations → action
  [giving a map [token to argument] | diverging | storing]
  [using given modes | current bindings | current storage] .

(1)   moderate ⟦ I:Identifier "=>" E:Expression ⟧ =
         give (the entire-mode-map of the given modes at the token of I) then
         | check either (it is the reference-mode, it is the copy-mode)
         | then access E
         or
         | check (it is the constant-mode)
         | then evaluate E
         then give map of the token of I to the given argument .

(2)   moderate ⟨ A_1:Association "," A_2:Associations ⟩ =
         | moderate A_1 and moderate A_2
         then give the disjoint-union of (the given map#1, the given map#2) .

16.2.3.7   Moderating Actual Parameters

- moderate _ :: Actuals → action
  [giving arguments | diverging | storing]
  [using given modes | current bindings | current storage] .

(1)   moderate ⟨ E:Expressions "," A:Associations ⟩ = moderate E and moderate A .

Some of the subtleties with tuples above could be avoided by using list [of argument] instead of argument*, but the semantic equations would be clumsier.

16.3   /AD/Semantic Entities (*continued*)

includes: Action Notation/Reflective .

16.3.1   Sorts (*continued*)

- entity = value | package | variable | type | function | procedure | □ .
- datum = entity | bindings | natural | escape-reason | mode | □ .

See Appendix A for the details of the modules specified below. You may ignore the details concerning function and procedure heads, which are only relevant for the semantics of full AD.

16.3.2   Subprograms

16.3.2.1   Modes

- mode   = constant-mode | copy-mode | reference-mode (*individual*) .
- modes   = (mode*, map [token to mode]) .
- combined-modes _ :: (modes, modes) → modes (*total*) .
- entire-mode-map _ :: modes → map [token to mode] (*total*) .

16.3.2.2   Arguments

- argument = value | variable .
- arguments = (argument*, [token to argument] map?) .
- copy-back _ :: map [token to variable] → action [completing | storing] .

16.3.2.3   Functions

- function of _   :: abstraction → function (*partial*) .
- function-abstraction _ :: function → abstraction (*total*) .
- parameterless _   :: function → function (*partial*) .
- parameterized _   :: function → function (*partial*) .

It is convenient to exploit the sort *terms* parameterless function and parameterized function, which are both subsorts of function, rather than introducing corresponding sort *constants*. Similarly for procedures, below.

16.3.2.4   Procedures

- procedure of _   :: abstraction → procedure (*partial*) .
- procedure-abstraction _ :: procedure → abstraction (*total*) .
- parameterless _   :: procedure → procedure (*partial*) .
- parameterized _   :: procedure → procedure (*partial*) .
- modalized _   :: (modes, procedure) → procedure (*partial*) .
- formal-modes _   :: procedure → modes (*partial*) .

16.3.3   Escapes

- escape-reason   = exit | return (*disjoint*) .
- exit   : escape-reason .
- return   = function-return | procedure-return (*disjoint*) .
- function-return of _ :: value → function-return (*total*) .
- returned-value _   :: function-return → value (*total*) .
- procedure-return   : return .

16.3.4   Errors

- error of _ :: string → error (*total*) .
- err _   :: string → action (*total*) .

The definition of err D given in Appendix A uses communicative action notation. For now, let us assume that err D = commit and then fail.

Summary

- *The semantics of a subprogram is essentially an abstraction. The encapsulated action elaborates the formal parameters using the arguments given by the actual parameters, and executes the body block.*

- *When there are different modes of parameter evaluation, the semantics of a subprogram includes the modes of its parameters as components.*

- *Name-mode parameters correspond to anonymous, parameterless functions, passed in constant-mode.*

- *For static bindings, abstractions are made into closures immediately, whereas for dynamic bindings this is left until just before calling.*

- *Returns are represented by escapes, which give data that distinguish them from escapes representing other constructs.*

Navigation

- *If you are curious about the full specification of the semantic entities used here, see the corresponding modules in Appendix A.*

- *Now look at Chapter 10, which introduces communicative actions, before proceeding with Part III.*

Exercises

1. The following syntax corresponds to the so-called λ-*calculus with atoms*:

   - Expression = Identifier | Atom |

                 ⟦ "λ" Identifier "." Expression ⟧ |

                 ⟦ Expression "(" Expression ")" ⟧ .

   - Identifier = □ .

   - Atom = □ .

   The intended semantics is that λ-abstractions ⟦ "λ" I "." E ⟧ evaluate to functions with single name-mode parameters. Atoms are assumed to evaluate to non-functional entities.

   (a) Give an action semantic description of this λ-calculus.

   (b) Argue that when the evaluation of E_2 does not depend on any bindings, the evaluation of the application ⟦ ⟦ "λ" I "." E ⟧ "(" E_2 ")" ⟧ is equivalent to that of the expression obtained by substituting E_2 for every occurrence of I in E, except inside further λ-abstractions on I.

   (c) Consider what modifications would be needed to change from name-mode to constant-mode parameter passing, where actual parameters in an application are always evaluated before the evaluation of body of the applied abstraction is started.

   (d) Modify your description of the λ-calculus so that the first time a parameter is evaluated, its value is recorded, to avoid recomputation with subsequent evaluations of that same parameter. Hint: use cells to store closures *or* atomic values.

2. Add name-mode parameter passing to parameterized procedures in AD, and specify the intended semantics.

3. Consider extending AD with the following abstract syntax:

grammar:

- Statement = □ | ⟦ "goto" Identifier ";" ⟧ |
                     ⟦ "begin" Statement$^+$ "<<" Identifier ">>" "end" ";" ⟧ .

The intended semantics is (roughly) that the identifier at the end of a block
labels that block, so that executing a goto statement with that identifier causes
a jump out of the block, whereafter execution continues normally.

(a) Specify semantic equations for the new constructs. Do any of the semantic
    equations already given for AD need changing? If so, which? You should
    assume here that the jump is only out of the most recent block execution
    with the specified label, which corresponds to dynamic scopes for label
    identifiers. Hint: it isn't necessary to bind label identifiers at all!

(b) Change your semantic equations so that when a goto statement occurs in a
    procedure body, executing it always exits to the same textually-enclosing
    block with the specified label, which corresponds to static scopes. Hint:
    allocate a cell then bind the label indentifier to it.

(c) Extend AD to allow labels on arbitrary statements, to be visible through-
    out the enclosing block. As in ADA, do not allow jumps *into* statements.
    Hint: define a subsidiary semantic function for 'jumping into' a statement
    sequence at a particular label.

Chapter 17

Tasks

- *Task declarations initiate concurrent processes, which can synchronize using entry calls and accept statements. The select statement may now iterate until an entry call can be accepted.*

- *The semantics of task declarations illustrates the use of the communicative action notation introduced in Chapter 10.*

- *Semantic entities now include agents, and various signals sent in messages. They also include entities that represent open alternatives of selections.*

Let us first consider the treatment of *input* and *output* in programming languages. By definition, the *input* of a program is the information that is supplied to it by the user; the *output* is the information that the user gets back. However, it is important to take into account not only *what* information is supplied, but also *when* the supply takes place. We may distinguish between so-called *batch* and *interactive* input-output.

With *batch* input, all the input to the program is supplied at the start of the program. The input may then be regarded as *stored*, in a file. Batch output is likewise accumulated in a file, and only given to the user when (if ever) the program terminates. On the other hand, *interactive* input is provided gradually, as a *stream* of data, while the program is running; the program may have to wait for further input data to be provided before it can proceed. Similarly, interactive output is provided to the user while the program is running, as soon as it has been determined. Interactive input-output allows later items of input to depend on earlier items of output. For instance, input may be stimulated by an output *prompt*.

We may regard batch input-output as merely a special case of interactive input-output: the program starts, and then immediately reads and stores the entire input; output is stored until the program is about to terminate, and then the entire output is

195

given to the user. The essential difference between batch and interactive input-output shows up in connection with programs that are intended to have the possibility of running 'for ever': batch input-output is not appropriate for the intended semantics of such programs. Familiar examples are traffic-light controllers, operating systems, and screen editors. These programs might, if allowed, read a never-ending stream of input, and emit a corresponding stream of output; in practice they also recognize some special input as a signal to stop. Moreover, once an item of output has been emitted, it cannot be revoked by the program, e.g., the traffic-light controller cannot *undo* the changing of a light.

Now suppose that several interactive programs may be run together, i.e., *concurrently*, and that data output by one program may be input by another. This gives a system of so-called *communicating processes*. There are many design issues in connection with languages for communicating processes. For instance, communication may be asynchronous, or may involve so-called *rendezvous*. The partners for communication may be specified directly, or indirectly by means of *channels*. There can be nondeterministic choices between alternative communications, and *time-outs*. Shared variables may or may not be permitted.

An aim of action semantics is to allow the semantics of all languages to be described straightforwardly. However, the communicative part of action notation is based on the notion of *direct, asynchronous* communication between distributed processes, because of its operational simplicity. To describe, say, synchronous channel-based communication, we have to introduce not only agents corresponding to the processes themselves, but also *auxiliary agents* representing the channels—and to find a *protocol* for asynchronous message passing such that the overall effect is essentially the intended synchronization. Similarly, shared storage is not built-in: allocation and assignment of variables shared between different processes has to be represented using communication primitives.

In practice, the explication of such high-level programming constructs in terms of asynchronous communicating actions is quite illuminating—more so than it would have been had the communicative part of action notation been based on some particular kind of synchronous communication, it seems. For instance, an action semantic description of CCS or CSP indicates that subsidiary arbiter agents are required for implementing synchronization (unless symmetry is broken somehow).

Tasks in ADA can synchronize and communicate with each other by means of *rendezvous*. One task must make a definite commitment to a rendezvous with another specified task, by means of an *entry* call. The other task must then execute a statement that *accepts* the entry, for the rendezvous to take place. The entry may determine some parameter values. Tasks are initialized dynamically, and they are allowed to *share* variables. There are many other features, such as delays, termination conditions, and selective waiting. Our illustrative language AD includes only a very simple version of tasks, focusing on the notion of rendezvous.

/AD

Abstract Syntax (*continued*)

Programs
needs: Expressions, Declarations.

Declarations (*continued*)

Statements (*continued*)

Semantic Functions (*continued*)

Programs
needs: Expressions, Declarations.

Declarations (*continued*)

Statements (*continued*)

Semantic Entities (*continued*)

Sorts (*continued*)

Tasks

Alternatives

Required Bindings

17.1 /AD/Abstract Syntax (*continued*)

17.1.1 Programs

grammar:

- Program = ⟦ Declaration⁺ Nominator ⟧ .

In legal ADA programs, the top-level declarations are compilation units, which are essentially just packages, subprograms, and tasks. Here we do not bother to exclude other sorts of declaration, such as constant and variable declarations. Let us assume that the nominator of a program indicates a main procedure, without parameters, to be called when the program is run.

17.1.2   Declarations (*continued*)

grammar:

- Declaration = □ | ⟦ "task" Identifier "is" Entry⁺ "end" ";" ⟧ |
  ⟦ "task" "body" Identifier "is" Block ";" ⟧ .
- Entry   = ⟦ "entry" Identifier ";" ⟧ .

Task heads are supposed to be declared before the corresponding bodies, although we don't bother to insist on this in our grammar above. We retain the entries of a task head only for the sake of familiarity, as they are irrelevant to our dynamic semantics.

17.1.3   Statements (*continued*)

grammar:

- Statement = □ | ⟦ Nominator "." Identifier ";" ⟧ |
  ⟦ "accept" Identifier ⟨ "do" Statement⁺ "end" ⟩⁷ ";" ⟧ |
  ⟦ "select" Alternatives
  ⟨ "else" Statement⁺ ⟩⁷ "end" "select" ";" ⟧ .

In Chapter 11 we already gave a semantics for else-less select statements in AD. Below, we give a *different* one, closer to the semantics of ADA, as well as describing select-else statements.

The statement ⟦ N "." I ⟧ might either be a call of a packaged parameterless procedure, or a call of entry I in task N. The semantic equations resolve this context-sensitive distinction. For simplicity, we omit parameterized entry calls.

The full syntax of alternatives in ADA *insists* that the statements of each alternative must start with an accept statement; delay statements and terminate statements are also allowed. In AD, an alternative *may* start with an accept statement, in which case the execution of the accept statement is treated essentially as part of the guard. Moreover, in AD we avoid issues related to timing, whose implementation-independent aspects are somewhat obscure.

17.2   /AD/Semantic Functions (*continued*)

17.2.1   Programs

introduces: run _ .

- run _ :: Program → action
  [completing | diverging | storing | communicating]
  [using current storage | current buffer] .

(1)   run $[\![$ D:Declaration$^+$ N:Nominator $]\!]$ =
     produce required-bindings hence
     furthermore elaborate D hence
       | give the entity nominated by N then
       | enact the procedure-abstraction of the given parameterless procedure
       | and then
       | send a message [to the user-agent] [containing the terminated-signal] .

The termination message sent above insists that the user should be able to notice
when the program has terminated; this might be useful when the user runs the
program on a remote agent. See the end of Appendix A for the definition of the
bindings of required identifiers in AD. The analogous definition for full ADA would
be substantially larger!

17.2.2   Declarations (*continued*)

17.2.2.1   Elaborating Declarations (*continued*)

- elaborate _ :: Declaration* $\rightarrow$ action
     [binding | diverging | storing | communicating]
     [using current bindings | current storage | current buffer] .

(1)   elaborate $[\![$ "task" I:Identifier "is" E:Entry$^+$ "end" ";" $]\!]$ =
     offer a contract [to any task-agent]
        [containing abstraction of the initial task-action] and then
       | receive a message [containing a task-agent] then
       | bind the token of I to
           the task yielded by the contents of the given message .

The action initial task-action is defined in **Semantic Entities/Tasks** below. Note
that the corresponding definition in Appendix A involves the sending of a begin-signal,
which is used in the full semantics of AD for synchronizing the tasks declared in a
block before starting to execute the block body.

(2)   elaborate $[\![$ "task" "body" I:Identifier "is" B:Block ";" $]\!]$ =
     send a message [to the task-agent bound to the token of I]
        [containing task of the closure of abstraction of execute B] .

Executions of task blocks receive all the bindings that were current where their body
was declared. These may include bindings to other tasks: a system of communicating
tasks can be set up by first declaring all the heads, then all the bodies. They may
also include bindings to variables; but attempts to assign to these variables, or to
inspect their values, always fail, because the cells referred to are not local to the

agent performing the action. It is a bit complicated to describe the action semantics
of distributed tasks that have access to shared variables—the task that declares a
variable has to act as a server for assignments and inspections—so we let AD deviate
from ADA in this respect.

17.2.3   Statements (*continued*)

introduces: exhaust _ , the selectability of _ .

17.2.3.1   Executing Statements (*continued*)

- execute _ :: Statement$^+$ → action
  [completing | escaping with an escape-reason | diverging | storing | communicating]
  [using current bindings | current storage | current buffer] .

(1)   execute ⟦ N:Nominator "." I:Identifier ";" ⟧ =
       give the entity nominated by N then
       │ │ produce the public-bindings of the given package hence
       │ │ enact the procedure-abstraction of
       │ │   the parameterless procedure bound to the token of I
       │ or
       │ │ send a message [to the given task-agent]
       │ │   [containing entry of the token of I] and then
       │ │ receive a message [from the given task-agent]
       │ │   [containing the done-signal] .

The above equation *replaces* the one specified for parameterless procedure calls in
Chapter 16. But it is essentially an extension: the original equation can be found
inside the new one.

(2)   execute ⟦ "accept" I:Identifier "end" ";" ⟧ =
       receive a message [from any task-agent]
           [containing entry of the token of I] then
       send a message [to the sender of the given message]
           [containing the done-signal] .

(3)   execute ⟦ "accept" I:Identifier "do" S:Statement$^+$ "end" ";" ⟧ =
       receive a message [from any task-agent]
           [containing entry of the token of I] then
       │ execute S and then
       │ send a message [to the sender of the given message]
       │   [containing the done-signal] .

Compare the following semantic equation with that given for select statements in Chapter 11. The one given here requires *iteration* in case none of the alternatives are open. This is fairly close to ADA, except that ADA insists that any conditions in guards only get evaluated once, thereby determining a fixed set of communication (or time-out) possibilities.

(4)   execute ⟦ "select" A:Alternatives "end" "select" ";" ⟧ =
     | unfolding
     | | exhaust A and then unfold
     trap
     | enact the alternative-abstraction of the given alternative .

The following semantics for select-else statements allows normal termination in case all alternatives are exhausted.

(5)   execute ⟦ "select" A:Alternatives "else" S:Statement$^+$ "end" "select" ";" ⟧ =
     | exhaust A and then
     | escape with alternative of the closure of abstraction of execute S
     trap
     | enact the alternative-abstraction of the given alternative .

17.2.3.2 Exhausting Alternatives

- exhaust _ :: Alternatives → action
  [escaping with an alternative | diverging | storing | communicating]
  [using current bindings | current storage | current buffer] .

(1)   exhaust S:Statement$^+$ =
     give the selectability of S then
     | | check the given truth-value and then
     | | escape with alternative of the closure of abstraction of execute S
     | or
     | | check not the given truth-value .

(2)   exhaust ⟦ "when" E:Expression "=>" S:Statement$^+$ ⟧ =
     evaluate E then
     | check the given truth-value and then exhaust S
     | or
     | check not the given truth-value .

(3)   exhaust ⟨ A_1:Alternative "or" A_2:Alternatives ⟩ = exhaust A_1 and exhaust A_2 .

Notice the use of _ and _ , rather than _ or _ ! This specifies that an implementation is obliged to go through all the cases, but the order is left open, and testing the remaining alternatives may be abandoned as soon as an open alternative has been found. With _ or _ instead, expression evaluation in guards might commit the performance prematurely to an alternative that is later found not to be open. Moreover, it wouldn't be possible to specify an action corresponding to the select-else statement, because failure cannot be trapped (asymmetrically), in contrast to escape.

17.2.3.3   Selectability

- the selectability of _ :: Statement$^+$ → yielder [of truth-value] [using current buffer] .

(1)   the selectability of ⟨ S_1:Statement S_2:Statement$^+$ ⟩ = the selectability of S_1 .

(2)   the selectability of ⟦ "accept" I:Identifier X:⟨ "do" Statement$^+$ ⟩$^?$ ";" ⟧ = the token of I is entered in the current buffer .

(3) S & ⟦ "accept" Identifier ⟨ "do" Statement$^+$ ⟩$^?$ ";" ⟧ = nothing ⇒ the selectability of S:Statement = true .

This last semantic equation demonstrates a convenient way to abbreviate a large number of similar equations.

17.3   /AD/Semantic Entities (*continued*)

includes: Action Notation/Communicative .

17.3.1   Sorts (*continued*)

- entity   = value | package | variable | type | function | procedure | task .
- datum   = entity | bindings | natural | escape-reason | mode | alternative | message | entry | error .
- sendable = agent | task | entry | signal | error | □ .

We still leave sendable open, since standard action notation has already included some data in it.

Appendix A gives the details of the remaining modules.

17.3.2 Tasks

- task-agent $\leq$ agent .
- task of _ :: abstraction $\rightarrow$ task (*total*) .
- task-abstraction _ :: task $\rightarrow$ abstraction (*total*) .
- signal = done-signal | terminated-signal (*individual*) .
- entry of _ :: token $\rightarrow$ entry (*total*) .
- _ is entered in _ :: entry, buffer $\rightarrow$ truth-value (*total*) .
- initial task-action =
  | send a message [to the contracting-agent]
  | [containing the performing-agent] and then
  | receive a message [from the contracting-agent]
  | [containing a task]
  then enact the task-abstraction of
      the task yielded by the contents of the given message .

17.3.3 Alternatives

- alternative of _ :: abstraction $\rightarrow$ alternative (*partial*) .
- alternative-abstraction _ :: alternative $\rightarrow$ abstraction (*total*) .

17.3.4 Required Bindings

- required-bindings = disjoint-union of (
      map of "TRUE" to true,
      map of "FALSE" to false,
      map of "BOOLEAN" to boolean-type,
      map of "MININT" to integer-number min-integer,
      map of "MAXINT" to integer-number max-integer,
      map of "INTEGER" to integer-type,
      map of "REAL" to real-type,
      map of "CHARACTER" to character-type) .

Summary

- *Tasks are represented by agents, and entries by combinations of agents and tokens.*

- *Task declarations are first configured, then the task bodies are sent to the selected task agent as closures incorporating the appropriate bindings.*

- *A rendezvous can be represented by a pair of asynchronous message transmissions.*

- *Selective waiting involves iteratively inspecting the current buffer.*

- *Selecting between alternatives is represented by an exhaustive search for an open alternative, the order being implementation-dependent and with the possibility of terminating the search as soon as an open alternative has been found.*

Navigation

- *Now see Appendix A for the complete action semantics of AD. You might like to compare the semantic equations given there with those given in the preceding chapters, to check that no large-scale modifications were ever necessary during the gradual development of our semantic description.*

- *Then test your ability to formulate a complete action semantic description of a small programming language! See Appendix G for a suggestion.*

- *You may independently proceed to Part IV for a conclusion, which includes a discussion of the relation between action semantics and other frameworks.*

Exercises

1. Change the semantics of tasks so that the execution of the block that initiates some tasks terminates only when all the tasks have themselves terminated. Consider adding termination statements (as in ADA) as alternatives of selection statements.

2. Propose syntax and semantics for interactive input-output between top-level tasks and the user agent.

3. Tasks in ADA may share variables. Consider how the action semantics of AD would need changing to allow shared variables.

4. ADA has delay statements. Discuss the (implementation-independent) semantics of 'real-time' constructs, and how it might be represented in action semantic descriptions.

Part IV

Conclusion

Part IV concludes by briefly relating action semantics to other frameworks, and by sketching its development. It cites the main sources for action semantics and the related frameworks, and mentions some current projects.

Chapter 18

Other Frameworks

- *Denotational semantics has poor pragmatic features, due to its use of the λ-notation.*

- *Several so-called algebraic frameworks are essentially operational.*

- *Genuinely axiomatic frameworks are prone to incompleteness and inconsistency.*

- *Operational semantics is useful; action semantics makes it easier.*

Action semantics is not the only available framework for giving formal semantic descriptions of programming languages. Other frameworks include denotational semantics, various kinds of algebraic semantics, axiomatic semantics, and operational semantics. What is *wrong* with them all? Why should one prefer action semantics—at least for describing full-scale, realistic programming languages?

Let us look *briefly* at most of the other frameworks in turn, pointing out their major defects in comparison to action semantics. To make the discussion accessible to those not familiar with the various frameworks, we indicate their main features, and cite primary references. However, a full appreciation of the comparisons requires in-depth familiarity with both action semantics and the other frameworks, as well as a more thorough discussion than can be provided here.

Almost all frameworks for formal semantics are based on context-free abstract syntax, although the notations that they use to specify abstract syntax are quite varied. The grammars that we use in action semantic descriptions perhaps have some significant advantages over other ways of specifying abstract syntax. But our main interest here is in the essential differences concerning the specification of *semantics*, once abstract syntax has been specified, so let us not pursue this point further.

Concerning *formality*, the inherent disadvantages of informal semantic descriptions were discussed in Chapter 1. You should by now be able to see for yourself the extent to which action semantics combines the *strengths* of informal descriptions—readability, comprehensibility, direct relation to programming concepts—with the essential feature of *formality*. Hence we do not discuss informal descriptions any further.

18.1 Denotational Semantics

Denotational semantics was the starting point for the development of action semantics, so it is hardly surprising that there are substantial similarities between the two frameworks, as well as some significant differences.

Both frameworks involve semantic functions that map abstract syntax, compositionally, to semantic entities. Semantic functions can also be regarded as syntax-directed translations, but it is better to focus on the semantic entities themselves, rather than on how they are expressed. The semantic entity corresponding to a particular phrase in denotational semantics is called its *denotation*. Both frameworks use semantic equations to define the semantic functions. Even the notation $[\![\ldots]\!]$ for abstract syntax trees in action semantics corresponds closely to the use of these so-called emphatic brackets for separating syntactic from semantic notation in denotational descriptions.

The essential difference between denotational and action semantics concerns the nature of semantic *entities*, and the notation used to express them. You know by now about the actions used to represent the semantics of programs and their phrases in action semantics, and about action notation. Denotational semantics uses *higher-order functions* on so-called Scott-domains as semantic entities, and it uses a rich, typed *λ-notation* to express particular functions, together with the values on which the functions are defined. For a summary of denotational semantics and λ-notation, see for example my chapter in the *Handbook of Theoretical Computer Science* [Mos90]; for a fuller account, I recommend Schmidt's book [Sch86].

Higher-order functions on Scott-domains have a rich and elegant mathematical theory, which can be useful when one has to prove that particular phrases enjoy certain semantical properties. Unfortunately, however, the functions required to represent the semantics of the usual constructs of programming languages tend to be rather complex. This stems from the fact that the basic operations on functions provided by the λ-notation—composition, tupling, application, abstraction, etc.—do *not* correspond directly to fundamental concepts of programming languages. These operations may be appropriate for representing the semantics of mathematical formalisms, such as

Church's λ-calculus, and of pure, lazy functional programming languages, but they are so far removed from the constructs of conventional imperative and concurrent programming languages that their use to represent the semantics of these constructs requires elaborate *coding* techniques, which can be quite obscure to the lay reader.

For instance, there are two main techniques for representing the basic concept of sequential execution: strict composition of functions on states, and reverse composition of functions on continuations. In fact the functions composed typically have further arguments, representing context-dependent information, such as the current bindings; this makes the pattern of composition really quite complex, even for representing something so simple as sequencing.

The complexity of purely functional representations makes it difficult to *read* the semantic equations that describe the semantics of a conventional programming language. It is even more difficult to comprehend their operational *implications*—primarily because λ-abstraction corresponds to call-by-name parameter passing, not call-by-value. But the really serious pragmatic problem with denotational descriptions of practical programming languages concerns their poor *modifiability* and *extensibility*. Not only are concepts such as sequencing represented by *complex* patterns of function composition and application, but also it may be necessary to replace these by radically different (although systematically related) patterns when one modifies or extends the features of the described language. For instance, in all textbooks on denotational semantics so far, the simple semantic equations for expression evaluation that are first presented have to be completely reformulated when declarations and statements are added. In a student text, this may be tolerable, although difficult to motivate. In the middle of developing a semantic description of a realistic programming language, it would certainly be discouraging, to say the least, to have to make large-scale reformulations of previous work.

A conventional denotational semantic description is essentially a largish functional program, written in a rather poor programming style where almost all parts of the program are sensitive to the exact structure of the 'data types' involved. It is possible to alleviate some of the pragmatic problems of denotational semantics by introducing *auxiliary notation* that corresponds to action primitives and combinators, defining the interpretation of this action notation as higher-order functions, using the usual λ-notation, instead of defining it operationally as we did in Appendix C. It is instructive to compare this hybrid[1] of denotational and action semantics [Mos91b] with the conventional denotational approach [Mos90]. But note that one can go *too far* in this direction: introducing an *ad hoc* auxiliary operation for *each* language construct

---

[1]Dubbed 'denotactional semantics' by some students at the IFIP WG2.2 Seminar in Petropolis, Brazil, 1989!

merely shifts the content of the semantic equations to the definition of the auxiliary operations, without achieving any improvements in pragmatics.

The use of an adequate auxiliary notation essentially hides the detailed structure of the underlying data types from the semantic equations—turning them almost into *abstract* data types. This greatly improves the comprehensibility, modifiability, and extensibility of the semantic equations, but not that of the definitions of the auxiliary operations: they may still have to be changed considerably when adding new operations, needed to describe an extended language.

An alternative approach to improving the techniques of denotational semantics has been developed by Moggi [Mog89], exploiting the category-theoretic notion of a *monad*. He provides a number of monad constructors that correspond to the main techniques used in denotational semantics for representing the semantics of programming concepts as higher-order functions, and these constructors can be combined in various ways. However, it remains to be seen to what extent these elegant theoretical ideas can form the basis for a practical framework for semantic description, and whether they can be made accessible to programmers, and others, who are not so well acquainted with category theory.

The problems of denotational semantics are not confined to purely pragmatic ones. For instance, it may sometimes be impossible to give even a *reasonably* abstract denotational semantics of a programming language using functions as semantic entities; this seems to be generally the case when using so-called resumptions to represent statement execution, because different numbers of computation steps give different resumptions. Moreover, the treatment of unbounded nondeterminism requires a weaker form of *continuity* than that which is usually assumed. Actually, the whole notion of continuity, which is the basis of domain theory, is only well-motivated in the case that a semantics determines the possible behaviours of a *single* implementation. But in reality, programming languages have implementation-dependent features, and standards must therefore allow a class of non-isomorphic implementations; such a class need not be representable by a single continuous function, in general.

Action semantics was developed so as to avoid the problems that arise when using denotational semantics for realistic programming languages. The use of the standard action notation, rather than the λ-notation, in the semantic equations allows good modifiability and extensibility, as well as readability and comprehensibility—as illustrated by the action semantics of AD in Appendix A and its gradual development in Part III. And although the full action notation may seem rather large, its kernel isn't that much bigger than the full, applied λ-notation used in conventional denotational semantics.

The operational definition of action notation doesn't involve notions of continuity, so there is no problem with catering for unbounded nondeterminism. Action equivalence provides sufficient abstractness to verify simple laws that fail to hold for resumptions. But the general theory of action notation has not yet been fully developed, and at the time of writing it is not known whether the degree of abstractness provided by action equivalence is high enough for general use in program verification.

Conventional denotational semantics uses the continuations technique. The original motivation for continuations was to deal with the semantics of jumps and labels, although the use of continuations in programming has since become popular in its own right , and continuation-handling primitives been incorporated in the programming language SCHEME [RC+86]. Actually, traps and escapes are quite adequate to express the semantics of jumps: a jump to a label consists of escaping out of blocks—perhaps relinquishing locally-allocated resources on the way, which is somewhat awkward to ensure with continuations—until the level of the label is reached, whereupon statement execution continues normally from the labelled statement. However, the action semantic description of unrestricted continuation-passing in SCHEME would not be so easy, and this is certainly a shortcoming of action semantics. It could be remedied, by adding notation for handling continuations to action notation, but the structural operational semantics of action notation would become more complicated.

Initial experiments with semantics-directed compiler generation based on action semantics [Pal92, BMW92] are encouraging. Action semantics makes evident properties that have to be verified by careful analysis of the semantic equations when using denotational semantics, for instance 'single-threadedness' of the store [Sch85].

We could discuss several further points of contrast between denotational and action semantics, for instance the extent to which descriptions can be recycled, so as to reduce the amount of new material needed when describing new languages; but the above should be sufficient for our purposes here. So let us proceed to consider variants on denotational semantics, and then some other frameworks.

18.2 VDM

VDM, The Vienna Development Method [BJ82], has an elaborate notation called , which can be used to give denotational descriptions of programming languages, as well as for specifying more general software. Although there are quite a few variants of META-IV, these share a substantial, partly-standardized notation that provides declarative and imperative syntax (e.g., let-constructions, storage allocation, sequencing, exception-handling) as well as a variety of familiar data types, such as trees, sets, and mappings. The treatment of exceptions in action semantics was directly inspired by that in META-IV, although our **trap** combinator is a bit simpler than META-IV's. The operational implications of this notation are more immediate than those of pure λ-notation, but as it is a supplement to, rather than a replacement for, the λ-notation, the inherent modularity of descriptions in META-IV is no better than that of traditional denotational descriptions. The fact that it has been possible to develop substantial[2] semantic descriptions in META-IV is a tribute to the discipline and energy of their authors, rather than evidence of modularity in META-IV.

18.3   Initial Algebra Semantics

Not to be confused with the initial algebra approach to specification of *abstract data types* [GTW78], the initial algebra semantics of programming languages [GTWW77] is closely related to denotational semantics. Essentially, it makes the algebraic nature of inductively-defined compositional semantic functions explicit: each semantic equation corresponds to the definition of an operation of a *target algebra*, and the *initiality* of abstract syntax among all such algebras ensures a unique *homomorphic* semantic function from it to the target algebra.

Initial algebra semantics has the advantage of focusing attention on how *entire* denotations are combined; in conventional denotational semantics, the usual style is to combine not denotations but the results of their *applications* to auxiliary values such as environments. However, definitions of target algebras are less perspicuous than the corresponding inductive definitions using semantic equations. Otherwise, the pragmatic and theoretical problems of initial algebra semantics are exactly the same as those of conventional denotational semantics, at least when denotations are higher-order functions expressed in the usual λ-notation.

18.4   Algebraic Semantics

A development of the initial algebra semantics discussed above is to consider classes of algebras satisfying some properties, such as the associativity of the statement sequencing operation [Gue81]. Such properties can be mostly specified as algebraic equations or inclusions. To deal with iteration and recursion, it is then appropriate to consider infinite program unfoldings, so that recursion equations can be solved either syntactically or semantically. The work on this approach mainly addresses foundational questions, and has not yet been applied to conventional programming languages. In fact it seems very difficult to obtain adequate algebraic axiomatizations of program equivalence for realistic languages.

---

[2]Some might say overwhelming

18.5   Abstract Semantic Algebras

My own earlier work on abstract semantic algebras [Mos83] uses algebraic axioms
to *define* the intended interpretation of an action notation, rather than using an
operational semantics for that purpose. This is easier than axiomatizing program
equivalence at the level of program syntax, because the constructs can be chosen
carefully, and once-and-for-all: they are not dictated by the programming languages
to be described.

I later realized that my *limiting complete* axioms for action equivalence were essentially operational transition rules in disguise, and this led to the development of
action semantics in its present form. Since the difference between abstract semantic
algebras and action semantics only concerns the foundations of action notation, the
pragmatics of the two frameworks are the same—although the version of action notation used with abstract semantic algebras was unfortunately somewhat more difficult
to use and understand than the present version.

Mason and Talcott [MT91] make a useful investigation of laws for functional programs with memory effects. The language that they deal with consists of the call-by-
value λ-calculus, enriched with atoms that allocate memory cells and store values in
them. This language is quite expressive, for example streams and objects can be represented in it. They define the operational semantics of the language by a reduction
system on contexts, representing memory states syntactically by sequences of applications of allocation and storing atoms, and show that operational equivalence satisfies
a number of useful laws. Compared to action semantics, Mason and Talcott provide
a rich theory for a rather restricted action notation, whereas we provide a (currently)
weak theory for a much richer notation. Although they aim to apply their theory to
reasoning about actor systems [Agh86], the extent to which their notation would be
useful for expressing the semantics of other programming languages is unclear.

18.6   First-Order Identities

The seminal paper by Wand [Wan80] uses algebraic axioms to define program equivalence, but quite indirectly: auxiliary operations, corresponding to semantic functions,
are introduced, and it is their applications to programs and other auxiliary entities
that are axiomatized. The axioms resemble semantic equations, but those given
for iterative constructs are non-compositional, and the framework is more closely
related to operational semantics than to denotational or action semantics. A similar
approach was proposed in connection with the CIP project [BPW87], and by Goguen
and Parsaye-Ghomi [GPG81].

The pragmatics of these approaches are comparable to those of denotational semantics: the modifiability and extensibility of specifications are poor. Note in particular that despite the modularization used by Goguen and Parsaye-Ghomi, the semantic equations are still sensitive to the style of model—they would require extensive reformulation if the described language were extended with some form of jumps, for instance. The modules are used only for pointing out minor reusable parts of the description, such as the specification of finite maps that are used to represent storage.

18.7 Evolving Algebras

This framework [Gur91] employs algebras—more precisely, first-order structures—to represent the configurations of operational transition systems. It provides a particularly concise and expressive notation for updates on complex structures, whereby there is no need to mention parts of structures that are to remain unchanged; this gives some useful modularity to specifications. Transition rules are usually conditional on details of the current configuration, and several rules can be applied at once.

All the structure resides in the configurations, including the program syntax and a pointer that indicates the current place of execution. There is no semantic decomposition or analysis of programs: the reader has to imagine how the presence of the program in the initial configuration will affect the computations,as determined by the transition rules. Evolving algebras can be regarded as the antithesis of action semantics, as they emphasize configurations at the expense of actions.

Experiments have shown that evolving algebras can be used to describe the semantics of practical programming languages, such as C and PROLOG. However, the algebras involved are quite large, and despite the succinct notation for structure updates, the rules get rather large and complicated.

18.8 Structural Operational Semantics

Structural operational semantics, SOS, was developed for use in describing programming languages by Plotkin [Plo81, Plo83]. The framework of so-called natural semantics developed by Kahn [Kah87] is a particular discipline of SOS, related to inference rules for natural deduction in logic. Astesiano [Ast91] provides a newer exposition, see also the SMoLCS framework [AR87]. The main feature is that although configurations involve program syntax, transitions are specified in a structural fashion that keeps track of control *implicitly*, avoiding the need for a control pointer into the entire program tree. The possible transitions for a compound phrase depend on the possible transitions for some or all of the subphrases, which gives a compositional flavour to SOS specifications—without achieving a truly compositional semantics, however. An SOS is usually presented as a logic with axioms and inference rules for the possibility of transitions between configurations. Alternatively, one can use Horn clause axioms together with the standard inference rules of Horn clause logic.

The definition of action notation in Appendix C is based on structural operational semantics (using Horn clause axioms). An action semantic description of a programming language can therefore be regarded as an easy way of defining an SOS for it, by *reducing* the language to action notation—although of course the syntactic components of configurations now involve action primitives and combinators, rather than the original program phrases. Essentially, the action combinators correspond to particular patterns in SOS rules. For example, A_1 and then A_2 corresponds to the pattern where only transitions involving A_1 are considered until a terminal configuration is reached, whereupon A_2 is considered—as specified, once and for all, in our Appendix C. By reducing the described programming language to action notation, one avoids repetitious specification of such patterns, as well as having standard symbols by which to represent them.

The pragmatic aspects of SOS are acceptable, as witnessed by the current popularity of the framework. However, this is partly due to the widespread exploitation of some elaborate *conventions* concerning propagation (of exceptions, for instance) whose formal status is rather dubious. Without these conventions, SOS descriptions are much more cumbersome, and can be tedious to read. The modifiability and extensibility of SOS descriptions are not as good as for action semantics, although somewhat better than for denotational semantics.

18.9   Hoare Logic

Sometimes referred to simply as axiomatic semantics, Hoare logic [Cou90] is concerned with partial correctness assertions about the values of variables: $\{P\}S\{Q\}$ asserts that when the variables satisfy condition P before the execution of statement S, then they will satisfy condition Q afterwards—provided that the execution terminates. The semantics of a statement S then essentially consists of all pairs (P, Q) of conditions such that $\{P\}S\{Q\}$ is provable—a somewhat inaccessible entity.

The pragmatic aspects of Hoare logic are poor, at least for giving semantic descriptions of practical programming languages. The inference rules for common constructs of high-level programming languages, such as procedures with parameters, are unwieldy.

18.10   Weakest Preconditions

With Dijkstra's approach to semantics [Dij75] one specifies for each statement S a *predicate transformer* that for each postcondition Q gives the corresponding weakest precondition P. This means that when P holds before S executed, the execution is guaranteed to terminate with Q holding.

Although the conditions considered are the same as those used in Hoare logic, weakest precondition semantics is an example of *denotational* semantics, where denotations are simply taken to be predicate transformers, which can be represented as continuous functions on power domains. Weakest precondition semantics is well-suited to program verification, and to specification-driven program design, but other pragmatic aspects are poor, and the few experiments with giving such semantic descriptions of practical programming languages have led to rather inaccessible documents.

Summary

- *Action semantics rules—OK?*

Chapter 19

Development

- *The original motivation for the development of action semantics was dissatisfaction with pragmatic aspects of denotational semantics.*

- *Early work on abstract semantic algebras focused on the use of algebraic axioms to specify the intended interpretation of action notation.*

- *Although the concrete form of action notation has varied greatly, the underlying primitives and combinators have remained rather stable.*

- *The adoption of a meta-notation based on unified algebras simplified the algebraic specification of generic abstract data types, and allowed the use of operations on sorts in actions.*

- *The provision of a structural operational semantics for action notation emphasized the operational essence of action notation, and allowed the verification of algebraic laws.*

- *Recent enhancements of action semantics concern the grammars for specifying abstract syntax, action notation for communication and indirect bindings, and the notation for sorts of actions.*

- *Current and future projects involve: the action semantic description of various programming languages; the implementation of systems supporting the creation, editing, checking, and interpretation of descriptions; action semantics directed compiler generation; and the further investigation of the theory of action notation.*

- *The author welcomes comments on action semantics, and maintains a mailing list.*

This concluding chapter explains the original motivation for the development of action semantics. It then gives what amounts to an annotated bibliography for action semantics and for its precursor, a framework called *abstract semantic algebras*. Finally, it describes current work, and invites you to participate in the future development of action semantics.

19.1   Origins

First, my own background: I was fortunate to be studying at the University of Oxford when Scott and Strachey started the development of denotational semantics in 1969 [Sco70, SS71]. I became an enthusiastic follower of the approach, and the first paper I wrote provided a fairly complete denotational description of ALGOL60 [Mos74]. My thesis work was on the use of denotational semantic descriptions in compiler generation [Mos75, Mos76], and I carried on to develop a prototype semantics implementation system called SIS [Mos79].

SIS, which is now obsolete, took denotational descriptions as input. It transformed a denotational description into a λ-expression which, when applied to the abstract syntax of a program, could be reduced to a λ-expression that represented the semantics of the program. This expression could be regarded as the 'code' of the program for the λ-reduction machine that SIS provided. By applying the code to some input, and reducing again, one could get the output of the program according to the semantics.

In the mid 1970's, denotational semantics was generally regarded as the most promising framework for semantic description. Adequate techniques had been developed for representing the semantics of all common (and many uncommon) constructs of programming languages. It was expected that before long, every major programming language would have a complete denotational description, which could be given as input to SIS to provide (inefficient but) correct implementations.

However, this expectation was not fulfilled; far from it! The few large-scale denotational descriptions that were formulated generally exploit many semi-formal notational conventions, for instance omitting domain injection functions; they also omit the precise definitions of various primitive functions, such as those representing storage allocation, and they make serious simplifying assumptions about the syntax of the described language. For it is discouragingly tedious to give fully-formal, complete denotational descriptions of realistic programming languages!

I started to look for the cause of this malady. My diagnosis was that the direct use of the λ-notation in semantic equations was to blame, since it made the semantic equations directly dependent on the structure of denotations: whether they were functions of environments, stores, continuations, etc. The lack of modularity made large-scale descriptions very difficult to manage. I had already become familiar with algebraic specification of abstract data types, so I tried to transfer the techniques to denotational semantics, with the aim of improving the modularity of descriptions, and thereby their other pragmatic aspects.

These ideas developed gradually in the following papers . The list is comprehensive, except that it omits some Danish student reports.

Making denotational semantics less concrete [Mos77]

Note: This tentative paper states one of the main ideas of action semantics—the use of standard combinators in semantic equations—fairly clearly. It introduces primitives for giving values and updating variables, and combinators corresponding to sequencing of statement execution and expression evaluation, as well as (deterministic) choice and iteration; and it gives examples of the kind of algebraic laws that could be used to define their intended interpretation. It also shows how a conventional denotational semantics can be recovered (as a 'concrete implementation') by defining the primitives and combinators as auxiliary operations, using λ-notation.

A constructive approach to compiler correctness [Mos80]

Abstract: It is suggested that denotational semantic definitions of programming languages should be based on a small number of abstract data types, each embodying a fundamental concept of computation. Once these fundamental abstract data types have been implemented in a particular target language (e.g., stack-machine code), it is a simple matter to construct a correct compiler for any source language from its denotational semantic definition. The approach is illustrated by constructing a compiler similar to the one which was proved correct by Thatcher, Wagner & Wright [TWW79].

A semantic algebra for binding constructs [Mos81]

Abstract: This paper presents a semantic algebra, suitable for use in giving the denotational semantics of various forms of declarations and binding constructs in programming languages. The emphasis of the paper is on the development of semantic descriptions which are easy to understand at an intuitive level, being based on algebraic operators corresponding to fundamental concepts of programming languages.

Models for abstract semantic algebras [BS82]

Abstract: Denotational models are given for a specific set of abstract semantic algebras. The possibility of systematically combining such models is discussed. Finally a unifying model is provided—the existence of which makes consistency of the involved abstract semantic algebras more likely.

Abstract semantic algebras! [Mos83]

Abstract: A new approach to the formal semantic description of programming language semantics is described and illustrated. 'Abstract semantic algebras' are just algebraically-specified abstract data types whose operations correspond to fundamental concepts of programming languages. The values of abstract semantic algebras are taken as the meanings of programs in Denotational (or Initial Algebra) Semantics, instead of using Scott domains. This leads to semantic descriptions that clearly exhibit the underlying conceptual analysis, and which are rather easy to modify and extend. Some basic abstract semantic algebras corresponding to fundamental concepts of programming languages are given; they could be used in the description of many different programming languages.

A basic abstract semantic algebra [Mos84]

Abstract: It seems that there are some pragmatic advantages in using Abstract Semantic Algebras (ASAs) instead of λ-notation in denotational semantics. The values of ASAs correspond to 'actions' (or 'processes'), and the operators correspond to primitive ways of combining actions. There are simple ASAs for the various independent 'facets' of actions: a functional ASA for data-flow, an imperative ASA for assignments, a declarative ASA for bindings, etc. The aim is to obtain general ASAs by systematic combination of these simple ASAs.

Here we specify a basic ASA that captures the common features of the functional, imperative and declarative ASAs—and highlights their differences. We discuss the correctness of ASA specifications, and sketch the proof of the consistency and (limiting) completeness of the functional ASA, relative to a simple model. Some familiarity with denotational semantics and algebraic specifications is assumed.

Executable semantic descriptions [Wat86]

Abstract: We describe how the denotational semantics of a programming language can be executed directly, if it is expressed in a suitable functional programming language such as ML. We also apply Mosses' idea of 'semantic algebras' to construct semantic descriptions that are significantly more modular and understandable than usual. The possibility of executing a language's semantic description directly supports a methodology of language design that we advocate: express the design as a formal language description, and use this to test and refine the design, before becoming committed to constructing a compiler.

The potential use of action semantics in standards [MW86]

Abstract:Current standards for programming languages generally use informal, rather than formal, semantic descriptions. Possible reasons for this are discussed. Action Semantics, which has been developed from Denotational Semantics and Abstract Semantic Algebras, has some features that may make it more attractive for use in standards than other formal approaches. This paper describes and motivates Action Semantics, and gives some realistic examples of its use.

Note: This position paper contributed to a report by an ISO working subgroup [BNM+89], listed below.

The action semantics of ML and Amber [Mar86]

Abstract: Parts of the programming languages ML and AMBER are described with the Action Semantics approach. The descriptions are used as a basis for discussion of Action Semantics as a tool for describing programming languages.

Note: See also [Wat88].

The use of action semantics [MW87]

Abstract: Formal descriptions of semantics have so far failed to match the acceptance and popularity of formal descriptions of syntax. Thus, in current standards for programming languages, syntax is usually described formally but semantics informally, despite the greater danger of impreciseness in the description of semantics. Action Semantics, which has been developed from Denotational Semantics and Abstract Semantic Algebras, has some features that may make it more attractive than other semantic formalisms. This paper describes and motivates Action Semantics, and gives some realistic examples of its use.

An action semantics for Joyce [BL87]

Abstract: This report gives an Action-Semantic description of the dynamic semantics of the concurrent, CSP- and PASCAL-based programming language JOYCE. The modularity of an Action-Semantic description is investigated by trying to reuse part of an existing Action-Semantic description of PASCAL as a basis for the semantic description of JOYCE.

It is concluded that the reusability of an Action-Semantic description is good. Also, introducing concurrency in an Action-Semantic description seems to be easy.

Modularity in action semantics [Mos88]

Abstract: The concept of *modularity* is examined, and its pragmatic significance discussed. Then a recently-developed framework for the semantic description of programming languages, called *Action Semantics*, is presented, and illustrated with a modest example. It is shown that action semantic descriptions have considerably greater modularity than ordinary denotational descriptions. Finally, related work is assessed.

An action semantics of Standard ML [Wat88]

Abstract: Action semantics is a form of denotational semantics that is based on abstract semantic algebras rather than Scott domains and λ-notation. It allows formal descriptions of programming languages to be written that are unusually readable and modular. This paper presents an action-semantic description of Standard ML, as evidence for the claimed merits of action semantics. Milner's structural operational semantics of the same language is used as a basis for comparison.

An action semantics for inheritance [Pal88]

Abstract: This report is concerned with three things: actions semantics, inheritance, BETA. Familiarity with them is not required: we attempt to give the reader an understanding of the use of action semantics, the nature of inheritance, and the semantics of BETA.

Action semantics of CCS and CSP [CO88]

Abstract: We investigate whether Action Semantics is capable of describing the concurrent aspects of 'Calculus of Communicating Systems' and 'Communicating

Sequential Processes'. We treat the two languages separately. In contrast to 'Communicating Sequential Processes' it turns out that we cannot describe all synchronization situations in 'Calculus of Communicating Systems' *fully* distributed. We doubt that it is possible. We conclude that Action Semantics is sufficient to describe the concurrent aspects of the two languages.

The action semantics description tool [RZ89]

Abstract: A case study of Action Semantics and an analysis of its ability to describe the dynamic semantics of programming languages.

Realistic compiler generation [Lee89]

Note: This book is based on *High-Level Semantics*, which is essentially a variant of action semantics, especially suited to the purposes of compiler generation for conventional programming languages.

A view of formal semantics [BNM+89]

Abstract: When writing a programming language standard, one must achieve comprehensibility and correctness in the face of complexity. Achieving both with informal methods requires an almost nonexistent combination of technical and literary skills. Because informal methods are inadequate, resort is often made to formal ones. This report outlines the major styles of formal semantic definitions, describes several specific definition methods, and enumerates various attempts to produce formal semantic definitions of real standardized languages. Until formal definition techniques improve, we recommend that standards contain both complete formal and complete informal language definitions, whenever feasible.

Unified algebras and action semantics [Mos89a]

Abstract: The recently-developed framework of Unified Algebras [Mos89c, Mos89b] is intended for axiomatic specification of abstract data types. In contrast, the somewhat older framework of Action Semantics (earlier known as 'Abstract Semantic Algebras') is for denotational specification of programming languages. This paper gives an introduction to the main features of Unified Algebras and Action Semantics, and discusses the relation between them. The two frameworks both exploit nondeterministic choice in unconventional ways.

Category sorted algebra-based action semantics [ES90a]

Abstract: In a series of papers, Mosses and Watt define *action semantics*, a metalanguage for high-level, domain-independent formulation of denotational semantics definitions. Action semantics hides details about domain structure (e.g., direct semantics domains vs. continuation semantics domains vs. resumption semantics domains) and coercions (e.g., integers into reals, injections of summands into sum domains) to encourage readability and modifiability. Action semantics notation is of interest as a programming language of itself, for its components (called *actions*) are polymorphic operators that can be composed in several fundamental ways. We formulate a model for action semantics based on Reynolds' *category-sorted algebra*. In the model, actions are natural transformations, and the composition operators are compositions in a 'category of actions'. We use the model to prove semantic soundness and completeness of a unification-based, decidable type inference algorithm for action semantics expressions.

Type inference for action semantics [ES90b]

Abstract: This paper presents our variant of action semantics and its typing system. We give the type inference algorithms, state properties that action semantics expressions satisfy, give soundness and completeness properties, and explain why they hold for type inference on action semantics expressions. We also present a small example.

Action semantics-based language design [Sch90]

Abstract: Mosses and Watt's action semantics and Tennent's language extension principles are used to formulate a language design methodology: first, a language core, consisting of data types and control structures, is defined; then naming constructs are introduced. The structure of the language core is based upon principles of action semantics, and the naming constructs are based upon the language extension principles. The design of an example imperative language is given, and finally, the mathematical structure of action semantics is examined.

Keywords: action semantics; facets; abstraction, parameterization, correspondence, and qualification principles.

A practical introduction to denotational semantics [Mos91b]

Abstract: The intention here is to give a thorough introduction to the basic formalism of Denotational Semantics, and to explain some of the techniques that are used in applications. A novel feature of the presentation here is the exploitation of a particular auxiliary notation (inspired by the author's work on Action Semantics) that improves some of the pragmatic aspects of denotational descriptions.

19.2   Current Status

The book you are reading is the first comprehensive and definitive published presentation of the action semantics framework. It originated from unpublished lecture notes, the first version of which I wrote in 1980. The papers cited above are based on intermediate versions of the framework, in which action notation had a somewhat different appearance compared to the present version. However, the fundamental primitives and combinators and their intended interpretation have remained quite stable since about 1985, when my collaboration with David Watt began, so most of the action semantic descriptions referred to above should be accessible (with some effort) to you after reading this book. Please note that some of them are out of print.

The following works are based on essentially the same version of action notation as used here, and are thus immediately accessible.

Programming Languages Syntax and Semantics [Wat91]

Abstract: *Programming Languages Syntax and Semantics* introduces methods for formally specifying the syntax and semantics of programming languages.

Chapter 2 introduces the topic of syntax, covering both context-free grammars and regular expressions. Chapters 3–5 introduce denotational semantics, the most commonly used method for specifying semantics. Chapter 6 introduces algebraic semantics, applying it to specify abstract data types. Chapters 7–8 introduce action semantics, a new method that promises to make semantic specifications unusually readable. The text concentrates on practical specification techniques, but the underlying theory is covered where appropriate.

Numerous examples, exercises, and case studies support the text.

An introduction to action semantics [Mos91a]

Abstract: Formal semantics is a topic of major importance in the study of programming languages. Its applications include documenting language design, establishing standards for implementations, reasoning about programs, and generating compilers.

These notes introduce *action semantics*, a recently-developed framework for formal semantics. The primary aim of action semantics is to allow *useful* semantic descriptions of *realistic* programming languages.

Keywords: semantic descriptions, action semantics, action notation, data notation, algebraic specifications, modules, unified algebras.

Note: The illustrations deal with the semantic description of the same programming constructs as [Mos91b], which form a subset of those dealt with in [Mos90]. The three papers provide an adequate basis for comparison of the three different styles of semantic description.

Real-time action [Kri91]

Abstract: The behavior of a real-time system depends on the scheduler used. The order in which tasks are executed depends on the characteristics such as ready time, deadline etc. We describe a language in which the readiness and deadlines can be specified. A scheduling policy using the task characteristics can be defined. To study the effect of schedulers on a system a notation should allow for the specification of time, processes, and scheduling. In this paper we show the applicability of Action Notation for specifying real-time behavior.

Semantics driven computer architecture [BPTS91]

Abstract: The performance achievements of RISC designs are the result of the application of compilation technology to computer architecture. In this paper we discuss how further gains can be obtained through the application of language semantics to machine organization. One optimized version of a semantic-architecture is a MISD machine, a class of architecture not previously considered.

Extraction of strong typing laws from action semantics definitions [DS92]

Abstract: We describe a method that automatically extracts a type checking semantics, encoded as a set of type inference rules, from a category sorted algebra-based action semantics definition of a programming language. The type inference rules are guaranteed to enforce strong typing, since they are based on an underlying metasemantics for action semantics, which uses typing functions and natural transformations to give meaning. Next, we use the type checking semantics to extract a dynamic semantics definition from the original action semantics definition. We present an example.

A provably correct compiler generator [Pal92]

Abstract: We have designed, implemented, and proven the correctness of a compiler-generator that accepts action semantic descriptions of imperative programming languages. The generated compilers emit absolute code for an abstract RISC machine language that currently is assembled into code for the SPARC and HP Precision Architecture. Our machine language needs no run-time type-checking and is thus more realistic than those considered in previous compiler proofs. We use solely algebraic specifications; proofs are given in the initial model. This paper gives an overview of its author's forthcoming PhD thesis.

ACTRESS: an action semantics directed compiler generator [BMW92]

Abstract: We report progress on the development of ACTRESS, a compiler-generator based on action semantics. A number of modules have been implemented in SML. These can be composed to construct either a compiler for action notation or a simple compiler generator. We also outline current and future developments that will improve the quality of the generated compilers.

Pascal: Action Semantics [MW92]

Abstract: This document gives a formal semantic description of ISO Standard Pascal (Level 0), using Action Semantics. It demonstrates the applicability of Action Semantics to practical programming languages.

The description should be intelligible even to language users who have little prior knowledge of Action Semantics. Nevertheless the description is fully formal, and specifies Pascal's semantics precisely enough for the needs of more sophisticated language users, such as implementors. The description could be used to generate correct, prototype compilers and interpreters for Pascal, and to reason about program equivalence.

19.3   Projects

Several projects involving tools related to action semantics have already started. For instance, Watt and his group at University of Glasgow are developing a system for action semantics directed compiler generation, described in [BMW92] (see above). At Aarhus University we are developing a system, provisionally called SAS, for processing action semantics descriptions in various ways, including interpretation of programs according to their action semantics (following [Mos79]). Schmidt and his group at Kansas State University are continuing their study of type inference for action notation [ES90b, DS92].

A long-term project is to develop the *theory* of action notation. Any help in this enterprise will be gratefully accepted!

Finally, there is still the project initiated by those who were developing denotational semantics in Oxford in the early 1970's: to provide

formal semantic descriptions of *all* major programming languages!

We didn't get very far with that using denotational semantics. Perhaps the better pragmatic features of action semantics—especially concerning reusability—will allow this project to be completed, at last...

19.4   Mailing List

If you would like to receive abstracts of future papers on action semantics, please send an e-mail message to me at the Internet address **pdmosses@daimi.aau.dk** with subject-line **AS mailing list**, giving your full name and *postal address*. Please use TEX/LATEX commands to represent accented and other non-English letters. Those using unreliable e-mail routes might like to prompt an automatic acknowledgment, for instance by inserting a **Return-Receipt-To:** field with their own Internet address. Of course, if you don't have easy access to e-mail, you are welcome to send me a letter by post instead.

I would also like to hear any comments that you have on this book, or on the action semantics framework in general. Please notify me of any errata that you find (using subject-line **AS errata** if by e-mail). In return I will send you an up-to-date list of corrigenda.

Finally, if you write a paper that involves action semantics, kindly send me a copy of it, together with full bibliographical details.

Appendices

Appendices

Appendix A

AD Action Semantics

- AD *is a medium-scale, high-level programming language. Syntactically, it is a sublanguage of* ADA.

- *The specified action semantics for* AD *constructs does not always correspond exactly to the semantics described in the* ADA *Reference Manual. For instance, parameter passing modes are left implementation-dependent in* ADA, *but not in* AD.

- *The action semantic description of* AD *given here collects and extends the fragmented illustrations given throughout Part III. It also provides the full algebraic specifications of all the semantic entities used in Part III.*

- *Some of the actions specified in Part III are respecified here with some extra subactions. For example, the action representing the execution of a block statement now synchronizes with locally-declared tasks before starting to execute the block body, and relinquishes locally-declared variables afterwards.*

- *The description of* AD *allows assessment of the pragmatic qualities of action semantics: readability, comprehensibility, modularity, modifiability, etc.*

- *To extend the description of* AD *to an accurate description of* ADA *would be a major project, the feasibility of which remains to be seen.*

- *The modular structure of the description is specified first, in the order in which the modules are presented, which is mostly bottom-up.*

231

Abstract Syntax

    Identifiers

    Literals

    Expressions   needs: Identifiers, Literals.

    Statements   needs: Identifiers, Expressions, Declarations.

    Declarations   needs: Identifiers, Expressions, Statements, Types.

    Types   needs: Identifiers, Expressions.

    Programs   needs: Expressions, Declarations.

Semantic Functions needs: Abstract Syntax, Semantic Entities.

    Identifiers

    Literals

    Expressions   needs: Identifiers, Literals.

    Statements   needs: Identifiers, Expressions, Declarations.

    Declarations   needs: Identifiers, Expressions, Statements, Types.

    Types   needs: Identifiers, Expressions.

    Programs   needs: Expressions, Declarations.

Semantic Entities

    Sorts   needs: Values, Variables, Types, Packages, Subprograms, Tasks, Alternatives, Escapes, Errors.

    Values   needs: Numbers, Characters, Accesses, Arrays, Records.

    Variables   needs: Values, Types, Arrays, Records.

    Types   needs: Arrays, Records.

    Numbers

    Characters

    Accesses   needs: Values, Variables.

    Arrays   needs: Values, Variables, Types, Numbers.

    Records   needs: Values, Variables, Types.

    Packages   needs: Sorts, Values, Variables, Types, Subprograms, Tasks.

    Subprograms

        Modes

        Arguments   needs: Values, Variables.

        Functions   needs: Values, Arguments.

        Procedures   needs: Modes, Arguments.

    Tasks

    Alternatives   needs: Escapes.

    Escapes   needs: Values.

    Errors

    Required Bindings needs: Numbers, Types.

A.1 Abstract Syntax

needs: Data Notation/Characters/ASCII (letter , digit , graphic-character).
closed.
grammar:

A.1.1 Identifiers

- Identifier   = □ .
- Word   = Reserved-Word | Identifier (*disjoint*) .
- Word   = ⟦ letter ⟨ letter | digit ⟩* ⟧ .
- Reserved-Word = "abs" | "accept" | "access" | "all" | "and" | "array" | "begin" |
  "body" | "constant" | "declare" | "do" | "else" | "end" | "entry" |
  "exit" | "function" | "if" | "in" | "is" | "loop" | "mod" |
  "new" | "not" | "null" | "of" | "or" | "out" | "package" |
  "procedure" | "record" | "rem" | "return" | "select" | "task" |
  "then" | "type" | "use" | "when" | "while" | "xor" .

A.1.2 Literals

- Literal   = Numeric-Literal | Character-Literal | String-Literal .
- Numeric-Literal   = ⟦ digit+ ⟧ | ⟦ digit+ '.' digit+ ⟧ .
- Character-Literal = ⟦ ''' graphic-character ''' ⟧ .
- String-Literal   = ⟦ '"' graphic-character* '"' ⟧ .

A.1.3 Expressions

- Nominator   = Identifier | ⟦ Nominator "." Identifier ⟧ .
- Name   = Identifier | ⟦ Name "." Identifier ⟧ |
  ⟦ Name "." "all" ⟧ | ⟦ Name "(" Actuals ")" ⟧ .
- Expression   = Literal | "null" | Name | ⟦ "new" Nominator ⟧ |
  ⟦ "(" Expressions ")" ⟧ | ⟦ "(" Associations ")" ⟧ |
  ⟦ Unary-Operator Expression ⟧ |
  ⟦ Expression Binary-Operator Expression ⟧ |
  ⟦ Expression Control-Operator Expression ⟧ .
- Expressions   = ⟨ Expression ⟨ "," Expression ⟩* ⟩ .
- Association   = ⟦ Identifier "=>" Expression ⟧ .
- Associations   = ⟨ Association ⟨ "," Association ⟩* ⟩ .
- Actuals   = Expressions | Associations | ⟨ Expressions "," Associations ⟩ .
- Unary-Operator   = "+" | "−" | "abs" | "not" .
- Binary-Operator = "+" | "−" | "&" | "*" | "/" | "mod" | "rem" |
  "=" | "/=" | "<" | "<=" | ">" | ">=" |
  "and" | "or" | "xor" .
- Control-Operator = ⟨ "and" "then" ⟩ | ⟨ "or" "else" ⟩ .

A.1.4　Statements

- Statement = ⟦ "null" ";" ⟧ | ⟦ Name ":=" Expression ";" ⟧ |
  ⟦ "if" Expression "then" Statement$^+$ ⟨ "else" Statement$^+$ ⟩$^?$ "end" "if" ";" ⟧ |
  ⟦ "select" Alternatives ⟨ "else" Statement$^+$ ⟩$^?$ "end" "select" ";" ⟧ |
  ⟦ ⟨ "while" Expression ⟩$^?$ "loop" Statement$^+$ "end" "loop" ";" ⟧ | ⟦ "exit" ";" ⟧ |
  ⟦ ⟨ "declare" Declaration$^+$ ⟩$^?$ "begin" Statement$^+$ "end" ";" ⟧ |
  ⟦ Identifier ";" ⟧ | ⟦ Nominator "(" Actuals ")" ";" ⟧ |
  ⟦ "return" Expression$^?$ ";" ⟧ | ⟦ Nominator "." Identifier ";" ⟧ |
  ⟦ "accept" Identifier ⟨ "do" Statement$^+$ "end" ⟩$^?$ ";" ⟧ .
- Block = ⟨ Declaration* "begin" Statement$^+$ "end" ⟩ .
- Alternative = Statement$^+$ | ⟦ "when" Expression "=>" Statement$^+$ ⟧ .
- Alternatives = ⟨ Alternative ⟨ "or" Alternative ⟩* ⟩ .

A.1.5　Declarations

- Declaration = ⟦ Identifier ":" "constant" Nominator$^?$ ":=" Expression ";" ⟧ |
  ⟦ Identifier ":" Nominator ⟨ ":=" Expression ⟩$^?$ ";" ⟧ |
  ⟦ "type" Identifier "is" Type ";" ⟧ |
  ⟦ "package" Identifier "is" Declaration$^+$ "end" ";" ⟧ |
  ⟦ "task" Identifier "is" Entry$^+$ "end" ";" ⟧ |
  ⟦ "function" Identifier ⟨ "(" Formals ")" ⟩$^?$
  "return" Nominator ⟨ "is" Block ⟩$^?$ ";" ⟧ |
  ⟦ "procedure" Identifier ⟨ "(" Formals ")" ⟩$^?$ ⟨ "is" Block ⟩$^?$ ";" ⟧ |
  ⟦ Body-Kind "body" Identifier "is" Block ";" ⟧ |
  ⟦ "use" Nominator ";" ⟧ .
- Body-Kind = "package" | "task" | "procedure" | "function" .
- Entry = ⟦ "entry" Identifier ";" ⟧ .
- Formal = ⟦ Identifier ":" Mode$^?$ Nominator ⟧ .
- Formals = ⟨ Formal ⟨ ";" Formal ⟩* ⟩ .
- Mode = "in" | ⟨ "in" "out" ⟩ | "out" .

A.1.6　Types

- Type = ⟦ "(" Enumerands ")" ⟧ |
  ⟦ "array" "(" Expression ".." Expression ")" "of" Nominator ⟧ |
  ⟦ "record" Component-Type$^+$ "end" "record" ⟧ |
  ⟦ "access" Nominator ⟧ .
- Enumerands = ⟨ Identifier ⟨ "," Identifier ⟩* ⟩ .
- Component-Type = ⟦ Identifier ":" Nominator ";" ⟧ .

A.1.7　Programs

- Program = ⟦ Declaration$^+$ Nominator ⟧ .

A.2 Semantic Functions

A.2.1 Identifiers

introduces: the token of _ .

- the token of _ :: Identifier → token .

(1) the token of I:Identifier = string & uppercase I .

A.2.2 Literals

introduces: the value of _ .

- the value of _ :: Literal → value .

A.2.2.1 Numerals

- the value of _ :: Numeric-Literal → number .

(1) the value of $[\![\ d{:}\text{digit}^+\ ]\!]$ = integer-number of decimal $[\![\ d\ ]\!]$.

(2) the value of $[\![\ d_1{:}\text{digit}^+\ \text{'.'}\ d_2{:}\text{digit}^+\ ]\!]$ =
    real-number of the sum of (decimal $[\![\ d_1\ ]\!]$,
        the product of (decimal $[\![\ d_2\ ]\!]$,
            the exponent of (decimal "10", the negation of the count of d_2))) .

A.2.2.2 Characters

- the value of _ :: Character-Literal → character .

(1) the value of $[\![\ \text{'''}\ c{:}\text{graphic-character}\ \text{'''}\ ]\!]$ = c .

A.2.2.3 Strings

- the value of _ :: String-Literal → string-array .

(1) the value of $[\![\ \text{'"'}\ s{:}\text{graphic-character}^*\ \text{'"'}\ ]\!]$ = array of s .

A.2.3 Expressions

introduces: the entity nominated by _ , investigate _ , access _ , evaluate _ , moderate _ ,
    the unary-operation-result of _ , the binary-operation-result of _ .

A.2.3.1 Nominators

- the entity nominated by _ :: Nominator → yielder [of bindable] [using current bindings] .

(1)   the entity nominated by I:Identifier = the entity bound to the token of I .

(2)   the entity nominated by ⟦ N:Nominator "." I:Identifier ⟧ =
      the entity bound to the token of I receiving
      the public-bindings of the package yielded by the entity nominated by N .

A.2.3.2 Investigating Names

- investigate _ :: Name → action
      [giving a (package | value | variable | parameterized function) |
      diverging | storing | communicating | redirecting]
      [using current bindings | current storage | current buffer | current redirections] .

(1)   investigate I:Identifier =
      give the entity bound to the token of I then
      | give the given (package | value | variable | parameterized function) or
      | enact the function-abstraction of the given parameterless function .

(2)   investigate ⟦ N:Name "." I:Identifier ⟧ =
      investigate N then
      | | produce the public-bindings of the given package or
      | | produce the component-bindings of
      | | the record accessible from the given (value | variable)
      hence investigate I .

(3)   investigate ⟦ N:Name "." "all" ⟧ =
      evaluate N then give the accessed-variable of the given access .

(4)   investigate ⟦ N:Name "(" A:Actuals ")" ⟧ =
      | investigate N and evaluate A
      then
      | give the component of
      | (the array accessible from the given (value | variable)#1,
      | the index-value yielded by the rest of the given data) or
      | enact the application of
      | the function-abstraction of the given parameterized function#1
      | to the arguments yielded by the rest of the given data .

A.2.3.3 Accessing Expressions

- access _ :: Expression → action
      [giving a variable | diverging | storing | communicating | redirecting]
      [using current bindings | current storage | current buffer | current redirections] .

(1)   access N:Name = investigate N then give the given variable .

(2) E & Name = nothing ⇒ access E:Expression = err "Illegal program" .

A.2.3.4 Evaluating Expressions

- evaluate _ :: Expression → action
  [giving a value | diverging | storing | communicating | redirecting]
  [using current bindings | current storage | current buffer | current redirections] .

(1) evaluate I:Identifier =
   give the entity bound to the token of I then
   | give (the given value | the value assigned to the given variable) or
   | enact the function-abstraction of the given parameterless function .

(2) evaluate ⟦ N:Name "." I:Identifier ⟧ =
   | investigate N then
   | | produce the public-bindings of the given package or
   | | produce the component-bindings of
   | | | the record accessible from the given (value | variable)
   | hence evaluate I .

(3) evaluate ⟦ N:Name "." "all" ⟧ =
   evaluate N then
   give the value assigned to the variable accessible from the given access .

(4) evaluate ⟦ N:Name "(" A:Actuals ")" ⟧ =
   | investigate N and evaluate A
   then
   | give the component of
   | | (the given array-value#1,
   | | | the index-value yielded by the rest of the given data) or
   | give the value assigned to the component of
   | | (the array-variable accessible from the given (access | variable)#1,
   | | | the index-value yielded by the rest of the given data) or
   | enact the application of
   | | the function-abstraction of the given parameterized function#1
   | | to the arguments yielded by the rest of the given data .

(5) evaluate L:Literal = give the value of L .

(6) evaluate "null" = give the null-access .

(7) evaluate ⟦ "new" N:Nominator ⟧ =
   allocate for the type yielded by the entity nominated by N then
   give access to the given variable .

(8) evaluate ⟦ "(" E:Expression ")" ⟧ = evaluate E .

(9) evaluate ⟦ "(" E:⟨Expression "," Expressions⟩ ")" ⟧ =
   evaluate E then give array of the given value$^+$.

(10) evaluate ⟦ "(" A:Associations ")" ⟧ =
   evaluate A then give record of the bindings yielded by the given map .

(11) evaluate ⟦ O:Unary-Operator E:Expression ⟧ =
   evaluate E then give the unary-operation-result of O .

(12) evaluate ⟦ E_1:Expression O:Binary-Operator E_2:Expression ⟧ =
   | evaluate E_1 and evaluate E_2
   then give the binary-operation-result of O .

(13) evaluate $[\![$ E_1:Expression "or" "else" E_2:Expression $]\!]$ =
      evaluate E_1 then
        | | check the given truth-value then give true
        | or
        | | check not the given truth-value then evaluate E_2 .

(14) evaluate $[\![$ E_1:Expression "and" "then" E_2:Expression $]\!]$ =
      evaluate E_1 then
        | | check the given truth-value then evaluate E_2
        | or
        | | check not the given truth-value then give false .

- evaluate _ :: Expressions → action
  [giving value$^+$ | diverging | storing | communicating | redirecting]
  [using current bindings | current storage | current buffer | current redirections] .

(15) evaluate ⟨ E_1:Expression "," E_2:Expressions ⟩ = evaluate E_1 and evaluate E_2 .

A.2.3.5   Evaluating Associations

- evaluate _ :: Associations → action
  [giving a map [token to value] | diverging | storing | communicating | redirecting]
  [using current bindings | current storage | current buffer | current redirections] .

(1) evaluate $[\![$ I:Identifier "=>" E:Expression $]\!]$ =
     evaluate E then give map of the token of I to the given value .

(2) evaluate ⟨ A_1:Association "," A_2:Associations ⟩ =
    | evaluate A_1 and evaluate A_2
    then give the disjoint-union of (the given map#1, the given map#2) .

A.2.3.6   Evaluating Actual Parameters

- evaluate _ :: Actuals → action
  [giving arguments | diverging | storing | communicating | redirecting]
  [using current bindings | current storage | current buffer | current redirections] .

(1) evaluate ⟨ E:Expressions "," A:Associations ⟩ = evaluate E and evaluate A .

A.2.3.7 Moderating Expressions

- moderate _ :: Expressions → action
  [giving argument$^+$ | diverging | storing | communicating | redirecting]
  [using given modes | current bindings | current storage | current buffer | current redirections] .

(1) moderate *E*:Expression =
  give the first of the given modes then
  | | check either (it is the reference-mode, it is the copy-mode) then access *E*
  | or
  | | check (it is the constant-mode) then evaluate *E* .

(2) moderate ⟨ E_1:Expression "," E_2:Expressions ⟩ =
  moderate E_1 and
  | give the rest of the given modes then moderate E_2 .

A.2.3.8 Moderating Associations

- moderate _ :: Associations → action
  [giving a map [token to argument] | diverging | storing | communicating | redirecting]
  [using given modes | current bindings | current storage | current buffer | current redirections] .

(1) moderate ⟦ *I*:Identifier "=>" *E*:Expression ⟧ =
  give (the entire-mode-map of the given modes at the token of *I*) then
  | | check either (it is the reference-mode, it is the copy-mode) then access *E*
  | or
  | | check (it is the constant-mode) then evaluate *E*
  then give map of the token of *I* to the given argument .

(2) moderate ⟨ A_1:Association "," A_2:Associations ⟩ =
  | moderate A_1 and moderate A_2
  then give the disjoint-union of (the given map#1, the given map#2) .

A.2.3.9 Moderating Actual Parameters

- moderate _ :: Actuals → action
  [giving arguments | diverging | storing | communicating | redirecting]
  [using given modes | current bindings | current storage | current buffer | current redirections] .

(1) moderate ⟨ *E*:Expressions "," *A*:Associations ⟩ = moderate *E* and moderate *A* .

A.2.3.10   Operating Unary Operators

- the unary-operation-result of _ :: Unary-Operator → yielder [of value] [using given value] .

(1)   the unary-operation-result of "+" = the given number .
(2)   the unary-operation-result of "−" = the negation of the given number .
(3)   the unary-operation-result of "abs" = the absolute of the given number .
(4)   the unary-operation-result of "not" = not the given truth-value .

A.2.3.11   Operating Binary Operators

- the binary-operation-result of _ :: Binary-Operator → yielder [of value] [using given (value,value)] .

(1)   the binary-operation-result of "+" =
          the sum of (the given number#1, the given number#2) .
(2)   the binary-operation-result of "−" =
          the difference of (the given number#1, the given number#2) .
(3)   the binary-operation-result of " & " =
          the concatenation of (the given array#1, the given array#2) .
(4)   the binary-operation-result of "∗" =
          the product of (the given number#1, the given number#2) .
(5)   the binary-operation-result of "/" =
          the quotient of (the given number#1, the given number#2) .
(6)   the binary-operation-result of "mod" =
          the modulo of (the given number#1, the given number#2) .
(7)   the binary-operation-result of "rem" =
          the remainder of (the given number#1, the given number#2) .
(8)   the binary-operation-result of "=" =
          the given value#1 is the given value#2 .
(9)   the binary-operation-result of "/=" =
          not (the given value#1 is the given value#2) .
(10) the binary-operation-result of "<" =
          the given number#1 is less than the given number#2 .
(11) the binary-operation-result of "<=" =
          not (the given number#1 is greater than the given number#2) .
(12) the binary-operation-result of ">" =
          the given number#1 is greater than the given number#2 .
(13) the binary-operation-result of ">=" =
          not (the given number#1 is less than the given number#2) .
(14) the binary-operation-result of "and" =
          both of (the given truth-value#1, the given truth-value#2) .
(15) the binary-operation-result of "or" =
          either of (the given truth-value#1, the given truth-value#2) .
(16) the binary-operation-result of "xor" =
          not (the given truth-value#1 is the given truth-value#2) .

A.2.4   Statements

introduces: execute _ , exhaust _ , the selectability of _ .

A.2.4.1   Executing Statements

- execute _ :: Statement$^+$ → action
  [completing | escaping with an escape-reason | diverging | storing | communicating | redirecting]
  [using current bindings | current storage | current buffer | current redirections] .

(1)   execute ⟨ S_1:Statement S_2:Statement$^+$ ⟩ = execute S_1 and then execute S_2 .

(2)   execute ⟦ "null" ";" ⟧ = complete .

(3)   execute ⟦ N:Name ":=" E:Expression ";" ⟧ =
  | access N and evaluate E
  then assign the given value#2 to the given variable#1 .

(4)   execute ⟦ "if" E:Expression "then" S:Statement$^+$ "end" "if" ";" ⟧ =
  evaluate E then
  | | check the given truth-value and then execute S
  | or
  | | check not the given truth-value .

(5)   execute ⟦ "if" E:Expression "then" S_1:Statement$^+$ "else" S_2:Statement$^+$ "end" "if" ";" ⟧ =
  evaluate E then
  | | check the given truth-value and then execute S_1
  | or
  | | check not the given truth-value and then execute S_2 .

(6)   execute ⟦ "select" A:Alternatives "end" "select" ";" ⟧ =
  | unfolding
  | | exhaust A and then unfold
  | trap
  | | enact the alternative-abstraction of the given alternative .

(7)   execute ⟦ "select" A:Alternatives "else" S:Statement$^+$ "end" "select" ";" ⟧ =
  | exhaust A and then
  | escape with alternative of the closure of abstraction of execute S
  | trap
  | | enact the alternative-abstraction of the given alternative .

(8)   execute ⟦ "loop" S:Statement$^+$ "end" "loop" ";" ⟧ =
  | unfolding
  | | execute S and then unfold
  | trap
  | | check there is given an exit
  | or
  | | check there is given a return and then escape with it .

(9) execute ⟦ "while" *E*:Expression "loop" *S*:Statement⁺ "end" "loop" ";" ⟧ =
   unfolding
    | evaluate *E* then
    | | check the given truth-value and then execute *S* and then unfold
    | or
    | | check not the given truth-value
   trap
    | check there is given an exit
    or
    | check there is given a return and then escape .

(10) execute ⟦ "exit" ";" ⟧ = escape with an exit .

(11) execute ⟦ "begin" *S*:Statement⁺ "end" ";" ⟧ = execute *S* .

(12) execute ⟦ "declare" *B*:⟨Declaration⁺ "begin" Statement⁺ "end" ⟩ ";" ⟧ = execute *B* .

(13) execute ⟦ *I*:Identifier ";" ⟧ =
   enact the procedure-abstraction of the parameterless procedure bound to the token of *I* .

(14) execute ⟦ *N*:Nominator "(" *A*:Actuals ")" ";" ⟧ =
   give the entity nominated by *N* then
    | give the procedure-abstraction of the given procedure and
    | give the formal-modes of the given parameterized procedure then
    | moderate *A*
   then enact the application of the given abstraction#1
       to the arguments yielded by the rest of the given data .

(15) execute ⟦ "return" ";" ⟧ = escape with a procedure-return .

(16) execute ⟦ "return" *E*:Expression ";" ⟧ =
   evaluate *E* then escape with function-return of the given value .

(17) execute ⟦ *N*:Nominator "." *I*:Identifier ";" ⟧ =
   give the entity nominated by *N* then
    | produce the public-bindings of the given package hence
    | enact the procedure-abstraction of
    | the parameterless procedure bound to the token of *I*
    or
    | send a message [to the given task-agent] [containing entry of the token of *I*] and then
    | receive a message [from the given task-agent] [containing the done-signal] .

(18) execute ⟦ "accept" *I*:Identifier "end" ";" ⟧ =
   receive a message [from any task-agent] [containing entry of the token of *I*] then
   send a message [to the sender of the given message] [containing the done-signal] .

(19) execute ⟦ "accept" *I*:Identifier "do" *S*:Statement⁺ "end" ";" ⟧ =
   receive a message [from any task-agent] [containing entry of the token of *I*] then
    | execute *S* and then
   send a message [to the sender of the given message] [containing the done-signal] .

A.2.4.2 Executing Blocks

- execute _ :: Block → action
  [escaping with an escape-reason | diverging | storing | communicating | redirecting]
  [using current bindings | current storage | current buffer | current redirections] .

(1) execute ⟨ "begin" S:Statement$^+$ "end" ⟩ = execute S .

(2) execute ⟨ D:Declaration$^+$ "begin" S:Statement$^+$ "end" ⟩ =
    furthermore elaborate D hence
     | synchronize D and then execute S and then relinquish D
     trap
     | relinquish D and then escape with the given escape-reason .

A.2.4.3 Exhausting Alternatives

- exhaust _ :: Alternatives → action
  [escaping with an alternative | diverging | storing | communicating | redirecting]
  [using current bindings | current storage | current buffer | current redirections] .

(1) exhaust S:Statement$^+$ =
    give the selectability of S then
     | check the given truth-value and then
     | escape with alternative of the closure of abstraction of execute S
     or
     | check not the given truth-value .

(2) exhaust ⟦ "when" E:Expression "=>" S:Statement$^+$ ⟧ =
    evaluate E then
     | check the given truth-value and then exhaust S
     or
     | check not the given truth-value .

(3) exhaust ⟨ A_1:Alternative "or" A_2:Alternatives ⟩ = exhaust A_1 and exhaust A_2 .

A.2.4.4 Selectability of Accept-Statements

- the selectability of _ :: Statement$^+$ → yielder [of truth-value] [using current buffer] .

(1) the selectability of ⟨ S_1:Statement S_2:Statement$^+$ ⟩ = the selectability of S_1 .

(2) the selectability of ⟦ "accept" I:Identifier X:⟨ "do" Statement$^+$ ⟩$^?$ ";" ⟧ =
    the token of I is entered in the current buffer .

(3) S & ⟦ "accept" Identifier ⟨ "do" Statement$^+$ ⟩$^?$ ";" ⟧ = nothing ⇒
    the selectability of S:Statement = true .

A.2.5   Declarations

introduces: elaborate _ , relinquish _ , synchronize _ , the mode of _ , the modes of _ , actualize _ .

A.2.5.1   Elaborating Declarations

- elaborate _ :: Declaration* → action
    [binding | diverging | storing | communicating | redirecting]
    [using current bindings | current storage | current buffer | current redirections] .

(1)   elaborate $\langle D_1$:Declaration D_2:Declaration$^+ \rangle$ = elaborate D_1 before elaborate D_2 .

(2)   elaborate $\langle \rangle$ = complete .

(3)   elaborate ⟦ I:Identifier ":" "constant" N:Nominator$^?$ ":=" E:Expression ";" ⟧ =
    evaluate E then bind the token of I to the given value .

(4)   elaborate ⟦ I:Identifier ":" N:Nominator ";" ⟧ =
    allocate a variable for the type yielded by the entity nominated by N
    then bind the token of I to the given variable .

(5)   elaborate ⟦ I:Identifier ":" N:Nominator ":=" E:Expression ";" ⟧ =
    | allocate a variable for the type yielded by the entity nominated by N
    | and evaluate E
    then
    | bind the token of I to the given variable#1 and
    | assign the given value#2 to the given variable#1 .

(6)   elaborate ⟦ "type" I:Identifier "is" T:Type ";" ⟧ =
    typify T then bind the token of I to the given type .

(7)   elaborate ⟦ "package" I:Identifier "is" D:Declaration$^+$ "end" ";" ⟧ =
    elaborate D hence
    indirectly bind the token of I to package of the current bindings .

(8)   elaborate ⟦ "package" "body" I:Identifier "is" D:Declaration*
                "begin" S:Statement$^+$ "end" ";" ⟧ =
    | furthermore
    | produce the public-bindings of the package bound to the token of I before
    | | elaborate D hence
    | | redirect the token of I to the privatization of
    | | (the package bound to the token of I, the current bindings)
    | | and rebind
    hence
    | synchronize D and then execute S .

(9)   elaborate ⟦ "function" I:Identifier "return" N:Nominator "is" B:Block ";" ⟧ =
    recursively bind the token of I to
        parameterless function of the closure of abstraction of
        | execute B and then err "No returned value"
        trap give the returned-value of the given function-return .

(10) elaborate ⟦ "function" *I*:Identifier "(" *F*:Formals ")"
          "return" *N*:Nominator "is" *B*:Block ";" ⟧ =
   recursively bind the token of *I* to
      parameterized function of the closure of abstraction of
        furthermore actualize *F* thence
          | execute *B* and then err "No returned value"
         trap give the returned-value of the given function-return .

(11) elaborate ⟦ "procedure" *I*:Identifier "is" *B*:Block ";" ⟧ =
   recursively bind the token of *I* to
      parameterless procedure of the closure of abstraction of
        execute *B*
        trap check there is given a procedure-return .

(12) elaborate ⟦ "procedure" *I*:Identifier "(" *F*:Formals ")" "is" *B*:Block ";" ⟧ =
   recursively bind the token of *I* to
      parameterized modalized (the modes of *F*,
        procedure of the closure of abstraction of
          furthermore actualize *F* thence
            execute *B*
           trap check there is given a procedure-return
          and then copy-back the given map [token to variable]) .

(13) elaborate ⟦ "function" *I*:Identifier "return" *N*:Nominator ";" ⟧ =
   indirectly bind the token of *I* to
      parameterless function-head of the closure of abstraction of
      furthermore give the empty-map .

(14) elaborate ⟦ "function" *I*:Identifier "(" *F*:Formals ")"
          "return" *N*:Nominator ";" ⟧ =
   indirectly bind the token of *I* to
      parameterized function-head of the closure of abstraction of
      furthermore actualize *F* .

(15) elaborate ⟦ "procedure" *I*:Identifier ";" ⟧ =
   indirectly bind the token of *I* to
      parameterless procedure-head of the closure of abstraction of
      furthermore give the empty-map .

(16) elaborate ⟦ "procedure" *I*:Identifier "(" *F*:Formals ")" ";" ⟧ =
   indirectly bind the token of *I* to
      parameterized modalized (the modes of *F*,
        procedure-head of the closure of abstraction of
        furthermore actualize *F*) .

(17) elaborate ⟦ "function" "body" *I*:Identifier "is" *B*:Block ";" ⟧ =
   redirect the token of *I* to
      function of (the function-head bound to the token of *I*,
        abstraction of
          | execute *B* and then err "No returned value"
        trap give the returned-value of the given function-return) .

(18) elaborate ⟦ "procedure" "body" *I*:Identifier "is" *B*:Block ";" ⟧ =
        redirect the token of *I* to
                procedure of (the procedure-head bound to the token of *I*,
                        abstraction of
                            | | execute *B*
                            | trap check there is given a procedure-return
                            | and then copy-back the given map [token to variable]) .

(19) elaborate ⟦ "task" *I*:Identifier "is" *E*:Entry⁺ "end" ";" ⟧ =
        offer a contract [to any task-agent] [containing abstraction of the initial task-action] and then
            | receive a message [containing a task-agent] then
            | bind the token of *I* to the task yielded by the contents of the given message .

(20) elaborate ⟦ "task" "body" *I*:Identifier "is" *B*:Block ";" ⟧ =
        send a message [to the task-agent bound to the token of *I*]
                [containing task of the closure of abstraction of execute *B*] .

(21) elaborate ⟦ "use" *N*:Nominator ";" ⟧ =
        produce the public-bindings of the package yielded by the entity nominated by *N* .

A.2.5.2   Relinquishing Variable Declarations

- relinquish _ :: Declaration⁺ → action
    [completing | storing]
    [using current bindings | current storage] .

(1) relinquish ⟨ *D₁*:Declaration *D₂*:Declaration⁺ ⟩ = relinquish *D₁* and relinquish *D₂* .

(2) relinquish ⟦ *I*:Identifier ":" *N*:Nominator *X*:⟨ ":=" Expression ⟩? ";" ⟧ =
        dispose of the variable bound to the token of *I* .

(3) relinquish ⟦ "package" *I*:Identifier "is" *D*:Declaration⁺ "end" ";" ⟧ =
        dispose of the package bound to the token of *I* .

(4) *D*: ⟦ Identifier ":" "constant" Nominator? ":=" Expression ";" ⟧ |
        ⟦ "type" Identifier "is" Type ";" ⟧ |
        ⟦ "task" Identifier "is" Entry⁺ "end" ";" ⟧ |
        ⟦ "function" Identifier ⟨ "(" Formals ")" ⟩? "return" Nominator ⟨ "is" Block ⟩? ";" ⟧ |
        ⟦ "procedure" Identifier ⟨ "(" Formals ")" ⟩? ⟨ "is" Block ⟩? ";" ⟧ |
        ⟦ Body-Kind "body" Identifier "is" Block ";" ⟧ |
        ⟦ "use" Nominator ";" ⟧ ⇒
    relinquish *D* = complete .

A.2.5.3 Synchronizing Task Declarations

- synchronize _ :: Declaration$^+$ → action
  [completing | diverging | communicating | redirecting]
  [using current bindings | current buffer | current redirections] .

(1) synchronize ⟨ D_1:Declaration D_2:Declaration$^+$ ⟩ = synchronize D_1 and synchronize D_2 .

(2) synchronize ⟦ "task" "body" I:Identifier "is" B:Block ";" ⟧ =
  receive a message [from the task-agent bound to the token of I] [containing the begin-signal] .

(3) D: ⟦ Identifier ":" "constant" Nominator$^?$ ":=" Expression ";" ⟧ |
  ⟦ Identifier ":" Nominator ⟨ ":=" Expression ⟩$^?$ ";" ⟧ |
  ⟦ "type" Identifier "is" Type ";" ⟧ |
  ⟦ "package" Identifier "is" Declaration$^+$ "end" ";" ⟧ |
  ⟦ "task" Identifier "is" Entry$^+$ "end" ";" ⟧ |
  ⟦ "function" Identifier ⟨ "(" Formals ")" ⟩$^?$ "return" Nominator ⟨ "is" Block ⟩$^?$ ";" ⟧ |
  ⟦ "procedure" Identifier ⟨ "(" Formals ")" ⟩$^?$ ⟨ "is" Block ⟩$^?$ ";" ⟧ |
  ⟦ ("package" | "procedure" | "function") "body" Identifier "is" Block ";" ⟧ |
  ⟦ "use" Nominator ";" ⟧ ⟹

  synchronize D = complete .

A.2.5.4 Modes

- the mode of _ :: Mode$^?$ → mode .

(1) the mode of ⟨ ⟩ = the constant-mode .
(2) the mode of "in" = the constant-mode .
(3) the mode of ⟨ "in" "out" ⟩ = the copy-mode .
(4) the mode of "out" = the reference-mode .

A.2.5.5 Modes of Formal Parameters

- the modes of _ :: Formals → modes .

(1) the modes of ⟦ I:Identifier ":" M:Mode$^?$ N:Nominator ⟧ =
  (the mode of M, map of the token of I to the mode of M).

(2) the modes of ⟨ F_1:Formal ";" F_2:Formals ⟩ =
  the combined-modes of (the modes of F_1, the modes of F_2) .

A.2.5.6   Actualizing Formal Parameters

- actualize _ :: Formals → action
     [binding | giving a map [token to variable] | storing]
     [using given arguments | current bindings | current storage] .

(1)   actualize ⟦ *I*:identifier ":" *M*:"in"? *N*:Nominator ⟧ =
        bind the token of *I* to the value yielded by
              (the first of the given arguments | (the given map at the token of *I*))
        and give the empty-map .

(2)   actualize ⟦ *I*:identifier ":" "out" *N*:Nominator ⟧ =
        bind the token of *I* to the variable yielded by
              (the first of the given arguments | (the given map at the token of *I*))
        and give the empty-map .

(3)   actualize ⟦ *I*:identifier ":" "in" "out" *N*:Nominator ⟧ =
        │ give the variable yielded by
        │   (the first of the given arguments | (the given map at the token of *I*))
        │ and allocate a variable for the type yielded by the entity nominated by *N*
        then
        │ bind the token of *I* to the given variable#2 and
        │ give map of the token of *I* to the given variable#1 and
        │ assign (the value assigned to the given variable#1) to the given variable#2 .

(4)   actualize ⟨ *F₁*:Formal ";" *F₂*:Formals ⟩ =
        │ actualize *F₁* and
        │ │ give (the rest of the given (argument,arguments) | the given map)
        │ │ then actualize *F₂*
        │ then give the disjoint-union of (the given map#1, the given map#2) .

A.2.6   Types

introduces: typify _ , enumerate _ , the component-types of _ .

A.2.6.1   Typifying Types

- typify _ :: Type → action
     [giving a type | binding | diverging | storing | communicating | redirecting]
     [using current bindings | current storage | current buffer | current redirections] .

(1)   typify ⟦ "(" *E*:Enumerands ")" ⟧ =
        give the enumeration-type and
        │ give 0 then enumerate *E* .

(2)   typify ⟦ "array" "(" *E₁*:Expression ".." *E₂*:Expression ")" "of" *N*:Nominator ⟧ =
        │ evaluate *E₁* and evaluate *E₂* and give the entity nominated by *N*
        then give array-type of the given (index-value, index-value, type) .

(3)   typify ⟦ "record" *C*:Component-Type⁺ "end" "record" ⟧ =
        give record-type of the component-types of *C* .

(4)   typify ⟦ "access" *N*:Nominator ⟧ = give the access-type .

A.2.6.2   Enumerating Constants

- enumerate _ :: Enumerands → action
    [binding] [using given natural] .

(1)   enumerate I:Identifier =
        bind the token of I to integer-number of the given natural .

(2)   enumerate ⟨ I:Identifier "," E:Enumerands ⟩ =
        enumerate I and
        | give the successor of the given natural then enumerate E .

A.2.6.3   Component Types

- the component-types of _ :: Component-Type$^+$ → yielder
    [of map [token to type]] [using current bindings] .

(1)   the component-types of ⟦ I:Identifier ":" N:Nominator ";" ⟧ =
        map of the token of I to the type yielded by the entity nominated by N .

(2)   the component-types of ⟨ C_1:Component-Type C_2:Component-Type$^+$ ⟩ =
        the disjoint-union of (the component-types of C_1, the component-types of C_2) .

A.2.7   Programs

introduces: run _ .

- run _ :: Program → action
    [completing | diverging | storing | communicating | redirecting]
    [using current storage | current buffer | current redirections] .

(1)   run ⟦ D:Declaration$^+$ N:Nominator ⟧ =
        produce required-bindings hence
        furthermore elaborate D hence
        | synchronize D and then
        | give the entity nominated by N then
        | enact the procedure-abstraction of the given parameterless procedure
        and then send a message [to the user-agent] [containing the terminated-signal] .

A.3 Semantic Entities

includes: **Action Notation.**

A.3.1 Sorts

introduces: entity .

- entity = value | variable | type | package |
  function | procedure | task (*disjoint*) .
- datum = entity | alternative | escape-reason | mode | bindings |
  message | entry | set [task-agent] | error | natural | □ .
- token = string of (uppercase letter, (uppercase letter | digit)*) .
- bindable = entity | function-head | procedure-head .
- storable = simple-value .
- sendable = agent | task | entry | signal | error | □ .

A.3.2 Values

introduces: value , simple-value .
includes: **Data Notation/Instant/Distinction** (value *for* s , _ is _).

- value   = simple-value | array-value | record-value (*disjoint*) .
- simple-value = truth-value | number | character | access (*disjoint*) .

A.3.3 Variables

introduces: variable , simple-variable ,
            assign _ to _ , the _ assigned to _ , allocate _ for _ , dispose of _ .

- variable   = simple-variable | array-variable | record-variable (*disjoint*) .
- assign _ to _   :: yielder [of value], yielder [of variable] → action [storing] .
- the _ assigned to _ :: value, yielder [of variable] → yielder [of value] .
- allocate _ for _   :: variable, yielder [of type] → action [giving a variable | storing] .
- dispose of _   :: yielder [of variable] → action [storing] .

(1) simple-variable = cell .

(2) assign (Y_1:yielder [of value]) to (Y_2:yielder [of variable]) =
    store the simple-value yielded by Y_1 in the simple-variable yielded by Y_2 or
    assign the array-value yielded by Y_1 to the array-variable yielded by Y_2 or
    assign the record-value yielded by Y_1 to the record-variable yielded by Y_2 .

(3) the ($v \leq$value) assigned to (Y:yielder [of variable]) =
    the (v & simple-value) stored in the simple-variable yielded by Y |
    the (v & array-value) assigned to the array-variable yielded by Y |
    the (v & record-value) assigned to the record-variable yielded by Y .

(4) allocate ($v \le$ variable) for (Y:yielder [of type]) =
   | check there is the simple-type yielded by Y and then
   | allocate a (v & simple-variable) or
   | allocate a (v & array-variable) for the array-type yielded by Y or
   | allocate a (v & record-variable) for the record-type yielded by Y .

(5) dispose of (Y:yielder [of variable]) =
       unreserve the simple-variable yielded by Y or
       dispose of the array-variable yielded by Y or
       dispose of the record-variable yielded by Y .

A.3.4 Types

introduces: type , simple-type , boolean-type , character-type ,
        enumeration-type , integer-type , real-type , access-type .

- type   = simple-type | array-type | record-type (*disjoint*) .
- simple-type = boolean-type | character-type | enumeration-type |
            integer-type | real-type | access-type (*individual*) .

A.3.5 Numbers

introduces: number , integer-number , real-number , min-integer , max-integer ,
        integer-number of _ , real-number of _ , negation _ , absolute _ ,
        sum _ , difference _ , product _ , quotient _ , modulo _ , remainder _ .

- number   = integer-number | real-number .
- min-integer , max-integer : integer .
- integer-number of _   :: integer $\to$ integer-number (*partial*) .
- real-number of _   :: rational $\to$ real-number (*partial*) .
- negation _ , absolute _   :: number $\to$ number (*partial*) .
- sum _ , difference _ , product _ , quotient _ ::
              number^2 $\to$ number (*partial*) .
- modulo _ , remainder _ :: integer-number^2 $\to$ integer-number (*partial*) .
- _ is _ , _ is less than _ , _ is greater than _ ::
              integer-number, integer-number $\to$ truth-value (*total*) ,
              real-number, real-number $\to$ truth-value (*total*) .

(1) i : integer [min min-integer] [max max-integer] $\Rightarrow$ integer-number of i : integer-number .

(2) i : integer [min successor max-integer] $\Rightarrow$ integer-number of i = nothing .

(3) i : integer [max predecessor min-integer] $\Rightarrow$ integer-number of i = nothing .

(4) real-number of (r:approximation) : real-number .

(5) real-number of (r:interval approximation) : real-number of (approximately r) .

(6) integer-number of i : integer-number $\Rightarrow$

   (1)   negation integer-number of i = integer-number of negation i ;

   (2)   absolute integer-number of i = integer-number of absolute i .

(7)   integer-number of i_1 : integer-number ;   integer-number of i_2 : integer-number $\Rightarrow$

    (1)   sum (integer-number of i_1, integer-number of i_2) = integer-number of sum (i_1, i_2) ;

    (2)   difference (integer-number of i_1, integer-number of i_2) = integer-number of difference (i_1, i_2) ;

    (3)   product (integer-number of i_1, integer-number of i_2) = integer-number of product (i_1, i_2) ;

    (4)   quotient (integer-number of i_1, integer-number of i_2) =
          integer-number of integer-quotient (i_1, i_2) ;

    (5)   modulo (integer-number of i_1, integer-number of i_2) =
          integer-number of integer-modulo (i_1, i_2) ;

    (6)   remainder (integer-number of i_1, integer-number of i_2) =
          integer-number of integer-remainder (i_1, i_2) .

(8)   real-number of r : real-number $\Rightarrow$

    (1)   negation real-number of r = real-number of negation r ;

    (2)   absolute real-number of r = real-number of absolute r .

(9)   real-number of r_1 : real-number ;   real-number of r_2 : real-number $\Rightarrow$

    (1)   sum (real-number of r_1, real-number of r_2) : real-number of sum (r_1, r_2) ;

    (2)   difference (real-number of r_1, real-number of r_2) : real-number of difference (r_1, r_2) ;

    (3)   product (real-number of r_1, real-number of r_2) : real-number of product (r_1, r_2) ;

    (4)   quotient (real-number of r_1, real-number of r_2) : real-number of quotient (r_1, r_2) .

(10) integer-number of i_1 : integer-number ;   integer-number of i_2 : integer-number $\Rightarrow$

    (1)   integer-number of i_1 is integer-number of i_2 = i_1 is i_2 ;

    (2)   integer-number of i_1 is less than integer-number of i_2 = i_1 is less than i_2 ;

    (3)   integer-number of i_1 is greater than integer-number of i_2 = i_1 is greater than i_2 .

(11) real-number of r_1 : real-number ;   real-number of r_2 : real-number $\Rightarrow$

    (1)   real-number of r_1 is real-number of r_2 = r_1 is r_2 ;

    (2)   real-number of r_1 is less than real-number of r_2 = r_1 is less than r_2 ;

    (3)   real-number of r_1 is greater than real-number of r_2 = r_1 is greater than r_2 .

A.3.6   Characters

includes: **Data Notation/Characters/ASCII** (character) ,
           Data Notation/Strings/Alphanumerics (uppercase _ , decimal _) .

A.3.7   Accesses

introduces: access , null-access , access to _ , accessed-variable _ , the _ accessible from _ .

- null-access   : access .
- access to _   :: variable → access (*total*) .
- accessed-variable _   :: access → variable (*partial*) .
- the _ accessible from _ :: (value | variable), yielder [of value | variable] →
                yielder [of value | variable] .

(1) access to v:variable : access .

(2) a = access to v $\Rightarrow$ accessed-variable of a:access = v .

(3) accessed-variable of null-access = nothing .

(4) access to v:variable is null-access = false .

(5) access to v_1:variable is access to v_2:variable = v_1 is v_2 .

(6) the ($v{\leq}$(value | variable)) accessible from (Y:yielder [of value | variable]) =
      (the v yielded by Y) |
      (the v yielded by the accessed-variable of the access yielded by Y) |
      (the v yielded by the accessed-variable of
          the access assigned to the simple-variable yielded by Y) .

A.3.8 Arrays

introduces: array , index-value , empty-array , array-value , string-array , array-variable ,
              array of _ , _ offset by _ , component _ , concatenation _ , array-type ,
              array-type of _ , lower index-value _ , upper index-value _ , component-type _ .

- array   = array-value | array-variable .
- index-value   = integer-number .
- empty-array   = array of ( ) .
- string-array $\leq$ array-value .
- array of _   :: ( ) $\rightarrow$ array (*total*) ,
                     value$^+$ $\rightarrow$ array-value (*partial*) ,
                     variable$^+$ $\rightarrow$ array-variable (*partial*) ,
                     character$^+$ $\rightarrow$ string-array (*partial*) .
- _ offset by _   :: array-value, index-value $\rightarrow$ array-value (*total*) ,
                     array-variable, index-value $\rightarrow$ array-variable (*total*) .
- component _   :: (array-value, index-value) $\rightarrow$ value (*partial*) ,
                     (array-variable, index-value) $\rightarrow$ variable (*partial*) .
- concatenation _   :: array-value^2 $\rightarrow$ array-value (*partial, associative, unit is* empty-array) .
- _ is _   :: array-value, array-value $\rightarrow$ truth-value (*total*) ,
                     array-variable, array-variable $\rightarrow$ truth-value (*total*) .
- array-type of _   :: (index-value^2, type) $\rightarrow$ array-type (*total*) .
- lower index-value _ , upper index-value _ ::
                     array-type $\rightarrow$ index-value (*total*) .
- component-type _ :: array-type $\rightarrow$ type (*total*) .

(1) count of v is greater than max-integer = false $\Rightarrow$ array of (v:(value* | variable*)) : array .

(2) string-array = array of character* .

(3) array of v offset by integer-number 0 = array of v .

(4) empty-array offset by n:integer-number = empty-array .

(5) (array of v offset by m:integer-number) offset by n:integer-number = array of v offset by n .

(6) a = array of v offset by n $\Rightarrow$
component $(a$:array, i:integer-number$)$ = component# difference (i, n) of v .

(7) a_1 = array of v_1 offset by n_1 ; a_2 = array of v_2 offset by n_2 ;   count of v_1 is greater than 0 $\Rightarrow$
concatenation $(a_1$:array-value, a_2:array-value$)$ = array of (v_1, v_2) offset by n_1 .

(8) a_1 = array of v_1 offset by n_1 ; a_2 = array of v_2 offset by n_2 $\Rightarrow$
$(a_1$:array-value$)$ is $(a_2$:array-value$)$ = v_1 is v_2 .

(9) t = array-type of (m, n, t') $\Rightarrow$

      (1)   lower index-value t:array-type = m ;

      (2)   upper index-value t:array-type = n ;

      (3)   component-type t:array-type = t' .

privately introduces: components _ , respectively assign _ to _ ,
                         the values respectively assigned to _ ,
                         allocate component-variables for _ from _ to _ ,
                         dispose of all _ .

(10) assign $(Y_1$:yielder [of array-value]$)$ to $(Y_2$:yielder [of array-variable]$)$ =
      respectively assign the components of Y_1 to the components of Y_2 .

(11) the $(v{\leq}$array-value$)$ assigned to $(Y$:yielder [of array-variable]$)$ =
      the v yielded by array of
          the values respectively assigned to the components of Y .

(12) allocate $(v{\leq}$array-variable$)$ for $(Y$:yielder [of array-type]$)$ =
     | give the lower index-value of Y and
     | allocate component-variables for the component-type of Y
     | from the lower index-value of Y to the upper index-value of Y
   then give (array of the variable* yielded by the rest of the given data
          offset by the given index-value#1) .

(13) dispose of $(Y$:yielder [of array-variable]$)$ = dispose of all the components of Y .

(14) a = array of v $\Rightarrow$ components of a:array = v .

(15) respectively assign $(Y_1$:yielder [of value*]$)$ to $(Y_2$:yielder [of variable*]$)$ =
     | check $(Y_1$ is $(\ ))$ and check $(Y_2$ is $(\ ))$
     or
     | assign the first of Y_1 to the first of Y_2 and
     | respectively assign the rest of Y_1 to the rest of Y_2 .

(16) the values respectively assigned to $(Y$:yielder [of variable*]$)$ =
     when Y is $(\ )$ then $(\ )$ |
     (the value assigned to the first of Y, the values respectively assigned to the rest of Y) .

(17) allocate component-variables for $(Y_1$:yielder [of type]$)$
     from $(Y_2$:yielder [of index-value]$)$ to $(Y_3$:yielder [of index-value]$)$ =
     | check $(Y_2$ is greater than $Y_3)$ and then give $(\ )$
     or
     | check not $(Y_2$ is greater than $Y_3)$ and then
     | | allocate a variable for Y_1 and
     | | allocate component-variables for Y_1 from sum $(Y_2$, integer-number of 1) to Y_3 .

(18) dispose of all $(Y$:yielder [of variable*]$)$ =
     check $(Y$ is $(\ ))$ or
     | dispose of the first of Y and
     | dispose of all the rest of Y .

A.3.9   Records

introduces: record , empty-record , record-value , record-variable ,
                record of _ , component-bindings _ , disjoint-union _ , record-type ,
                record-type of _ , component-type-bindings _ .

- record   = record-value | record-variable .
- empty-record   = record of empty-map .
- record of _   :: empty-map → record (*total*) ,
                          map [token to value] → record-value (*total*) ,
                          map [token to variable] → record-variable (*total*) .
- component-bindings _   :: record-value → map [token to value] (*total*) ,
                          record-variable → map [token to variable] (*total*) .
- disjoint-union _   :: record-value^2 → record
                          (*partial, associative, commutative, unit is* empty-record) .
- _ is _   :: record-value, record-value → truth-value (*total*) ,
                          record-variable, record-variable → truth-value (*total*) .
- record-type of _   :: map [token to type] → record-type (*total*) .
- component-type-bindings _ :: record-type → map [token to type] (*total*) .

(1) r = record of m ⇒ component-bindings of r:record = m .

(2) r_1 = record of m_1 ; r_2 = record of m_2 ⇒
     disjoint-union (r_1:record, r_2:record) = record of disjoint-union of (m_1, m_2) .

(3) r_1 = record of m_1 ; r_2 = record of m_2 ⇒ (r_1:record) is (r_2:record) = m_1 is m_2 .

(4) r = record-type of m ⇒ component-type-bindings of r:record = m .

privately introduces: assign _ to _ from _ , the value-bindings assigned to _ from _ ,
                        allocate variable-bindings for _ from _ , dispose of _ from _ .

(5)   assign (Y_1:yielder [of record-value]) to (Y_2:yielder [of record-variable]) =
      check (the mapped-set of the component-bindings of Y_1 is
         the mapped-set of the component-bindings of Y_2) and then
      assign the component-bindings of Y_1 to the component-bindings of Y_2
         from the elements of the mapped-set of the component-bindings of Y_1 .

(6)   the (v≤record-value) assigned to (Y:yielder [of record-variable]) =
      the v yielded by record of
         the value-bindings assigned to the component-bindings of Y
            from the elements of the mapped-set of the component-bindings of Y .

(7)   allocate (v≤record-variable) for (Y:yielder [of record-type]) =
      allocate variable-bindings for the component-type-bindings of Y
         from the elements of the mapped-set of the component-type-bindings of Y
      then give (the v yielded by record of the given map [token to variable]) .

(8)   dispose of (Y:yielder [of record-variable]) =
      dispose of the component-bindings of Y
         from the elements of the mapped-set of the component-bindings of Y .

(9)   assign (Y_1:yielder [of map [token to value]]) to (Y_2:yielder [of map [token to variable]])
      from (Y_3:yielder [of token*]) =
      | check (Y_3 is ( ))
      or
      | assign (Y_1 at the first of Y_3) to (Y_2 at the first of Y_3) and
      | assign Y_1 to Y_2 from the rest of Y_3 .

(10) the value-bindings assigned to (Y_1:yielder [of map [token to variable]])
         from (Y_2:yielder [of token*]) =
         when Y_2 is ( ) then empty-map |
         disjoint-union of (map of the first of Y_2 to the value assigned to (Y_1 at the first of Y_2),
            the value-bindings assigned to Y_1 from the rest of Y) .

(11) allocate variable-bindings for (Y_1:yielder [of map [token to type]])
         from (Y_2:yielder [of token*]) =
         | check (Y_2 is ( )) and then give empty-map
         or
         | give the first of Y_2 and
         | allocate a variable for (Y_1 at the first of Y_2) and
         | allocate variable-bindings for Y_1 from the rest of Y_2
         | then give disjoint-union of (map of the given token#1 to the given variable#2,
            the given map#3) .

(12) dispose of (Y_1:yielder [of map [token to variable]) from (Y_2:yielder [of token*]) =
         check (Y_2 is ( )) or
         | dispose of (Y_1 at the first of Y_2) and
         | dispose of Y_1 from the rest of Y_2 .

A.3.10   Packages

introduces: package , package of _ , privatization _ , public-bindings _ , dispose of _ .

- package of _   :: bindings → package (*total*) .
- privatization _   :: package, bindings → package (*partial*) .
- public-bindings _   :: package → bindings (*total*) .
- dispose of _   :: package → action [completing | storing] .

(1)   intersection (mapped-set of public-bindings of p, mapped-set of b) = empty-set $\Rightarrow$
     privatization (p:package, b:bindings) : package .

(2) p = package of b $\Rightarrow$ public-bindings p:package = b .

(3) p = privatization (package of b, b') $\Rightarrow$ public-bindings p:package = b .

privately introduces: private-bindings _ , dispose of _ from _ .

(4) p = package of b $\Rightarrow$ private-bindings p:package = empty-map .

(5) p = privatization (package of b, b') $\Rightarrow$ private-bindings p:package = b' .

(6)   dispose of (Y:yielder [of package]) =
        give disjoint-union of (the public-bindings of Y, the private-bindings of Y) then
        dispose of the given bindings from the elements of the mapped-set of the given bindings .

(7)   dispose of (Y_1:yielder [of map [token to bindable-entity]]) from (Y_2:yielder [of token*]) =
      check (Y_2 is ( )) or
      | dispose of (Y_1 at the first of Y_2) and
      | dispose of Y_1 from the rest of Y_2 .

(8)   dispose of (Y:yielder [of bindable-entity]) =
      dispose of the variable yielded by Y or
      dispose of the package yielded by Y or
      check there is the (value | type | subprogram | task) yielded by Y .

A.3.11   Subprograms

A.3.11.1   Modes

introduces: mode , modes , combined-modes _ , entire-mode-map _ ,
            constant-mode , reference-mode , copy-mode .

- mode   = constant-mode | copy-mode | reference-mode   (*individual*) .
- modes   = (mode*, map [token to mode]) .
- combined-modes _ :: (modes, modes) → modes (*total*) .
- entire-mode-map _ :: modes → map [token to mode] (*total*) .

includes: **Data Notation/Instant/Distinction** (mode *for* s , _ is _).

(1)   combined-modes (t_1:mode*, m_1:map [token to mode], t_2:mode*, m_2:map [token to mode]) =
       (t_1, t_2, disjoint-union of (m_1, m_2)) .

(2)   entire-mode-map (t:mode*, m:map [token to mode]) = m .

(3)   distinct (constant-mode, reference-mode, copy-mode) = true .

A.3.11.2   Arguments

introduces: argument , arguments , copy-back _ .

- argument   = value | variable .
- arguments   = (argument*, [token to argument] map$^?$) .
- copy-back _ :: map [token to variable] → action [completing | storing] .

privately introduces: copy-back _ from _ .

(1)   copy-back (Y:yielder [of map [token to variable]]) =
      copy-back Y from the elements of the mapped-set of Y .

(2)   copy-back (Y_1:yielder [of map [token to variable]]) from (Y_2:yielder [of token*]) =
      check (Y_2 is ( )) or
      | assign (the value assigned to the variable bound to the first of Y_2)
      | to the variable yielded by (Y_1 at the first of Y_2) and then
      | dispose of the variable yielded by (Y_1 at the first of Y_2) and then
      | copy-back Y_1 from the rest of Y_2 .

A.3.11.3   Functions

introduces: function , function of _ , function-abstraction _ ,
            parameterless _ , parameterized _ , function-head , function-head of _ .

- function of _   :: abstraction → function (*partial*) .
- function-abstraction _   :: function → abstraction (*total*) .
- parameterless _ , parameterized _ :: function → function (*partial*) .
- function-head of _   :: abstraction → function-head (*partial*) .
- function of _   :: (function-head, abstraction) → function (*partial*) .
- parameterless _ , parameterized _ :: function-head → function-head (*partial*) .

(1) a : action [giving a value | diverging | storing | communicating | redirecting]
             [using given arguments | current storage | current buffer | current redirections] $\Rightarrow$
     function of abstraction of a : function .

(2) f = function of a $\Rightarrow$ the function-abstraction of f:function = a .

(3) f = function of a $\Rightarrow$ parameterless f:function : function ; parameterized f:function : function .

(4) f = parameterless function of a $\Rightarrow$ the function-abstraction of f:function = a .

(5) f = parameterized function of a $\Rightarrow$ the function-abstraction of f:function = a .

(6) a : action [binding] [using given arguments | current storage] $\Rightarrow$
     function-head of abstraction of a : function-head .

(7) h = function-head of a $\Rightarrow$
     function of (h:function-head, a':abstraction) = function of (a thence a') .

(8) h = function-head of a $\Rightarrow$
     parameterless h:function-head : function ; parameterized h:function-head : function .

(9) function of (parameterless h:function-head, a:abstraction) = parameterless function of (h, a) .

(10) function of (parameterized h:function-head, a:abstraction) = parameterized function of (h, a) .

A.3.11.4 Procedures

introduces: procedure , procedure of _ , procedure-abstraction _ ,
                  parameterless _ , parameterized _ , modalized _ ,
                  formal-modes _ , procedure-head , procedure-head of _ .

- procedure of _   :: abstraction $\rightarrow$ procedure (*partial*) .
- procedure-abstraction _   :: procedure $\rightarrow$ abstraction (*total*) .
- parameterless _ , parameterized _ :: procedure $\rightarrow$ procedure (*partial*) .
- modalized _   :: (modes, procedure) $\rightarrow$ procedure (*partial*) .
- formal-modes _   :: procedure $\rightarrow$ modes (*partial*) .
- procedure-head of _   :: abstraction $\rightarrow$ procedure-head (*partial*) .
- procedure of _   :: (procedure-head, abstraction) $\rightarrow$ procedure (*partial*) .
- parameterless _ , parameterized _ :: procedure-head $\rightarrow$ procedure-head (*partial*) .
- modalized _   :: (modes, procedure-head) $\rightarrow$ procedure-head (*partial*) .

(1) a : action [completing | diverging | storing | communicating | redirecting]
             [using given arguments | current storage | current buffer | current redirections] $\Rightarrow$
     procedure of abstraction of a : procedure .

(2) p = procedure of a $\Rightarrow$ the procedure-abstraction of p:procedure = a .

(3) p = procedure of a $\Rightarrow$
     parameterless p:procedure : procedure ; parameterized p:procedure : procedure .

(4) p = parameterless procedure of a $\Rightarrow$ the procedure-abstraction of p:procedure = a .

(5) p = parameterized procedure of a $\Rightarrow$ the procedure-abstraction of p:procedure = a .

(6) p = parameterized modalized (m:modes, procedure of a) $\Rightarrow$

    (1) the procedure-abstraction of p:procedure = a ;

    (2) the formal-modes of p:procedure = m .

(7) a : action [binding | storing] [using given arguments | current storage] $\Rightarrow$
procedure-head of abstraction of a : procedure-head .

(8) h = procedure-head of a $\Rightarrow$
procedure of (h:procedure-head, a':abstraction) = procedure of (a thence a') .

(9) h = procedure-head of a $\Rightarrow$
parameterless h:procedure-head : procedure ;
parameterized h:procedure-head : procedure .

(10) procedure of (parameterless h:procedure-head, a:abstraction) =
      parameterless procedure of (h, a) .

(11) procedure of (parameterized h:procedure-head, a:abstraction) =
      parameterized procedure of (h, a) .

(12) procedure of (parameterized modalized (m:modes, h:procedure-head), a:abstraction) =
      parameterized modalized (m, procedure of (h, a)) .

A.3.12 Tasks

introduces: task-agent , task , task of _ , task-abstraction _ , initial task-action ,
             signal , begin-signal , done-signal , terminated-signal ,
             entry , entry of _ , _ is entered in _ .

- task-agent $\leq$ agent .
- task of _   :: abstraction $\rightarrow$ task (*total*) .
- task-abstraction _ :: task $\rightarrow$ abstraction (*total*) .
- signal   = begin-signal | done-signal | terminated-signal (*individual*) .
- initial task-action : action .
- entry of _   :: token $\rightarrow$ entry (*total*) .
- _ is entered in _ :: entry, buffer $\rightarrow$ truth-value (*total*) .

(1) t = task of a $\Rightarrow$ task-abstraction t:task = a .

(2) initial task-action =
        | send a message [to the contracting-agent] [containing the performing-agent] and then
        | receive a message [from the contracting-agent] [containing a task]
        then
        | send a message [to the contracting-agent] [containing the begin-signal] and then
        | enact the task-abstraction of the task yielded by the contents of the given message .

(3) entry of k_1:token is entry of k_2:token = k_1 is k_2 .

(4) e:entry is entered in empty-list = false .

(5) e:entry is entered in list of m:message [containing an entry] = e is the contents of m .

(6) e:entry is entered in list of m:message [containing a signal | agent | task] = false .

(7) e:entry is entered in concatenation (b_1:buffer, b_2:buffer) =
      either (e is entered in b_1, e is entered in b_2) .

A.3.13   Alternatives

introduces: alternative , alternative of _ , alternative-abstraction _ .

- alternative of _   :: abstraction → alternative (*partial*) .
- alternative-abstraction _   :: alternative → abstraction (*total*) .

(1) a : action [completing | escaping with an escape-reason |
                   diverging | storing | communicating | redirecting]
                   [using current storage | current buffer | current redirections] ⇒
      alternative of abstraction of a : alternative .

(2) a = alternative of a' ⇒ the alternative-abstraction of a:alternative = a' .

A.3.14   Escapes

introduces: escape-reason , exit , return , function-return ,
              function-return of _ , returned-value _ , procedure-return .

- escape-reason   = exit | return (*disjoint*) .
- exit   : escape-reason .
- return   = function-return | procedure-return   (*disjoint*) .
- function-return of _ :: value → function-return (*total*) .
- returned-value _   :: function-return → value (*total*) .
- procedure-return   : return .

(1) e = function-return of v ⇒ the returned-value of e:function-return = v .

A.3.15   Errors

introduces: error , error of _ , err _ .

- error of _ :: string → error (*total*) .
- err _   :: string → action (*total*) .

(1)   err s:string = send a message [to the user-agent] [containing error of s] and then fail .

A.3.16   Required Bindings

introduces: required-bindings .

- required-bindings : map [token to value | type] .

(1)   required-bindings = disjoint-union of (map of "TRUE" to true,
                                            map of "FALSE" to false,
                                            map of "BOOLEAN" to boolean-type,
                                            map of "MININT" to integer-number min-integer,
                                            map of "MAXINT" to integer-number max-integer,
                                            map of "INTEGER" to integer-type,
                                            map of "REAL" to real-type,
                                            map of "CHARACTER" to character-type) .

Appendix B

Action Notation

- *The specification of the algebraic properties of action notation in this Appendix is divided into modules as shown on the next page.*

- *The body of each module introduces symbols, highlights their principal properties, and lists their secondary properties.*

- *The properties specified are sufficient to reduce the full action notation to a kernel, whose abstract syntax and structural operational semantics are defined in Appendix C.*

- *The specified properties of the kernel action notation hold for the notion of action equivalence defined at the end of Appendix C. The algebraic theory of action notation is not yet fully developed, although it may already be adequate for verifying the semantic correctness of simple program optimizations.*

- *Action notation supports concurrency, but without introducing a combinator for it, so there are no algebraic properties concerning the sending and receipt of messages, or the fulfilment of contracts.*

- *The module **Facets** deserves special mention. It defines a moderately expressive notation for subsorts of actions, with reference to outcomes and incomes, and similarly for yielders. This notation is specified axiomatically; the expected correspondence with the operational semantics of action notation has not yet been proved. Nevertheless, the axiomatic specification of the subsort notation provides useful documentation of the sorts of yielders to be used in primitive actions, and of the various facets of the action combinators.*

261

Basic

    Actions   needs: Yielders.
    Yielders   needs: Data.
    Data   .

Functional   includes: Basic.

    Actions   needs: Yielders.
    Yielders   needs: Data.
    Data   .

Declarative   includes: Basic.

    Actions   needs: Yielders.
    Yielders   · needs: Data.
    Data   .

Imperative   includes: Basic.

    Actions   needs: Yielders.
    Yielders   · needs: Data.
    Data   .

Reflective   includes: Basic, Functional, Declarative.

    Actions   needs: Yielders.
    Yielders   needs: Data.
    Data   .

Communicative includes: Basic, Reflective.

    Actions   needs: Yielders.
    Yielders   needs: Data.
    Data   .

Directive   includes: Basic, Declarative, Reflective.

    Actions   needs: Yielders.
    Yielders   needs: Data.
    Data   .

Hybrid   includes: Functional, Declarative, Imperative,
                        Reflective, Communicative, Directive.

    Actions   needs: Yielders.
    Yielders   needs: Data.
    Data   .

Facets   needs: Hybrid.

    Outcomes   needs: Incomes.
    Incomes   .
    Actions   needs: Outcomes, Incomes.
    Yielders   needs: Outcomes, Incomes.
    Unfolding   needs: Outcomes, Incomes, Actions.

B.1 Basic

B.1.1 Actions

introduces: action , primitive-action , complete , escape , fail , commit , diverge , unfold , unfolding _ , indivisibly _ , _ or _ , _ and _ , _ and then _ , _ trap _ .

- action $\geq$ primitive-action .
- complete   : primitive-action .
- escape   : primitive-action .
- fail   : primitive-action .
- commit   : primitive-action .
- diverge   : action .
- unfold   : action .
- unfolding _   :: action $\rightarrow$ action (*total*) .
- indivisibly _   :: action $\rightarrow$ action (*partial*) .
- _ or _   :: action, action $\rightarrow$ action (*total, associative, commutative, idempotent, unit is* fail) .
- _ and _   :: action, action $\rightarrow$ action (*total, associative, unit is* complete) .
- _ and then _ :: action, action $\rightarrow$ action (*total, associative, unit is* complete) .
- _ trap _   :: action, action $\rightarrow$ action (*total, associative, unit is* escape) .

(1) A : complete | escape | commit | fail $\Rightarrow$ indivisibly $A = A$.

(2)   indivisibly indivisibly A:action = indivisibly A .

(3)   indivisibly diverge = nothing .

(4)   escape and diverge = escape or diverge .

(5) A : escape | fail | diverge $\Rightarrow$ A and then A':action = A .

(6) A : complete | fail | diverge $\Rightarrow$ A trap A':action = A .

B.1.2 Yielders

introduces: yielder , the _ yielded by _ , *data-operation* .

- yielder $\geq$ data .
- the _ yielded by _ :: data, yielder $\rightarrow$ yielder .
- *data-operation*   :: yielder, ... $\rightarrow$ yielder .

(1)   the data yielded by ($Y \leq$yielder) = Y .

(2)   the ($d \leq$data) yielded by the ($d' \leq$data) yielded by ($Y \leq$yielder) = the d & d' yielded by Y .

(3)   the ($d \leq$data) yielded by ($d' \leq$data) = d & d' .

B.1.3   Data

introduces: datum , distinct-datum , data , a _ , an _ , the _ , of _ , some _ .
includes: **Data Notation/General.**
includes: **Data Notation/Instant/Distinction** (distinct-datum *for* s) .

- datum $\leq$ component .
- datum $\geq$ truth-value | rational | character | list |
                     set | map | abstraction (*disjoint*) .
- distinct-datum $\leq$ datum .
- distinct-datum $\geq$ truth-value | rational | character | list [distinct-datum] |
                     set [distinct-datum] | map [distinct-datum to distinct-datum] .
- data   = datum* .
- a _ , an _ , the _ , of _ , some _ :: data $\rightarrow$ data (*total*) .

(1)   distinct (t:truth-value, r:rational, c:character, l:list [distinct-datum],
          s:set [distinct-datum], m:map [distinct-datum to distinct-datum]) = true .

(2) $x \leq$ datum ; x & list = nothing $\Rightarrow$ $x \leq$ item .

(3) $x \leq$ distinct-datum ; x & set = nothing $\Rightarrow$ $x \leq$ nonset-element .

(4) $x \leq$ datum ; x & map = nothing $\Rightarrow$ $x \leq$ nonmap-range .

(5) $d \leq$ data $\Rightarrow$ a $d = d$;   an $d = d$;   the $d = d$;   of $d = d$; some $d = d$.

B.2   Functional

B.2.1   Actions

introduces: give _ , escape with _ , regive , choose _ , check _ , _ then _ .

- give _   :: yielder $\rightarrow$ primitive-action .
- escape with _ :: yielder $\rightarrow$ primitive-action .
- regive   : primitive-action .
- choose _   :: yielder $\rightarrow$ primitive-action .
- check _   :: yielder $\rightarrow$ primitive-action .
- _ then _   :: action, action $\rightarrow$ action (*total, associative, unit is* regive) .

(1)   give ( ) = complete ;   give nothing = fail .

(2)   give (Y:yielder) and give (Y':yielder) = give (Y, Y') .

(3)   escape with (Y:yielder) = give Y then escape .

(4)   escape = escape with the given data .

(5)   regive = give the given data .

(6)   choose (d:data) = give d ;   choose nothing = fail .

(7)   check (Y:yielder) = give the true yielded by Y then give () .

(8)   check true = complete ;   check false = fail .

(9) A : fail | escape | diverge $\Rightarrow$ A then A':action = A .

(10)   (A:action then give ( )) and A':action = A' and (A then give ( )) .

B.2.2   Yielders

introduces: given _ , given _#_ , it , them .

- given _   :: data → yielder (*strict*) .
- given _#_ :: datum, positive-integer → yielder (*strict*) .
- it   : yielder .
- them   : yielder .

(1)   given ($d{\leq}$data) = the d yielded by the given data .

(2)   given ($d{\leq}$datum)#(p:positive-integer) = the d yielded by component#p of the given data .

(3)   given ($d{\leq}$datum)#1 = given d .

(4)   it = the given datum ;   them = the given data .

B.2.3   Data

introduces: data .

- data = datum* .

B.3   Declarative

B.3.1   Actions

introduces: bind _ to _ , unbind _ , rebind , produce _ ,
                   furthermore _ , _ moreover _ , _ hence _ , _ before _ .

- bind _ to _   :: yielder, yielder → primitive-action .
- unbind _   :: yielder → primitive-action .
- rebind   : primitive-action .
- produce _   :: yielder → primitive-action .
- furthermore _ :: action → action (*total*) .
- _ moreover _ :: action, action → action (*total, associative, unit is* complete) .
- _ hence _   :: action, action → action (*total, associative, unit is* rebind) .
- _ before _   :: action, action → action (*total, associative, unit is* complete) .

(1)   rebind = produce the current bindings .

(2)   furthermore A:action = rebind moreover A .

(3)   furthermore (A_1:action before A_2:action) hence A_3:action =
         furthermore A_1 hence furthermore A_2 hence A_3 .

(4)   give ((Y_1:yielder) receiving (Y_2:yielder)) = produce Y_2 hence give Y_1 .

(5)   produce empty-map = complete .

(6)   produce map of (Y_1:yielder) to (Y_2:yielder) = bind Y_1 to Y_2 .

(7)   produce (Y_1:yielder) and produce (Y_2:yielder) = produce disjoint-union (Y_1, Y_2) .

(8)   produce (Y_1:yielder) moreover produce (Y_2:yielder) = produce overlay (Y_2, Y_1) .

(9)   produce (Y_1:yielder) hence produce (Y_2:yielder) = produce (Y_2 receiving Y_1) .

(10) produce (b:bindings) hence (produce (Y_1:yielder) before produce (Y_2:yielder)) =
        produce overlay (Y_2 receiving overlay (Y_1 receiving b, b), Y_1 receiving b) .

B.3.2   Yielders

introduces: current bindings , the _ bound to _ , _ receiving _ .

- current bindings : yielder .
- the _ bound to _ :: bindable, yielder → yielder .
- _ receiving _   :: yielder, yielder → yielder (*total*) .

(1)   the (d≤bindable) bound to (Y:yielder) ≥
           the d yielded by (current bindings at the token yielded by Y) .

(2)   (Y:yielder) receiving current bindings = Y .

B.3.3   Data

introduces: bindings , token , bindable , unknown , known _ .

- bindings ≥ map [token to bindable | unknown] .
- token   ≤ distinct-datum .
- bindable ≤ data .
- unknown : datum .
- known _ :: bindings → bindings (*total*) .

(1)   unknown & bindable = nothing .

(2)   known empty-map = empty-map .

(3)   known map of t:token to unknown = empty-map .

(4)   known map of t:token to d:bindable = map of t to d .

(5)   known disjoint-union (b_1:bindings, b_2:bindings) = disjoint-union (known b_1, known b_2) .

B.4   Imperative

B.4.1   Actions

introduces: store _ in _ , unstore _ , reserve _ , unreserve _ .

- store _ in _ :: yielder, yielder → primitive-action .
- unstore _   :: yielder → primitive-action .
- reserve _   :: yielder → primitive-action .
- unreserve _ :: yielder → primitive-action .

c, c': cell ; c is $c' = $ false ; d, d': storable $\Rightarrow$

(1)   indivisibly (reserve c and then store d in c and then give the storable stored in c) =
indivisibly (reserve c and then store d in c and then give d) ;

(2)   indivisibly (reserve c and then store d in c and then store d' in c) =
indivisibly (reserve c and then store d' in c) ;

(3)   indivisibly (reserve c and then store d in c and then unreserve c) =
indivisibly (reserve c and then unreserve c) ;

(4)   indivisibly (reserve c and then store d in c and then store d' in c') =
indivisibly (reserve c and then store d' in c' and then store d in c) ;

(5)   indivisibly (reserve c and then store d in c and then unstore c) =
indivisibly (reserve c) ;

(6)   indivisibly (reserve c and then give the datum stored in c) =
indivisibly (reserve c and then give uninitialized) .

B.4.2   Yielders

introduces: current storage , the _ stored in _ .

- current storage   : yielder .
- the _ stored in _ :: storable, yielder $\rightarrow$ yielder .

(1)   the ($d \leq$ storable) stored in (Y:yielder) =
     the d yielded by (current storage at the cell yielded by Y) .

B.4.3   Data

introduces: storage , cell , storable , uninitialized , initialized _ .

- storage   = map [cell to storable | uninitialized] .
- cell $\leq$ distinct-datum .
- storable $\leq$ data .
- uninitialized : datum .
- initialized _ :: storage $\rightarrow$ storage (*total*) .

(1)   uninitialized & storable = nothing .

(2)   initialized empty-map = empty-map .

(3)   initialized map of c:cell to uninitialized = empty-map .

(4)   initialized map of c:cell to d:storable = map of c to d .

(5)   initialized map of (s_1:storage, s_2:storage) = disjoint-union (initialized s_1, initialized s_2) .

B.5   Reflective

B.5.1   Actions

introduces: enact _ .

- enact _ :: yielder → primitive-action .

(1)   enact the application of the closure of abstraction of A:action to the given data $= A$.

B.5.2   Yielders

introduces: application _ to _ , closure _ .

- application _ to _ :: yielder, yielder → yielder .
- closure _   :: yielder → yielder .

(1)   application (Y_1:yielder) to (Y_2:yielder) = (provision Y_2) then Y_1 .
(2)   closure (Y:yielder) = (production current bindings) hence Y .
(3)   closure (application (Y_1:yielder) to (Y_2:yielder)) = application (closure Y_1) to Y_2 .

B.5.3   Data

introduces: abstraction , abstraction of _ , *action-operation* , provision _ , production _ .

- abstraction   ≤ datum .
- abstraction of _ :: action → abstraction (*total*) .
- *action-operation* :: abstraction, ... → abstraction (*total*) .
- provision _   :: data → abstraction (*total*) .
- production _   :: bindings → abstraction (*total*) .

(1)   *action-operation* (abstraction of A:action) = abstraction of (*action-operation* A) .
(2)   (abstraction of A_1:action) *action-operation* (abstraction of A_2:action) =
        abstraction of (A_1 *action-operation* A_2) .
(3)   provision d:data = abstraction of give d .
(4)   production b:bindings = abstraction of produce b .

B.6   Communicative

B.6.1   Actions

introduces: send _ , remove _ , offer _ , patiently _ .

- send _   :: yielder → primitive-action .
- remove _   :: yielder → primitive-action .
- offer _   :: yielder → primitive-action .
- patiently _ :: action → action (*partial*) .

(1) patiently complete = complete ;   patiently escape = escape ;   patiently fail = diverge .

(2) patiently A:action = patiently indivisibly A .

(3) m:message $\Rightarrow$

    (1) indivisibly (remove m and then check (m is in set of items of current buffer)) = indivisibly (remove m and then give false) ;

    (2) indivisibly (check (m is in set of items of current buffer) and then remove m) = indivisibly (remove m) .

B.6.2 Yielders

introduces: current buffer , performing-agent , contracting-agent .

- current buffer : yielder .
- performing-agent , contracting-agent : yielder .

B.6.3 Data

introduces: agent , user-agent , buffer , communication , message , sendable , contract , contents _ , sender _ , receiver _ , serial _ , _ [containing _] , _ [from _] , _ [to _] , _ [at _] .

- agent $\leq$ distinct-datum .
- user-agent   : agent .
- buffer   = list [message] .
- communication $\leq$ distinct-datum .
- communication = message | contract .
- sendable $\leq$ data .
- sendable   = abstraction | agent | $\square$.
- contents _   :: message $\rightarrow$ sendable (*total*) , contract $\rightarrow$ abstraction (*total*) .
- sender _   :: communication $\rightarrow$ agent (*total*) .
- receiver _   :: message $\rightarrow$ agent (*total*) , contract $\rightarrow$ agent (*strict, linear*) .
- serial _   :: communication $\rightarrow$ natural (*total*) .
- _ [containing _] :: message, sendable $\rightarrow$ message (*partial*) , contract, abstraction $\rightarrow$ contract (*partial*) .
- _ [from _]   :: communication, agent $\rightarrow$ communication (*partial*) .
- _ [to _]   :: message, agent $\rightarrow$ message (*partial*) , contract, agent $\rightarrow$ contract (*strict*) .
- _ [at _]   :: communication, natural $\rightarrow$ communication (*partial*) .

(1) $d \leq$ data $\Rightarrow$ $(m\leq$message$)$ [containing d] $\leq m$.

(2) $a \leq$ agent $\Rightarrow$ $(m\leq$message$)$ [from a] $\leq m$.

(3) $a \leq$ agent $\Rightarrow$ $(m\leq$message$)$ [to a] $\leq m$.

(4) $n \leq$ natural $\Rightarrow$ $(m\leq$message$)$ [at n] $\leq m$.

privately introduces: message of _ , contract of _ .

(5)   message of _ :: data, agent, agent, natural $\to$ message .

(6)   message of $(d$:sendable, a:agent, a':agent, n:natural) : message .

(7)   contract of _ :: abstraction, agent, agent, natural $\to$ contract .

(8)   contract of $(d$:abstraction, a:agent, $a' \leq$agent, n:natural) : contract .

(9) $m =$ message of $(d, a, a', n) \leq$ message $\Rightarrow$

    (1)   contents $m = d$; m [containing d'] = message of $(d \& d', a, a', n)$;

    (2)   sender $m = a$; m [from a''] = message of $(d, a \& a'', a', n)$;

    (3)   receiver $m = a'$; m [to a''] = message of $(d, a, a' \& a'', n)$;

    (4)   serial $m = n$; m [at n'] = message of $(d, a, a', n \& n')$.

(10) $c =$ contract of $(d, a, a', n) \leq$ contract $\Rightarrow$

    (1)   contents $c = d$; c [containing d'] = contract of $(d \& d', a, a', n)$;

    (2)   sender $c = a$; c [from a''] = contract of $(d, a \& a'', a', n)$;

    (3)   receiver $c = a'$; c [to a''] = contract of $(d, a, a' \& a'', n)$;

    (4)   serial $c = n$; c [at n'] = contract of $(d, a, a', n \& n')$.

B.7   Directive

B.7.1   Actions

introduces: indirectly bind _ to _ , redirect _ to _ ,
                undirect _ , recursively bind _ to _ , indirectly produce _ .

- indirectly bind _ to _   :: yielder, yielder $\to$ primitive-action .
- redirect _ to _   :: yielder, yielder $\to$ primitive-action .
- recursively bind _ to _ :: yielder, yielder $\to$ primitive-action .
- undirect _   :: yielder $\to$ primitive-action .
- indirectly produce _   :: yielder $\to$ primitive-action .

(1)   redirect $(Y$:yielder) to $(d$:bindable) and then redirect Y to d':bindable = redirect Y to d' .

(2)   redirect $(Y$:yielder) to $(d$:bindable) and then undirect Y = undirect Y .

(3)   recursively bind $(Y_1$:yielder) to $(Y_2$:yielder) =
    | furthermore indirectly bind Y_1 to unknown
   hence
    | redirect Y_1 to Y_2 and bind Y_1 to the redirection bound to Y_1 .

(4)   indirectly produce map of $(i$:indirection) to $(Y$:yielder) = redirect i to Y .

B.7.2   Yielders

introduces: current redirections , indirect closure _ .

- current redirections : redirections .
- indirect closure _   :: abstraction → abstraction (*total*) .

(1)   indirect closure *a*:abstraction = (the production of the current redirections) and then *a* .

(2)   the (*d*≤bindable) bound to (*Y* :yielder) =
       the *d* yielded current bindings at *Y* |
       the *d* yielded by (current redirections at (current bindings at *Y*)) .

B.7.3   Data

introduces: redirections , indirection , indirect production _ .

- redirections   = map [indirection to bindable | unknown] .
- indirection   ≤ distinct-datum .
- indirect production _ :: redirections → abstraction (*total*) .
- bindings   = map [token to bindable | unknown | indirection] .

(1)   indirection & (bindable | unknown) = nothing .

(2)   known map of *t*:token to *i*:indirection = map of *t* to *i* .

(3)   indirect production *r*:redirections = abstraction of indirectly produce *r* .

B.8   Hybrid

B.8.1   Actions

introduces: allocate _ , receive _ , subordinate _ ,
                _ and then moreover _ , _ then moreover _ , _ thence _ , _ then before _ .

- allocate _   :: yielder → action .
- receive _   :: yielder → action .
- subordinate _   :: yielder → action .
- _ and then moreover _ :: action, action → action (*total, associative, unit is* complete) .
- _ then moreover _   :: action, action → action (*total, associative, unit is* regive) .
- _ thence _   :: action, action → action (*total, associative, unit is* (regive and rebind)) .
- _ then before _   :: action, action → action (*total, associative, unit is* regive) .

(1)   allocate (*Y* ≤yielder) =
       indivisibly
       | choose a *Y* [not in the mapped-set of the current storage] [on the performing-agent] then
       | | reserve the given cell and give it .

(2)   receive (*Y* ≤yielder) =
       patiently
       | choose a *Y* [in set of items of the current buffer] then
       | | remove the given message and give it .

privately introduces: subordinate-action .

(3)   subordinate ($Y \leq$yielder) =
> offer a contract [to Y] [containing abstraction of subordinate-action] and then
> | receive a message [from Y] [containing an agent] then
> | give the contents of the given message .

(4)   subordinate-action =
> send a message [to the contracting-agent] [containing the performing-agent] then
> receive a message [from the contracting-agent] [containing an abstraction] then
> enact the contents of the given message .

(5)   reserve (Y:yielder) = reserve the cell [on the performing-agent] yielded by Y .

(6)   unreserve (Y:yielder) = unreserve the cell [on the performing-agent] yielded by Y .

(7)   store (Y_1:yielder) in (Y_2:yielder) =
> store Y_1 in the cell [on the performing-agent] yielded by Y_2 .

B.8.2   Yielders

(1)   the ($d \leq$storable) stored in (Y:yielder) = the d stored in Y [on the performing-agent] .

(2)   current storage = the map [cell [on the performing-agent] to storable] yielded by current storage .

B.8.3   Data

introduces: owner _ , _ [on _] .

- owner _ :: cell | indirection $\rightarrow$ agent (*total*) .
- _ [on _] :: agent, cell $\rightarrow$ cell (*partial*) ,
            agent, indirection $\rightarrow$ indirection (*partial*) .

(1) a:(cell | indirection) [on a:agent] = when a is owner of x then x .

B.9   Facets

B.9.1   Outcomes

introduces: outcome , giving _ , escaping with _ , binding , completing , escaping ,
            failing , committing , storing , communicating , redirecting , diverging .

- outcome   = giving data | escaping with data | binding |
                    failing | committing | storing |
                    communicating | redirecting | diverging (*disjoint*) .
- giving _   :: data $\rightarrow$ outcome (*strict, linear*) .
- escaping with _ :: data $\rightarrow$ outcome (*strict, linear*) .
- completing   = giving ( ) .
- escaping   = escaping with given data .
- failing   = nothing .
- committing $\leq$ storing & communicating & redirecting .

B.9.2 Incomes

introduces: income .

- income = given data | current bindings | current storage |
  current buffer | current redirections .
- given _ :: data → income (*strict, linear*) .
- given _#_ :: data, positive-integer → income (*strict, linear*) .
- given data = given datum#positive-integer .
- given datum = given datum#1 .

B.9.3 Actions

introduces: _ [_] , _ [using _] .

- _ [_] :: action, outcome → action .
- _ [using _] :: action, income → action .

$O, O_1, O_2 \leq$ outcome ; $I, I_1, I_2 \leq$ income ; $A, A_1, A_2 \leq$ action $\Rightarrow$

(1) A [outcome] $= A$;

(2) A [O_1] [O_2] $= A$ [O_1 & O_2] ;

(3) A_1 [O_1] & A_2 [O_2] $= (A_1$ & $A_2)$ [O_1 & O_2] ;

(4) A [using income] $= A$;

(5) A [using I_1] [using I_2] $= A$ [using I_1 & I_2] ;

(6) A_1 [using I_1] & A_2 [using I_2] $= (A_1$ & $A_2)$ [using I_1 & I_2] ;

$G_1, G_2 \leq$ given data ; $B_1, B_2 \leq$ bindings ;
$C_1, C_2 \leq$ current storage | current buffer | current redirections ;
$\bar{G}_1, \bar{G}_2 \leq$ current bindings | current storage | current buffer | current redirections ;
$\bar{B}_1, \bar{B}_2 \leq$ given data | current storage | current buffer | current redirections ;
$d, d_1, d_2 \leq$ data; $E_1' \leq$ escaping with data ; $B_1' \leq$ binding ;
$C', C_1' \leq$ storing | communicating | redirecting ; $U_1' \leq$ diverging ;
$\bar{G}', \bar{G}_1', \bar{G}_2' \leq$ escaping with data | binding | storing | communicating | redirecting | diverging ;
$\bar{E}_1' \leq$ giving data | binding | storing | communicating | redirecting | diverging ;
$\bar{B}_1' \leq$ giving data | escaping with data | storing | communicating | redirecting | diverging ;
$\bar{U}' \leq$ giving data | escaping with data | binding | storing | communicating | redirecting $\Rightarrow$

(7) A [binding | $\bar{G}'$] $= A$ [completing | binding | $\bar{G}'$] ;

(8) A [committing | C'] $= A$ [completing | committing | C'] ;

(9) A [storing | C'] $= A$ [completing | storing | C'] ;

(10) A [communicating | C'] $= A$ [completing | communicating | C'] ;

(11) A [redirecting | C'] $= A$ [completing | redirecting | C'] ;

(12) complete   : action [giving ( )] [using nothing] ;

(13) escape   : action [escaping with given data] [using given data] ;

(14) fail   : action [failing] [using nothing] ;

(15) commit   : action [committing] [using nothing] ;

(16) diverge   : action [diverging] [using nothing] ;

(17) give _   :: yielder [of d] [using I] $\rightarrow$ action [giving d] [using I] ;

(18) escape with _   :: yielder [of d] [using I] $\rightarrow$ action [escaping with d] [using I] ;

(19) regive   : action [giving data] [using given data] ;

(20) choose _   :: yielder [of d] [using I] $\rightarrow$ action [giving d] [using I] ;

(21) check _   :: yielder [of truth-value] [using I] $\rightarrow$ action [giving ( ) | failing] [using I] ;

(22) bind _ to _   :: yielder [of token] [using I_1], yielder [of bindable] [using I_2] $\rightarrow$
                            action [binding] [using I_1 | I_2] ;

(23) unbind _   :: yielder [of token] [using I] $\rightarrow$ action [binding] [using I] ;

(24) rebind   : action [binding] [using current bindings] ;

(25) produce _   :: yielder [of bindings] [using I] $\rightarrow$ action [binding] [using I] ;

(26) store _ in _   :: yielder [of storable] [using I_1], yielder [of cell] [using I_2] $\rightarrow$
                            action [storing] [using I_1 | I_2] ;

(27) unstore _   :: yielder [of cell] [using I] $\rightarrow$ action [storing] [using I] ;

(28) reserve _   :: yielder [of cell] [using I] $\rightarrow$ action [storing] [using I] ;

(29) unreserve _   :: yielder [of cell] [using I] $\rightarrow$ action [storing] [using I] ;

(30) enact _   :: yielder [of abstraction [O_2] [using C_2]] [using I_1] $\rightarrow$
                            action [O_2 | diverging] [using I_1 | C_2] ;

(31) send _   :: yielder [of message] [using I] $\rightarrow$ action [communicating] [using I] ;

(32) remove _   :: yielder [of message] [using I] $\rightarrow$ action [communicating] [using I] ;

(33) offer _   :: yielder [of contract] [using I] $\rightarrow$ action [communicating] [using I] ;

(34) indirectly bind _ to _ :: yielder [of token] [using I_1], yielder [of bindable | unknown] [using I_2] $\rightarrow$
                                action [binding | redirecting] [using I_1 | I_2] ;

(35) redirect _ to _   :: yielder [of token] [using I_1], yielder [of bindable | unknown] [using I_2] $\rightarrow$
                            action [redirecting] [using I_1 | I_2 | current bindings] ;

(36) recursively bind _ to _ :: yielder [of token] [using I_1], yielder [of bindable] [using I_2] $\rightarrow$
                                action [binding | redirecting] [using I_1 | I_2] ;

(37) undirect _   :: yielder [of token] [using I] $\rightarrow$ action [redirecting] [using I] ;

(38) indirectly produce _ :: yielder [of redirections] [using I] $\rightarrow$
                            action [redirecting] [using I] ;

(39) allocate _   :: yielder [of $d \leq$ cell] [using I] $\rightarrow$ action [giving d | storing] [using I] ;

(40) receive _   :: yielder [of $d \leq$ message] [using I] $\rightarrow$
                            action [giving d | communicating] [using I] ;

(41) subordinate _   :: yielder [of $d \leq$ agent] [using I] $\rightarrow$
                            action [giving d | communicating] [using I] ;

(42) indivisibly _ :: action $[\bar{U}']$ [using I] $\to$ action $[\bar{U}']$ [using I] ;

(43) furthermore _ :: action $[O]$ [using I] $\to$ action $[O \mid$ binding$]$ [using I] ;

(44) patiently _ :: action $[\bar{U}']$ [using I] $\to$ action $[\bar{U}' \mid$ diverging$]$ [using I] ;

(45) _ or _ :: action $[O_1]$ [using I_1], action $[O_2]$ [using I_2] $\to$
action $[O_1 \mid O_2]$ [using $I_1 \mid I_2$] ;

(46) _ and _ :: action [giving $d_1 \mid \bar{G}'_1$] [using I_1],
action [giving $d_2 \mid \bar{G}'_2$] [using I_2] $\to$
action [giving $(d_1, d_2) \mid \bar{G}'_1 \mid \bar{G}'_2$] [using $I_1 \mid I_2$] ;

(47) _ and then _ :: action [giving $d_1 \mid \bar{G}'_1$] [using I_1],
action [giving $d_2 \mid \bar{G}'_2$] [using I_2] $\to$
action [giving $(d_1, d_2) \mid \bar{G}'_1 \mid \bar{G}'_2$] [using $I_1 \mid I_2$] ;

(48) _ trap _ :: action [escaping with $d_1 \mid \bar{E}'_1$] [using I_1],
action $[O_2]$ [using given $d_2 \mid \bar{G}_2$] $\to$
action $[\bar{E}'_1 \mid O_2]$ [using $I_1 \mid \bar{G}_2$] ;

(49) _ then _ :: action [giving $d_1 \mid \bar{G}'_1$] [using I_1],
action $[O_2]$ [using given $d_2 \mid \bar{G}_2$] $\to$
action $[\bar{G}'_1 \mid O_2]$ [using $I_1 \mid \bar{G}_2$] ;

(50) _ moreover _ :: action [giving $d_1 \mid \bar{G}'_1$] [using I_1],
action [giving $d_2 \mid \bar{G}'_2$] [using I_2] $\to$
action [giving $(d_1, d_2) \mid \bar{G}'_1 \mid \bar{G}'_2$] [using $I_1 \mid I_2$] ;

(51) _ hence _ :: action [giving $d_1 \mid B'_1 \mid C'_1 \mid U'_1$] [using I_1],
action [giving $d_2 \mid \bar{G}'_2$] [using $B_2 \mid \bar{B}_2$] $\to$
action [giving $(d_1, d_2) \mid C'_1 \mid U'_1 \mid \bar{G}'_2$] [using $I_1 \mid \bar{B}_2$] ;

(52) _ before _ :: action [giving $d_1 \mid \bar{G}'_1$] [using I_1],
action [giving $d_2 \mid \bar{G}'_2$] [using I_2] $\to$
action [giving $(d_1, d_2) \mid \bar{G}'_1 \mid \bar{G}'_2$] [using $I_1 \mid I_2$] ;

(53) _ and then moreover _ :: action [giving $d_1 \mid \bar{G}'_1$] [using I_1],
action [giving $d_2 \mid \bar{G}'_2$] [using I_2] $\to$
action [giving $(d_1, d_2) \mid \bar{G}'_1 \mid \bar{G}'_2$] [using $I_1 \mid I_2$] ;

(54) _ then moreover _ :: action [giving $d_1 \mid \bar{G}'_1$] [using I_1],
action $[O_2]$ [using given $d_2 \mid \bar{G}_2$] $\to$
action $[\bar{G}'_1 \mid O_2]$ [using $I_1 \mid \bar{G}_2$] ;

(55) _ thence _ :: action [giving $d_1 \mid B'_1 \mid C'_1 \mid U'_1$] [using I_1],
action $[O_2]$ [using given $d_2 \mid B_2 \mid C_2$] $\to$
action $[C'_1 \mid U'_1 \mid O_2]$ [using $I_1 \mid C_2$] ;

(56) _ then before _ :: action [giving $d_1 \mid \bar{G}'_1$] [using I_1],
action $[O_2]$ [using given $d_2 \mid \bar{G}_2$] $\to$
action $[\bar{G}'_1 \mid O_2]$ [using $I_1 \mid \bar{G}_2$] .

B.9.4   Yielders

introduces: _ [_] , _ [using _] .

- _ [_]   :: yielder, data → yielder .
- _ [using _] :: yielder, income → yielder .

$d, d_1, d_2 \leq$ data ; $I, I_1, I_2 \leq$ income ; $Y, Y_1, Y_2 \leq$ yielder $\Rightarrow$

(1) Y [data] $= Y$;

(2) Y [d_1] [d_2] $= Y$ [d_1 & d_2] ;

(3) Y_1 [d_1] & Y_2 [d_2] $= (Y_1$ & $Y_2)$ [d_1 & d_2] ;

(4) Y [using income] $= Y$;

(5) Y [using I_1] [using I_2] $= Y$ [using I_1 & I_2] ;

(6) Y_1 [using I_1] & Y_2 [using I_2] $= (Y_1$ & $Y_2)$ [using I_1 & I_2] ;

(7)   data $=$ data [using nothing] ;

$B_1, B_2 \leq$ current bindings ; $R \leq$ current redirections ;
$\bar{G}_1 \leq$ current bindings | current storage | current buffer | current redirections ;
$\bar{B}, \bar{B}_1 \leq$ given data | current storage | current buffer | current redirections ;
$\bar{R} \leq$ given data | current bindings | current storage | current buffer ;
$d, d_1, d_2 \leq$ data ; $O, O_1 \leq$ outcome $\Rightarrow$

(8)   given _   :: $d \to$ yielder [of d] [using given d] ;

(9)   given _#_   :: $d \leq$ datum, p:positive-integer $\to$ yielder [of d] [using given $d\#p$] ;

(10) it   : yielder [of datum] [using given datum] ;

(11) them   : yielder [of data] [using given data] ;

(12) current bindings   : yielder [of bindings] [using current bindings] ;

(13) the _ bound to _   :: d_1, yielder [of $d \leq$ token] [using I] $\to$
                                yielder [of d_1] [using current bindings | I] ;

(14) _ receiving _   :: yielder [of d_1] [using B_1 | $\bar{B}_1$], yielder [of $d \leq$ bindings] [using I_2] $\to$
                                yielder [of d_1] [using $\bar{B}_1$ | I_2] ;

(15) current storage   : yielder [of storage] [using current storage] ;

(16) the _ stored in _   :: d_1, yielder [of $d \leq$ cell] [using I] $\to$
                                yielder [of d_1] [using current storage | I] ;

(17) application _ to _   :: yielder [of abstraction [O_1] [using given d_1 | $\bar{G}_1$]] [using I_1],
                                yielder [of d_2] [using I_2] $\to$
                                yielder [of abstraction [O_1] [using $\bar{G}_1$]] [using I_1 | I_2] ;

(18) closure _   :: yielder [of abstraction [O] [using B | $\bar{B}$]] [using I] $\to$
                                yielder [of abstraction [O] [using $\bar{B}$]] [using I | current bindings] ;

(19) current buffer   : yielder [of buffer] [using current buffer] ;

(20) performing-agent   : yielder [of agent] [using nothing] ;

(21) contracting-agent   : yielder [of agent] [using nothing] ;

(22) current redirections   : yielder [of redirections] [using current redirections] ;

(23) indirect closure _   :: yielder [of abstraction [O] [using R | $\bar{R}$]] [using I] $\to$
                                yielder [of abstraction [O] [using $\bar{R}$]] [using I | current redirections] .

B.9.5 Unfolding

needs: Basic/Actions, Basic/Facets.

privately introduces: _ ⓒ _ .

- _ ⓒ _ :: action, action → action (*total*) .

The auxiliary action operation A ⓒ A_0 substitutes A_0 for 'free' occurrences of unfold in A. It is used to let facet restrictions propagate out of unfoldings, and to express the main law concerning unfolding.

A, A_0, A_1, A_2 : action ; $O \leq$ outcome ; $I \leq$ income $\Rightarrow$

(1)   unfold $[O]$ [using I] : action $[O]$ [using I] ;

(2) A ⓒ unfold $[O]$ [using I] : action $[O]$ [using I] $\Rightarrow$
      unfolding A : action $[O$ | diverging] [using I] ;

(3)   unfolding $A = A$ ⓒ (unfolding A) ;

(4) A:primitive-action ⓒ $A_0 = A$;

(5)   unfold ⓒ $A_0 = A_0$;

(6)   (unfolding A) ⓒ $A_0 =$ unfolding A ;

(7)   (indivisibly A) ⓒ $A_0 =$ indivisibly (A ⓒ A_0) ;

(8)   (furthermore A) ⓒ $A_0 =$ furthermore (A ⓒ A_0) ;

(9)   (patiently A) ⓒ $A_0 =$ patiently (A ⓒ A_0) ;

(10)   (A_1 or A_2) ⓒ $A_0 = (A_1$ ⓒ A_0) or (A_2 ⓒ A_0) ;

(11)   (A_1 and A_2) ⓒ $A_0 = (A_1$ ⓒ A_0) and (A_2 ⓒ A_0) ;

(12)   (A_1 and then A_2) ⓒ $A_0 = (A_1$ ⓒ A_0) and then (A_2 ⓒ A_0) ;

(13)   (A_1 trap A_2) ⓒ $A_0 = (A_1$ ⓒ A_0) trap (A_2 ⓒ A_0) ;

(14)   (A_1 then A_2) ⓒ $A_0 = (A_1$ ⓒ A_0) then (A_2 ⓒ A_0) ;

(15)   (A_1 moreover A_2) ⓒ $A_0 = (A_1$ ⓒ A_0) moreover (A_2 ⓒ A_0) ;

(16)   (A_1 hence A_2) ⓒ $A_0 = (A_1$ ⓒ A_0) hence (A_2 ⓒ A_0) ;

(17)   (A_1 before A_2) ⓒ $A_0 = (A_1$ ⓒ A_0) before (A_2 ⓒ A_0) ;

(18)   (A_1 and then moreover A_2) ⓒ $A_0 = (A_1$ ⓒ A_0) and then moreover (A_2 ⓒ A_0) ;

(19)   (A_1 then moreover A_2) ⓒ $A_0 = (A_1$ ⓒ A_0) then moreover (A_2 ⓒ A_0) ;

(20)   (A_1 thence A_2) ⓒ $A_0 = (A_1$ ⓒ A_0) thence (A_2 ⓒ A_0) ;

(21)   (A_1 then before A_2) ⓒ $A_0 = (A_1$ ⓒ A_0) then before (A_2 ⓒ A_0) .

Appendix C

Operational Semantics
of Action Notation

- *The abstract syntax of a kernel action notation is the basis for its formal semantic description. The full action notation can be reduced to the kernel by using some of the algebraic properties specified in Appendix B.*

- *The specification of semantic entities shows what kind of states are needed to support action performance.*

- *The structural operational semantics of action notation gives the formal definition of action performance.*

- *The definition of observational and testing equivalence on actions relates the operational semantics of action notation to the algebraic properties specified in Appendix B.*

The standard action notation used in action semantics allows direct expression of control, dataflow, scopes of bindings, changes to storage, and communication between distributed agents. It is therefore to be expected that this Appendix, which contains its complete operational semantic description, makes a formidable document. The modular structure is shown on the next page. The modules are followed by the definition of observational and testing equivalence.

Whereas standard action notation is semantically rich, the kernel of action notation is syntactically of only moderate size. This is revealed by the grammar specifying the abstract syntax of the kernel. There are eight fundamental binary combinators, and four hybrid combinators. Disregarding the unfolding notation used to abbreviate infinite action terms, there are only two unary combinators in the kernel. There are about 20 primitive actions, most of which take one or two yielders as arguments. This together gives a kernel notation for actions which is about twice as large as the applied λ-notation generally used in denotational semantics [Mos90].

Abstract Syntax

    Actions   **needs: Yielders, Data.**

    Yielders   **needs: Actions, Data.**

    Data   .

Semantic Entities

    Acting   **needs: Abstract Syntax.**

    States   **needs: Acting.**

    Commitments   .

    Processing   **needs: States, Acting.**

Semantic Functions **needs: Abstract Syntax, Semantic Entities.**

    Data   .

    Yielders   **needs: Data.**

    Actions

        Simple   **needs: Yielders, Data.**

            Basic   .

            Functional   .

            Declarative .

            Imperative   .

            Reflective   .

            Communicative .

            Directive

        Compound   **needs: Actions/Simple, Data.**

            Stepping   .

            Simplifying .

            Unfolding   .

            Giving   .

            Receiving

      Processes   **needs: Actions.**

C.1   Abstract Syntax

The grammar below specifies the abstract syntax of a *kernel* of action notation. The general laws in Appendix B define the remaining notation for actions and yielders in terms of the kernel notation. They also specify the notation for data, algebraically.

As usual, the nonterminal symbols of the grammar are capitalized, and the terminal symbols are quoted, to avoid confusion between notation for syntactic and semantic entities.

The abstract syntax of notation for data is left open, so the user of action notation may add nonstandard data notation. A uniform abstract syntax is adopted for applications of unary and binary data operations. The operational semantics of action notation does not depend on the details of notation for data, only on the existence of its intended interpretation.

closed   except Data .
grammar:

C.1.1   Actions

- Action   = Simple-Action | ⟦ Action-Prefix Action ⟧ | ⟦ Action Action-Infix Action ⟧ .
- Simple-Action   = Constant-Action | ⟦ Simple-Prefix Yielder ⟧ |
                 ⟦ To-Prefix Yielder "to" Yielder ⟧ | ⟦ "store" Yielder "in" Yielder ⟧ .
- Constant-Action = "complete" | "escape" | "fail" | "commit" | "unfold" .
- Simple-Prefix   = "give" | "choose" | "produce" | "unbind" |
                 "unstore" | "reserve" | "unreserve" |
                 "enact" | "send" | "remove" | "offer" |
                 "undirect" | "indirectly produce" .
- To-Prefix   = "bind" | "indirectly bind" | "redirect" .
- Action-Prefix   = "unfolding" | "indivisibly" | "patiently" .
- Action-Infix   = "or" | "and" | "and then" | "then" | "trap" |
                 "moreover" | "and then moreover" | "then moreover" |
                 "hence" | "thence" | "before" | "then before" .

C.1.2   Yielders

- Yielder   = Data-Constant | Abstraction |
             ⟦ Data-Unary "(" Yielder ")" ⟧ |
             ⟦ Data-Binary "(" Yielder "," Yielder ")" ⟧ |
             ⟦ "if" Yielder "then" Yielder "else" Yielder ⟧ |
             ⟦ "the" Data "yielded by" Yielder ⟧ | ⟦ Yielder "receiving" Yielder ⟧ |
             "them" | "current bindings" | "current storage" | "current buffer" |
             "current redirections" | "performing-agent" | "contracting-agent" .
- Abstraction = Yielder | ⟦ "abstraction of" Action ⟧ | ⟦ Abs-Prefix Yielder ⟧ |
                 ⟦ Action-Prefix Abstraction ⟧ | ⟦ Abstraction Action-Infix Abstraction ⟧ .
- Abs-Prefix   = "provision" | "production" | "indirect production" .

C.1.3 Data

- Data   = Data-Constant | ⟦ Data-Unary "(" Data ")" ⟧ |
                 ⟦ Data-Binary "(" Data "," Data ")" ⟧ |
                 ⟦ "if" Data "then" Data "else" Data ⟧ | □ .
- Data-Constant = □ .
- Data-Unary   = □ .
- Data-Binary = □ .

C.2   Semantic Entities

In contrast to semantic entities used in action semantic descriptions, those used in operational semantics involve *syntactic* components, representing what remains to be performed.

The specifications below use standard data notation for tuples, maps, etc. For convenience, they also use data sorts that were specified algebraically in Appendix B, such as data and bindings—but they do *not* use actions at all, of course.

includes: **Data Notation** .
includes: **Action Notation/*/Data** (Abstracting *for* abstraction) .

C.2.1   Acting

Acting is a generalization of Action. The new constructs include Terminated entities, which stand for the outcome of the performance of a subaction, and may contain data and bindings. They also include Action entities with attached data and bindings. The classification of Action-Infix into Sequencing, Interleaving, and Normal is for later use.

grammar:

- Acting   = Terminated | Intermediate .
- Terminated   = Completed | Escaped | Failed .
- Completed   = ⟨ "completed" data bindings⟩ .
- Escaped   = ⟨ "escaped" data⟩ .
- Failed   = "failed" .
- Intermediate = Simple-Action | ⟦ Action-Prefix Acting ⟧ | ⟦ Acting Action-Infix Acting ⟧ |
                 ⟨Action data⟩ | ⟨Action bindings⟩ | ⟨Action data bindings⟩ |
                 ⟦ Acting ("before" | "then before") Acting bindings ⟧ | ⟨ "redirect" redirections⟩ .
- Sequencing   = "and then" | "then" | "trap" |
                 "and then moreover" | "then moreover" |
                 "hence" | "thence" | "before" | "then before" .
- Interleaving = "and" | "moreover" .
- Normal   = "and" | "and then" | "then" |
                 "moreover" | "and then moreover" | "then moreover" |
                 "hence" | "thence" | "before" | "then before" .
- Abstracting = ⟦ "abstraction of" Acting ⟧ .

C.2.2   States

A state represents a point in the performance of an action. The local information corresponds to the current stable and permanent information of the performing agent, the transient data and bindings being incorporated in the acting component of the state. The natural number component serves as a serial number to distinguish messages sent between the same agents. The agent components correspond to the performing agent and the contracting agent, respectively. Note that (Action, info) ≤ state.

introduces: state , local-info , info .
(1)   state = (Acting, local-info) .
(2)   local-info = (redirections, storage, natural, buffer, agent, agent) .
(3)   info = (data, bindings, local-info) .

C.2.3   Commitments

A commitment is either uncommitted, or a list indicating that a committing action has been performed together with any communications that are to be emitted by the agent. The standard data operations concatenation _ and items _ are already defined on lists, so we need only to extend them to uncommitted arguments.

introduces: commitment , committing , committed , commitment of _ ,
               uncommitted , concatenation _ , items _ .
(1)   commitment = committing | uncommitted (*disjoint*) .
(2)   committing = list [of communication] .
(3)   committed = empty-list .
(4)   commitment of c:communication* = list of c .
(5)   uncommitted : commitment .
(6)   concatenation _ :: commitment^2 → commitment (*unit is* uncommitted) .
(7)   items uncommitted = ( ) .

C.2.4 Processing

A processing entity represents an ideal snapshot of a distributed system of agents. It consists of a tuple of delayed events. The use of a tuple instead of a set is merely for notational convenience, the order of the events is immaterial.

The active agents are implicit in the processing. The time forever is used as a delay when an agent reaches a terminated state. When c is a tuple of communications, c delayed natural is the processing sort where each communication in c has an arbitrary natural number as delay. Similarly for s delayed natural, where s is a state.

The arbitrary finite delays are attached to state transitions and communications when they are initiated, to represent 'true concurrency' and the lack of synchrony. Processing is finite initially, and it remains finite thereafter. Each agent in the system can only be making one state transition at once, although the number of agents concurrently making transitions is unbounded. Each communication being transmitted is distinguished by a serial number, determined locally on emission.

introduces: processing , initial-processing _ , agents _ ,
event , time , forever , _ delayed _ , undelayed _ .

(1) (1) processing = (event delayed time)* .

(2) initial-processing (A:Acting) =
undelayed (A, empty-map, empty-map, 0, empty-list, user-agent, user-agent) .

(2) (1) agents _ :: processing $\rightarrow$ agent* .

(2) agents ( ) = ( ) .

(3) agents (p_1, p_2) = (agents p_1, agents p_2) .

(4) agents (c:communication delayed t:time) = ( ) .

(5) $s = (x, a_1$:agent, a_2:agent) $\Rightarrow$ agents (s:state delayed t:time) = a_1 .

(3) (1) event = communication **|** state .

(2) time = natural **|** forever .

(3) forever : time .

(4) _ delayed _ :: state, time $\rightarrow$ processing (*total*) ,
communication*, natural $\rightarrow$ processing .

(5) (c:communication) delayed (n:natural) : processing .

(6) (c_1:communication$^+$, c_2:communication$^+$) delayed ($t{\leq}$natural) =
(c_1 delayed t, c_2 delayed t) .

(7) ( ) delayed ($t{\leq}$time) = ( ) .

(8) undelayed e:event = e delayed 0 .

C.3   Semantic Functions

The 'semantic functions' below correspond to a *structural operational semantics*. They are, in general, *not* compositional—in contrast to those in action semantics. See Section 3.4 for an introduction to the style of specification used here, which is algebraic.

C.3.1   Data

For a data term d with abstract syntax D, we expect entity $D = d$. Given the full specification of Data, the corresponding semantic equations could be generated automatically.

introduces: entity _ , unary-operation _ _ , binary-operation _ _ _ _ .

- entity _ :: Data → data .

(1) entity $[\![$ O:Data-Unary "$($" D:Data "$)$" $]\!]$ = unary-operation O (entity D) .

(2) entity $[\![$ O:Data-Binary "$($" D_1:Data "," D_2:Data "$)$" $]\!]$ =
         binary-operation O (entity D_1) (entity D_2) .

(3) entity $[\![$ "if" D_1:Data "then" D_2:Data "else" D_3:Data $]\!]$ =
         if (truth-value & entity D_1) then entity D_2 else entity D_3 .

- unary-operation _ _ :: Data-Unary, data → data .
- binary-operation _ _ _ :: Data-Binary, data, data → data .

C.3.2   Yielders

The evaluation of yielders is compositional, but note that yielders occurring in the action of an abstraction do *not* get evaluated.

introduces: evaluated _ .

- evaluated _ :: (Yielder, info) → data .

(1) evaluated (Y:Data-Constant, i:info) = entity Y .

(2) evaluated ($[\![$ O:Data-Unary "$($" Y:Yielder "$)$" $]\!]$, i:info) = unary-operation O (evaluated (Y i)) .

(3) evaluated ($[\![$ O:Data-Binary "$($" Y_1:Yielder "," Y_2:Yielder "$)$" $]\!]$, i:info) =
         binary-operation O (evaluated (Y_1, i)) (evaluated (Y_2, i)) .

(4) evaluated ($[\![$ "if" Y_1:Yielder "then" Y_2:Yielder "else" Y_3:Yielder $]\!]$, i:info) =
         if (truth-value & evaluated (Y_1, i)) then evaluated (Y_2, i) else evaluated (Y_3, i) .

(5) evaluated ($[\![$ "the" D:Data "yielded by" Y:Yielder $]\!]$, i:info) = entity D & evaluated (Y, i) .

(6) evaluated ($[\![$ Y_1:Yielder "receiving" Y_2:Yielder $]\!]$, d:data, b:bindings, l:local-info) =
         evaluated (Y_1, d, bindings & evaluated (Y_2, d, b, l), l) .

(7) $i = (d$:data, b:bindings, r:redirections, s:storage, n:natural, q:buffer, a_1:agent, a_2:agent) $\Rightarrow$
         evaluated ("them", i:info) = d ;
         evaluated ("current bindings", i:info) = b ;
         evaluated ("current storage", i:info) = s ;
         evaluated ("current buffer", i:info) = q ;
         evaluated ("current redirections", i:info) = r ;
         evaluated ("performing-agent", i:info) = a_1 ;
         evaluated ("contracting-agent", i:info) = a_2 .

(8)   evaluated ($\llbracket$ "abstraction of" A:Action $\rrbracket$, i:info) = $\llbracket$ "abstraction of" A $\rrbracket$.

(9)   evaluated $(Y, i) = d$: data $\Rightarrow$
      evaluated ($\llbracket$ "provision" Y:Yielder $\rrbracket$, i:info) = $\llbracket$ "abstraction of" "completed" d empty-map $\rrbracket$.

(10) evaluated $(Y, i) = b$: bindings $\Rightarrow$
      evaluated ($\llbracket$ "production" Y:Yielder $\rrbracket$, i:info) = $\llbracket$ "abstraction of" "completed" ( ) b $\rrbracket$.

(11) evaluated $(Y, i) = r$: redirections $\Rightarrow$
      evaluated ($\llbracket$ "indirect production" Y:Yielder $\rrbracket$, i:info) = $\llbracket$ "abstraction of" "redirect" r $\rrbracket$.

(12) evaluated $(Y, i) = \llbracket$ "abstraction of" A:Acting $\rrbracket$ $\Rightarrow$
      evaluated ($\llbracket$ O:Action-Prefix Y:Yielder $\rrbracket$, i) = $\llbracket$ "abstraction of" $\llbracket$ O A $\rrbracket$ $\rrbracket$.

(13) evaluated $(Y_1, i) = \llbracket$ "abstraction of" A_1:Acting $\rrbracket$;
      evaluated $(Y_2, i) = \llbracket$ "abstraction of" A_2:Acting $\rrbracket$ $\Rightarrow$
      evaluated ($\llbracket$ Y_1:Yielder O:Action-Infix Y_2:Yielder $\rrbracket$, i) = $\llbracket$ "abstraction of" $\llbracket$ A_1 O A_2 $\rrbracket$ $\rrbracket$.

C.3.3   Actions

run s is the sort of terminated states reachable from indivisible performances starting from the intermediate state s, together with the concatenated commitments made by each step. stepped s is the sort of states obtained from performing the first transition from the intermediate state s. Both functions are undefined on terminated states.

introduces: run _ , stepped _ .

- run _ :: state $\rightarrow$ (Terminated, local-info, commitment) .

(1)   stepped $(A, l) \geq (A'$:Intermediate, l':local-info, c':commitment) ;
      run $(A', l') \geq (A''$:Terminated, l'':local-info, c'':commitment) $\Rightarrow$
      run $(A$:Acting, l:local-info) $\geq$ $(A'', l''$, concatenation $(c', c''))$.

(2)   stepped $(A, l) \geq (A'$:Terminated, l':local-info, c':commitment) $\Rightarrow$
      run $(A$:Acting, l:local-info) $\geq (A', l', c')$.

- stepped _ :: state $\rightarrow$ (state, commitment) .

(3)   stepped $(A$:Terminated, l:local-info) = nothing .

C.3.3.1   Simple

(1) $i = (d$:data, b:bindings, l:local-info) ;
      evaluated (Y, i) = nothing $\Rightarrow$
      stepped ($\llbracket$ P:Simple-Prefix Y:Yielder $\rrbracket$, i:info) =
      stepped ($\llbracket$ P:To-Prefix Y:Yielder "to" Y_2:Yielder $\rrbracket$, i:info) =
      stepped ($\llbracket$ P:To-Prefix Y_1:Yielder "to" Y:Yielder $\rrbracket$, i:info) =
      stepped ($\llbracket$ "store" Y:Yielder "in" Y_2:Yielder $\rrbracket$, i:info) =
      stepped ($\llbracket$ "store" Y_1:Yielder "in" Y:Yielder $\rrbracket$, i:info) =
          ("failed", l, uncommitted) .

When evaluated (Y, i) is a vacuous sort different to nothing, the action being performed is regarded as ill-formed, and no transition at all is defined.

C.3.3.1.1   Basic

(1) stepped ("complete", d:data, b:bindings, l:local-info) =
        ("completed", ( ), empty-map, l, uncommitted) .

(2) stepped ("escape", d:data, b:bindings, l:local-info) =
        ("escaped", d, l, uncommitted) .

(3) stepped ("fail", d:data, b:bindings, l:local-info) =
        ("failed", l, uncommitted) .

(4) stepped ("commit", d:data, b:bindings, l:local-info) =
        ("completed", ( ), empty-map, l, committed) .

(5) stepped ("unfold", d:data, b:bindings, l:local-info) = nothing .

C.3.3.1.2   Functional

(1) evaluated (Y, d, b, l) = d' : data $\Rightarrow$
     stepped ($[\![$ "give" Y:Yielder $]\!]$, d:data, b:bindings, l:local-info) =
        ("completed", d', empty-map, l, uncommitted) .

(2) evaluated (Y, d, b, l) $\geq d'$: data $\Rightarrow$
     stepped ($[\![$ "choose" Y:Yielder $]\!]$, d:data, b:bindings, l:local-info) $\geq$
        ("completed", d', empty-map, l, uncommitted) .

choose Y is the only primitive action whose performance is nondeterministic, with stepped giving a
proper sort of states when Y evaluates to a proper sort of data.

C.3.3.1.3   Declarative

(1) evaluated (Y_1, d, b, l) = t : token ;
     evaluated (Y_2, d, b, l) = v : bindable $\Rightarrow$
     stepped ($[\![$ "bind" Y_1 "to" Y_2 $]\!]$, d:data, b:bindings, l:local-info) =
        ("completed", ( ), map t to v, l, uncommitted) .

(2) evaluated (Y, d, b, l) = b' : bindings $\Rightarrow$
     stepped ($[\![$ "produce" Y:Yielder $]\!]$, d:data, b:bindings, l:local-info) =
        ("completed", ( ), b', l, uncommitted) .

(3) evaluated (Y, d, b, l) = t : token $\Rightarrow$
     stepped ($[\![$ "unbind" Y:Yielder $]\!]$, d:data, b:bindings, l:local-info) =
        ("completed", ( ), map t to unknown, l, uncommitted) .

C.3.3.1.4   Imperative

(1) evaluated (Y_1, d, b, l) = v : storable ;
     evaluated (Y_2, d, b, l) = c : cell ;
     l = (r:redirections, s:storage, $x!$) ; l' = (r, overlay (map c to v, s), x) $\Rightarrow$
     stepped ($[\![$ "store" Y_1 "in" Y_2 $]\!]$, d:data, b:bindings, l:local-info) =
        if c is in mapped-set of s
        then ("completed", ( ), empty-map, l', committed)
        else ("failed", l, uncommitted) .

(2)   evaluated $(Y, d, b, l) = c$: cell ;
 $l = (r$:redirections, s:storage, $x!)$; $l' = (r$, overlay (map c to uninitialized, s), $x) \Rightarrow$
 stepped ($\llbracket$ "unstore" $Y \rrbracket$, d:data, b:bindings, l:local-info) =
   if c is in mapped-set of s
   then ("completed", ( ), empty-map, l', committed)
   else ("failed", l, uncommitted) .

(3)   evaluated $(Y, d, b, l) = c$: cell ;
 $l = (r$:redirections, s:storage, $x!)$; $l' = (r$, disjoint-union (map c to uninitialized, s), $x) \Rightarrow$
 stepped ($\llbracket$ "reserve" $Y \rrbracket$, d:data, b:bindings, l:local-info) =
   if not (c is in mapped-set of s)
   then ("completed", ( ), empty-map, l', committed)
   else ("failed", l, uncommitted) .

(4)   evaluated $(Y, d, b, l) = c$: cell ;
 $l = (r$:redirections, s:storage, $x!)$; $l' = (r$, s omitting set of c, $x) \Rightarrow$
 stepped ($\llbracket$ "unreserve" $Y \rrbracket$, d:data, b:bindings, l:local-info) =
   if c is in mapped-set of s
   then ("completed", ( ), empty-map, l', committed)
   else ("failed", l, uncommitted) .

C.3.3.1.5 Reflective

(1)   evaluated $(Y, d, b, l) = \llbracket$ "abstraction of" A:Acting $\rrbracket \Rightarrow$
 stepped ($\llbracket$ "enact" Y:Yielder $\rrbracket$, d:data, b:bindings, l:local-info) =
   (given (received $(A$, empty-map), ( )), l) .

C.3.3.1.6 Communicative

(1)   evaluated $(Y, d, b, l) = m \le$ message ; m [from a_1] [at n] = m' : message ;
 $l = (r$:redirections, s:storage, n:natural, q:buffer, a_1:agent, a_2:agent) ;
 $l' = (r, s$, successor n, q, a_1, $a_2) \Rightarrow$
 stepped ($\llbracket$ "send" $Y \rrbracket$, d:data, b:bindings, l:local-info) =
   ("completed", ( ), empty-map, l', list of m') .

(2)   evaluated $(Y, d, b, l) = m$: message ;
 $l = (r$:redirections, s:storage, n:natural, q:buffer, a_1:agent, a_2:agent) ;
 $l' = (r, s, n, q$ omitting set of m, a_1, $a_2) \Rightarrow$
 stepped ($\llbracket$ "remove" $Y \rrbracket$, d:data, b:bindings, l:local-info) =
   if m is in set of items q
   then ("completed", ( ), empty-map, l', list of c)
   else ("failed", l, uncommitted) .

(3)   evaluated $(Y, d, b, l) = c \le$ contract ; c [from a_1] [at n] = c' : contract ;
 $l = (r$:redirections, s:storage, n:natural, q:buffer, a_1:agent, a_2:agent) ;
 $l' = (r, s$, successor n, q, a_1, $a_2) \Rightarrow$
 stepped ($\llbracket$ "offer" $Y \rrbracket$, d:data, b:bindings, l:local-info) =
   ("completed", ( ), empty-map, l', list of c') .

C.3.3.1.7   Directive

(1)   evaluated $(Y_1, d, b, l) = t$: token ;
     evaluated $(Y_2, d, b, l) = v$: bindable | unknown ;
     i : indirection [not in mapped-set r] ;
     $l = (r{:}\text{redirections}, x!)$; $l' = (\text{overlay (map } i \text{ to } v, r), x) \Rightarrow$
     stepped ($[\![$ "indirectly bind" Y_1 "to" Y_2 $]\!]$, d:data, b:bindings, l:local-info) $\geq$
         ("completed", ( ), map t to i, l', committed) .

(2)   evaluated $(Y_1, d, b, l) = t$: token ;
     evaluated $(Y_2, d, b, l) = v$: bindable | unknown ;
     $i = (b$ at $t)$: indirection ; $l = (r{:}\text{redirections}, x!)$; $l' = (\text{overlay (map } i \text{ to } v, r), x) \Rightarrow$
     stepped ($[\![$ "redirect" Y_1 "to" Y_2 $]\!]$, d:data, b:bindings, l:local-info) $=$
         ("completed", ( ), empty-map, l', committed) .

(3)   evaluated $(Y, d, b, l) = t$: token ;
     $i = (b$ at $t)$: indirection ; $l = (r{:}\text{redirections}, x!)$; $l' = (r$ omitting set of i, $x) \Rightarrow$
     stepped ($[\![$ "undirect" Y $]\!]$, d:data, b:bindings, l:local-info) $=$
         ("completed", ( ), empty-map, l', committed) .

(4)   evaluated $(Y, d, b, l) = r'$: redirections ;
     $l = (r{:}\text{redirections}, x!)$; $l' = (\text{overlay } (r', r), x) \Rightarrow$
     stepped ($[\![$ "indirectly produce" Y:Yielder $]\!]$, d:data, b:bindings, l:local-info) $=$
         ("completed", ( ), empty-map, l', committed) .

(5) $l = (r{:}\text{redirections}, x!)$; $l' = (\text{overlay } (r', r), x) \Rightarrow$
     stepped ("redirect", r':redirections, l:local-info) $=$
         ("completed", ( ), empty-map, l', committed) .

C.3.3.2   Compound

The function simplified is only applied to an intermediate compound acting A where an immediate component of A is the acting part of the result of applying stepped. The result is an acting equivalent to A, simplified for instance by propagating "failed". The specification of simplified $[\![$ A_1 O A_2 $]\!]$ when both A_1 and A_2 are terminated shows how the flow of transient and scoped information *out of* actions is determined by the various combinators.

unfolded $(A, [\![$ "unfolding" A $]\!])$ is used to replace occurrences of unfold by $[\![$ "unfolding" A $]\!]$ before performing A. Each unfolding takes a step, so performing $[\![$ "unfolding" "unfold" $]\!]$ takes infinitely-many steps.

given (A, d) is used to freeze the initial transient data given to A; similarly received (A, b) for bindings. The specification of given and received shows clearly how the flow of data and bindings *into* actions is determined by the various combinators

introduces: simplified _ , unfolded _ , given _ , received _ .

- simplified _ :: Acting $\rightarrow$ Acting .
- unfolded _ :: (Action, Action) $\rightarrow$ Action .
- given _ :: (Acting, data) $\rightarrow$ Acting .
- received _ :: (Acting, bindings) $\rightarrow$ Acting .

C.3.3.2.1 Stepping

(1) stepped ($[\![$ "unfolding" A:Action $]\!]$, d:data, b:bindings, l:local-info) =
(given (received (unfolded (A, $[\![$ "unfolding" A $]\!]$), b), d), l, uncommitted) .

(2) stepped ($[\![$ "indivisibly" A:Acting $]\!]$, l:local-info) = run (A, l) .

(3) run (A, l) $\geq$ ("failed", l':local-info, c':commitment) $\Rightarrow$
stepped ($[\![$ "patiently" A:Acting $]\!]$, l:local-info) $\geq$ ($[\![$ "patiently" A $]\!]$, l', c') .

(4) run (A, l) $\geq$ (A':(Completed | Escaped), l':local-info, c':commitment) $\Rightarrow$
stepped ($[\![$ "patiently" A:Acting $]\!]$, l:local-info) $\geq$ (A', l', c') .

(5) stepped (A_1, l) $\geq$ (A_1':Acting, l':local-info, c':commitment) ;
$[\![$ A_1 O A_2 $]\!]$: $[\![$ Intermediate Sequencing Intermediate $]\!]$ |
$[\![$ Intermediate Interleaving (Intermediate | Completed) $]\!]$ $\Rightarrow$
stepped ($[\![$ A_1 O A_2 $]\!]$, l:local-info) $\geq$ (simplified $[\![$ A_1' O A_2 $]\!]$, l', c') .

(6) stepped (A_2, l) $\geq$ (A_2':Acting, l':local-info, c':commitment) ;
$[\![$ A_1 O A_2 $]\!]$: $[\![$ (Intermediate | Completed) Interleaving Intermediate $]\!]$ $\Rightarrow$
stepped ($[\![$ A_1 O A_2 $]\!]$, l:local-info) $\geq$ (simplified $[\![$ A_1 O A_2' $]\!]$, l', c') .

(7) stepped (A_1, l) $\geq$ (A_1':Acting, l':local-info, uncommitted) ;
$[\![$ A_1 O A_2 $]\!]$: $[\![$ Intermediate "or" Intermediate $]\!]$ $\Rightarrow$
stepped ($[\![$ A_1 O A_2 $]\!]$, l:local-info) $\geq$ (simplified $[\![$ A_1' O A_2 $]\!]$, l', uncommitted) .

(8) stepped (A_2, l) $\geq$ (A_2':Acting, l':local-info, uncommitted) ;
$[\![$ A_1 O A_2 $]\!]$: $[\![$ Intermediate "or" Intermediate $]\!]$ $\Rightarrow$
stepped ($[\![$ A_1 O A_2 $]\!]$, l:local-info) $\geq$ (simplified $[\![$ A_1 O A_2' $]\!]$, l', uncommitted) .

(9) stepped (A_1, l) $\geq$ (A_1':Acting, l':local-info, c':committing) ;
$[\![$ A_1 O A_2 $]\!]$: $[\![$ Intermediate "or" Intermediate $]\!]$ $\Rightarrow$
stepped ($[\![$ A_1 O A_2 $]\!]$, l:local-info) $\geq$ (A_1', l', c') .

(10) stepped (A_2, l) $\geq$ (A_2':Acting, l':local-info, c':committing) ;
$[\![$ A_1 O A_2 $]\!]$: $[\![$ Intermediate "or" Intermediate $]\!]$ $\Rightarrow$
stepped ($[\![$ A_1 O A_2 $]\!]$, l:local-info) $\geq$ (A_2', l', c') .

C.3.3.2.2 Simplifying

(1) $[\![$ A_1' O A_2 $]\!]$: $[\![$ Failed Sequencing Intermediate $]\!]$ |
$[\![$ (Failed | Escaped) Interleaving (Intermediate | Completed) $]\!]$ |
$[\![$ Escaped Normal Intermediate $]\!]$ |
$[\![$ Completed "trap" Intermediate $]\!]$ |
$[\![$ (Completed | Escaped) "or" Intermediate $]\!]$ $\Rightarrow$
simplified $[\![$ A_1' O A_2 $]\!]$ = A_1' .

(2) $[\![$ A_1 O A_2' $]\!]$: $[\![$ (Intermediate | Completed) Interleaving (Failed | Escaped) $]\!]$ |
$[\![$ Intermediate "or" (Completed | Escaped) $]\!]$ $\Rightarrow$
simplified $[\![$ A_1 O A_2' $]\!]$ = A_2' .

(3) $[\![$ A_1' O A_2' $]\!]$: $[\![$ Intermediate Action-Infix Intermediate $]\!]$ $\Rightarrow$
simplified $[\![$ A_1' O A_2' $]\!]$ = $[\![$ A_1' O A_2' $]\!]$.

(4) simplified $[\![$ "failed" "or" A_2:Intermediate $]\!]$ = A_2 .

(5) simplified $[\![$ A_1:Intermediate "or" "failed" $]\!]$ = A_1 .

(6)   simplified ⟦ "completed" d_1:data b_1:bindings "and" "completed" d_2:data b_2:bindings ⟧ =
       ⟨ "completed" (d_1, d_2) (disjoint-union (b_1, b_2))⟩ .

(7)   simplified ⟦ A_1:Completed "and then" A_2:Intermediate ⟧ = ⟦ A_1 "and" A_2 ⟧ .

(8)   simplified ⟦ "completed" d_1:data b_1:bindings "then" A_2:Intermediate ⟧ =
       ⟦ "completed" ( ) b_1 "and" (given (A_2, d_1)) ⟧ .

(9)   simplified ⟦ "escaped" d_1:data "trap" A_2:Intermediate ⟧ = given (A_2, d_1) .

(10) simplified ⟦ "completed" d_1:data b_1:bindings "moreover" "completed" d_2:data b_2:bindings ⟧ =
       ⟨ "completed" (d_1, d_2) (overlay (b_2, b_1))⟩ .

(11) simplified ⟦ A_1:Completed "and then moreover" A_2:Intermediate ⟧ =
       ⟦ A_1 "moreover" A_2 ⟧ .

(12) simplified ⟦ "completed" d_1:data b_1:bindings "then moreover" A_2:Intermediate ⟧ =
       ⟦ "completed" ( ) b_1 "moreover" (given (A_2, d_1)) ⟧ .

(13) simplified ⟦ "completed" d_1:data b_1:bindings "hence" A_2:Intermediate ⟧ =
       ⟦ "completed" d_1 empty-map "and" (received (A_2, b_1)) ⟧ .

(14) simplified ⟦ "completed" d_1:data b_1:bindings "thence" A_2:Intermediate ⟧ =
       given (received (A_2, b_1), d_1) .

(15) simplified ⟦ "completed" d_1:data b_1:bindings "before" A_2:Intermediate b:bindings ⟧ =
       ⟦ "completed" d_1 b_1 "moreover" (received $(A_2,$ overlay (b_1, b))) ⟧ .

(16) simplified ⟦ "completed" d_1:data b_1:bindings "then before" A_2:Intermediate b:bindings ⟧ =
       ⟦ "completed" ( ) b_1 "moreover" (given (received $(A_2,$ overlay(b_1, b)), d_1)) ⟧ .

C.3.3.2.3   Unfolding

(1)   unfolded $(A_1$:Simple-Action, A_0:Action) = if A_1 is "unfold" then ⟦ "unfolding" A_0 ⟧ else A_1 .

(2)   unfolded (⟦ O:Action-Prefix A_1:Action ⟧, A_0) = ⟦ O (unfolded (A_1, A_0)) ⟧ .

(3)   unfolded (⟦ A_1:Action O:Action-Infix A_2:Action ⟧, A_0) =
       ⟦ (unfolded (A_1, A_0)) O (unfolded (A_2, A_0)) ⟧ .

C.3.3.2.4   Giving

(1)   given $(A$:Terminated, d:data) = A .

(2) A : Simple-Action | ⟦ "unfolding" Action ⟧ | ⟦ "redirect" redirections ⟧   ⇒
           given $(A, d$:data) = (A, d) ;
           given $(A, b$:bindings, d:data) = (A, d, b) .

(3) O:"indivisibly" | "patiently"   ⇒
       given (⟦ O A:Acting ⟧, d:data) = ⟦ O (given (A, d)) ⟧ .

(4) O : "and" | "and then" | "moreover" | "and then moreover" | "hence" | "before"   ⇒
       given (⟦ A_1:Acting O A_2:Acting ⟧, d:data) = ⟦ (given (A_1, d)) O (given (A_2, d)) ⟧ .

(5) O : "then" | "trap" | "then moreover" | "thence" | "then before"   ⇒
       given (⟦ A_1:Acting O A_2:Acting ⟧, d:data) = ⟦ (given (A_1, d)) O A_2 ⟧ .

C.3.3.2.5 Receiving

(1) received $(A:\text{Terminated}, b:\text{bindings}) = A$.

(2) $A : \text{Simple-Action} \mid [\![\text{ "unfolding" Action }]\!] \mid [\![\text{ "redirect" redirections }]\!] \Rightarrow$

   received $(A, b:\text{bindings}) = (A, b)$;

   received $(A, d:\text{data}, b:\text{bindings}) = (A, d, b)$.

(3) $O:\text{"indivisibly"} \mid \text{"patiently"} \Rightarrow$
   received $([\![O\ A:\text{Acting}]\!], b:\text{bindings}) = [\![O\ (\text{received } (A, b))]\!]$.

(4) $O : \text{"and"} \mid \text{"and then"} \mid \text{"then"} \mid \text{"trap"} \mid$
   $\text{"moreover"} \mid \text{"and then moreover"} \mid \text{"then moreover"} \Rightarrow$
   received $([\![A_1:\text{Acting}\ O\ A_2:\text{Acting}]\!], b:\text{bindings}) = [\![(\text{received } (A_1, b))\ O\ (\text{received } (A_2, b))]\!]$.

(5) $O : \text{"hence"} \mid \text{"thence"} \Rightarrow$
   received $([\![A_1:\text{Acting}\ O\ A_2:\text{Acting}]\!], b:\text{bindings}) = [\![(\text{received } (A_1, b))\ O\ A_2]\!]$.

(6) $O : \text{"before"} \mid \text{"then before"} \Rightarrow$
   received $([\![A_1:\text{Acting}\ O\ A_2:\text{Acting}]\!], b:\text{bindings}) = [\![(\text{received } (A_1, b))\ O\ A_2\ b]\!]$.

C.3.4 Processes

concluded p is used to define testing equivalence of actions. It gives the conclusive outcomes obtained by iteratively advancing the processing p until the user agent reaches a terminated state. Other (contracted) agents are *not* required to reach terminated states.

We may characterize an implementation of action notation as *safe* when, given a representation of any $A:\text{Action}$, either it diverges or it reaches a representation of some individual of concluded (initial-processing A). This definition allows the safe implementation of communicative actions on single processors, as well as that of uncommunicative actions on multi-processors. (Of course it allows the always-diverging implementation as well, but in practice, users are just as dissatisfied with extremely slow implementations as with diverging ones!)

advanced p deals with the undelayed communications and state transitions, and advances the delayed ones by one unit of time. It inserts each undelayed message in the buffer of the agent to which it was sent; several undelayed messages for the same agent are inserted in arbitrary order. Undelayed contracts are awarded to arbitrary agents that are not currently active. For each undelayed intermediate state in p, it produces a possible next state with an arbitrary delay. Any communications committed by the transition are given arbitrary delays too.

introduces: conclusion , concluded _ , advanced _ .

(1) conclusion = "completed" | "escaped" | "failed" .

- concluded _ :: processing → conclusion .

(2) $s = (c:\text{conclusion}, x!, \text{user-agent}, \text{user-agent}) \Rightarrow$
   concluded $(p:\text{processing}, \text{undelayed } s:\text{state}, p':\text{processing}) \ge c$.

(3) advanced $p \ge p'$: processing ; concluded $p' \ge c:\text{conclusion} \Rightarrow$
   concluded $p:\text{processing} \ge c$.

- advanced _ :: processing → processing .

(4) p_1, p_2 : processing ; e_1, e_2 : (event delayed time) ⇒
       advanced (p_1, e_1, e_2, p_2) = advanced (p_1, e_2, e_1, p_2) .

(5)   advanced (c:communication delayed t:positive-integer, p:processing) ≥
             (c delayed predecessor t, advanced p) .

(6) m : message [to a_1] ;
       s = ($x!$, q:buffer, a_1:agent, a_2:agent) ; s' = (x, list of (items q, m), a_1, a_2) ⇒
       advanced (undelayed m, s:state delayed t:time, p:processing) =
             advanced (s' delayed t, p) .

(7) m : message [to agent[not in set of agents of p]] ⇒
       advanced (undelayed m, p:processing) = advanced p .

(8) c : contract [to a≤agent] [from a_2:agent] [containing [["abstraction of" A:Acting]]] ;
       a_1 : a [not in set of agents of p] ;
       s = (given (received (A, empty-map), ( )), empty-map, empty-map, 0, empty-list, a_1, a_2) ⇒
       advanced (undelayed c, p:processing) ≥ (undelayed s, advanced p) .

(9) c : contract [to a≤agent] ;
       a [not in set of agents of p] = nothing ⇒
       advanced (undelayed c, p:processing) ≥ (undelayed c, advanced p) .

(10) p & (undelayed communication)$^+$ = nothing ⇒
       advanced (s:state delayed t:positive-integer, p:processing) =
             (s delayed predecessor t, advanced p) .

(11) p & (undelayed communication)$^+$ = nothing ⇒
       advanced (s:state delayed forever, p:processing) =
             (s delayed forever, advanced p) .

(12) p & (undelayed communication)$^+$ = nothing ;
       stepped s ≥ (s':(Intermediate, local-info), c:commitment) ⇒
       advanced (undelayed s:state, p:processing) ≥
             (items c delayed natural, s' delayed natural, advanced p) .

(13) p & (undelayed communication)$^+$ = nothing ;
       stepped s ≥ (s':(Terminated, local-info), c:commitment) ⇒
       advanced (undelayed s:state, p:processing) ≥
             (items c delayed natural, s' delayed forever, advanced p) .

The inclusion of s' delayed forever in the processing prevents the performing agent of the terminated state s' from ever being re-contracted.

C.4 Equivalence

The operational semantics of Action Notation determines the processing possibilities of each action. But this does not, by itself, provide a useful notion of *equivalence* between actions. For if two compound actions have exactly the same processing possibilities, it is easy to see that they must have the same compositional structure.

From a user's point of view, however, two actions may be considered equivalent whenever there is no *test* that reveals the differences in their processing possibilities. A test on an action may consist of performing it locally, and checking that it completes; or of subcontracting it to another agent, and demanding a certain pattern of communication. A class of tests, together with a criterion for the success, failure, or inconclusiveness of the processing of a test, induces a so-called *testing equivalence* on actions.

We expect the testing equivalence of actions to include various algebraic laws, such as associativity of the action combinators. Moreover, we expect it to be a *congruence*, i.e., preserved by the combinators. Then the laws can be used in algebraic reasoning to show that various compound actions are equivalent, perhaps justifying a *program transformation rule* for some language on the basis of its action semantics.

It is easy to show that our testing equivalence is in fact a congruence. Unfortunately, it is difficult to verify directly that testing equivalences includes particular laws: one would have to consider all possible tests on the actions involved in the laws! Instead, we define another, smaller equivalence called *bisimulation*, which can more easily be shown to include the intended laws, and then argue that bisimulation itself is included in our testing equivalence.

The techniques used here were developed by Park, Milner, de Nicola, and Hennessy, mainly in connection with studies of the specification calculus CCS. The notation and presentation below follow [Mil90], although note that here we have to deal with local information and commitments, as well as actions.

C.4.1 Bisimulation

First we define transition relations on states:

Definition C.1 *For each c :* commitment *let* $\xrightarrow{c} \subseteq$ state $\times$ state *be the* state transition relation *determined by* stepped _ *as follows:*

$$s \xrightarrow{c} s' \text{ iff } \text{stepped } s \geq (s',\, c) : (\text{state, commitment}) .$$

When c is uncommitted *we write* $\xrightarrow{}$ *instead of* $\xrightarrow{c}$.

Further, for each c : commitment *let* $\overset{c}{\Longrightarrow} \subseteq$ state $\times$ state *be the* observable *state transition relation defined by*

$$\overset{c}{\Longrightarrow} = \xrightarrow{}^* \ \xrightarrow{c} \ \xrightarrow{}^*$$

(where $R_1\, R_2$ denotes the composition of relations R_1, R_2 and R^* denotes the reflexive transitive closure of R).

Now we consider relations on actions, i.e., elements of Action:

Definition C.2 *Let $\mathcal{H}$ be the function over binary relations $R \subseteq$ Action×Action such that $(A_1, A_2) \in \mathcal{H}(R)$ iff, for all l:local-info,*

- *Whenever $(A_1, l) \xrightarrow{c} (A'_1, l')$ then,*
  - *$(A_2, l) \xRightarrow{c} (A'_1, l')$, if A'_1 : Terminated,*
  - *for some A'_2 with $(A'_1, A'_2) \in R$, $(A_2, l) \xRightarrow{c} (A'_2, l')$, otherwise;*
- *Whenever $(A_2, l) \xrightarrow{c} (A'_2, l')$ then,*
  - *$(A_1, l) \xRightarrow{c} (A'_2, l')$, if A'_2 : Terminated,*
  - *for some A'_1 with $(A'_1, A'_2) \in R$, $(A_1, l) \xRightarrow{c} (A'_1, l')$, otherwise.*

Definition C.3 *$R \subseteq$ Action × Action is a bisimulation if $R \subseteq \mathcal{H}(R)$.*
Let $\approx = \bigcup \{R \mid R \text{ is a bisimulation}\}$. When $A_1 \approx A_2$ we say that A_1 and A_2 are bisimilar.

Notice that two actions can only be bisimilar when they have similar transitions for *any* particular local information. In practice, this means that they must refer to exactly the same items of the current information.

Proposition C.1 *$\approx$ is the largest bisimulation, the largest fixed point of $\mathcal{H}$, and an equivalence relation.*

Proof: Using the monotonicity of $\mathcal{H}$. See [Mil90] for the details of a similar proof. □

Proposition C.2 *$\approx$ is a congruence for the constructs of action notation.*

Proof: From the definitions, and by constructing bisimulations containing the compound actions when subactions are bisimilar. For example, consider the combinator A' then A: we have to show that whenever $A_1 \approx A_2$ we get also A_1 then $A \approx A_2$ then A, and similarly for the other argument of _ then _ . It is enough to show that $\{(A_1 \text{ then } A, A_2 \text{ then } A) \mid A_1 \approx A_2; A, A_1, A_2: \text{Action}\}$ is a bisimulation. For any l:local-info, and any transition $(A_1, l) \xrightarrow{c} (A'_1, l')$ to a *terminated* state, we have $(A_2, l) \xRightarrow{c} (A'_1, l')$ and the result follows immediately. Similarly for transitions to *intermediate* states, only now $(A_2, l) \xRightarrow{c} (A'_2, l')$ for some A'_2 with $A'_1 \approx A'_2$. □

Proposition C.3 *The laws relating kernel actions given in Appendix B are included in $\approx$.*

Proof: By exhibiting for each law, a bisimulation that contains all instances of that law. □

The laws involving non-kernel constructs of action notation are regarded as definitions of those constructs, and there is nothing to prove concerning bisimilarity for them.

It should be noted that (for simplicity) bisimulation here is defined to be insensitive to the possibility of uncommitted divergence, i.e., an infinite sequence of $\xrightarrow{\ \ }$ state transitions.

C.4.2   Testing Equivalence

The basic idea of testing an action is to let it be performed in an arbitrary context. The result of processing a particular test may be that the action succeeds or fails to pass that test—or it may be that no conclusion is reached.

Let tests be initiated by the user agent. The user may either perform the tested action itself, or subcontract the performance to another agent. The latter possibility allows the communications of an action to be tested—in interaction not only with the user, but also with an unbounded number of other agents.

Rather than letting the user agent embed the tested action in an arbitrary context, we may just as well let the user agent start by giving an abstraction that incorporates the tested action. Thus:

Definition C.4 *The* testing *of an action A by an action A′ starts from*

     testing $(A, A') =$
         initial-processing $[\![\; [\![$ "give" $[\![$ "abstraction of" $A\;]\!]\;]\!]$ "then" $A'\;]\!]$.

We take the final state of the user as indicative of the outcome of the test, ignoring whether or not subcontracted agents have already terminated. Any completed or escaped state is regarded as success; any failed state is regarded as failure to pass the test. Divergence is regarded as being inconclusive.

Testing equivalence is now defined in terms of the operational semantics of actions as follows:

Definition C.5 *Two actions A_1, A_2 are* testing equivalent, *written $A_1 \equiv A_2$, iff for all actions A',*

     concluded (testing (A_1, A')) = concluded (testing (A_2, A')) .

Proposition C.4 $A_1 \approx A_2$ *implies* $A_1 \equiv A_2$.

Proof: Since bisimilarity is a congruence, we have

     testing $(A_1, A') \approx$ testing (A_2, A')

and from the definition of $\approx$ it can be seen that corresponding states involving bisimilar actions lead to identical possibilities of final states, and hence the same choice of outcomes.   □

Appendix D

Informal Summary
of Action Notation

- The systematic informal description of action notation summarizes Part II, and gives further details. It is intended for reference.

- To make it self-contained, it starts by repeating most of the introduction to the concepts of actions, data, and yielders given in Section 1.5.2.

- The symbols of action notation are explained below in the same order as they are introduced in Part II and Appendix B, as indicated below. See the start of Appendix B for a more detailed overview of the modular structure of action notation.

Action Notation

    Basic.
    Functional.
    Declarative.
    Imperative.
    Reflective.
    Communicative.
    Directive.
    Hybrid.
    Facets
        Outcomes.
        Incomes.
        Actions.
        Yielders.
        Unfolding.

Actions are essentially dynamic, *computational* entities. The *performance* of an action directly represents information processing behaviour and reflects the gradual, step-wise nature of computation. Items of data are, in contrast, essentially static, *mathematical* entities, representing pieces of information, e.g., particular numbers. Of course actions are 'mathematical' too, in the sense that they are abstract, formally-defined entities, analogous to abstract machines defined in automata theory. A *yielder* represents an *unevaluated* item of data, whose value depends on the *current information*, i.e., the previously-computed and input values that are available to the performance of the enclosing action. For example, a yielder might always evaluate to the datum currently stored in a particular cell, which could change during the performance of an action.

Actions

A performance of an action, which may be part of an enclosing action, either:

- *completes*, corresponding to normal termination (the performance of the enclosing action proceeds normally); or

- *escapes*, corresponding to exceptional termination (parts of the enclosing action are skipped until the escape is trapped); or

- *fails*, corresponding to abandoning the performance of an action (the enclosing action performs an alternative action, if there is one, otherwise it fails too); or

- *diverges*, corresponding to nontermination (the enclosing action also diverges).

Actions can be used to represent the semantics of programs: action performances correspond to possible program behaviours. Furthermore, actions can represent the (perhaps indirect) contribution that *parts* of programs, such as statements and expressions, make to the semantics of entire programs.

An action may be nondeterministic, having different possible performances for the same initial information. Nondeterminism represents implementation-dependence, where the behaviour of a program (or the contribution of a part of it) may vary between different implementations—or even between different instants of time on the same implementation. Note that nondeterminism does not imply actual randomness: each implementation of a nondeterministic behaviour may be absolutely deterministic.

The information processed by action performance may be classified according to how far it tends to be propagated, as follows:

- *transient*: tuples of data, corresponding to intermediate results;

- *scoped*: bindings of tokens to data, corresponding to symbol tables;

- *stable*: data stored in cells, corresponding to the values assigned to variables;

- *permanent*: data communicated between distributed actions.

Transient information is made available to an action for immediate use. Scoped information, in contrast, may generally be referred to throughout an entire action, although it may also be hidden temporarily. Stable information can be changed, but not hidden, in the action, and it persists until explicitly destroyed. Permanent information cannot even be changed, merely augmented.

When an action is performed, transient information is given only on completion or escape, and scoped information is produced only on completion. In contrast, changes to stable information and extensions to permanent information are made *during* action performance, and are unaffected by subsequent divergence, failure, or escape.

The different kinds of information give rise to so-called *facets* of actions, focusing on the processing of at most one kind of information at a time:

- the *basic* facet, processing independently of information (control flows);

- the *functional* facet, processing transient information (actions are *given* and *give* data);

- the *declarative* facet, processing scoped information (actions *receive* and *produce* bindings);

- the *imperative* facet, processing stable information (actions *reserve* and *unreserve* cells of storage, and *change* the data stored in cells); and

- the *communicative* facet, processing permanent information (actions *send* messages, *receive* messages in buffers, and offer *contracts* to *agents*).

These facets of actions are independent. For instance, changing the data stored in a cell—or even unreserving the cell—does not affect any bindings. There are, however, some *directive* actions, which process a mixture of scoped and stable information, so as to provide finite representations of self-referential bindings. There are also some *hybrid* primitive actions and combinators, which involve more than one kind of information at once, such as an action that both reserves a cell of storage and gives it as transient data.

The notation for specifying actions consists of action *primitives*, which may involve yielders, and action *combinators*, which operate on one or two *subactions*. See Section D.9.3 for an explanation of the notation for specifying *sorts* of actions.

Yielders

Yielders are entities that can be *evaluated* to yield data during action performance. The data yielded may depend on the current information, i.e., the given transients, the received bindings, and the current state of the storage and buffer. In fact action notation provides primitive yielders that evaluate to compound data (tuples, maps, lists) representing entire slices of the current information, such as the current state of storage. Evaluation cannot affect the current information.

Compound yielders can be formed by the application of data operations to yielders. The data yielded by evaluating a compound yielder are the result of applying the operation to the data yielded by evaluating the operands. For instance, one can form the sum of two number yielders. Items of data are a special case of data yielders, and always yield themselves when evaluated. See Section D.9.4 for an explanation of the notation for specifying *sorts* of actions.

Data

The information processed by actions consists of items of *data*, organized in structures that give access to the individual items. Data can include various familiar mathematical entities, such as truth-values, numbers, characters, strings, lists, sets, and maps. It can also include entities such as tokens, cells, and agents, used for accessing other items, and some compound entities with data components, such as messages and contracts. Actions themselves are not data, but they can be incorporated in so-called *abstractions*, which are data, and subsequently *enacted* back into actions. (Abstraction and enaction are a special case of so-called *reification* and *reflection*.) New kinds of data can be introduced *ad hoc*, for representing special pieces of information.

D.1 Basic Action Notation

Basic action notation is primarily concerned with specifying flow of control in performances of actions. It includes basic notation for data as well.

D.1.1 Actions

- *All primitive basic actions:*

  - Give no transients, except for **escape**.

  - Produce no bindings.

  - Make no changes to storage.

  - Do not communicate.

  - Redirect no bindings.

- *All basic action combinators are:*

  - Functionally conducting (see the basic action A_1 and A_2), except for A_1 **trap** A_2, which is functionally composing (see the functional action A_1 **then** A_2 in Section D.2.1).

  - Declaratively conducting (see the basic action A_1 and A_2).

- **complete**: a primitive basic action. Represents normal termination. Unit for A_1 and A_2, as well as for A_1 and then A_2.

  - Indivisible. Always completes.

- **escape**: a primitive basic action. Represents abnormal termination. Unit for A_1 **trap** A_2.

  - Indivisible. Always escapes.

  - Gives any given transients.

- **fail**: a primitive basic action. Represents abortion of the current alternative. Unit for A_1 **or** A_2.

  - Indivisible. Always fails.

- **commit**: a primitive basic action. Represents commitment to the current alternative, cutting away other current alternatives.

  - Indivisible. Always commits and completes.

- **diverge**: a basic action. Represents nontermination.

  - Always diverges.

- **unfold**: a dummy action, standing for the innermost enclosing unfolding.

- **unfolding** A: Represents the (in general, infinite) action formed by continually substituting A for unfold. (To avoid singularities in pathological cases, substitute **complete** and then A, rather than just A.)

- Performs A, but whenever the dummy action unfold is reached, A is performed in place of unfold.

- **indivisibly** A: a basic combination of action A. Represents that the steps of performing A are not interleaved with those of other actions performed by the same agent. Also ensures that the performance of A cannot be interrupted by an escape or failure occurring outside A. For use only when A cannot diverge.

  - *Indivisible*: A is performed as a single step.

- A_1 **or** A_2: a basic combination of actions A_1, A_2. Represents implementation-dependent choice; specializes to deterministic choice when one or the other of A_1, A_2 must fail.

  - Performs either A_1 or A_2. When the performed alternative fails without committing, it is ignored and the other alternative is performed instead.
  - All the transients given to the combination of A_1, A_2 are given to the performed alternative. On normal or abnormal termination, all the transients given by the performed alternative are given by the combined action.
  - All the bindings received by the combination of A_1, A_2 are received by the performed alternative. On normal termination, all the bindings produced by the performed alternative are produced by the combined action.

- A_1 **and** A_2: a basic combination of actions A_1, A_2. Represents implementation-dependent order of performance of indivisible subactions, specializing to independent performance when there is no interference between A_1 and A_2.

  - *Basically interleaving*: Performs both A_1, A_2, with arbitrary interleaving of their indivisible steps. An escape or a failure causes any remaining parts of the subactions to be skipped.
  - *Functionally conducting*: The transients given to the combination of A_1, A_2 is given to both A_1, A_2. On normal termination, all the transients given by A_1, A_2 is collected and given by the combined action—if both give one or more items of transients, these are tupled in the given order. On escape, only the transients given by the escape is given by the combined action.
  - *Declaratively conducting*: The bindings received by the combination of A_1, A_2 are received by both A_1, A_2. On normal termination, all the bindings produced by A_1, A_2 are collected and produced by the combined action—provided that the bindings are all for distinct tokens, otherwise the combined action fails.

- A_1 **and then** A_2: a basic combination of actions A_1, A_2. Represents dependency on normal termination.

  - *Basically (normal) sequencing*: Performs A_1 first. If A_1 completes, performs A_2.

- A_1 **trap** A_2: a basic action combination. Represents recovery from abnormal termination.

  - Performs A_1 first. If A_1 escapes, performs A_2.
  - Functionally composing (see the functional action A_1 then A_2 in Section D.2.1).

- **action**: the sort of all actions. See Section D.9.3 for notation for subsorts of action.

D.1.2   Yielders

- the d yielded by Y: a yielder, where d is a sort of data and Y is a yielder. When Y yields an individual, it yields that individual, provided that the individual is included in the sort, otherwise it yields nothing.

- Every *data-operation* (i.e., operation specified for arguments included in data) is extended to arguments of sort yielder. The application of a data operation to yielders yields whatever is yielded by applying the data operation to the data yielded by the arguments. For instance, sum (Y_1, Y_2) yields the numerical sum of whatever Y_1 and Y_2 yield.

- yielder: the sort of all yielders. See Section D.9.4 for notation for subsorts of yielder.

D.1.3   Data

- datum: a sort. Its individuals represent items of data. Left open, as it depends on the variety of information processed by the programs of a programming language. Includes generally-useful sorts from data notation (see Appendix E), except for tuples. Similarly for distinct-datum, the sort of datum whose individuals are distinguished by the operation _ is _ .

- data: a sort. Its individuals represent tuples, i.e., ordered collections of individuals of sort datum, which may also be processed as transient information (see Section D.2.3).

- a d: the same data as d. Only used to improve the readability of the notation. Similarly for an d, the d, of d, and some d. Thus an application of an operation op to arguments x can be written as $op\ x$, op of x, and the op of x. Note that the words 'the' and 'of' are obligatory parts of some other operation symbols. (Compare the HyperCard scripting language, HyperTalk [Goo87].)

D.2   Functional Action Notation

Functional action notation is primarily concerned with specifying the processing of transient information (data).

D.2.1   Actions

- *All primitive functional actions*:

  - Do not commit.

  - Produce no bindings.

  - Make no changes to storage.

  - Do not communicate.

  - Redirect no bindings.

- *All functional action combinators are*:

  - Declaratively conducting (see the basic action A_1 and A_2 in Section D.1.1).

- **give** Y: a primitive functional action, where Y is a data yielder. Represents creating a piece of transient information.

  - Indivisible. Completes when Y yields data. Fails when Y yields nothing.
  - Gives the data yielded by Y.

- **escape with** Y: a primitive functional action, where Y is a data yielder. Represents escaping with a piece of transient information, which may be used to distinguish different reasons for escape.

  - Indivisible. Escapes when Y yields data. Fails when Y yields nothing.
  - Gives the data yielded by Y.

- **regive**: a primitive functional action. Represents propagation of transient information, i.e., data. Unit for A_1 then A_2.

  - Indivisible. Always completes.
  - Gives any given data.

- **choose** Y: a functional action, where Y is a data yielder. Represents implementation-dependent choice between a possibly infinite collection of individual items of data.

  - Indivisible. Completes when Y yields a sort including a data individual. Fails when Y yields nothing.
  - Gives any individual data of the sort yielded by Y.

- **check** Y: a functional action, where Y is a truth-value yielder. Represents a guard checking that a condition is true.

  - Indivisible. Completes when Y yields true. Fails when Y yields false (or nothing).
  - Gives no data.

- A_1 **then** A_2: a functional combination of actions A_1, A_2. Represents passing on transient information normally.

  - Basically sequencing (see the basic action A_1 and then A_2 in Section D.1.1).
  - *Functionally composing*: The transients given to the combination of A_1, A_2 are given to A_1. Only the transients given by A_1 are given to A_2 (provided that A_2 is performed). Only the transients given by A_2 are given by the combined action.

D.2.2   Yielders

- **given** d: a data yielder, where d is a sort of data. Yields the transient data given to its evaluation, provided that the data is of sort d.

- **given** $d\#p$: a datum yielder, where d is a sort of datum and p is a positive integer. Yields the p'th component of the transient data given to its evaluation, provided that the datum is of sort d.

- it: a datum yielder. Yields the single datum given to its evaluation as a transient.

- them: a data yielder. Yields all the data given to its evaluation as transients.

D.2.3 Data

- data: a sort. Its individuals represent ordered collections, i.e., tuples, of individuals of sort datum, processed as transient information.

D.3 Declarative Action Notation

Declarative action notation is primarily concerned with specifying the processing of scoped information (bindings).

D.3.1 Actions

- *All primitive declarative actions*:

  - Do not commit.

  - Give no transients.

  - Make no changes to storage.

  - Do not communicate.

  - Redirect no bindings.

- *All declarative action combinators are*:

  - Functionally conducting (see the basic action A_1 and A_2 in Section D.1.1).

- bind T to Y: a primitive declarative action, where T is a token and Y is a yielder of bindable data. Represents creating a piece of scoped information.

  - Indivisible. Completes when Y yields data of sort bindable. Fails otherwise.

  - Produces the binding of the token T to the bindable data.

- unbind T: a primitive declarative action, where T is a token. Represents hiding a piece of scoped information, making a hole in its scope.

  - Indivisible. Completes.

  - Produces the binding of the token T to the datum unknown.

- rebind: a primitive declarative action. Represents propagation of scoped information. Unit for the declarative action A_1 hence A_2.

  - Indivisible. Always completes.

  - Produces all received bindings.

- produce Y: a primitive declarative action. Represents production of reified scoped information.

  - Indivisible. Completes when Y yields a datum of sort bindings.
  - Produces the bindings yielded by Y.

- furthermore A: a declarative combination of the action A. Represents propagating the received bindings, but letting bindings produced by A take precedence when there is a conflict.

  - Basically as A.
  - Functionally as A.
  - Declaratively as rebind moreover A.

- A_1 moreover A_2: a declarative combination of actions A_1, A_2. Like A_1 and A_2, but gives priority to bindings produced by A_2.

  - Basically interleaving (see the basic action A_1 and A_2 in Section D.1.1).
  - *Declaratively overlaying*: The bindings received by the combination of A_1, A_2 are received by both A_1, A_2. On normal termination the bindings produced by A_1, overlaid with those produced by A_2, are produced by the combined action.

- A_1 hence A_2: a declarative combination of actions A_1, A_2. Represents passing on scoped information, restricting the bindings received by A_2.

  - Basically sequencing (see the basic action A_1 and then A_2 in Section D.1.1).
  - *Declaratively composing*: The bindings received by the combination of A_1, A_2 are received by A_1. Only the bindings produced by A_1 are received by A_2 (provided that it is performed). Only the bindings produced by A_2 are produced by the combined action.

- A_1 before A_2: a declarative combination of actions A_1, A_2. Represents accumulating scoped information.

  - Basically sequencing (see the basic action A_1 and then A_2 in Section D.1.1).
  - *Declaratively accumulating*: The bindings received by the combination of A_1, A_2 are received by A_1. The bindings received by the combined action, overlaid with the bindings produced by A_1, are received by A_2 (provided that it is performed). On normal termination the bindings produced by A_1, overlaid with those produced by A_2, are produced by the combined action.

D.3.2   Yielders

- current bindings: a yielder of bindings maps. Yields the collection of bindings received by its evaluation.

- the d bound to T: a yielder of bindable data, where d is a sort of data and T is a token. Yields the data of sort d to which T is bound by the received bindings, if any.

- Y_1 receiving Y_2: a yielder, where Y_2 is a yielder of binding maps. Represents evaluation of Y_1 using reified bindings instead of current bindings.

D.3.3 Data

- bindings: a subsort of map. Its individuals represent collections of associations between tokens and bindable (or unknown) individuals. (Further entities, called indirections, are associated with tokens in connection with the directive actions in Section D.7.1.)

- token: a subsort of distinct-datum. Left unspecified, as it depends on the variety of identifiers of a programming language. (Usually, it is a subsort of string.)

- bindable: a subsort of data. Left open, as it depends on the variety of scoped information processed by the programs of a programming language.

- unknown: an individual datum, not of sort bindable. A binding of a token to unknown is used to conceal a binding of the token to other data.

- known b: the restriction of the bindings b obtained by omitting bindings of tokens to unknown.

D.4 Imperative Action Notation

Imperative action notation is primarily concerned with specifying the processing of stable information (storage).

D.4.1 Actions

- *All primitive imperative actions*:
  - Give no transients.
  - Produce no bindings.
  - Do not communicate.
  - Redirect no bindings.

- *There are no special imperative action combinators.*

- store Y_1 in Y_2: a primitive imperative action, where Y_1 is a yielder of storable data and Y_2 is a yielder of cells. Represents changing an atomic piece of stable information.

  - Indivisible. Commits and completes when Y_2 yields a reserved cell and Y_1 yields storable data. Fails otherwise.

  - Stores the storable yielded by Y_1 in the cell yielded by Y_2.

- unstore Y: a primitive imperative action, where Y is a yielder of cells. Represents destroying a piece of stable information.

    - Indivisible. Commits and completes when Y yields a reserved cell. Fails otherwise.

    - Stores the datum uninitialized in the cell yielded by Y.

- reserve Y: a primitive imperative action, where Y is a yielder of cells. Represents extending stable information with an extra, uninitialized piece.

    - Indivisible. Commits and completes when Y yields an unreserved cell. Fails otherwise.

    - Reserves the cell yielded by Y and stores the datum uninitialized in it.

- unreserve Y: a primitive imperative action, where Y is a cell yielder. Represents destroying stable information.

    - Indivisible. Commits and completes when Y yields a reserved cell. Fails otherwise.

    - Unreserves the cell yielded by Y.

D.4.2   Yielders

- current storage: a yielder of storage maps. Yields the state of storage.

- the d stored in Y: a yielder of storable data, where d is a sort of data and Y is a yielder of cells. Yields the data of sort d stored in the cell yielded by Y according to the current storage, provided that the cell is currently reserved.

D.4.3   Data

- storage: a subsort of map. Its individuals represents states of stable information, associating cells with storable (or uninitialized) individuals.

- cell: a subsort of distinct-datum. Its individuals represent the locations of pieces of stable information. Left loosely-specified, as the details are implementation-dependent.

- storable: a subsort of data. Left unspecified, as it depends on the variety of stable information processed by the programs of a programming language.

- uninitialized: an individual datum. Represents the absence of a stored datum in a reserved cell.

- initialized S: the restriction of the storage S obtained by omitting uninitialized cells.

D.5 Reflective Action Notation

Reflective action notation is concerned with specifying the *reification* of actions and information as abstractions, and with the *reflection* of abstractions as actions.

D.5.1 Actions

- enact Y: a reflective action, where Y is a yielder of abstractions. Represents performing an action in a context different from that of its occurrence.

  - Performs the action incorporated in the abstraction yielded by evaluating Y.
  - The performance of the incorporated action is given no data. (But see the abstraction yielder application d_1 to d_2.)
  - The performance of the incorporated action receives no bindings. (But see the abstraction yielder closure d.)

D.5.2 Yielders

- application d_1 to d_2: an abstraction, when d_1 is an abstraction and d_2 is data. Incorporates the same action as d_1, except that the incorporated action is given d_2 as transients whenever the abstraction is enacted. Represents supplying transients to an abstraction (precluding the supply of further transients).

  This operation extends to yielders Y_1, Y_2 in the usual way: it is evaluated by applying the above operation to the data yielded by evaluating Y_1, Y_2.

- closure d: an abstraction yielder, where d is an abstraction. Yields an abstraction which incorporates the same action as d, except that the incorporated action receives particular bindings whenever the abstraction is enacted. The bindings are those current for the evaluation of closure d.

  This operation extends to yielders Y in the usual way: it is evaluated by applying the above operation to the datum yielded by evaluating Y.

  The yielder closure abstraction of A represents reification of an action as an abstraction with static bindings. The action enact the closure of a given abstraction represents reflection of an abstraction with dynamic bindings (unless static bindings were already supplied to it). The action enact a given abstraction represents reflection of an abstraction with no bindings (unless static bindings were already supplied to it).

D.5.3 Data

- abstraction: the sort of datum that incorporates (i.e., reifies) an action. The incorporated action is performed when the abstraction is enacted (i.e., reflected).

- abstraction of A: an abstraction, where A is an action. Incorporates A. Represents (a pointer to) the 'code' implementing A. Yielders occurring in A do *not* get evaluated when the abstraction is evaluated: they are left for evaluation during the performance of the incorporated action.

- Every *action-operation* (i.e., operation specified for arguments included in action) is extended to arguments of sort abstraction, and thus to yielder. For example, if a_1 and a_2 are abstractions that incorporate actions A_1 and A_2 respectively, a_1 and then a_2 is the abstraction that incorporates the action A_1 and then A_2.

- provision d: an abstraction, where d is data. Incorporates the action give d. Useful when the argument is a yielder of data. For example, an evaluation of provision given data yields an abstraction which, when enacted, always gives the same data, namely that given to the evaluation.

- production d: an abstraction, where d is bindings or redirections. Incorporates the action produce d. Useful when the argument is a yielder of bindings. For example, an evaluation of production current bindings yields an abstraction which, when enacted, always reflects the bindings received by the evaluation.

D.6   Communicative Action Notation

Communicative action notation is primarily concerned with specifying the processing of permanent information (communications).

D.6.1   Actions

- *All primitive communicative actions*:

  - Give no transients.

  - Produce no bindings.

  - Make no changes to storage.

  - Redirect no bindings.

- *There is only a unary communicative action combinator.*

- send Y: a primitive communicative action, where Y yields a sort of message. Represents initiating the transmission of a message. The usual form of Y is a message [to Y_1] [containing Y_2], where Y_1 and Y_2 yield individuals.

  - Indivisible. Commits and completes when the sort of message yielded by Y includes a message from the current performer (with the next serial number). Fails otherwise.

  - Emits a message of the sort yielded by Y. The serial number of the message is the successor of that of the previous message sent (or contract offered) by the performing agent. Message transmission is reliable, but each message takes an implementation-dependent 'time' to arrive (so message transmission between two particular agents is not necessarily order-preserving).

- remove Y: a primitive communicative action, where Y is a yielder of individual messages. Represents that a particular message in the buffer has been processed and is to be discarded.

  - Indivisible. Commits and completes when the message yielded by Y is in the buffer. Fails otherwise.

  - Removes the message yielded by Y from the buffer.

- offer Y: a primitive communicative action, where Y yields sort of contract. Represents initiating the arrangement of a contract with another, perhaps only partially specified, agent. The usual form of Y is a contract [to an agent] [containing abstraction of A], where A is the action to be performed according to the contract.

  - Indivisible. Commits and completes when the sort of contract yielded by Y includes an individual contract from the performer. Fails otherwise.

  - Gives no data.

  - Requests the arrangement of a contract of the sort yielded by Y. Offered contracts are distinguished by serial numbers, as with sent messages. The arrangement of a contract takes an implementation-dependent 'time', which must be finite when there is a continually uncontracted agent of the specified sort.

- patiently A: a communicative action, where A is an action. Represents *busy waiting* while A fails. Only useful when A refers to information that may change due to some other action, for instance, the messages in the buffer.

  - Performs A indivisibly, but not indivisible itself. If the performance fails it tries again. Thus it diverges when A always fails.

  - Functionally as A.

  - Declaratively as A.

D.6.2 Yielders

- current buffer: a yielder of buffers. Yields the list of messages that have appeared in the buffer, but which have not yet been removed. The messages are listed in the order of their arrival in the buffer.

- performing-agent: a yielder of agents. Yields (the identity of) the agent that is performing the enclosing action.

- contracting-agent: a yielder of agents. Yields (the identity of) the agent that offered the contract to the performer.

D.6.3 Data

- **agent**: a sort of datum. An agent identifies a potential process of performing an action, representing a piece of distributed processing. It is loosely-specified, as the maximum number and distribution of processes is usually implementation-dependent.

  Each agent has its own buffer and storage. It is inactive until it accepts a contract to perform an action, whereafter it remains active for ever, even after the termination of the contracted action.

- **user-agent**: a distinguished agent. It corresponds to the environment of a program, providing input and accepting output. The user agent is initially the only agent with a contract.

- **buffer**: a sort of datum. A buffer is a list of messages sent to the same agent, in the order of their arrival.

- **communication**: a sort of datum. Individual communications represent information that can be transmitted by agents. Communications have components indicating their sender, receiver, and contents. Moreover, each communication is distinguished by a serial number determined by the sender.

- **message**: a subsort of communication. Messages can be sent directly from one agent to another.

- **sendable**: a sort of data. The data that can be the contents of messages sent between agents. Left open, as it depends on the variety of permanent information processed by the programs of a programming language. (Specified to include **abstraction** and **agent** to allow proper use of subordinate Y.)

- **contract**: a subsort of communication. Contracts can be offered by one agent to another (sort of) agent. The contents of a contract is the abstraction to be enacted by an agent accepting the contract.

- **contents** d: data, where d is a communication. The data contained in d.

- **sender** d: a datum, where d is a communication. The agent that sends d.

- **receiver** d: a datum, where d is a communication. The agent that receives d.

- **serial** d: a datum, where d is a communication. The serial number of d, determined locally when it is emitted.

- d [**containing** d_1]: a subsort of communication, where d_1 is a (sort of) data, and d is a sort of communication. It includes only those communications in d whose contents is (of sort) d_1.

- d [**from** d_1]: a subsort of communication, where d_1 is a (sort of) agent, and d is a sort of communication. It includes only those communications in d whose sender is (of sort) d_1.

- d [**to** d_1]: a subsort of communication, where d_1 is a (sort of) agent, and d is a sort of communication. It includes only those communications in d whose receiver is (of sort) d_1.

- d [**at** d_1]: a subsort of communication, where d_1 is a (sort of) natural number, and d is a sort of communication. It includes only those communications in d whose serial number is (of sort) d_1.

D.7 Directive Action Notation

Directive action notation is concerned with specifying the processing of a mixture of scoped and stable information, representing circular bindings by means of *redirections*.

D.7.1 Actions

- *All primitive directive actions*:

    - Give no transients.

    - Make no changes to storage.

    - Do not communicate.

- *There are no special directive action combinators.*

- indirectly bind T to Y: a primitive directive action, where T is a token and Y is a yielder. Represents creating a piece of scoped information for subsequent redirection.

    - Indivisible. Completes when Y yields data of sort bindable or the individual datum unknown. Fails otherwise.

    - Produces the binding of the token T to an indirection.

    - Augments the current redirections with the indirection, initialized to refer to the data yielded by Y.

- redirect T to Y: a primitive directive action, where T is a token and Y is a yielder. Represents redirecting a piece of scoped information so as to create a circular structure.

    - Indivisible. Completes when Y yields data of sort bindable or unknown. Fails otherwise.

    - Produces no bindings.

    - Redirects the indirection bound to T to refer to the data yielded by Y.

- undirect T: a primitive directive action, where T is a token. Indicates that an indirection can be reused.

    - Indivisible. Completes.

    - Produces no bindings.

    - Redirects the indirection bound to T to unknown, and makes it available for reuse.

- recursively bind T to Y: a directive action, where T is a token and Y is a yielder. Represents creating a piece of scoped information and redirecting it so as to create a circular structure. The yielder Y is evaluated in the scope of an indirect binding for T.

  - Indivisible. Completes when Y yields data of sort bindable (or unknown). Fails otherwise.

  - Produces the binding of the token T to an indirection.

  - Augments the current redirections with the indirection, initialized to refer to the data yielded by evaluating Y using the current bindings overlaid by the indirect binding for T.

- indirectly produce Y: a primitive directive action. Represents reflection of reified stable information.

  - Indivisible. Completes when Y yields a datum of sort redirections.

  - Makes the redirections yielded by Y.

D.7.2 Yielders

- current redirections: a map yielder. Yields the state of the redirections.

- indirect closure a: an abstraction yielder, where a is an abstraction. Yields an abstraction which incorporates the same action as a, except that the incorporated action has a snapshot of the current redirections, of use when the abstraction is to be enacted on another agent and the incorporated action depends on indirect bindings. (The indirections created on different agents are distinct, to avoid interference between the snapshot of redirections in an indirect closure and any redirections current on the agent where the closure is enacted.)

  This operation extends to yielders Y in the usual way: it is evaluated by applying the above operation to the datum yielded by evaluating Y.

D.7.3 Data

- redirections: a subsort of map. Its individuals represent collections of associations between indirections and bindable (or unknown) individuals.

- indirection: a subsort of distinct-datum. An indirection represents a point of circularity on a particular agent, but it can be re-produced on another agent (by a closure).

- indirect production d: an abstraction, where d is redirections. Incorporates the action indirectly produce d. Useful when d is a redirections yielder. For example, an evaluation of indirect production current redirections yields an abstraction which, when enacted, always reflects the redirections received by the evaluation.

D.8 Hybrid Action Notation

Hybrid action notation consists of some useful abbreviations for compound actions involving more than one kind of information, together with some hybrid combinators that mix various facets of the other combinators. There are also some hybrid data operations.

D.8.1 Actions

- allocate d: an imperative and functional action, where d is a sort of cell. Represents implementation-dependent choice and reservation of a cell of sort d.

  - Indivisible. Commits and completes when there is an unreserved cell of sort d. Fails otherwise.
  - Reserves some cell of sort d.
  - Gives the reserved cell.

- receive Y: a communicative and functional action, where Y yields a sort of message. Represents waiting for a message to arrive in the buffer. The usual form of Y is a restriction such as a message [from Y_1] [containing Y_2], where Y_1, Y_2 may yield sorts or individuals.

  - Patiently waits for a message of the sort yielded Y to arrive, then commits and completes. Otherwise diverges.
  - Chooses and gives any received message of the sort yielded by Y.
  - Removes the chosen message from the buffer.

- subordinate Y: a communicative and functional action, where Y yields a sort of agent. Represents offering a contract and ascertaining the identity of the accepting agent. The usual form of Y is some agent.

  - Fails only if the sort of agent yielded by Y is vacuous. Commits otherwise. Completes after a contract with an agent of the specified sort has been accepted. Diverges if the contract is never accepted.
  - On completion, gives the identity of the agent accepting the contract.
  - Offers a contract for an incorporated action that sends the identity of the accepting agent to the offering agent, waits for a message containing an abstraction (from the offering agent) and enacts the abstraction.

- A_1 and then moreover A_2: a basic and declarative hybrid combination of actions A_1, A_2. Like A_1 and then A_2 for control and transients, and like A_1 moreover A_2 for bindings.

- A_1 then moreover A_2: a declarative and functional hybrid combination of actions A_1, A_2. Like A_1 then A_2 for control and transients, and like A_1 moreover A_2 for bindings.

- A_1 thence A_2: a declarative and functional hybrid combination of actions A_1, A_2. Like A_1 then A_2 for control and transients, and like A_1 hence A_2 for bindings.

- A_1 then before A_2: a declarative and functional hybrid combination of actions A_1, A_2. Like A_1 then A_2 for transients, and like A_1 before A_2 for bindings.

D.8.2   Yielders

- *There are no hybrid yielders.*

D.8.3   Data

- owner d: an agent, where d is a cell or an indirection. The agent where it is located.

- d [on d_1]: a subsort of cell, where d_1 is a (sort of) agent, and d is a sort of cell. It includes only those cells in d whose owner is (of sort) d_1. Similarly when d is a (sort of) indirection.

D.9   Facets

The facets of actions and yielders are obtained by focusing on particular kinds of information. The notation summarized below is used for expressing *sorts* of actions and yielders.

D.9.1   Outcomes

- outcome: a sort of auxiliary entities, used for specifying sorts of actions. Sort union $O_1 \mid O_2$ combines outcomes. (The various outcomes below are disjoint, so there is no use for specifying their intersections.)

- giving d: allows normal termination that always gives transients included in the data sort d. completing abbreviates giving ( ), where ( ) is the empty tuple of data.

- escaping with d: allows abnormal termination that always gives transients included in the data sort d. escaping abbreviates escaping with data.

- binding: allows normal termination that optionally produces some bindings. The union outcome giving $d \mid$ binding allows normal termination that always gives transients of sort d and optionally produces some bindings. The use of binding alone implies completing.

- failing: ignored. (Most compound actions that use information fail when that information is not made available to their performance.)

- committing: allows commitment, independently of termination. Included in storing, communicating, and redirecting, which are analogous.

- diverging: allows nontermination. Actions without this sort of outcome are guaranteed to terminate, whereas those with this outcome might or might not terminate. Actions that contain any occurrence of unfolding or enact Y have this sort of outcome, unless they are equivalent to other actions that do not have it.

D.9.2 Incomes

- income: a sort of auxiliary entities, used for specifying sorts of actions and yielders. Sort union $I_1 \mid I_2$ combines incomes. (The various incomes below are disjoint, so there is no use for specifying their intersections.)

- given d: allows use of given transients of the data sort d. More specifically, the income given $d\#p$ specifies possible use of the p'th component of the given transients, this being of datum sort d.

- current bindings: allows use of received bindings.

- current storage: allows use of storage.

- current buffer: allows use of the message buffer.

- current redirections: allows use of indirect bindings.

D.9.3 Actions

- action: the sort of all actions. Its subsort primitive-action includes not only the actions described in this Appendix as primitive, but also compound actions that are equivalent to them, e.g., complete and then escape, which is equivalent to escape.

- $A\,[O]$: a sort of action, where A is a sort of action and O is a sort of outcome. Restricts A to those actions which, whenever performed, either fail or have an outcome whose termination properties and kind of information processing are included in O. Note that $A\,[O_1] \mid A\,[O_2]$ is generally a proper subsort of $A\,[O_1 \mid O_2]$, whereas $A\,[O_1]$ & $A\,[O_2]$ is the same sort as $A\,[O_1$ & $O_2]$, which can also be written as $A\,[O_1]\,[O_2]$.

- $A\,[\text{using } I]$: a sort of action, where I is a sort of income. Restricts A to those actions which, whenever performed, perhaps evaluate yielders that refer to the current information indicated by I. Compare $Y\,[\text{using } I]$, where Y is a sort of yielder, below.

D.9.4 Yielders

- yielder: the sort of all yielders.

- $Y\,[d]$: a sort of yielder, where Y is a sort of action and d is a sort of data. Restricts Y to those yielders which, whenever evaluated, yield data included in d. Note that the union sort $Y\,[d_1] \mid Y\,[d_2]$ is generally a proper subsort of $Y\,[d_1 \mid d_2]$, whereas $Y\,[d_1]$ & $Y\,[d_2]$ is the same sort as $Y\,[d_1$ & $d_2]$, which can also be written as $Y\,[d_1]\,[d_2]$.

- $Y\,[\text{of } d]$: equivalent to $Y\,[d]$, but a yielder [of an integer] reads a bit more naturally than yielder [integer].

- $Y\,[\text{using } I]$:_ [using _]_ [using _] a sort of yielder, where I is a sort of income. Restricts Y to those yielders which, whenever evaluated, refer at most to the current information indicated by I.

Appendix E

Data Notation

- *The algebraic specification of data notation given here is definitive. See Chapter 5 for an informal introduction to the various symbols. The occasional informal comment is inserted in the formal specification where appropriate.*

- *The specification is divided into nested modules. The order of presentation of the modules is such that earlier modules do not often refer to later ones. In fact the submodules could be presented in a strictly bottom-up manner, but this would make navigation more difficult.*

- *Reference to the module **Data Notation/General** includes all the specified modules except for the submodule **Characters/ASCII**, thus allowing specialization to alternative character sets. It also omits the **Instant** submodules, which are intended for use with the symbols translated to some specified sort.*

General	includes: Tuples, Truth-Values, Numbers, Characters/Alphanumerics, Lists, Strings, Trees, Sets, Maps.
Instant	
Distinction	includes: Truth-Values.
Partial Order	includes: Distinction.
Total Order	includes: Partial Order.
Tuples	
Generics	
Basics	includes: Generics, Numbers/Naturals/Basics.
Specifics	includes: Basics, Numbers/Naturals/Specifics.
Truth-Values	
Basics	
Specifics	includes: Basics.

Numbers

    Naturals

        Basics

        Specifics   includes: Basics.

    Integers

        Basics   includes: Naturals/Basics.

        Specifics   includes: Basics, Naturals.

    Rationals

        Basics   includes: Integers.

        Specifics   includes: Basics.

    Approximations

        Generics   includes: Rationals.

        Basics   includes: Generics.

Characters

    Basics

    Alphanumerics includes: Basics.

    ASCII   includes: Alphanumerics.

Lists

    Flat

        Generics

        Basics   includes: Generics.

        Specifics   includes: Basics.

    Nested

        Generics   includes: Flat/Generics.

        Basics   includes: Generics, Flat/Basics.

        Specifics   includes: Basics, Flat/Specifics.

Strings

    Basics   includes: Characters/Basics.

    Alphanumerics includes: Basics, Characters/Alphanumerics.

Syntax

    Basics   includes: Strings.

    Specifics   includes: Basics.

Sets

    Generics   .

    Basics   includes: Generics.

    Specifics   includes: Basics.

Maps

    Generics   includes: Sets/Generics.

    Basics   includes: Generics, Sets.

    Specifics   includes: Basics.

E.1   Instant

E.1.1   Distinction

introduces: s , _ is _ .

- s   = $\square$.
- _ is _ :: s, s $\rightarrow$ truth-value (*partial, commutative*) .

(1) x:s is x = true .

(2) x is y = true ; y : s ; y is z = true $\Rightarrow$ x:s is z:s = true .

(3) x is y = false $\Rightarrow$ (x:s) & (y:s) = nothing .

E.1.2   Partial Order

includes: Distinction (s , _ is _) .

introduces: _ is less than _ , _ is greater than _ .

- _ is _   :: s, s $\rightarrow$ truth-value (*total, commutative*) .
- _ is less than _   :: s, s $\rightarrow$ truth-value (*total*) .
- _ is greater than _ :: s, s $\rightarrow$ truth-value (*total*) .

(1) x:s is less than y:s = true $\Rightarrow$ y is less than x = false ; x is y = false .

(2) x:s is y:s = true $\Rightarrow$ x is less than y = false .

(3) x is less than y = true ; y : s ; y is less than z = true $\Rightarrow$ x:s is less than z:s = true .

(4) x:s is y:s = true ; y is less than z:s = true $\Rightarrow$ x is less than z = true .

(5) x:s is y:s = true ; z:s is less than y = true $\Rightarrow$ z is less than x = true .

(6) x:s is greater than y:s = y is less than x .

E.1.3 Total Order

includes: Partial Order (s , _ is _ , _ is less than _ , _ is greater than _) .
introduces: _ [min _] , _ [max _] .

- _ [min _] :: s, s → s (*partial*) .
- _ [max _] :: s, s → s (*partial*) .

(1) any (x is less than y, x:s is y:s, y is less than x) = true .
(2) (y:s) [min x:s] = when not (y is less than x) then y .
(3) (y:s) [max x:s] = when not (y is greater than x) then y .
(4) ($z \leq$ s) [min x:s] = z & s [min x] .
(5) ($z \leq$ s) [max x:s] = z & s [max x] .
(6) ($z \leq$ s) [min x:s] [max y:s] = z [max y] [min x] .
(7) y is less than x = true $\Rightarrow$ ($z \leq$ s) [min x:s] [max y:s] = nothing .

E.2 Tuples

E.2.1 Generics

introduces: component .

- component = $\square$.

open.

E.2.2 Basics

introduces: tuple , ( ) , (_ , _) , _$^?$, _* , _$^+$, _$^-$.

The symbol '(_ , _)' may be used as an infix '_ , _', omitting the parentheses, when this does not cause ambiguity. In particular, '(x, y, z)' is a legal way of writing '((x, y), z)'.

- tuple ≥ component .
- ( ) : tuple .
- (_ , _) :: tuple, tuple → tuple (*total, associative, unit is* ( )) .
- _$^?$ :: tuple → tuple .
- _* :: tuple → tuple .
- _$^+$ :: tuple → tuple .
- _$^-$ :: tuple, natural → tuple .

(1) $x^? = ( ) \mid x$;
$x^* = ( ) \mid x^+$;
$x^+ = x \mid (x^+, x^+)$;
$x^0 = ( )$; $x^{\text{successor } n:\text{natural}} = (x, x^n)$.

(2) component$^* = ( ) \mid$ component $\mid$ (component$^+$, component$^+$) (*disjoint*) .

closed except Generics .

E.2.3   Specifics

introduces: count _ , first _ , rest _ , reverse _ , rotate _ _ , shuffle _ ,
                component#_ _ , components from #_ _ , components from #_ to #_ _ ,
                equal _ , distinct _ , strictly-increasing _ , strictly-decreasing _ .

includes: **Instant/Distinction** (tuple *for* s , _ is _) .

includes: **Instant/Partial Order** (component *for* s , _ is _ , _ is less than _) .

- count _   :: tuple $\rightarrow$ natural (*total*) .
- first _   :: tuple $\rightarrow$ component (*partial*) .
- rest _   :: tuple $\rightarrow$ tuple (*partial*) .
- reverse _   :: tuple $\rightarrow$ tuple (*total, injective*) .
- rotate _ _ :: natural, tuple $\rightarrow$ tuple (*total*) .
- shuffle _   :: tuple $\rightarrow$ tuple (*strict, linear*) .

rotate n t shifts the tuple t left n times, putting the first component at the end each time. shuffle t is the sort union of all the individual permutations of the tuple t.

(1)   count ( ) = 0 ;   count (c:component) = 1 ;
     count (t_1:tuple, t_2:tuple) = sum (count t_1, count t_2) .

(2)   first ( ) = nothing ;   first (c:component, t:tuple) = c .

(3)   rest ( ) = nothing ;   rest (c:component, t:tuple) = t .

(4)   reverse ( ) = ( ) ;   reverse c:component = c ;
     reverse (t_1:tuple, t_2:tuple) = (reverse t_2, reverse t_1) .

(5)   rotate 0 (t:tuple) = t ;   rotate (n:natural) ( ) = ( ) ;   rotate (n:natural) (c:component) = c ;
     rotate (successor (n:natural)) (c:component, t:tuple) = rotate n (t, c) .

(6)   shuffle ( ) = ( ) ;   shuffle c:component = c ;
     shuffle (c:component, t:tuple) = rotate (natural [max count t]) (c, shuffle t) .

- equal _   :: (component$^+$, component$^+$) $\rightarrow$ truth-value (*partial, commutative*) .
- distinct _   :: (component$^+$, component$^+$) $\rightarrow$ truth-value (*partial, commutative*) .
- strictly-increasing _ :: (component$^+$, component$^+$) $\rightarrow$ truth-value (*partial*) .
- strictly-decreasing _ :: (component$^+$, component$^+$) $\rightarrow$ truth-value (*partial*) .
- _ is _   :: tuple, tuple $\rightarrow$ truth-value (*partial*) .

(7)   equal (x:component, y:component) = x is y ;
     equal (x:component$^+$, y:component, z:component$^+$) = both (equal (x, y), equal (y, z)) .

(8)   distinct (x:component, y:component) = not (x is y) ;
     distinct (x:component$^+$, y:component, z:component$^+$) =
         all (distinct (x, y), distinct (x, z), distinct (y, z)) .

(9)   strictly-increasing (x:component, y:component) = x is less than y ;

(10) strictly-increasing (x:component$^+$, y:component, z:component$^+$) =
         both (strictly-increasing (x, y), strictly-increasing (y, z)) .

(11) strictly-decreasing (x:component, y:component) = x is greater than y ;
     strictly-decreasing (x:component$^+$, y:component, z:component$^+$) =
         both (strictly-decreasing (x, y), strictly-decreasing (y, z)) .

(12) ( ) is t:component$^+$ = false ;
   (c_1:component, t_1:tuple) is (c_2:component, t_2:tuple) = both (c_1 is c_2, t_1 is t_2) .

- component#_ _   :: positive-integer, tuple → component (*partial*) .
- components from #_ _   :: positive-integer, tuple → tuple (*partial*) .
- components from #_ to #_ _ :: positive-integer, positive-integer, tuple → tuple (*partial*) .

(13) component#i:positive-integer ( ) = nothing ;
   component#1 (c:component, t:tuple) = c ;
   component#successor i:positive-integer (c:component, t:tuple) = component#i t .

(14) components from #i:positive-integer ( ) = nothing ;
   components from #1 t:tuple = t ;
   components from #successor i:positive-integer (c:component, t:tuple) = components from #i t .

(15) components from #i:positive-integer to #j:positive-integer ( ) = nothing ;
   components from #1 to #1 t:tuple = component#1 t ;
   components from #1 to #successor j:positive-integer (c:component, t:tuple) =
      (c, components from #1 to #j t) ;
   components from #successor i:positive-integer
         to #successor j:positive-integer (c:component, t:tuple) =
      components from #i to #j t ;
   components from #successor i:positive-integer to #1 t = ( ) .

E.3   Truth-Values

E.3.1   Basics

introduces: truth-value , true , false .

- truth-value = true | false (*individual*) .

closed.

E.3.2   Specifics

introduces: if _ then _ else _ , when _ then _ , there is _ , not _ , both _ , either _ , all _ , any _ .
includes: **Instant/Distinction** (truth-value *for* s , _ is _) .
needs: **Tuples/Basics** .   truth-value $\leq$ component .

- if _ then _ else _ :: truth-value, x, $y \rightarrow x \mid y$ (*linear*) .
- when _ then _   :: truth-value, $x \rightarrow x$ (*partial*) .
- there is _   :: $x \rightarrow$ true (*total*) .
- not _   :: truth-value $\rightarrow$ truth-value (*total, injective*) .
- both _   :: (truth-value, truth-value) $\rightarrow$ truth-value
  (*total, associative, commutative, idempotent, unit is* true) .
- either _   :: (truth-value, truth-value) $\rightarrow$ truth-value
  (*total, associative, commutative, idempotent, unit is* false) .
- all _   :: truth-value$^{*} \rightarrow$ truth-value
  (*total, associative, commutative, idempotent, unit is* true) .
- any _   :: truth-value$^{*} \rightarrow$ truth-value
  (*total, associative, commutative, idempotent, unit is* false) .
- _ is _   :: truth-value, truth-value $\rightarrow$ truth-value (*total*) .

(1)   (if t:truth-value then x else y) = when t then x | when not t then y .

(2)   (when true then x) = x ;   (when false then x) = nothing .

(3)   (there is x!) = true ;   (there is nothing) = nothing .

(4)   (not true) = false ;   (not not t:truth-value) = t .

(5)   both (t:truth-value, u:truth-value) = if t then u else false ;
      both (t:truth-value, u:truth-value) = true $\Rightarrow$ t = true .

(6)   either (t:truth-value, u:truth-value) = if t then true else u ;
      either (t:truth-value, u:truth-value) = false $\Rightarrow$ t = false .

(7)   all (s_1:truth-value, s_2:truth-value) = both (s_1, s_2) .

(8)   any (s_1:truth-value, s_2:truth-value) = either (s_1, s_2) .

(9)   true is false = false .

E.4   Numbers

E.4.1   Naturals

E.4.1.1   Basics

introduces: natural , positive-integer , successor _ , 0 .

- 0   : natural .
- successor _ :: natural $\rightarrow$ positive-integer (*total, injective*) .

(1)   natural = 0 | positive-integer (*disjoint*) .

(2)   positive-integer = successor natural .

closed.

E.4.1.2 Specifics

introduces: 1 , 2 , 3 , 4 , 5 , 6 , 7 , 8 , 9 ,
                _0 , _1 , _2 , _3 , _4 , _5 , _6 , _7 , _8 , _9 ,
                sum _ , product _ , exponent _ , integer-quotient _ , integer-remainder _ .

includes: Instant/Total Order (natural *for* s , _ is _ , _ is less than _) .

needs: Tuples/Basics .   natural $\leq$ component .

- 1 , 2 , 3 , 4 , 5 , 6 , 7 , 8 , 9 : natural .
- _0 , _1 , _2 , _3 , _4 , _5 , _6 , _7 , _8 , _9 :: natural $\rightarrow$ natural (*total*) .
- sum _   :: natural* $\rightarrow$ natural (*total, associative, commutative, unit is* 0) .
- product _   :: natural* $\rightarrow$ natural (*total, associative, commutative, unit is* 1).
- exponent _   :: (natural, natural) $\rightarrow$ natural (*total*).
- integer-quotient _   :: (natural, natural) $\rightarrow$ natural (*partial*) .
- integer-remainder _ :: (natural, natural) $\rightarrow$ natural (*partial*) .

(1)   1 = successor 0 ;   2 = successor 1 ;   3 = successor 2 ;   4 = successor 3 ;
     5 = successor 4 ;   6 = successor 5 ;   7 = successor 6 ;   8 = successor 7 ;
     9 = successor 8 ;   10 = successor 9 .

(2)   (n:natural)0 = product (n, 10) ;
     (n:natural)1 = sum (product (n, 10), 1) ;
     ...
     (n:natural)9 = sum (product (n, 10), 9) .

(3)   sum _ :: natural*, positive-integer $\rightarrow$ positive-integer ;
     sum (n:natural, 1) = successor n .

(4)   product _ :: positive-integer* $\rightarrow$ positive-integer ;
     product (n:natural, 0) = 0 ;
     product (m:natural, successor n:natural) = sum (m, product (m, n)) .

(5)   exponent (m:natural, 0) = 1 ;
     exponent (m:natural, successor n:natural) = product (m, exponent (m, n)) .

(6)   integer-quotient (n:natural, 0) = nothing ;
     integer-remainder (n:natural, 0) = nothing .

(7) m is less than p = true ; m, n : natural ; p : positive-integer $\Rightarrow$

     (1)   integer-quotient (sum (product (n, p), m), p) = n ;
     (2)   integer-remainder (sum (product (n, p), m), p) = m .

(8)   0 is p:positive-integer = false ;
     successor m:natural is successor n:natural = m is n .

(9)   0 is less than p:positive-integer = true ;
     n:natural is less than 0 = false ;
     successor m:natural is less than successor n:natural = m is less than n .

(10) natural [min m:natural] = m | natural [min successor m] (*disjoint*) ;
      natural [max successor m:natural] = natural [max m] | successor m (*disjoint*) .

(11) natural [min 0] = natural ;   natural [max 0] = 0 .

E.4.2   Integers

E.4.2.1   Basics

introduces: integer , negative-integer , nonzero-integer , predecessor _ .

- successor _   :: integer → integer (*total, injective*) .
- predecessor _ :: integer → integer (*total, injective*) .

(1)   integer = 0 | nonzero-integer (*disjoint*) .
(2)   nonzero-integer = positive-integer | negative-integer (*disjoint*) .
(3)   successor _ :: negative-integer → 0 | negative-integer .
(4)   predecessor _ :: 0 | negative-integer → negative-integer ,
                 positive-integer → natural .
(5)   successor predecessor *i*:integer = *i* ;   predecessor successor *i*:integer = *i* .
closed.

E.4.2.2   Specifics

introduces: negation _ , absolute _ , difference _ .
includes: **Instant/Total Order** (integer *for* s , _ is _ , _ is less than _) .
needs: **Tuples/Basics** .   integer ≤ component .

- negation _   :: integer → integer (*total*) .
- absolute _   :: integer → natural (*total*) .
- sum _   :: integer* → integer (*total, associative, commutative, unit is* 0) .
- difference _   :: (integer, integer) → integer (*total*) .
- product _   :: integer* → integer (*total, associative, commutative, unit is* 1) .
- exponent _   :: (integer, natural) → integer (*total*) .
- integer-quotient _   :: (integer, integer) → integer (*partial*) .
- integer-remainder _ :: (integer, integer) → integer (*partial*) .

(1)   negation 0 = 0 ;
      negation successor *i*:integer = predecessor negation *i* ;
      negation negation *i*:integer = *i* ;
      negation positive-integer = negative-integer .
(2)   absolute *n*:natural = *n* ;   absolute negation *n*:natural = *n* .
(3)   sum (*i*:integer, 1) = successor *i* ;   sum (*i*:integer, negation 1) = predecessor *i* .
(4)   difference (*i*:integer, *j*:integer) = sum (*i*, negation *j*) .
(5)   product (0, *i*:integer) = 0 ;
      product (negation *i*:integer, *j*:integer) = negation product (*i*, *j*) ;
      product (sum (*i*:integer, *j*:integer), *k*:integer) = sum (product (*i*, *k*), product (*j*, *k*)) .
(6)   exponent (negation *i*:integer, product (2, *n*:natural)) = exponent (*i*, product (2, *n*)) .
(7)   exponent (negation *i*:integer, successor product (2, *n*:natural)) =
          negation exponent (*i*, successor product (2, *n*)) .

(8) integer-quotient (i:integer, 0) = nothing ;
     integer-quotient (negation i:integer, j:integer) = negation integer-quotient (i, j) ;
     integer-quotient (i:integer, negation j:integer) = negation integer-quotient (i, j) .

(9) integer-remainder (i:integer, 0) = nothing ;
     integer-remainder (negation i:integer, j:integer) = negation integer-remainder (i, j) ;
     integer-remainder (i:integer, negation j:integer) = integer-remainder (i, j) .

(10) i, j : integer $\Rightarrow$ sum (product (integer-quotient (i, j), j), integer-remainder (i, j)) = i .

(11) m:negative-integer is 0 = false ;
     negation i:integer is negation j:integer = i is j ;
     m:negative-integer is p:positive-integer = false ;
     sum (i:integer, j:integer) is sum (i, k:integer) = j is k .

(12) m:negative-integer is less than 0 = true ;
     negation i:integer is less than negation j:integer = j is less than i ;
     sum (i:integer, j:integer) is less than sum (i, k:integer) = j is less than k .

(13) integer [min m:integer] = m | integer [min successor m] (*disjoint*) ;
     integer [max successor m:integer] = integer [max m] | successor m (*disjoint*) .

E.4.3 Rationals

E.4.3.1 Basics

introduces: rational , nonzero-rational , positive-rational , negative-rational , quotient _ .

- quotient _ :: integer, nonzero-integer $\rightarrow$ rational (*total*) .

(1) rational = 0 | nonzero-rational (*disjoint*) .

(2) nonzero-rational = positive-rational | negative-rational (*disjoint*).

(3) positive-integer $\leq$ positive-rational ;   negative-integer $\leq$ negative-rational .

(4) quotient _ :: positive-integer, positive-integer $\rightarrow$ positive-rational,
                 negative-integer, positive-integer $\rightarrow$ negative-rational,
                 integer, 0 $\rightarrow$ nothing .

(5) quotient (negation i:integer, j:nonzero-integer) = negation quotient (i, j) .

(6) quotient (i:integer, negation j:nonzero-integer) = negation quotient (i, j) .

(7) quotient (product (i:nonzero-integer, j:integer), product (i, k:integer)) = quotient (j, k) .

(8) quotient (i:integer, 1) = i .   quotient (0, i:nonzero-integer) = 0 .

closed.

E.4.3.2 Specifics

introduces: truncation _ , fraction _ .
includes: **Instant/Total Order** (rational *for* s , _ is _ , _ is less than _) .
needs: **Tuples/Basics** . rational ≤ component .

- quotient _ :: rational, nonzero-rational → rational (*total*) .
- truncation _ :: rational → integer (*total*) .
- fraction _ :: rational → rational (*total*) .
- negation _ :: nonzero-rational → nonzero-rational (*total*) .
- absolute _ :: nonzero-rational → positive-rational (*total*) .
- sum _   :: rational* → rational (*total, associative, commutative, unit is* 0) .
- difference _ :: (rational, rational) → rational (*total*) .
- product _   :: rational* → rational (*total, associative, commutative, unit is* 1) .
- exponent _ :: (rational, integer) → rational (*partial*) .

(1) quotient _ :: positive-rational, positive-rational → positive-rational,
        negative-rational, positive-rational → negative-rational,
        rational, 0 → nothing .

(2) truncation quotient (i:integer, j:nonzero-integer) = integer-quotient (i, j) .

(3) fraction quotient (i:integer, j:nonzero-integer) = quotient (integer-remainder (i, j), j) .

(4) negation quotient (r:rational, n:nonzero-rational) = quotient (negation r, n) .

(5) absolute p:positive-rational = p ;   absolute n:negative-rational = negation n .

(6) sum (r:rational, quotient (q:rational, n:nonzero-rational)) =
        quotient (sum (product (r, n), q), n) .

(7) difference (q:rational, r:rational) = sum (q, negation r) .

(8) product (r:rational, quotient (q:rational, n:nonzero-rational)) = quotient (product (r, q), n) .

(9) exponent (quotient (q:rational, n:nonzero-rational), i:integer) =
        quotient (exponent (q, i), exponent(n, i)) ;

     exponent (quotient (q:rational, n:nonzero-rational), negation p:positive-integer) =
            exponent (quotient (n, q), p) .

(10) quotient (r:rational, quotient (q:nonzero-rational, n:nonzero-rational)) =
        quotient (product (r, n), q) ;

     quotient (quotient (q:rational, n:nonzero-rational), r:nonzero-rational) =
        quotient (q, product (n, r)) .

(11) product (p:nonzero-rational, q:rational) is product (p, r:rational) = q is r .

(12) product (p:positive-rational, q:rational) is less than product (p, r:rational) = q is less than r .

E.4.4 Approximations

E.4.4.1 Generics

introduces: approximation , min-approximation , max-approximation .

- approximation $\leq$ rational .
- min-approximation, max-approximation : approximation .

(1) approximation [min min-approximation] [max max-approximation] = approximation .

open.

E.4.4.2 Basics

introduces: interval _ , approximately _ .

- interval _   :: rational → rational (*strict*) .
- approximately _ :: rational → rational (*strict, linear*) .

The sort interval r is the smallest closed subsort of rational that includes the sort r, whereas approximately r is an interval whose bounds are of sort approximation, or nothing when r is entirely outside the interval from min-approximation to max-approximation

(1) $r \leq$ rational $\Rightarrow$ $r \leq$ interval r .
(2) $s, t : r \leq$ rational $\Rightarrow$ rational [min s] [max t] $\leq$ interval r .
(3) $x :$ rational $\Rightarrow$ $x :$ approximately x .
(4) $x :$ rational $\Rightarrow$ interval approximately $x =$ approximately x .
(5) $x :$ approximation $\Rightarrow$ approximately $x = x$.
(6) $x :$ interval $y ;$ $y \leq$ approximation $\Rightarrow$ approximately $x \leq$ interval y .
(7) x is greater than max-approximation = true $\Rightarrow$ approximately x:rational = nothing .
(8) x is less than min-approximation = true $\Rightarrow$ approximately x:rational = nothing .

E.5 Characters

E.5.1 Basics

introduces: character , character of _ , code _ .
includes: **Instant/Partial Order** (character *for* s , _ is _ , _ is less than _) .
needs: **Numbers/Naturals** .

- character   = □ .
- character of _ :: natural → character (*partial, injective*) .
- code _   :: character → natural (*total, injective*) .

(1) character of code c:character = c .
(2) c:character is c':character = code c is code c' .
(3) c:character is less than c':character = code c is less than code c' .

open.

E.5.2   Alphanumerics

introduces: digit , letter , lowercase _ , uppercase _ .

- character $\geq$ digit | letter (*disjoint*) .
- digit   = '0' | '1' | '2' | '3' | '4' | '5' | '6' | '7' | '8' | '9' (*individual*) .
- letter   = lowercase letter | uppercase letter (*disjoint*) .
- lowercase letter = 'a' | ... | 'z' (*individual*) .
- uppercase letter = 'A' | ... | 'Z' (*individual*) .
- lowercase _   :: character $\rightarrow$ character (*total*) .
- uppercase _   :: character $\rightarrow$ character (*total*) .

needs: **Tuples** .   character $\leq$ component .

(1)   distinct (d:digit, l:lowercase letter, u:uppercase letter) = true .

(2)   strictly-increasing ('0', '1', ..., '9') = true ;

(3)   strictly-increasing ('a', 'b', ..., 'z') = true ;

(4)   strictly-increasing ('A', 'B', ..., 'Z') = true .

(5)   uppercase 'a' = 'A' ;   lowercase 'A' = 'a' ;

     ...

     uppercase 'z' = 'Z' .   lowercase 'Z' = 'z' .

(6)   lowercase lowercase l:letter = lowercase l ;   uppercase uppercase l:letter = uppercase l .

(7) c & letter = nothing $\Rightarrow$ lowercase c:character = c ; uppercase c:character = c .

open.

E.5.3   ASCII

introduces: graphic-character , control _ , control-character , format-effector .

needs: **Strings/Alphanumerics** .

- code _   :: character $\rightarrow$ natural [max octal "177"] (*total, injective*) .
- character   = graphic-character | control-character .
- graphic-character = ' ' | '!' | '"' | '#' | '\$' | '%' | '&' | ''' |
            '(' | ')' | '*' | '+' | ',' | '_' | '.' | '/' |
            digit | ':' | ';' | '<' | '=' | '>' | '?' |
            '@' | uppercase letter | '[' | '\\' | ']' | '^' | '_' |
            '`' | lowercase letter | '{' | '|' | '}' | '~' (*individual*) .
- control _   :: '@' | uppercase letter | '[' | '\\' | ']' | '^' | '_' | '?' $\rightarrow$ control-character
            (*total, injective*) .
- format-effector   = control ('I' | 'J' | 'K' | 'L' | 'M') .

(1) c & ('@' | uppercase letter | '[' | '\\' | ']' | '^' | '_' | '?') = nothing $\Rightarrow$ control c:character = nothing .

(2)   code control '@' = octal "000" ;   code control 'A' = octal "001" ;   ...

     code ' '   = octal "040" ;   ...

     code '~'   = octal "176" ;   code control '?' = octal "177" .

closed.

E.6 Lists

E.6.1 Flat

E.6.1.1 Generics

introduces: item .
- item = □ .

open.

E.6.1.2 Basics

introduces: flat-list , list of _ .
needs: Tuples/Basics . item ≤ component .

- flat-list = list of item* .
- list of _ :: item* → flat-list (*total, injective*) .

(1) item & flat-list = nothing .
closed except Generics .

E.6.1.3 Specifics

introduces: _ [_] , items _ , head _ , tail _ , empty-list , concatenation _ .
includes: Instant/Distinction (list *for* s , _ is _) .
needs: Tuples . flat-list ≤ component .

- _ [_]   :: flat-list, item → flat-list .
- items _   :: flat-list → item* (*total, injective*) .
- head _   :: flat-list → item (*partial*) .
- tail _   :: flat-list → flat-list (*partial*) .
- empty-list   : flat-list .
- concatenation _ :: flat-list* → flat-list (*total, associative, unit is* empty-list) .

needs: Numbers/Naturals .
(1) $(l \leq$ flat-list$) [i \leq$ item $] = l$ & list of i^* .
(2) $l =$ list of $i \Rightarrow$ items l:flat-list $= i$.
(3) head of l:flat-list $=$ component#1 items l .
(4) tail of l:flat-list $=$ list of components from #2 items l .
(5) empty-list $=$ list of ( ) .
(6) concatenation (l_1:flat-list, l_2:flat-list) $=$ list of (items l_1, items l_2) .
(7) l_1:flat-list is l_2:flat-list $=$ items l_1 is items l_2 .

E.6.2 Nested

E.6.2.1 Generics

introduces: leaf .
  • leaf = item | □ .
open.

E.6.2.2 Basics

introduces: list , tree .
needs: **Tuples/Basics** . tree ≤ component .

  • list   = list of tree* .
  • tree   = leaf | list (*disjoint*) .
  • list of _ :: tree* → list (*total, injective*) .
closed   except Generics .

E.6.2.3 Specifics

introduces: _ [_] , branches _ , leaves _ , head _ , tail _ , empty-list , concatenation _ _ .
includes: **Instant/Distinction** (tree *for* s , _ is _) .
needs: **Tuples** .

  • _ [_]   :: list, tree → list .
  • branches _   :: list → tree* (*total, injective*) .
  • leaves _   :: tree* → leaf* (*total*) .
  • head _   :: list → tree (*partial*) .
  • tail _   :: list → list (*partial*) .
  • empty-list   : list .
  • concatenation _ :: list* → list (*total, associative, unit is* empty-list) .

needs: Numbers/Naturals .
(1) (l≤list) [t≤tree] = l & list of t^* .
(2) branches list of t:tree* = t .
(3) leaves l:leaf = l ;   leaves list of t:tree* = leaves t .
     leaves ( ) = ( ) ;   leaves (t_1:tree*, t_2:tree*) = (leaves t_1, leaves t_2) .
(4) head of l:list = component#1 branches l .
(5) tail of l:list = list of components from #2 branches l .
(6) empty-list = list of ( ) .
(7) concatenation (l_1:list, l_2:list) = list of (branches l_1, branches l_2) .
(8) l_1:list is l_2:list = branches l_1 is branches l_2 ;
     x:leaf is l:list = false .

E.7 Strings

E.7.1 Basics

introduces: string , string of _ , characters _ , " " , _ ˆ _ .
includes: Instant/Distinction (string *for* s , _ is _) .
needs: Tuples/Basics, Lists/Flat . character $\leq$ item .

- string $\quad$ = flat-list [character] .
- string of _ $\quad$ :: character* $\to$ string (*total, injective*) .
- characters _ :: string $\to$ character* (*total, injective*) .
- " " $\qquad$: string .
- _ ˆ _ $\qquad$ :: string, string $\to$ string (*total, associative, unit is* " ") .
- _ is _ $\qquad$ :: string, string $\to$ truth-value (*total*) .

(1) $\quad$ " " = empty-list .

(2) $\quad$ string of c:character* = list of c .

(3) $\quad$ characters s:string = items s .

(4) $\quad$ $(s_1$:string$)$ ˆ $(s_2$:string$)$ = concatenation $(s_1,\ s_2)$.

The notation "c" abbreviates string of 'c'. Moreover, for $n \geq 2$, the notation "$c_1 \ldots c_n$" abbreviates "c_1" ˆ $\ldots$ ˆ "c_n" .

E.7.2 Alphanumerics

introduces: lowercase _ , uppercase _ , decimal _ , octal-digit , octal _ .
needs: Tuples/Basics, Numbers/Naturals .

- lowercase _ :: string $\to$ string (*total*) .
- uppercase _ :: string $\to$ string (*total*) .
- decimal _ $\quad$ :: string of digit$^+$ $\to$ natural (*total*) .
- octal _ $\qquad$ :: string of octal-digit$^+$ $\to$ natural (*total*) .
- octal-digit $\;$ = '0' | '1' | '2' | '3' | '4' | '5' | '6' | '7' .

(1) $\quad$ lowercase " " = " " ; $\quad$ lowercase string of c:character = string of lowercase c ;
$\qquad$ lowercase $(s_1$:string ˆ s_2:string$)$ = lowercase s_1 ˆ lowercase s_2 .

(2) $\quad$ uppercase " " = " " ; $\quad$ uppercase string of c:character = string of uppercase c ;
$\qquad$ uppercase $(s_1$:string ˆ s_2:string$)$ = uppercase s_1 ˆ uppercase s_2 .

(3) $\quad$ decimal "0" = 0 ; $\quad$ decimal "1" = 1 ; $\quad$ decimal "2" = 2 ; $\quad$ decimal "3" = 3 ; $\quad$ decimal "4" = 4 ;
$\qquad$ decimal "5" = 5 ; $\quad$ decimal "6" = 6 ; $\quad$ decimal "7" = 7 ; $\quad$ decimal "8" = 8 ; $\quad$ decimal "9" = 9 ;
$\qquad$ decimal $(s$:string of digit$^+$ ˆ string of d:digit$)$ =
$\qquad\qquad$ sum (product (10, decimal s), decimal (string of d)) .

(4) $\quad$ octal (string of d:octal-digit) = decimal (string of d) ; $\quad$ octal "8" = nothing ; $\quad$ octal "9" = nothing ;
$\qquad$ octal $(s$:string of octal-digit$^+$ ˆ string of d:octal-digit$)$ =
$\qquad\qquad$ sum (product (8, octal s), octal (string of d)) .

E.8   Syntax

E.8.1   Basics

introduces: syntax-tree .
needs: **Lists/Nested** .   syntax-tree ≤ tree .
- syntax-tree = character | list [syntax-tree] (*disjoint*) .

E.8.2   Specifics

introduces: $[\![\,]\!]$, $[\![\,_\,]\!]$, $[\![\,_\,_\,]\!]$, ... , $\langle\,\rangle$, $\langle\,_\,\rangle$, $\langle\,_\,_\,\rangle$, ...
includes: **Instant/Distinction** (syntax-tree *for* s , _ is _) .
needs: **Tuples/Basics** .

- $[\![\,]\!]$: syntax-tree .
- $[\![\,_\,]\!]$ :: syntax-tree* → syntax-tree (*total*) .
- $[\![\,_\,_\,]\!]$ :: syntax-tree*, syntax-tree* → syntax-tree (*total*) .
  ...
- $\langle\,\rangle$: syntax-tree* .
- $\langle\,_\,\rangle$ :: syntax-tree* → syntax-tree* (*total*) .
- $\langle\,_\,_\,\rangle$ :: syntax-tree*, syntax-tree* → syntax-tree* (*total*) .
  ...
- _ is _   :: syntax-tree, syntax-tree → truth-value (*total*) .

(1) $[\![\,]\!]$ = empty-list .
   $[\![\ t{:}\text{syntax-tree}^*\ ]\!]$ = list of t .
   $[\![\ t_1{:}\text{syntax-tree}^*\ t_2{:}\text{syntax-tree}^*\ ]\!]$ = list of (t_1, t_2) .
   ...

(2) $\langle\,\rangle$ = ( ) .
   $\langle\ t{:}\text{syntax-tree}^*\ \rangle$ = t .
   $\langle\ t_1{:}\text{syntax-tree}^*\ t_2{:}\text{syntax-tree}^*\ \rangle$ = (t_1, t_2) .
   ...

This specification is schematic. It may be regarded as an abbreviation for an infinite specification. Only a finite part of it is needed in practice.

E.9   Sets

E.9.1   Generics

introduces: nonset-element .
includes: **Instant/Distinction** (nonset-element *for* s , _ is _) .
- nonset-element = □ .
- _ is _   :: nonset-element, nonset-element → truth-value (*total*) .
open.

E.9.2 Basics

introduces: set , element , set of _ .
needs: Tuples/Basics . element ≤ component .

- set = set of element* .
- element = nonset-element | set (*disjoint*) .
- set of _ :: element* → set (*total*) .

(1) set of (e:element*, e_1:element, e_2:element, e':element*) = set of (e, e_2, e_1, e') .

(2) e_1 is e_2 = true ⇒ set of (e:element*, e_1:element, e_2:element, e':element*) = set of (e, e_1, e') .

closed except Generics .

E.9.3 Specifics

introduces: _ [_] , elements _ , empty-set , disjoint-union _ , union _ , difference _ , intersection _ ,
_ restricted to _ , _ omitting _ , _ [in _] , _ [not in _] , _ is in _ , _ is included in _ .
includes: Instant/Partial Order (set *for* s , _ is _ , _ is included in _ *for* _ is less than _) .
needs: Tuples, Lists .

- _ [_] :: set, element → set .
- elements _ :: set → element* (*strict, linear*) .
- empty-set : set .
- disjoint-union _ :: set* → set (*partial, associative, commutative, unit is* empty-set) .
- union _ :: set* → set (*total, associative, commutative, idempotent,*
  unit is empty-set) .
- difference _ :: set, set → set (*total*) .
- intersection _ :: set$^+$ → set (*total, associative, commutative, idempotent*) .
- _ restricted to _ :: list [element], set → list [element] (*total*) .
- _ omitting _ :: list [element], set → list [element] (*total*) .
- _ [in _] :: element, set → element (*partial*) .
- _ [not in _] :: element, set → element (*partial*) .
- _ is in _ :: element, set → truth-value (*total*) .
- _ is included in _ :: set, set → truth-value (*total*) .
- _ is _ :: set, set → truth-value (*total*) .

(1) (s≤set) [e≤element] = s & set of e^* .

(2) s = set of e:element* ; distinct e = true ⇒ elements (s:set) = shuffle e .

(3) empty-set = set of ( ) .

(4) disjoint-union (s:set, t:set) = when intersection (s, t) is empty-set then union (s, t) .

(5) union (set of e_1:element*, set of e_2:element*) = set of (e_1, e_2) .

(6) difference.(empty-set, s:set) = empty-set ;
difference (s:set, empty-set) = s ;
difference (set of e:element, s:set) = if e is in s then empty-set else set of e ;
difference (union (s:set, t:set), u:set) = union (difference (s, u), difference (t, u)) .

(7)   intersection (empty-set, s:set) = empty-set ;
      intersection (set of e:element, s:set) = if e is in s then set of e else empty-set ;
      intersection (union (s:set, t:set), u:set) = union (intersection (s, u), intersection (t, u)) .
(8)   empty-list restricted to s:set = empty-list ;
      empty-list omitting s:set = empty-list .
(9)   concatenation (list of e:element, l:list) restricted to s:set =
          if e is in s then concatenation (list of e, l restricted to s) else l restricted to s ;
      concatenation (list of e:element, l:list) omitting s:set =
          if not (e is in s) then concatenation (list of e, l omitting s) else l omitting s .
(10) (e:element) [in s:set] = when e is in s then e ;
      (e:element) [not in s:set] e:element = when not (e is in s) then e .
(11) e:element is in empty-set = false ;
      e:element is in union (s:set, t:set) = either ((e is in s), (e is in t)) .
(12) s:set is included in t:set = union (s, t) is t .
(13) empty-set is set of e:element$^+$ = false ;
      union (set of e:element, s:set) is t:set =
          both ((e is in t), (difference (s, set of e) is difference (t, set of e))) .

E.10   Maps

E.10.1   Generics

introduces: nonmap-range .
  • nonmap-range = □ .
open.

E.10.2   Basics

introduces: map , range , map of _ to _ , empty-map , disjoint-union _ , mapped-set _ .
needs: **Tuples/Basics** .   map ≤ component .

  • map   = disjoint-union (map of element to range)* .
  • range   = nonmap-range | map (*disjoint*) .
  • map of _ to _   :: element, range $\rightarrowtail$ map (*total, injective*) .
  • empty-map   : map .
  • disjoint-union _ :: map* $\rightarrow$ map (*partial, associative, commutative, unit is* empty-map) .
  • mapped-set _   :: map $\rightarrow$ set (*total*) .

(1) disjoint-union ( ) = empty-map ;

   disjoint-union (map of e:element to r:range) = map of e:element to r:range .

   intersection (mapped-set m_1, mapped-set m_2) is empty-set = true $\Rightarrow$
   disjoint-union (m_1:map, m_2:map) : map .

   intersection (mapped-set m_1, mapped-set m_2) is empty-set = false $\Rightarrow$
   disjoint-union (m_1:map, m_2:map) = nothing .

(2) mapped-set empty-map = empty-set ;

   mapped-set map of e:element to r:range = set of e ;

   mapped-set disjoint-union (m_1:map, m_2:map) =
       disjoint-union (mapped-set m_1, mapped-set m_2) .

closed   except Generics .

E.10.3   Specifics

introduces: _ [_ to _] , _ at _ , overlay _ , _ restricted to _ , _ omitting _ .

includes: **Instant/Distinction** (map *for* s , _ is _) .

needs: **Tuples/Basics** .

- _ [_ to _]   :: map, element, range → map .
- _ at _   :: map, element → range (*partial*) .
- overlay _   :: map* → map (*total, associative, idempotent, unit is* empty-map) .
- _ restricted to _ :: map, set → map (*total*) .
- _ omitting _   :: map, set → map (*total*) .

(1) (m≤map) [e≤element to r≤range] = m & disjoint-union (map of e to r)* .

(2) empty-map at e:element = nothing ;

   map of e':element to r:range at e:element = when e is e' then r ;

   disjoint-union (m:map, m':map) at e:element =
       when there is disjoint-union (m, m') then ((m at e) | (m' at e)) .

(3) overlay (m:map, m':map) = disjoint-union (m, m' omitting mapped-set m) .

(4) empty-map restricted to s:set = empty-map ;

   map of e:element to r:range restricted to s:set = if e is in s then map of e to r else empty-map ;

   disjoint-union (m:map, m':map) restricted to s:set =
       when there is disjoint-union (m, m')
       then disjoint-union (m restricted to s, m' restricted to s) .

(5) empty-map omitting s:set = empty-map ;

   map of e:element to r:range omitting s:set = if e is in s then empty-map else map of e to r ;

   disjoint-union (m:map, m':map) omitting s:set =
       when there is disjoint-union (m, m') then disjoint-union (m omitting s, m' omitting s) .

(6) empty-map is m:disjoint-union (map of element to range)$^+$ = false ;

   map of e_1:element to r_1:range is map of e_2:element to r_2:range =
       if e_1 is e_2 then r_1 is r_2 else false ;

   disjoint-union (map of e:element to r:range, m:map) is m':map =
       when not (e is in mapped-set m) then
       if not (e is in mapped set m') then false
       else both ((r is (m' at e)), (m is (m' omitting set of e))) .

Appendix F

Meta-Notation

- *The meta-notation used in this book consists of positive Horn clauses, constraints, and modules, together with some convenient abbreviations.*

- *The informal summary of the meta-notation given in this Appendix provides a concise explanation of each construct.*

- *The description of the formal abbreviations used in the meta-notation reduces the meta-notation to a simple kernel.*

- *A context-free grammar specifies the abstract syntax of the meta-notation, and suggests its concrete syntax.*

- *The logic used for reasoning about the meta-notation consists of the standard inference rules for Horn clause logic with equality, together with some Horn clause axioms.*

- *The formal semantics of the meta-notation is, unfortunately, out of the scope of this book.*

F.1 Informal Summary

Meta-notation is for specifying formal notation: what symbols are used, how they may be put together, and their intended interpretation.

Our meta-notation here supports a *unified* treatment of sorts and individuals: an individual is treated as a special case of a sort. Thus operations can be applied to sorts as well as individuals. A vacuous sort represents the lack of an individual, in particular the *undefined* result of a partial operation. Sorts may be related by inclusion; sort equality is just mutual inclusion. But a sort is not determined just by the set of individuals that it includes: it has an *intension*, stemming from the way it is expressed. For example, the sort of those natural numbers that are in the range of the successor operation may be distinct from the sort of those that have a well-defined reciprocal, even though their sets of individuals are the same.

The meta-notation provides (positive) Horn clauses and (initial) constraints—explained below—for specifying the intended interpretation of symbols. Specifications may be divided into mutually-dependent and nested modules, presented incrementally in any order.

F.1.1 Vocabulary

The vocabulary of the meta-notation consists of constant and operation symbols, variables, titles, and special marks.

F.1.1.1 Symbols

Symbols are of two forms: quoted or unquoted. Quoted symbols always stand for constants. A doubly-quoted symbol "..." may quote an arbitrary sequence ... of graphic characters—except that it must be properly balanced with respect to quotation marks. A singly-quoted symbol '.' may only quote a single character.

In unquoted symbols the underline character _ indicates the positions of arguments. Symbols without _ *always* stand for constants. Unquoted symbols are written here in this sans-serif font. They must not contain quotation marks at all, and they must be balanced with respect to brackets ( ), [ ], etc. A symbol may not consist entirely of _'s.[1] An operation symbol is classified as an *infix* when it both starts and ends with a _ , and as a *prefix* or *postfix* when it only ends, respectively starts, with a _ . It is called an *outfix* when _ only occurs internally.

There is one built-in constant symbol, nothing, and there are two built-in infix operation symbols, _ | _ , _ & _ .

F.1.1.2 Variables

Variables are sequences of letters, here written in *this italic font*, optionally followed by primes ' and/or a numerical subscript or suffix.

F.1.1.3 Titles

Titles are sequences of words, here capitalized and written in **This Bold Font**.

F.1.1.4 Marks

The marks used in the meta-notation consist of:

> , . ; : :- ! :: ( ) = ≤ ≥ → ⇒ □ / /* (*continued*) **closed except open**
> **grammar: includes: introduces: needs: privately**
> *associative commutative disjoint for idempotent individual*
> *injective linear partial restricted strict total unit is* .

A pair of grouping parentheses ( ) may be replaced by a vertical line to the left of the grouped material. Horizontal lines may be used to separate formal specification from interspersed informal comments, but they are not obligatory. Reference numbers for parts of specifications have no formal significance.

F.1.1.5 ASCII Representation

Fonts are simply ignored in the ASCII representation of the formatted meta-notation, since it is unlikely that ambiguity could arise.

---

[1]unless some of them are raised or lowered.

Double quotes "..." may be represented by the ASCII double quote character "...", or by double ASCII single (backward and forward) quote characters `` ``...'' ``. The special double brackets $[\![$ $]\!]$ used in grammars can be represented in various ways: by `[[` `]]`, by `{` `}`, or simply by `[` `]` when no confusion can arise.

Subscripts in variables are not lowered in the ASCII representation. When both subscripts and primes are used in the formatted meta-notation, let the primes be put after the (raised) subscript.

The only other marks belonging to the meta-notation that need special treatment are $\leq \geq \to \Rightarrow$ $\square$. These are represented in ASCII by `=< >= -> =>` `[]` respectively.

F.1.2   Sentences

A sentence is essentially a Horn clause involving formulae that assert equality, sort inclusion, or individual inclusion between the values of terms. The variables occurring in the terms range over all values, not only over individuals. The universal quantification is left implicit.

F.1.2.1   Terms

Terms consist essentially of constant symbols, variables, and applications of operation symbols to subterms. We use *mixfix* notation, writing the application of an operation symbol $S_0\_\dots\_S_n$ to terms $T_1,\dots,T_n$ as $S_0 T_1 \dots T_n S_n$. Infixes have weaker precedence than prefixes, which themselves have weaker precedence than postfixes. Moreover, infixes are grouped to the left, so we may write $x \mid y \mid z$ without parentheses. Grouping parentheses ( ) may be freely inserted for further disambiguation.

The value of a term is determined by the interpretation of the variables that occur in it. Such a value may be an individual (which is regarded as a special kind of sort), a vacuous sort, or a proper sort that includes some individuals.

The value of the constant nothing is a vacuous sort, included in all other sorts. Operations map sorts to sorts, preserving sort inclusion. $\_\mid\_$ is sort union and $\_\&\_$ is sort intersection; they are the join and meet, respectively, of the sort lattice, and enjoy the usual properties of set union and intersection: associativity, commutativity, idempotency, and distribution over each other (De Morgan's laws). Moreover, nothing is the unit for $\_\mid\_$. There is no point in having a unit for $\_\&\_$, as it would be a sort that includes everything.

F.1.2.2   Formulae

$T_1 = T_2$ asserts that the values of the terms T_1 and T_2 are the same (individuals or sorts).

$T_1 \leq T_2$ asserts that the value of the term T_1 is a subsort of that of the term T_2; so does $T_2 \geq T_1$. Sort inclusion is the partial order of the sort lattice.

$T_1 : T_2$ asserts that the value of the term T_1 is an individual included in the (sort) value of the term T_2; so does $T_2 :\!\!- T_1$. Thus $T : T$ merely asserts that the value of T is an individual. This can be abbreviated to T ! .

The mark $\square$ (read as 'filled in later') in a term abbreviates the other side of the enclosing equation. Thus $T_2 = T_1 \mid \square$ specifies the same as $T_2 = T_1 \mid T_2$ (which is equivalent to $T_2 \geq T_1$).

The mark *disjoint* following an equation or inclusion $T = T_1 \mid \dots \mid T_n$ abbreviates equations asserting vacuity of the pairwise intersections of the T_i. The mark *individual* abbreviates equations asserting that each T_i is an individual, as well as their disjointness.

$F_1 ; \dots ; F_n$ is the conjunction of the formulae $F_1, \dots, F_n$. Conjunctions with a common term may be abbreviated, e.g., $x, y : z$ abbreviates $x : z ; y : z$ and $x : y = z$ abbreviates $x : y ; y = z$.

F.1.2.3 Clauses

A (generalized positive Horn) clause $F_1; \ldots; F_m \Rightarrow C_1; \ldots; C_n$, where $m, n \geq 1$, asserts that whenever all the antecedent formulae F_i hold, so do *all* the consequent clauses (or formulae) C_j. Note that clauses cannot be nested to the left of $\Rightarrow$, so $F_1 \Rightarrow F_2 \Rightarrow F_3$ is unambiguously grouped as $F_1 \Rightarrow (F_2 \Rightarrow F_3)$.

We restrict the interpretation of a variable V to individuals of some sort T in a clause C by specifying $V:T \Rightarrow C$. Alternatively we may simply replace some occurrence of V as an argument in C by $V:T$. We restrict V to subsorts of T by writing $V \leq T$ instead of $V:T$.

F.1.2.4 Functionalities

A functionality clause $S :: T_1, \ldots, T_n \rightarrow T$ specifies that the value of any application of S is included in T whenever the values of the argument terms are included in the T_i. It does *not* by itself indicate whether the value might be an individual, a proper sort, or a vacuous sort.

Such a functionality may be augmented by the following attributes (described more precisely in Section F.2.2.2):

total: the value is an individual when all arguments are individuals of the appropriate sorts; moreover, S is *strict* and *linear*.

partial: as for *total*, except that the value may also be a vacuous sort when all the arguments are individuals.

restricted: the arguments are restricted to the specified sorts, so overloading is prohibited;

strict: the value is nothing when any argument is nothing;

linear: the value on a union of two sorts is the union of the values on each sort separately (but not necessarily for intersections);

injective: not only is the operation one-one on individual arguments (whenever the result is non-vacuous) but also the value on an intersection of two sorts is the intersection of the values on each sort separately—for *total* operations, this latter property corresponds roughly to one-oneness.

When S is binary, we may use the following attributes (following OBJ3): *associative, commutative, idempotent*, and *unit is* U. These attributes have a similar meaning when S is unary and the argument sort is a tuple sort, such as T^+ or T^2. (See Appendix E for the notation for tuples, which is not regarded as a part of the meta-notation itself.)

In all cases, the attributes only apply when all arguments are included in the sorts specified in the functionality. For instance, consider:

```
product _ ::
       (number, number) → number (total, associative, commutative, unit is 1) ,
       (matrix, matrix) → matrix (partial, associative) .
```

which also illustrates how several functionalities for the same symbol can be specified together.

It is straightforward to translate ordinary many-sorted algebraic specifications into our meta-notation, using functionalities and attributes; similarly for order-sorted specifications [GM86] written in OBJ3 [GW88].

F.1.3   Specifications

A modular specification S is of the form $B\ M_1 \ldots M_n$, where B is a basic specification, and the M_i are modules. Either B or the M_i (but not both) may be absent. B is inherited by all the M_i.

Each symbol stands for the same value or operation throughout a specification—except for symbols introduced *privately*. All the symbols (but not the variables) used in a module have to be explicitly introduced: either in the module itself, or in an outer basic specification, or in a referenced module.

F.1.3.1   Basic Specifications

A basic specification B may introduce symbols, assert sentences, and impose (initial) constraints on subspecifications. The meta-notation for basic specifications is as follows.

introduces: $O_1, \ldots, O_n$. introduces the indicated symbols, which stand for constants and/or operations. Also **privately introduces:** $O_1, \ldots, O_n$. introduces the indicated symbols, but here the enclosing module translates them to *new* symbols, so that they cannot clash with symbols specified in other modules.

C . asserts the clause C as an axiom, to hold for any assignment of values to the variables that occur in it. Omitting C gives the empty specification, made visible by a period.

$B_1 \ldots B_n$ specifies all that the basic specifications $B_1, \ldots, B_n$ specify, i.e., it is their union. The order of the B_i is irrelevant, so symbols may be used before they are introduced.

includes: $R_1, \ldots, R_n$. specifies the same as all the modules indicated by the references R_i. **needs:** $R_1, \ldots, R_n$. is similar to **includes:** $R_1, \ldots, R_n$. , except that it is not transitive: symbols introduced in the modules referenced by the R_i are not regarded as being automatically available for use in modules that reference the enclosing module.

grammar: S augments the basic specification S with standard specifications of strings and syntax trees from Appendix E, and with the introduction of each constant symbol that occurs as the left hand side of an equation in S. Similarly when S is a series of modules.

closed . specifies the constraint that the enclosing module is to have a *standard* (i.e., initial) interpretation. This means that it must be possible, using the specified symbols, to express every *individual* that is included in some expressible sort (*no junk*), and moreover that terms have equal/included/individual values only when that logically follows from the specified axioms (*no confusion*). **closed except** $R_1, \ldots, R_n$. specifies a similar constraint, but leaves the (sub)modules referenced by the R_i open, so that they may be specialized in extensions of the specification. **open** . merely indicates that the enclosing module is not to be closed.

F.1.3.2   Modules

A module M is of the form $I\ S$, where I is a title (or a series of titles, separated by /) that identifies the specification S.

Modules may be specified incrementally, in any order. To show that a module is continuing an earlier specification with the same identification, the mark (*continued*) may be appended to its title.

Modules may also be nested, in which case an inner module inherits the basic specifications of all the enclosing modules, and the series of titles that identifies the immediately enclosing module. Titles of enclosing modules are not inherited by a module whose title starts with a /.

Parameterization of modules is rather implicit: unconstrained submodules, specified as **open** . , can always be specialized

A series of titles $I_1/\ldots/I_n$ refers to a module (together with all its submodules). A common prefix of the titles of the enclosing module and of the referenced module may be omitted. In particular, sibling modules in a nest can be referenced using single titles. $R/(I_1, \ldots, I_n)$ refers to the collection of modules $R/I_1, \ldots, R/I_n$.

$I\,(O_1'\ for\ O_1, \ldots, O_n'\ for\ O_n)$ refers to the same module as the title(s) I, but with all the symbols O_i translated to O_i'. Each O_i must be specified by the module referenced by I. Identity translations $O_i\ for\ O_i$ may be abbreviated to S_i, as in $I\,(O_1, \ldots, O_n)$ which indicates that the module referenced by I specifies at least all the symbols $O_1, \ldots, O_n$.

F.2 Formal Abbreviations

The full meta-notation, summarized in Section F.1, consists of a simple kernel, together with some formal abbreviations whose use can make specifications less tedious.

This section explains how to expand the abbreviations so as to reduce specifications from the full meta-notation to the kernel. The expansions may be performed in any order. Formally, they correspond to a confluent and terminating set of term rewriting rules, such that normal forms are kernel specifications.

F.2.1 Specifications

1. (*continued*) is ignored at the end of titles of modules.

2. The reference $R/(I_1, \ldots, I_n)$ abbreviates $(R/I_1), \ldots, (R/I_n)$. /* in a reference abbreviates $R/(I_1, \ldots, I_n)$ where the I_i are all the titles of specified submodules of the module(s) referenced by R.

3. **needs:** $R_1, \ldots, R_n$. abbreviates **includes:** $R_1, \ldots, R_n$ . . (The visibility restriction on symbols provided by using **needs:** instead of **includes:** is not formalized here.)

4. A symbol O occurring alone in a translation abbreviates $O\ for\ O$.

5. **grammar:** $(O_1 = T_1. \ \ldots \ O_n = T_n.)$, where the O_i are constant symbols and the T_i are terms, abbreviates the specification:

   > **includes:** /Data Notation/Syntax.
   > **introduces:** $O_1, \ldots, O_n$.
   > $O_1 = T_1. \ \ldots \ O_n = T_n$.

   Similarly when the equations are divided into modules.

6. **open** . is ignored. (It should be checked that the enclosing module is not also specified to be closed, but that is not formalized here.)

F.2.2   Sentences

Let $O(\!| T_1, \ldots, T_n |\!)$ be the term obtained by replacing the n occurrences of _ in the operation symbol O by the terms $T_1, \ldots, T_n$ in that order. (This is meta-meta-notation! We assume that the special brackets $(\!| \,\, |\!)$ do not occur in user-specified operation symbols.)

F.2.2.1   Formulae

1. $T_2 \geq T_1$ abbreviates the formula $T_1 \leq T_2$.

2. $T_2 :\!\!- T_1$ abbreviates the formula $T_1 : T_2$.

3. $T \, !$ abbreviates the formula $T : T$.

4. $T_1, \ldots, T_n : T$ abbreviates the formulae $T_1 : T ; \ldots; T_n : T$. Similarly for the other relations.

5. $T_1 : T_2 = T_3$ abbreviates the formulae $T_1 : T_2 ; T_2 = T_3$. Similarly for other combinations of relations.

6. $T = \ldots \square \ldots$ abbreviates the formula $T = \ldots T \ldots$.

7. *disjoint* in $T = T_1 \mid \ldots \mid T_n$ (*disjoint*) abbreviates the formulae $T_i \, \& \, T_j =$ nothing, for $1 \leq i < j \leq n$.

8. *individual* in $T = T_1 \mid \ldots \mid T_n$ (*individual*) abbreviates the formulae $T_i : T_i$, for $1 \leq i \leq n$, as well as the formulae $T_i \, \& \, T_j =$ nothing, for $1 \leq i < j \leq n$.

9. $\ldots O(\!| \ldots, V\!:\!T, \ldots |\!) \ldots$, where V is a variable, abbreviates the clause
   $V\!:\!T \,\Rightarrow\, \ldots O(\!| \ldots, V, \ldots |\!) \ldots$, and similarly for the other relations.

F.2.2.2   Functionalities

1. $O :: F_1, \ldots, F_n$. abbreviates the clauses $O :: F_1$. $\ldots$ $O :: F_n$ . .

2. $O :: T_1, \ldots, T_n \to T \, (A_1, \ldots, A_m)$. abbreviates the clauses

$$O :: T_1, \ldots, T_n \to T \, .$$
$$O :: T_1, \ldots, T_n \to T \, (A_1) \, .$$
$$\ldots$$
$$O :: T_1, \ldots, T_n \to T \, (A_m) \, .$$

3. $O :: T_1, \ldots, T_n \to T$ abbreviates the clause $O(\!| T_1, \ldots, T_n |\!) \leq T$.

4. $O :: T_1, \ldots, T_n \to T \, (total)$. abbreviates the clauses

$$O :: T_1, \ldots, T_n \to T \, (partial) \, .$$
$$x_1\!:\!T_1 ; \ldots; x_n\!:\!T_n \,\Rightarrow\, O(\!| x_1, \ldots, x_n |\!) : T \, .$$

Here and below the x_i are distinct variables not otherwise occurring in the (unabbreviated) enclosing specification.

5. $O :: T_1, \ldots, T_n \to T \, (partial)$. abbreviates the clauses

$$O :: T_1, \ldots, T_n \to T \, (strict, linear) \, .$$
$$x_1\!:\!T_1 ; \ldots; x_n\!:\!T_n ; x : O(\!| x_1, \ldots, x_n |\!) \,\Rightarrow\, O(\!| x_1, \ldots, x_n |\!) : T \, .$$

6. $O :: T_1, \ldots, T_n \to T$ (*restricted*) . abbreviates the clause

$$O(\!|x_1, \ldots, x_n|\!) = O(\!|x_1 \,\&\, T_1, \ldots, x_n \,\&\, T_n|\!) .$$

7. $O :: T_1, \ldots, T_n \to T$ (*strict*) . abbreviates the clauses

$$O(\!|\text{nothing}, T_2, \ldots, T_n|\!) = \text{nothing} .$$

$$\ldots$$

$$O(\!|T_1, \ldots, T_{n-1}, \text{nothing}|\!) = \text{nothing} .$$

8. $O :: T_1, \ldots, T_n \to T$ (*linear*) . abbreviates the clause

$$x_1, x_1' \le T_1 ; \ldots ; x_n, x_n' \le T_n \Rightarrow$$
$$O(\!|x_1 \mid x_1', x_2, \ldots, x_n|\!) = O(\!|x_1, x_2, \ldots, x_n|\!) \mid O(\!|x_1', x_2, \ldots, x_n|\!) ;$$
$$\ldots ;$$
$$O(\!|x_1, \ldots, x_n \mid x_n'|\!) = O(\!|x_1, \ldots, x_n|\!) \mid O(\!|x_1, \ldots, x_n'|\!) .$$

9. $O :: T_1, \ldots, T_n \to T$ (*injective*) . abbreviates the two clauses

$$x_1, x_1' : T_1 ; \ldots ; x_n, x_n' : T_n ;$$
$$O(\!|x_1, \ldots, x_n|\!) = O(\!|x_1', \ldots, x_n'|\!) ;$$
$$O(\!|x_1, \ldots, x_n|\!) : T \Rightarrow$$
$$x_1 = x_1' ; \ldots ; x_n = x_n' .$$

$$x_1, x_1' \le T_1 ; \ldots ; x_n, x_n' \le T_n \Rightarrow$$
$$O(\!|x_1 \,\&\, x_1', x_2, \ldots, x_n|\!) = O(\!|x_1, x_2, \ldots, x_n|\!) \,\&\, O(\!|x_1', x_2, \ldots, x_n|\!) ;$$
$$\ldots ;$$
$$O(\!|x_1, \ldots, x_n \,\&\, x_n'|\!) = O(\!|x_1, \ldots, x_n|\!) \,\&\, O(\!|x_1, \ldots, x_n'|\!) .$$

10. $O :: T, T \to T$ (*associative*) . abbreviates the clause

$$x_1, x_2, x_3 : T \Rightarrow O(\!|x_1, O(\!|x_2, x_3|\!)|\!) = O(\!|O(\!|x_1, x_2|\!), x_3|\!) .$$

Similarly, for unary operations on tuples, $O :: T^2 \to T$ (*associative*) . abbreviates the clause

$$x_1, x_2, x_3 : T \Rightarrow O(x_1, O(x_2, x_3)) = O(O(x_1, x_2), x_3) .$$

For unary operations on nonempty tuples, $O :: T^+ \to T$ (*associative*) . abbreviates *also* the clause

$$x_1, x_2, x_3 : T^+ \Rightarrow O(x_1, x_2, x_3) = O(O(x_1, x_2), x_3) .$$

and similarly for $O :: T^* \to T$ (*associative*) .

11. $O :: T, T \to T_0$ (*commutative*) . abbreviates the clause

$$x_1, x_2 : T \Rightarrow O(\!|x_1, x_2|\!) = O(\!|x_2, x_1|\!) .$$

The expansion when O is a unary operation on tuples is analogous to that given for *associative* above.

12. $O :: T, T \to T$ (*idempotent*) . abbreviates the clause

$$x : T \Rightarrow O(\!|x, x|\!) = x .$$

The expansion when O is a unary operation on tuples is analogous to that given for *associative* above.

13. $O :: T, T \rightarrow T$ (*unit is* U) . abbreviates the clause

$$x : T \Rightarrow (\ O(\!|x, U|\!) = x \ ; \ O(\!|U, x|\!) = x\ ) .$$

The expansion when O is a unary operation on tuples is analogous to that given for *associative* above. That is, when the argument sort is the sort of pairs T^2 the clause is

$$x : T \Rightarrow O(x, U) = x \ ; \ O(U, x) = x .$$

When the argument sort is T^+, the following clause is added:

$$x : T \Rightarrow O(x) = x .$$

When the argument sort is T^*, the following further clause is added:

$$O(\ ) = U .$$

F.3   Abstract Syntax

The following context-free grammar can be interpreted as specifying the abstract syntax of our entire meta-notation. It is written in the meta-notation itself, using the notation for strings and trees provided by data notation Appendix E.

The terminal symbols used in the abstract syntax grammar correspond almost exactly to the marks that we use to write specifications in the meta-notation. (The only exception is the use of ⟦ Symbol "⟨" Terms "⟩" ⟧ to indicate the application of an operation symbol to arguments, which avoids a messy specification of mixfix notation.) Thus the grammar can be regarded as specifying the concrete syntax of the meta-notation, as well as its abstract syntax—up to disambiguation of grouping, anyway.

The specification of the sorts italic-letter and boldface-letter is omitted. The grammar is otherwise complete, apart from the sort Symbol, which has been intentionally left open.

grammar:

Symbol	= "nothing" | "_|_" | "_&_" | □ .
Symbols	= ⟨ Symbol ⟨ "," Symbol ⟩* ⟩ .
Variable	= ⟦ italic-letter$^+$ digit* $'''^*$ ⟧ .
Title	= ⟦ boldface-letter$^+$ ⟨ ' ' boldface-letter$^+$ ⟩$^+$ ⟧ .
Term	= Variable | Symbol | ⟦ Symbol "⟨" Terms "⟩" ⟧ | ⟦ "(" Term ")" ⟧ | ⟦ Variable Relator Term ⟧ | ⟦ Variable "!" ⟧ | "□" .
Terms	= ⟨ Term ⟨ "," Term ⟩* ⟩ .
Formula	= ⟦ Terms ⟨ Relator Term ⟩$^+$ ⟧ | ⟦ Term "!" ⟧ | ⟦ Term Relator Term "(" Disjoiner ")" ⟧ .
Relator	= "=" | "≤" | "∴" | "≥" | "∵" .
Disjoiner	= "*disjoint*" | "*individual*" .
Clause	= Formula | ⟦ Formula ⟨ ";" Formula ⟩* "⇒" Clause ⟨ ";" Clause ⟩* ⟧ | ⟦ Symbols "::" Functionality ⟨ "," Functionality ⟩* ⟧ .
Functionality	= ⟦ Terms "→" Term ⟨ "(" Attribute ⟨ "," Attribute ⟩* ")" ⟩ ⟧ .
Attribute	= "*total*" | "*partial*" | "*restricted*" | "*strict*" | "*linear*" | "*injective*" "*associative*" | "*commutative*" | "*idempotent*" | ⟨ "*unit is*" Term ⟩ .
Basic	= ⟦ "privately"$^?$ "introduces:" Symbols "." ⟧ | ⟦ Clause$^?$ "." ⟧ | ⟦ ⟨ "includes:" | "needs:" ⟩ References "." ⟧ | ⟦ "closed" "." ⟧ | ⟦ "open" "." ⟧ | ⟦ "closed" "except" References "." ⟧ | ⟦ "grammar:" ⟨ Basic$^+$ | Module$^+$ ⟩ ⟧ .
References	= ⟨ Reference ⟨ "," Reference ⟩* ⟩ .
Reference	= Path | ⟦ Path "(" Translation ⟨ "," Translation ⟩* ")" ⟧ .
Path	= Title | ⟦ "/" Title ⟧ | ⟦ Path "/" Title ⟧ | ⟦ Path "/" "*" ⟧ | ⟦ Path "/" "(" Path ⟨ "," Path ⟩* ")" ⟧ .
Translation	= ⟦ Symbol ⟨ "*for*" Symbol ⟩$^?$ ⟧ .
Module	= ⟦ Path Specification ⟧ .
Specification	= Basic$^+$ | ⟦ Basic* Module$^+$ ⟧ .

F.4 Logic

The following axioms characterize the essential properties of the basic operations and relations provided by the meta-notation. The axioms are not intended to be independent of each other: all interesting general properties are specified.

A consequence of the axioms below is that all models are *distributive lattices* with *bottoms*. However, individuals are *not* necessarily *atoms* of the lattice, just above the bottom. That property, which holds for singletons in the lattice of sets ordered by inclusion, cannot be captured by positive Horn clauses alone.

(1) $x = y \,;\, y = z \;\Rightarrow\; x = z$.

$x = y \;\Rightarrow\; y = x$.

$x = x$.

(2) $x \leq y \,;\, y \leq z \;\Rightarrow\; x \leq z$.

$x \leq y \,;\, y \leq x \;\Rightarrow\; x = y$.

$x \leq x$.

nothing $\leq x$.

(3) $x : x \,;\, x \leq y \;\Rightarrow\; x : y$.

$x : y \;\Rightarrow\; x : x \,;\, x \leq y$.

$x :$ nothing $\;\Rightarrow\; y = z$.

(4) $x \mid (y \mid z) = (x \mid y) \mid z$.

$x \mid y = y \mid x$.

$x \mid x = x$.

$x \mid$ nothing $= x$.

$x \leq z \,;\, y \leq z \;\Rightarrow\; x \mid y \leq z$.

$x \leq x \mid y$.

(5) $x \,\&\, (y \,\&\, z) = (x \,\&\, y) \,\&\, z$.

$x \,\&\, y = y \,\&\, x$.

$x \,\&\, x = x$.

$x \,\&\,$ nothing $=$ nothing .

$z \leq x \,;\, z \leq y \;\Rightarrow\; z \leq x \,\&\, y$.

$x \,\&\, y \leq x$.

(6) $x \,\&\, (y \mid z) = (x \,\&\, y) \mid (x \,\&\, z)$.

$x \mid (y \,\&\, z) = (x \mid y) \,\&\, (x \mid z)$.

Furthermore, for each introduced operation symbol O of n arguments the following axioms are provided, for $i = 1$ to n:

$$x_i \leq x_i' \;\Rightarrow\; O(\!|x_1, \ldots, x_i, \ldots, x_n|\!) \leq O(\!|x_1, \ldots, x_i', \ldots, x_n|\!) .$$

Finally, the inference rules of Horn clause logic with equality are simply: *Modus Ponens* (from the formulae $F_1, \ldots, F_m$ and the clause $F_1; \ldots; F_m \Rightarrow G_1; \ldots; G_n$ infer $G_1, \ldots, G_n$); the substitutivity of terms proved equal; and the instantiation of clauses by substituting terms for variables.

Appendix G

Assessment

- *This Appendix gives some examples of possible course assessment projects. They concern* MODULA-3, ADA, *and functional programming languages. Your lecturer or supervisor might either let you choose between them, or designate which one you are to attempt.*

- *Your completion of such a project not only documents your active participation in the course, it also serves some important pedagogical purposes. For instance, it gives you the opportunity to revise the material already covered, it helps you appreciate the inherent modularity of action semantic descriptions, and it lets you check whether you have indeed acquired a working knowledge of action semantics.*

- *You are advised to finish the description of straightforward constructs before proceeding to the more challenging ones. Try to reuse the description of* AD *as much as possible!*

- *At Aarhus, the students are expected to work in groups of two or three, handing in as much as they can manage after 25 hours work—without sacrificing quality for quantity! They are given access to the LATEX formatting macros used for the semantic descriptions in this book, and to the LATEX source for Appendix A.*

G.1   Modula-3

The reference for MODULA-3 is

Modula-3 Report (revised)
Research Report 52, Digital Systems Research Center,
Palo Alto, California, November 1989.

The following overview of MODULA-3 is taken from the Preface of the Report:

The goal of Modula-3 is to be as simple and safe as it can be while
meeting the needs of modern system programmers. Instead of exploring
new features, we studied the features from the Modula family of languages
that have proven themselves in practice and tried to simplify them and fit
them into a harmonious language. We found that most of the successful
features were aimed at one of two main goals: greater robustness, and a
simpler, more systematic type system.

Modula-3 descends from Mesa, Modula-2, Cedar, and Modula-2+. It
also resembles its cousins Object Pascal, Oberon, and Euclid.

Modula-3 retains one of Modula-2's most successful features, the provision for explicit interfaces between modules. It adds objects and classes,
exception handling, garbage collection, lightweight processes (or *threads*),
and the isolation of unsafe features.

You should restrict your attention to some small, but preferably useful, sublanguage of
Modula-3. Several MODULA-3 constructs are very similar to AD constructs. Thanks
to the good modularity of action semantics, it should be possible for you to reuse the
semantic description of these constructs in Appendix A, with only minor modifications. The choice of constructs to be described is up to you. However, you should
include either *exceptions* or *objects*, to make sure that you deal with at least some
constructs not to be found in AD.

G.2   Ada

The reference for ADA is:

Reference Manual for the Ada Programming Language,
ANSI/MIL-STD 1815 A, January 1983.

You should extend AD with some further ADA constructs. For example:

1. Discriminants and Variant Records.

2. Array Slices.

3. Exceptions.

4. Task Termination.

5. Goto Statements and Labels.

If any changes are required to Appendix A to accommodate the chosen constructs, you should specify them clearly.

G.3   A Functional Programming Language

There are several possibilities, including:

1. Standard ML:[1]

    The Definition of Standard ML,
    Robin Milner, Mads Tofte, and Robert Harper,
    MIT Press, 1990.

2. FL, son of FP [Bac78]:

    FL Language Manual, Parts 1 and 2,
    John Backus, John H. Williams, and Ed L. Wimmers,
    Report RJ 7100, IBM Almaden Research Center, October 1989.

3. Scheme, a language related to Lisp:

    The Revised[3] Report on the Algorithmic Language Scheme,
    J. Rees, W. Clinger, et al.,
    ACM SIGPLAN Notices, volume 21, number 12, pages 37–79, 1986.

4. Miranda, a lazy language:

    An Overview of Miranda,
    David A. Turner,
    ACM SIGPLAN Notices, volume 21, number 12, pages 158–166, 1986.

---

[1]Strongly recommended, unless you are already familiar with one of the others.

Bibliography

[Agh86]   Gul Agha. *Actors: A Model of Concurrent Computation in Distributed Systems.* MIT Press, 1986.

[ANS83]   ANSI. *Reference Manual for the Ada Programming Language, ANSI/MIL-STD 1815 A*, 1983.

[AR87]   Egidio Astesiano and Gianna Reggio. SMoLCS driven concurrent calculi. In *TAPSOFT'87, Proc. Int. Joint Conf. on Theory and Practice of Software Development, Pisa, Volume 1*, number 249 in Lecture Notes in Computer Science. Springer-Verlag, 1987.

[Ast91]   Egidio Astesiano. Inductive and operational semantics. In Neuhold and Paul [NP91], pages 51–136.

[Bac78]   John Backus. Can programming be liberated from the von Neumann style? a functional style and its algebra of programs. *Communications of the ACM*, 21:613–641, 1978.

[BJ82]   Dines Bjørner and Cliff B. Jones, editors. *Formal Specification & Software Development.* Prentice-Hall, 1982.

[Bjø83]   Dines Bjørner, editor. *Formal Description of Programming Concepts II, Proc. IFIP TC2 Working Conference, Garmisch-Partenkirchen, 1982.* IFIP, North-Holland, 1983.

[BL87]   Susanne Bondesen and Søren Laursen. An Action Semantics for Joyce. Internal Report DAIMI IR–72, Computer Science Dept., Aarhus University, 1987. Out of print.

[BMW92]   Deryck F. Brown, Hermano Moura, and David A. Watt. ACTRESS: an action semantics directed compiler generator. Accepted for the *International Workshop on Compiler Construction*, Paderborn, October 1992; a summary is to appear in *Functional Programming Glasgow 1991*, BCS/Springer Workshops in Computer Science, 1992.

350

[BNM+89] Hendrik J. Boom, Claus Bendix Nielsen, Andrew D. McGettrick, Peter D. Mosses, Charles Rattray, Robert D. Tennent, and David A. Watt. A view of formal semantics. *Computer Standards and Interfaces*, 9, 1989.

[BPTS91] Peter L. Bird, Uwe F. Pleban, Nigel P. Topham, and Henrik Scheuer. Semantics driven computer architecture. In *Proc. Int. Conf. on Parallel Computing, London*. North-Holland, 1991.

[BPW87] Manfred Broy, Peter Pepper, and Martin Wirsing. On the algebraic definition of programming languages. *ACM Transactions on Programming Languages and Systems*, 9:54–99, 1987.

[BS82] Inger Bohlbro and Michael I. Schwartzbach. Models for abstract semantic algebras. Internal Report DAIMI IR–44, Computer Science Dept., Aarhus University, 1982. Out of print.

[CO88] Søren Christensen and Michael Hoffmann Olsen. Action semantics of "CCS" and "CSP". Internal Report DAIMI IR–82, Computer Science Dept., Aarhus University, 1988.

[Cou90] Patrick Cousot. Methods and logics for proving programs. In J. van Leeuwen, A. Meyer, M. Nivat, M. Paterson, and D. Perrin, editors, *Handbook of Theoretical Computer Science*, volume B, chapter 15. Elsevier Science Publishers, Amsterdam; and MIT Press, 1990.

[Dij75] E. W. Dijkstra. Guarded commands, non-determinacy, and formal derivations of programs. *Communications of the ACM*, 18:453–457, 1975.

[DR81] J. Diaz and I. Ramos, editors. *Proc. Int. Coll. on Formalization of Programming Concepts, Peñiscola*, number 107 in Lecture Notes in Computer Science. Springer-Verlag, 1981.

[DS92] Kjung-Goo Doh and David A. Schmidt. Extraction of strong typing laws from action semantics definitions. In *ESOP'92, Proc. European Symposium on Programming, Rennes*, number 582 in Lecture Notes in Computer Science, pages 151–166. Springer-Verlag, 1992.

[ES90a] Susan Even and David A. Schmidt. Category sorted algebra-based action semantics. *Theoretical Computer Science*, 77:73–96, 1990.

[ES90b] Susan Even and David A. Schmidt. Type inference for action semantics. In *ESOP'90, Proc. European Symposium on Programming, Copenhagen*, number 432 in Lecture Notes in Computer Science, pages 118–133. Springer-Verlag, 1990.

[FW84]   Daniel P. Friedman and Mitchell Wand. Reification: Reflection without meta-
            physics. In *Proc.ACM 1984 Symposium on Lisp and Functional Programming*,
            pages 348–355. ACM, 1984.

[Geh83]   Narain Gehani. *Ada: An Advanced Introduction*. Prentice-Hall, 1983. Includ-
            ing: Reference Manual for the Ada Programming Language.

[GM86]   Joseph A. Goguen and José Meseguer. Order-sorted algebra: Algebraic theory
            of polymorphism. *Journal of Symbolic Logic*, 51:844–845, 1986. Abstract.

[GM89]   Joseph A. Goguen and José Meseguer. Order-sorted algebra I: Equational
            deduction for multiple inheritance, overloading, exceptions and partial opera-
            tions. Technical Report SRI-CSL-89-10, Computer Science Lab., SRI Interna-
            tional, 1989.

[Goo87]   Danny Goodman. *The Complete HyperCard Handbook*. Bantam, 1987.

[GPG81]   Joseph A. Goguen and Kamran Parsaye-Ghomi. Algebraic denotational seman-
            tics using parameterized abstract modules. In Diaz and Ramos [DR81].

[GTW78]   J. A. Goguen, J. W. Thatcher, and E. G. Wagner. An initial algebra approach
            to the specification, correctness, and implementation of abstract data types.
            In Raymond T. Yeh, editor, *Current Trends in Programming Methodology*,
            volume IV. Prentice-Hall, 1978.

[GTWW77]   J. A. Goguen, J. W. Thatcher, E. G. Wagner, and J. B. Wright. Initial algebra
            semantics and continuous algebras. *Journal of the ACM*, 24:68–95, 1977.

[Gue81]   Irene Guessarian. *Algebraic Semantics*. Number 99 in Lecture Notes in Com-
            puter Science. Springer-Verlag, 1981.

[Gur91]   Yuri Gurevich. Evolving algebras, a tutorial introduction. *Bull. EATCS*,
            (43):264–284, February 1991.

[GW88]   Joseph A. Goguen and Timothy Winkler. Introducing OBJ3. Technical Report
            SRI-CSL-88-9, Computer Science Lab., SRI International, 1988.

[Kah87]   Gilles Kahn. Natural semantics. In *STACS'87, Proc. Symp. on Theoretical
            Aspects of Computer Science*, number 247 in Lecture Notes in Computer Sci-
            ence. Springer-Verlag, 1987.

[Kri91]   Padmanabhan Krishnan. Real-time action. In *Proc. Euromicro Workshop on
            Real-Time Systems*, 1991.

[Lee89]   Peter Lee. *Realistic Compiler Generation*. Foundations of Computing Series.
            MIT Press, 1989.

[Mar86]   Jan Mark. The action semantics of ML and Amber. Internal Report DAIMI IR–66, Computer Science Dept., Aarhus University, 1986.

[Mil90]   Robin Milner. Operational and algebraic semantics of concurrent processes. In van Leeuwen et al. [vLMN+90], chapter 19.

[Mog89]   Eugenio Moggi. Computational lambda-calculus and monads. In *LICS'89, Proc. 4th Ann. Symp. on Logic in Computer Science*, pages 14–23. IEEE, 1989.

[Mos74]   Peter D. Mosses. The mathematical semantics of Algol60. Tech. Mono. PRG–12, Programming Research Group, University of Oxford, 1974.

[Mos75]   Peter D. Mosses. *Mathematical Semantics and Compiler Generation*. D.Phil. dissertation, University of Oxford, 1975.

[Mos76]   Peter D. Mosses. Compiler generation using denotational semantics. In *MFCS'76, Proc. Symp. on Math. Foundations of Computer Science, Gdańsk*, number 45 in Lecture Notes in Computer Science. Springer-Verlag, 1976.

[Mos77]   Peter D. Mosses. Making denotational semantics less concrete. In *Proc. Int. Workshop on Semantics of Programming Languages, Bad Honnef*, pages 102–109. Abteilung Informatik, Universität Dortmund, 1977. Bericht nr. 41.

[Mos79]   Peter D. Mosses. SIS, Semantics Implementation System: Reference manual and user guide. Tech. Mono. MD–30, Computer Science Dept., Aarhus University, 1979. Out of print.

[Mos80]   Peter D. Mosses. A constructive approach to compiler correctness. In *ICALP'80, Proc. Int. Coll. on Automata, Languages, and Programming, Noordwijkerhout*, number 85 in Lecture Notes in Computer Science. Springer-Verlag, 1980.

[Mos81]   Peter D. Mosses. A semantic algebra for binding constructs. In Diaz and Ramos [DR81].

[Mos83]   Peter D. Mosses. Abstract semantic algebras! In Bjørner [Bjø83].

[Mos84]   Peter D. Mosses. A basic abstract semantic algebra. In *Proc. Int. Symp. on Semantics of Data Types, Sophia-Antipolis*, number 173 in Lecture Notes in Computer Science. Springer-Verlag, 1984.

[Mos88]   Peter D. Mosses. The modularity of action semantics. Internal Report DAIMI IR–75, Computer Science Dept., Aarhus University, 1988. Revised version of a paper presented at a CSLI Workshop on Semantic Issues in Human and Computer Languages, Half Moon Bay, California, March 1987 (proceedings unpublished).

[Mos89a]   Peter D. Mosses. Unified algebras and action semantics. In *STACS'89, Proc. Symp. on Theoretical Aspects of Computer Science, Paderborn*, number 349 in Lecture Notes in Computer Science. Springer-Verlag, 1989.

[Mos89b]   Peter D. Mosses. Unified algebras and institutions. In *LICS'89, Proc. 4th Ann. Symp. on Logic in Computer Science*, pages 304–312. IEEE, 1989.

[Mos89c]   Peter D. Mosses. Unified algebras and modules. In *POPL'89, Proc. 16th Ann. ACM Symp. on Principles of Programming Languages*, pages 329–343. ACM, 1989.

[Mos90]   Peter D. Mosses. Denotational semantics. In van Leeuwen et al. [vLMN+90], chapter 11.

[Mos91a]   Peter D. Mosses. An introduction to action semantics. Technical Monograph DAIMI PB–370, Computer Science Dept., Aarhus University, 1991. Lecture Notes for the Marktoberdorf Summer School, to be published in the Proceedings of the Summer School by Springer-Verlag (Series F).

[Mos91b]   Peter D. Mosses. A practical introduction to denotational semantics. In Neuhold and Paul [NP91], pages 1–49.

[Mos92]   Peter D. Mosses. The use of sorts in algebraic specifications. In *Proc. 8th Workshop on Abstract Data Types and 3rd COMPASS Workshop*, Lecture Notes in Computer Science. Springer-Verlag, 1992. To appear.

[MT91]   Ian Mason and Carolyn Talcott. Equivalence in functional languages with effects. *Journal of Functional Programming*, 1:287–327, 1991.

[MTH90]   Robin Milner, Mads Tofte, and Robert Harper. *The Definition of Standard ML*. MIT Press, 1990.

[MW86]   Peter D. Mosses and David A. Watt. The potential use of action semantics in standards. Technical Monograph DAIMI PB–206, Computer Science Dept., Aarhus University, 1986. Out of print.

[MW87]   Peter D. Mosses and David A. Watt. The use of action semantics. In Martin Wirsing, editor, *Formal Description of Programming Concepts III, Proc. IFIP TC2 Working Conference, Gl. Avernæs, 1986*. IFIP, North-Holland, 1987.

[MW92]   Peter D. Mosses and David A. Watt. Pascal: Action Semantics. Draft, Version 0.4 (a revised version is forthcoming), April 1992.

[NP91]   Ehrich J. Neuhold and Manfred Paul, editors. *Formal Description of Programming Concepts*. IFIP State-of-the-Art Report. Springer-Verlag, 1991.

[Pal88]   Jens Palsberg. *An Action Semantics for Inheritance.* M.Sc. dissertation, Aarhus University, 1988.

[Pal92]   Jens Palsberg. A provably correct compiler generator. In *ESOP'92, Proc. European Symposium on Programming, Rennes,* number 582 in Lecture Notes in Computer Science, pages 418–434. Springer-Verlag, 1992.

[Plo77]   Gordon D. Plotkin. LCF considered as a programming language. *Theoretical Computer Science,* 5:223–255, 1977.

[Plo81]   Gordon D. Plotkin. A structural approach to operational semantics. Lecture Notes DAIMI FN–19, Computer Science Dept., Aarhus University, 1981. Now available only from University of Edinburgh.

[Plo83]   Gordon D. Plotkin. An operational semantics for CSP. In Bjørner [Bjø83].

[RC+86]   J. Rees, W. Clinger, et al. The revised[3] report on the algorithmic language Scheme. *ACM SIGPLAN Notices,* 21(12):37–79, 1986.

[RZ89]   Jan Reher and Eld Zierau. The action semantics description tool. Internal Report DAIMI IR–90, Computer Science Dept., Aarhus University, 1989.

[Sch85]   David A. Schmidt. Detecting global variables in denotational specifications. *ACM Transactions on Programming Languages and Systems,* 7:299–310, 1985.

[Sch86]   David A. Schmidt. *Denotational Semantics: A Methodology for Language Development.* Allyn & Bacon, 1986.

[Sch90]   David A. Schmidt. Action semantics-based language design. In *Proc. SOFSEM'90 Winter School, Krkonose, Czechoslovakia,* 1990.

[Sco70]   Dana S. Scott. Outline of a mathematical theory of computation. In *Proc. Fourth Annual Princeton Conference on Information Sciences and Systems,* 1970. A revised and slightly expanded version is Tech. Mono. PRG–2, Programming Research Group, University of Oxford, 1970.

[SIG89]   SIGAda. Approved Ada language commentaries. *ACM Ada Letters,* IX(3), 1989.

[SS71]   Dana S. Scott and Christopher Strachey. Toward a mathematical semantics for computer languages. In *Proc. Symp. on Computers and Automata,* volume 21 of *Microwave Research Institute Symposia Series.* Polytechnic Institute of Brooklyn, 1971.

[Sto88]   Allen Stoughton. *Fully Abstract Models of Programming Languages.* Pitman & John Wiley, 1988.

[Tur86]   David A. Turner. An overview of Miranda. *ACM SIGPLAN Notices*, 21(12):158–166, 1986.

[TWW79]   J. W. Thatcher, E. G. Wagner, and J. B. Wright. More on advice on structuring compilers and proving them correct. In *ICALP'79, Proc. Int. Coll. on Automata, Languages, and Programming, Graz*, number 71 in Lecture Notes in Computer Science. Springer-Verlag, 1979.

[vLMN+90]   J. van Leeuwen, A. Meyer, M. Nivat, M. Paterson, and D. Perrin, editors. *Handbook of Theoretical Computer Science*, volume B. Elsevier Science Publishers, Amsterdam; and MIT Press, 1990.

[Wan80]   Mitchell Wand. First-order identities as a defining language. *Acta Informatica*, 14:337–357, 1980.

[Wat86]   David A. Watt. Executable semantic descriptions. *Software: Practice and Experience*, 16:13–43, 1986.

[Wat88]   David A. Watt. An action semantics of Standard ML. In *Proc. Third Workshop on Math. Foundations of Programming Language Semantics, New Orleans*, number 298 in Lecture Notes in Computer Science, pages 572–598. Springer-Verlag, 1988.

[Wat91]   David A. Watt. *Programming Language Syntax and Semantics*. Prentice-Hall, 1991.

[Wir90]   Martin Wirsing. Algebraic specification. In van Leeuwen et al. [vLMN+90], chapter 13.

[Wir91]   Martin Wirsing. Algebraic specification: Semantics, parameterization, and refinement. In Neuhold and Paul [NP91], pages 259–318.

[WM87]   David A. Watt and Peter D. Mosses. Pascal: Static Action Semantics. Draft, Version 0.31 (a revised version is planned), 1987.

Symbol Index

---

[1] *Italic* page numbers indicate *standard symbols* of action notation, data notation, or meta-notation; ordinary page numbers are used for symbols introduced either in the examples or in the operational semantics of action notation in Appendix C.

357

Concept Index

Printed in the United States
By Bookmasters